BURNETT

W9-BMU-639

Brown v. Board

Brown v. Board

*The Landmark Oral Argument Before
the Supreme Court*

Edited by Leon Friedman

THE NEW PRESS

NEW YORK
LONDON

Published in the United States by The New Press, New York, 2004
Distributed by W. W. Norton & Company, Inc., New York

ISBN 1-56584-913-2 (hc.)

The New Press was established in 1990 as a not-for-profit alternative to the large,
commercial publishing houses currently dominating the book publishing industry.
The New Press operates in the public interest rather than for private gain,
and is committed to publishing, in innovative ways, works of educational,
cultural, and community value that are often deemed insufficiently profitable.

The New Press
38 Greene Street, 4th floor
New York, NY 10013
www.thenewpress.com

In the United Kingdom:
6 Salem Road
London W2 4BU

Printed in the United States of America

2 4 6 8 10 9 7 5 3 1

CONTENTS

PREFACE

Leon Friedman

Fifty years after *Brown v. Board of Education* was decided, its importance in American legal and political history remains in question. It is certainly one of the most famous cases ever decided by the United States Supreme Court, ranking with *Marbury v. Madison* or *Miranda v. Arizona* as the case most Americans recognize. Chief Justice Earl Warren named it as one of the three most important cases decided by the Court when he acted as its chief. Judge Louis Pollak (former dean of both the Yale Law School and the University of Pennsylvania Law School) called it "the most important American act of government of any kind since the Emancipation Proclamation."

Does *Brown* deserve all of this praise today? At the time, the case eliminated the "separate but equal" doctrine, the key legal device for maintaining segregated schools in the Southern states (including such non-Southern states as Kansas and Delaware). But the concrete results achieved by the case—integration of elementary and secondary schools—have largely been reversed as a result of housing patterns and population shifts that resegregated schools in large metropolitan areas and because of white flight into the suburbs. In addition, later Supreme Court cases limited the remedies available to federal courts in formerly segregated school districts. Federal courts could not fashion inter-district remedies: sending students from one school district to another to reduce the degree of segregation (see *Milliken v. Bradley*, 418 U.S. 717 [1974]). No longer could federal courts undo the new segregated patterns, since they had not been caused by state laws. In a series of cases decided by the Burger and Rehnquist courts, *Pasadena Board of Education v. Spangler* (497 U.S. 424 [1976]), *Board of Education v. Dowell* (498 U.S. 237 [1991]), *Freeman v. Pitts* (505 U.S. 467 [1992]), and the final decision in *Missouri v. Jenkins* (515 U.S. 70 [1995]), the Court limited the remedies available to a federal court to a "good faith compliance" with a previously imposed desegregation decree "for a reasonable period of time." The assumption then arises that the "vestiges of segregation has been eliminated to the extent practicable."

By the 1990s segregation returned to almost all elementary and secondary schools in the nation, including the North. By 1996, black students were the majority in the public schools in most of the metropolitan large cities: over 90% of the students in public schools in Atlanta, New Orleans, San Antonio, Washington, D.C., and Richmond were minorities. In Chicago, 90% of public school students were minorities, and in New York City the figure was 84%. The white middle class sent their students to private schools. A recent law review article notes that in North Carolina, the student population in ten of fifty-four elementary schools in Winston-Salem was at least 80% black or greater. These school districts also had the highest poverty rate in the state. By contrast the schools with the highest white population had a far lower poverty rate. Gary Orfield surveys the widespread reversal throughout the States in his 1996 book *Dismantling Desegregation: The Quiet Reversal of Brown v. Board of Education.*

But the *Brown* case stands for more than the concrete results it achieved. From the end of Reconstruction to the 1950s, a vast legal structure was in place that effectively kept the black population in a second-class status. Laws segregated schools, parks, libraries, and public facilities, as well as places of public accommodations. It was a crime for a black person to go into places that the laws preserved for whites. Placing blacks in such an inferior position made it virtually impossible for them to use political power to correct their situation.

Education was clearly the heart of the problem. First, segregation in education affected the largest number of black citizens—the tens of millions of children of school age. Second, segregation and lack of political power by blacks necessarily led to inferior schools with few books or teachers, and no science labs or other teaching tools. It made it difficult or impossible for the black population to acquire the necessary skills to raise itself from its second-class status.

But separate schools were permitted by long-standing Supreme Court precedent so long as they were equal. John W. Davis argued for the State of South Carolina in one of the five cases that came before the Court under the *Brown v. Board of Education* rubric: ". . . somewhere, sometime to every principle comes a moment of repose when it has been so often announced, so confidently relied upon, so long continued, that it passes the limits of judicial discretion and disturbance. . . . We relied on the fact that this Court had not once but seven times, I think, pronounced in favor of the 'separate but equal' doctrine." (215)*

In the 1930s, a group of young lawyers educated at Howard Law School, led by Charles Houston, began a legal campaign to show that segregated schools by their very nature could not be equal. The lawyers belonged to the NAACP, which in 1939 set up a separate legal organization called the NAACP Legal Defense Fund, Inc., otherwise known as the "Inc. Fund." The first cases were brought against law schools, on the assumption that the Justices of the Supreme Court could appreciate whether a segregated black law school with limited resources was equal to the well-endowed schools that serviced the white population. The first such case reached the Supreme Court in 1938, argued by Charles Houston. It came from Missouri, which did not even have a law school but sent black students out of state to achieve a legal education. In an opinion by Chief Justice Hughes, the Court stated that, "The white resident is afforded legal education within the state; the negro resident having the same qualification is refused it there and must go outside the state to obtain it. This is a denial of the equality of legal right [protected by the equal protection clause]" (*Missouri ex rel Gaines v. Canada* [305 U.S. 337 349 (1938)]).

Later desegregation cases were argued by Thurgood Marshall, who became head of the Inc. Fund in the late 1930s. In *Sipuel v. Bd. of Regents of the University of Oklahoma* (332 U.S. 631 [1948]), the Court again emphasized that the State must provide equal legal education for black students. Finally in *McLaurin v. Oklahoma State Regents for Higher Education* (339 U.S. 336 [1950]), the Court held that a

---

* Numbers in parentheses refer to pages in this book.

black student could not be relegated to a separate screened-off seat in the lecture halls and a separate table in the library and dining room in the University of Oklahoma graduate school. In the same year, the Court decided *Sweatt v. Painter* (339 U.S. 629 [1950]), where it ordered the black plaintiff to be admitted to the Texas Law School on the same terms as white students.

At that point, the lawyers from the Inc. Fund believed that the next step was to attack other schools of higher education such as colleges or other professional schools. The purpose was to establish a series of precedents that could finally lead up to an attack on segregation in elementary schools. But in 1950, the local students and citizens took matters away from the strategy of the lawyers. As told in Richard Kluger's brilliant work "Simple Justice," a group of black parents in Clarendon County, South Carolina, led by Rev. Joseph DeLaine, demanded a school bus for their own children. (The white students had thirty busses to take them to school.) They commenced a lawsuit to demand equality of treatment, which soon became the test case to challenge the entire structure of segregated elementary and secondary schools.

The case was joined with another suit from Virginia, where high school students organized a strike in Prince Edward County, Virginia, complaining about the inadequate facilities in the black schools. Another suit was brought in Topeka, Kansas (the *Brown* case), another case in Delaware, and a final case in the District of Columbia.

The lower courts (except in Delaware) found against the black plaintiffs, generally relying upon three Supreme Court precedents: (a) *Plessy v. Ferguson* (163 U.S. 537 [1896]), the cornerstone of the "separate but equal" doctrine; (b) *Cumming v. County Board of Education* (175 U.S. 528 [1899]), which held that a Georgia County did not have to provide a separate high school for black students, and (c) *Gong Lum v. Rice* (275 U.S. 78 [1927]), a case when the Supreme Court unanimously held that a Chinese student could not attend the white schools but was required to attend the separate schools primarily attended by blacks.

The lower courts found that the facilities for black and white students were not equal in the districts in South Carolina and Virginia. But they noted that efforts were being made to equalize the schools. In the South Carolina case, the lower court noted that, ". . . under the leadership of Governor [James] Byrnes [a former Justice of the Supreme Court] the legislature of South Carolina had made provision for a bond issue of $75,000,000 with a 3 per cent sales tax to support it for the purpose of equalizing educational opportunities and facilities throughout the state and of meeting the problem of equal educational opportunities for Negro children where this has not been done." *Briggs v. Elliott* (98 F.Supp. 529, 531 [E.D. S.Car. 1951]). (John W. Davis, arguing for the State of South Carolina in the Supreme Court, made a major argument based on these efforts of the State). The lower court rejected the argument that elementary schools should be treated the same way as the professional schools. "The problem of segregation as applied to graduate and professional education is essentially different from that involved in segregation in education at the lower levels." It further noted:

> The problem of segregation at the common school level is a very different one. At this level, as good education can be afforded in Negro schools as in white schools. . . . Moreover, education at this level is not a matter of voluntary choice on the part of the student but of compulsion by the state. The student is taken from the control of the

family during school hours by compulsion of law and placed in control of the school, where he must associate with his fellow students. The law thus provides that the school shall supplement the work of the parent in the training of the child and in doing so it is entering a delicate field and one fraught with tensions and difficulties. In formulating educational policy at the common school level, therefore, the law must take account, not merely of the matter of affording instruction to the student, but also of the wishes of the parent as to the upbringing of the child and his associates in the formative period of childhood and adolescence. If public education is to have the support of the people through their legislatures, it must not go contrary to what they deem for the best interests of their children. (98 F.Supp. at 535)

Only the Delaware judges and Judge J. Waries Waring, a courageous district court judge from South Carolina, dissented from this analysis and would have declared segregation in education inherently unconstitutional. (Judge Waring left South Carolina immediately after writing his dissent because of the intense hostility directed toward him because of his decisions favoring equal rights.)

These were the cases that made up the School Desegregation cases argued before the Supreme Court, first in 1952, again in 1953, and finally in 1955, on the remedies to be afforded.

The arguments before the Court are important documents of legal history, social science, and political theory. In addition, they contain some of the most important and eloquent instances of legal argument before the Court. The chief lawyer representing the South was John W. Davis, former Democratic presidential candidate in 1924, leader of the American bar, founder of a major law firm, who argued before the Supreme Court more times than any lawyer had done before and declined a nomination to the Supreme Court in the 1920s because it would involve too great a cut of his income as an attorney. He was a native of West Virginia and believed in the principles of segregation. He was enlisted by Governor James Byrnes to argue the case for South Carolina.

His chief opponent was Thurgood Marshall, who was forty-four when he argued the *Brown* case in 1952. He had argued five cases in the Court before *Brown,* including *Sweatt v. Painter, McLaurin,* and *Sipuel.* There were six other attorneys arguing for the plaintiffs in the other cases, Robert Carter (later appointed as a federal district court judge in New York), Spottswood Robinson III (later a Court of Appeals judge in Washington), James Nabrit (Dean of the Howard Law School and later United States Deputy Representative to the United Nations), Jack Greenberg (later Director of the Inc. Fund and a Columbia Law School Professor), and Louis Redding and George E. C. Hayes, private practitioners.

The arguments contained many brilliant bursts of legal rhetoric, sharp exchanges between lawyers and judges, steady focusing on the key legal issue by the Inc. Fund lawyers, as well as many ironic touches (such as the segregationist lawyers quoting Dr. W. E. B. DuBois in support of their position (60–61)). John W. Davis was at the height of his powers. He argued in the second round of arguments in 1953:

> Neither this Court nor any other court, I respectfully submit, can sit in the chairs of the legislature of South Carolina and mold its educational map. If it is found to be in its present form unacceptable, the State of South Carolina must devise the alternative.

It establishes the schools, it pays the funds, and it has the sole power to educate its citizens. . . .

Let me say this for the State of South Carolina. It does not come here as Thad Stevens would have wished in sack cloth and ashes. It believes that its legislation is not offensive to the Constitution of the United States.

It is confident of its good faith and intention to produce equality for all of its children of whatever race or color. It is convinced that the happiness, the progress and the welfare of these children is best promoted in segregated schools, and it thinks it a thousand pities that by this controversy there should be urged the return to an experiment which gives no more promise of success today than when it was written into their Constitution during what I call the tragic era [of Reconstruction].

I am reminded—and I hope it won't be treated as a reflection on anybody—of Aesop's fable of the dog and the meat. The dog, with a fine piece of meat in his mouth, crossed a bridge and saw the shadow in the stream and plunged for it and lost both substance and shadow.

Here is equal education, not promised, not prophesied, but present. Shall it be thrown away on some fancied question of racial prestige? (216)

Thurgood Marshall was not to be outdone. His argument was solid, with few flourishes:

Those same kids in Virginia and South Carolina—and I have seen them do it—they play in the streets together, they play on their farms together, they go down the road together, they separate to go to school, they come out of school and play ball together. They have to be separated in school.

There is some magic to it. You can have them voting together, you can have them not restricted because of law in the houses they live in. You can have them going to the same state university and the same college, but if they go to elementary and high school, the world will fall apart. And it is the exact same argument that has been made to this Court over and over again

They can't take race out of this case. From the day this case was filed until this moment, nobody has in any form or fashion . . . done anything to distinguish this statute from the Black Codes, which they must admit, because nobody can dispute, say anything anybody wants to say, one way or the other, the Fourteenth Amendment was intended to deprive the states of power to enforce Black Codes or anything else like it.

We charge that they are Black Codes. They obviously are Black Codes if you read them. They haven't denied that they are Black Codes, so if the Court wants to very narrowly decide this case, they can decide it on that point.

So whichever way it is done, the only way that this Court can decide this case in opposition to our position, is that there must be some reason which gives the state the right to make a classification that they can make in regard to nothing else in regard to Negroes, and we submit the only way to arrive at this decision is to find that for some reason Negroes are inferior to all other human beings.

Nobody will stand in the Court and urge that, and in order to arrive at the decision that they want as to arrive at, there would have to be some recognition of a reason why of all of the multitudinous groups of people in this country you have to single out Negroes and give them this separate treatment. (239)

During the first argument in 1952, Chief Justice Fred M. Vinson presided over the case. His questions during oral argument showed he was not sympathetic to the black students' position. He focused on the impracticality of ordering desegregation. He asked one of the Inc. Fund lawyers: "If you did not have the facilities [to equalize facilities] and did not have the teachers, how would you take care of them?" (78)

As we now know from Richard Kluger's book and from studies of Justices Burton's and Jackson's notes, the Court was badly split after the first argument, with Vinson and Reed opposed to overturning segregation (primarily because of the impracticality of any remedy), four others in favor, and the others undecided. At that point Justice Frankfurter thought up the idea of postponing decision by ordering reargument the next term, based on five new questions to be answered by the parties. Two of the questions seemed to favor the Southern states and three seemed to favor the plaintiffs.

By the time reargument occurred the next year, an important change had taken place on the Court: Earl Warren replaced Fred Vinson as Chief Justice. That change turned out to be decisive in the final outcome in the case. Chief Justice Warren came from a political background, not a legal one—attorney general of California, Governor, Republican vice-presidential candidate in 1948. He had never served as a judge. But as a politician, he knew he had to create a consensus. He knew that the prevailing sentiment among the other Justices was to avoid recriminations for the past and to arrange for a peaceful transition in the schools.

Although some of the Justices were prepared to write strong attacks on segregation and Justice Reed was insistent on dissenting, Chief Justice Warren waged a quiet campaign to issue a unanimous decision that did not look backward, that would outlaw segregation in the schools and that would postpone the difficult issues of implementation for another time. He succeeded. He enlisted Justices Clark and Jackson by preparing an opinion that did not look backward and did not attack the South for its past transgressions or go through an elaborate legal and historical analysis on the meaning of the equal protection clause. The final decision read:

> In approaching this problem, we cannot turn the clock back to 1868 when the Amendment was adopted, or even to 1896 when *Plessy v. Ferguson* was written. We must consider public education in the light of its full development and its present place in American life throughout the Nation. Only in this way can it be determined if segregation in public schools deprives these plaintiffs of the equal protection of the laws. (347 U.S. at 492–493)

With respect to Justice Reed, Chief Justice Warren took him out to lunch (with Justice Burton) about twenty times after the argument was held. When the opinion was ready, Warren asked Reed: "Stan, you're all by yourself in this now. You've got to decide whether it's really the best thing for the country."

The final opinion, issued on May 17, 1954, is short, quiet, and nonaccusatory.

> We come then to the question presented: Does segregation of children in public schools solely on the basis of race, even though the physical facilities and other 'tangible' factors may be equal, deprive the children of the minority group of equal educational opportunities? We believe that it does.

> In *McLaurin v. Oklahoma State Regents*, . . . the Court, in requiring that a Negro admitted to a white graduate school be treated like all other students, again resorted to

intangible considerations: 'his ability to study, to engage in discussions and exchange views with other students, and, in general, to learn his profession.' Such considerations apply with added force to children in grade and high schools. To separate them from others of similar age and qualifications solely because of their race generates a feeling of inferiority as to their status in the community that may affect their hearts and minds in a way unlikely ever to be undone.

We conclude that in the field of public education the doctrine of 'separate but equal' has no place. Separate educational facilities are inherently unequal. Therefore, we hold that the plaintiffs and others similarly situated for whom the actions have been brought are, by reason of the segregation complained of, deprived of the equal protection of the laws guaranteed by the Fourteenth Amendment. (347 U.S. at 493–94)

Thereafter, the Court heard argument again on the type of decree that should be entered to implement the decision. The lawyers for the Southern states made the most racist remarks imaginable, insisting that black students cannot be placed in the same classroom as white students because of the low scores of black students on intelligence tests and the high incidence of syphilis and gonorrhea and the "promiscuity" of the black population.

When the decree was finally issued, in May, 1955, it did not establish any deadlines for compliance with the *Brown* decision and gave the school districts time to work out a plan for desegregation:

The courts may consider problems related to administration, arising from the physical condition of the school plant, the school transportation system, personnel, revision of school districts and attendance areas into compact units to achieve a system of determining admission to the public schools on a nonracial basis, and revision of local laws and regulations which may be necessary in solving the foregoing problems. They will also consider the adequacy of any plans the defendants may propose to meet these problems and to effectuate a transition to a racially nondiscriminatory school system. During this period of transition, the courts will retain jurisdiction of these cases.

The judgments below . . . are accordingly reversed and the cases are remanded to the District Courts to take such proceedings and enter such orders and decrees consistent with this opinion as are necessary and proper to admit to public schools on a racially nondiscriminatory basis with all deliberate speed the parties to these cases.

The rest of the history of *Brown* is found in the decades of "massive resistance" by the Southern states, the use of every device imaginable to resist integration, including closing the schools in Prince Edward County, the Virginia district that was part of the original group of *Brown* cases. It was not until Congress included a provision in the 1964 Civil Rights Act that required compliance with desegregation orders of federal courts as a condition of receiving federal education funds that any real advance was made in eliminating segregation. In addition, the Supreme Court gave federal courts wide power to order bussing to implement a desegregation decree in *Swann v. Charlotte-Mecklenburg Bd. of Educ.* (402 U.S. 1 [1971]). By 1972–73, 91% of Southern schools were desegregated, that is, they had some minority students attending. The figure is deceptive, however, since the large majority (62%) of black students attended schools that were primarily attended by minorities, and 32.7% were in schools that were 90% minority.

So is *Brown* a failure? In legal terms, it destroyed the chief weapon that the Southern states had used to ghettoize the black population. "Separate but equal" was found to be illegal and unconstitutional because legal separation by race was necessarily stigmatic. When the states told the black population to stay on its side of the line and deprived it of voting power and furthermore made it a crime for whites to marry blacks or associate intimately with them, it established a virtually impregnable system of apartheid. *Brown* undercut the foundation of that structure. Not only were separate schools unconstitutional, but so were separate parks, libraries, and public facilities of all kind. Blacks could not legally be kept apart or kept down.

Brown was one of the sparks that ignited the Civil Rights Movement. From *Brown,* came the Montgomery bus boycott in 1955, which was about keeping blacks separate on busses. Then came the lunch-counter sit-ins in 1961, which attacked forced separation in restaurants. Then came the Civil Rights demonstrations in Birmingham in 1963, which also attacked separate facilities. By that time, Congress was forced to legislate in accordance with the developing Civil Rights campaign. The 1964 Civil Rights Act prohibited discrimination in places of public accommodation, in employment, and in any program that received federal funds. The 1965 Voting Rights Act broke down the last legal barriers to voting.

Brown could not solve all the problems created by a hundred years of legal restriction and societal separation. Indeed, it could not even solve the problem of segregation in schools. But it is there as a first, necessary step that we should celebrate on its fiftieth anniversary.

LEON FRIEDMAN
November 2003

THE *BROWN* DECISION AND ITS DISCONTENTS

Waldo E. Martin, Jr.

Today the 1954 *Brown v. the Board of Education* decision mandating the end of Jim Crow schools and by implication the end of Jim Crow America is represented as a mixed triumph, if a triumph at all. Similarly, *Brown* is increasingly characterized of late as a legal decision with a mixed legacy at best, a legacy of failure at worst. The evidence for this ambivalence is clear and compelling. All around us, in far too many ways, in spite of *Brown* and comparable antiracist successes, we can see Jim Crow America resurrected under different guises: some even postmodern and allegedly liberal, allegedly progressive. In fact, as the old saying goes, the more things have changed, in crucial ways the more they have remained the same. Yet when viewed within the context of its post–World War II historical moment, the origins, consequences, and meanings, the hope and promise of *Brown,* can be glimpsed anew.

The fact that fifty years after the original ruling, American schools are as racially segregated and as unequal as they were in 1954 is sobering. Far too many African-American and Latino students today attend lousy schools where they are essentially being warehoused, disrespected, mis- and undereducated. Our society has rendered these children disposable, and as a result their future prospects are dim. The ubiquitous and enduring calls for education reform to address these kinds of serious educational challenges typically gloss over the depth and severity of the problem. As a society, we consistently fail to grapple with the structural inequalities of class privilege and white racial privilege that brace not just the public schools but also the society and culture of which those schools are but a consequence.

The notion of finally fulfilling the grand and historic public school mission of providing a quality education for all American children, regardless of race, ethnicity, class, or station, was fundamental to the vision animating *Brown.* Realizing that optimistic mission meant revitalizing the central educational mission of these schools. This revitalized commitment to equal educational opportunity meant making available at every level all the necessary energies and resources to help realize such a lofty aim. First-rate public schools demanded nothing less than first-rate public support all around.

Providing the full and untrammeled opportunity for equal education for all children, envisioned by *Brown,* is thus a profound and inspiring, not to mention exceedingly lofty and difficult, goal. Commitment to this vision has also meant seriously reviving the civic mission of public schools as social institutions committed to weaving together into a singular people the nation's diverse racial, ethnic, class, and neighborhood strands. In other words, this aspect of *Brown's* broad educational vision of equal educational opportunity has meant a related yet vital commitment to a kind of social engineering: knitting America's diverse peoples firmly together so that they might better understand one another and work together. The ultimate goal here has been to move us as a nation toward a collective understanding of the American Dream of social betterment, not just an individualistic vision of that dream.

Unfortunately, as previously noted, America's public schools have by and large continued to reflect the inequalities that stratify the larger society. The democratic and egalitarian goals of America's public schools remain to a large extent underrealized, when not unrealized. Whether viewed from an educational, civic, and social standpoint or some combined standpoint, the results have too often been disappointing, if not dispiriting. Rather than engines of upward mobility, these schools have too often become cogs in the wheels of an increasingly global economy with the best jobs either reserved for a highly educated elite or shipped abroad. As a result, vast and growing numbers of America's children are being educated to fit into an economy of low-wage, dead-end service jobs, and social lives of diminished hope and shuttered aspiration.

Change is imperative. Yet the kind of legal and constitutional change epitomized by *Brown* can neither substitute for nor camouflage the crying need for substantive systemic change. The disgraceful American records on integration more generally, as well as school integration more specifically, are a case in point. Courts can rule on the legality and constitutionality of positions, and can even mandate steps to be taken to implement those rulings. But absent the national will and the national leadership to realize those rulings, hoped-for progress will languish. Add to the mix active white opposition and justifiable black skepticism, and you have several of the crucial ingredients for the undistinguished history of school integration since the *Brown* decision.

Still, the tendency to equate the *Brown* decision with the whole of the history of integration, notably school integration, is flawed and misleading. In and of itself, that decision is neither responsible for the too-few subsequent moments of integration's success nor the too-many subsequent moments of integration's failure. That revealing and often sordid history must be read against the kaleidoscopic historical backdrop of America's ongoing racial quagmire. In effect, the hope and promise of *Brown* has foundered on the shoals of American's foundering commitment to equality and justice, not to mention freedom. In other words, the failure of integration is America's failure, not the failure of *Brown*. Put another way, to the extent that it has been a failure, the decision has failed society because society has failed the decision.

The hope and promise of *Brown,* in this view, has to date been subverted and squandered by a leadership and a citizenry whose responsibility it has been to make integration happen. The failure, therefore, is neither with the decision's powerful egalitarian and democratic vision nor the committed and visionary lawyers who bequeathed it to us. Rather, the failure rests with the decision makers and the rest of us. The problem rests with those who were entrusted with the power to make integration happen but have instead lacked commitment to, even opposed, the vision of integration, not to mention having working against it and thus undermined its realization.

The foregoing argument that we have failed *Brown,* that *Brown* has not failed us, reflects the assumption of a guiding principle that making integration work has been a vital national goal. This argument thus assumes the absolute centrality of and a firm commitment to bringing about integration at every level. This evolving integrationism would be a multitiered endeavor proceeding in tandem on various related levels simultaneously. These levels would include a historical process proceeding politically, economically, socially, and culturally, as well as racially, ethnically, religiously, and classwise. In fact, though, the post-*Brown* history of integration exposes the assumption of a national commitment to integration to be idealistic, perhaps overstated, and maybe even illusory, if not downright delusory.

It is highly debatable that we as a nation have ever actually agreed upon first principles in the matter of integration. The concept emerged in the second half of the twentieth century as part of the postwar American national ethos critically spurred on by a variety of movements for social change, most importantly the Modern Civil Rights Movement. All of this transpired, however, without the kind of coherent national discussion that might have led to a national consensus regarding a set of guiding first principles. What is integration? Do we as a nation really want integration? If we truly do, how do we go about making it a reality? Given the lack of clarity on these foundational issues, it is no wonder that in terms of theory and practice, we have often drifted, been sidetracked, and stumbled badly. This very lack of clarity has only aided and abetted the maintenance of an unequal and unfair status quo, leading to a history of integration replete with ambiguity, ambivalence, half-baked schemes, missed opportunities, rank opportunism, and outright opposition.

It is useful to see *Brown* as a peak in an ongoing Black Freedom Struggle dating back to the arrival of the first Africans on these shores in the seventeenth century. Needless to say, innumerable peaks and valleys have marked the path of the long-term struggle since then. For sure, because of the massive black grassroots insurgency of the Civil Rights (1945–1965) and Black Power (1966–1975) years, that continuing struggle has witnessed a more progressive turn of events generally. The same can be said of the last decades of the twentieth century, in many ways a Post–Civil Rights, Post–Black Power era. Unfortunately, the path of integration, especially school integration, belies on balance a positive assessment, in spite of a few modest gains. On this front, as on so many others, the struggle continues.

When framed as an indispensable episode in the emergence of the modern phase of the Civil Rights Movement, *Brown* is a truly peak moment. The series of cases that culminated in the *Brown* victory owed to a multitiered strategy launched in the 1930s by the brilliant and prescient Charles Houston, Dean of Howard University's Law School. First, Houston and his cohorts envisioned legal and constitutional struggle, or judicial activism, as part and parcel of the ongoing Black Freedom Struggle. Spearheaded by the legal arm of the National Association for the Advancement of Colored People, this approach attracted an impressive array of black legal talent. This black judicial activism was seen as intimately related to and thus complementing other forms of black activism, such as collective protest. In practice as well as theory, the law—the veritable rule of law—had to be made to function as an effective weapon on behalf of the Black Freedom Struggle in close conjunction with the other components of that struggle. The more elite paths of struggle forged in the judicial arena were intimately interwoven with the more grassroots paths forged in the streets.

Second, Houston's strategy encompassed the training of a first-rate cadre of black lawyers to do the demanding yet necessary legal work. He clearly understood that the daunting challenge of dismantling Jim Crow demanded that blacks themselves rely principally upon themselves, not others, be they white allies or friends, radicals or progressives. As evidenced throughout the long and winding trajectory of the Black Freedom Struggle, here again the collective strategy of black self-help proved imperative. For Houston; his like-minded colleagues, including William Hastie; and exceptional students like Thurgood Marshall and Robert L. Carter; black civil rights lawyers needed to be committed to making the law work on behalf of the Black Freedom Struggle.

Third, what Houston and his cohorts artfully crafted was a way to marry civil rights litigation to the emerging mass black insurgency: to connect formally and strategically the legal struggle to the developing grassroots social movement. Throughout the thirties and forties, the overriding objective of the NAACP lawyers' strategy was a gradualist approach of destroying over time the separate but equal fiction of Jim Crow by making its practice financially impossible as well as unlawful. The master plan was to render Jim Crow unworkable by demanding that the separate world of Southern blacks be made truly equal in every respect to that of Southern whites. Equalization, as this strategy was called, yielded many triumphs throughout the thirties and forties, as various blatant manifestations of this racist discrimination, such as lower salaries for black teachers compared to white teachers, were ruled unlawful.

In part inspired by the militant black spirit of the World War II era, the NAACP lawyers shifted gears and developed a more aggressive strategy: a withering frontal assault on the citadel of Jim Crow itself. This uncompromising strategy was an all-out attack on the *Plessy v. Ferguson* doctrine itself, a vicious doctrine that had rationalized the separate but equal lie bracing Jim Crow since the turn of the century. The key constitutional argument was that the separate and unequal reality of Jim Crow schools was a fundamental denial of black children's, indeed all blacks', Fourteenth Amendment–protected right to equal citizenship. The legal and constitutional triumph of *Brown* not only overturned the *Plessy* dictum, but it also maintained persuasively that separate schools harmed white as well as black children, all whites as well as all blacks, indeed all Americans. Integrated public schools were envisioned, therefore, as a necessary step in the direction of a more egalitarian, more democratic, and, in turn, integrated society.

The year 1955 witnessed the Supreme Court dodging the question of the appropriate remedy in the *Brown* case in its "with all deliberate speed" formulation. The states of the former Confederacy interpreted that ambiguous evasion as further reason to mount a Massive Resistance Campaign to school integration. Until the federal government intervened in the late sixties to begin to enforce Southern school integration, it languished. After a brief period of halting progress toward school integration, largely in the 1970s and mostly in the South, we have of late witnessed the resegregation of America's public schools and, as a result, seen growing evidence of increasingly race-based and class-based inequality and injustice.

The legacy of *Brown* has indeed been mixed at best, a failure at worst. In the end, however, that very legacy, whether seen as failed or mixed, illuminates and signifies an even larger question: What kind of society do we really want? Do we really want a truly egalitarian and democratic society? Until we as a nation can commit ourselves to a concerted national effort to a more egalitarian and a more democratic society, our schools will continue to replicate, even exacerbate, inequality and injustice.

Brown v. Board

JUSTICES PRESENT AT ARGUMENT

Chief Justice Fred Vinson
(participated only in 1952 argument)

(1890–1953) Member, House of Representatives (1924–1929; 1931–1938); United States Circuit Judge, District of Columbia Court of Appeals, 1938–1943; Secretary of the Treasury, 1945–1946; Chief Justice of the United States, 1946–1953.

Earl Warren
(participated in 1953 and 1955 arguments)

(1891–   ) Attorney General, State of California, 1939–1943; Governor of California, 1943–1953; Republican candidate for Vice President of United States, 1948; Chief Justice of the United States, 1953–1969.

Hugo L. Black

(1886–   ) United States Senator from Alabama, 1927–1937; Associate Justice, United States Supreme Court, 1937–

Stanley F. Reed

(1884–   ) Solicitor General of United States, 1935–1938; Associate Justice, United States Supreme Court, 1938–1957.

Felix Frankfurter

(1882–1965) Professor, Harvard Law School, 1914–1939; Associate Justice, United States Supreme Court, 1939–1962.

William O. Douglas

(1898–   ) Commissioner, Securities and Exchange Commission, 1934–1936, Chairman, 1936–1939; Associate Justice, United States Supreme Court, 1939–

Robert H. Jackson
(participated in 1952 and 1953 arguments)

(1892–1954) General Counsel, Bureau of Internal Revenue; Assistant Attorney General of United States, 1936–1938; Solicitor General of United States, 1938–1939; Attorney General, Jan. 1940–June 1941; Associate Justice, United States Supreme Court, 1941–1954; Chief Counsel to prosecute war criminals before International Military Tribunal at Nuremburg, 1946–1947.

Harold H. Burton

(1888–1964) Mayor of Cleveland, Ohio, 1935–1940; United States Senator from Ohio, 1941–1945; Associate Justice, United States Supreme Court, 1945–1958.

Tom C. Clark

(1899–   ) Assistant Attorney General of United States, 1943–1945; Attorney General, 1945–1949; Associate Justice, United States Supreme Court, 1949–1967.

Sherman Minton

(1890–1965) United States Senator from Indiana, 1935–1941. United States Circuit Judge, Seventh Circuit Court of Appeals, 1941–1949; Associate Justice, United States Supreme Court, 1949–1956.

John Marshall Harlan
(participated only in 1955 argument)

(1899–   ) United States Circuit Judge, Second Circuit Court of Appeals, 1954–1955; Associate Justice, United States Supreme Court, 1955–

ATTORNEYS FOR PLAINTIFFS

Robert L. Carter

Assistant Counsel, NAACP Legal Defense and Educational Fund, Inc. at the time of the argument in Brown v. Board of Education; subsequently General Counsel for NAACP.

Thurgood Marshall

Director-Counsel of the NAACP Legal Defense and Educational Fund, Inc., 1940–1961; United States Circuit Judge for the Second Circuit Court of Appeals, 1961–1965; Solicitor General of United States, 1965–1967; Associate Justice, United States Supreme Court, 1967–

Spottswood Robinson, III

Southeast Regional Counsel NAACP Legal Defense and Educational Fund, Inc., 1951–1960; Dean, Howard University Law School, 1960–1964; Member United States Commission on Civil Rights, 1961–1966; United States Circuit Judge for the District of Columbia Court of Appeals, 1966–

George E. C. Hayes

Private practice Washington D.C.; Member of Board of Directors of NAACP Legal Defense and Educational Fund, Inc.

James Nabrit

Professor, Howard University Law School, 1936–1956; Dean 1958–1960; President, Howard University, 1960–1967; United States Deputy Representative to United Nations, 1966–1967.

Louis L. Redding

Private Practice, Wilmington, Del.

Jack Greenberg

Assistant Counsel, NAACP Legal Defense and Educational Fund, Inc., 1949–1961; Director-Counsel, 1961–

ATTORNEYS FOR DEFENDANTS

Paul E. Wilson   Assistant Attorney General, State of Kansas.

Harold R. Fatzer   Attorney General, State of Kansas, 1949–1956; Justice, Supreme Court of Kansas, 1956–

John W. Davis   Member, House of Representatives, 1911–1915; Solicitor General of United States, 1913–1918; Ambassador to Great Britian, 1918–1921; Member of law firm of Davis, Polk, Wardwell, Sunderland & Kiendl, 1921–1955; Democratic candidate for President, 1924; President of American Bar Association, 1922; declined nomination to United States Supreme Court, 1922.

Robert McC. Figg, Jr.   Counsel for Board of Trustees of Clarendon County, South Carolina School District.

S. E. Rogers   Counsel for Board of Trustees of Clarendon County, South Carolina School District.

T. Justin Moore   Counsel for Prince Edward County Virginia School System; Member of firm of Hunton, Williams, Gay, Powell & Gibson of Richmond, Va.

Archibald G. Robertson   Counsel for Prince Edward County Virginia School System; Member of firm of Hunton, Williams, Gay, Powell & Gibson of Richmond, Va.

J. Lindsay Almond   Member, House of Representatives, 1946–1948; Attorney General, State of Virginia, 1948–1957; Governor, State of Virginia, 1958–1962; Judge, United States Court of Customs and Patent Appeals, 1962–

Milton Korman   Assistant Corporation Counsel, District of Columbia.

H. Albert Young   Attorney General, State of Delaware.

Joseph D. Craven   Attorney General, State of Delaware.

COUNSEL FOR *AMICI*

J. Lee Rankin

Assistant Attorney General, Department of Justice, 1953–1956; Solicitor General of United States, 1956–1961; Chief Counsel, Warren Commission, 1963–1964; Corporation Counsel, City of New York, 1966–

Simon E. Sobeloff

Chief Judge, Maryland Court of Appeals, 1952–1954; Solicitor General of United States, 1954–1956; United States Circuit Judge for the Fourth Circuit Court of Appeals, 1956–   , Chief Judge since 1958.

Richard Ervin

Attorney General, State of Florida; Justice, Florida Supreme Court, 1964.

Ralph E. Odum

Assistant Attorney General, State of Florida.

I. Beverly Lake

Assistant Attorney General, State of North Carolina.

Thomas J. Gentry

Attorney General, State of Arkansas.

Mac Q. Williamson

Attorney General, State of Oklahoma.

C. Ferdinand Sybert

Attorney General, State of Maryland, 1954–1961; Judge, Court of Appeals, Maryland, 1961.

John Ben Shepperd

Attorney General, State of Texas.

Burnell Waldrep

Assistant Attorney General, State of Texas.

1952   ARGUMENT

IN THE SUPREME COURT OF THE UNITED STATES

October Term, 1952

OLIVER BROWN, MRS. RICHARD LAWTON, MRS. SADIE EMMANUEL, ET AL
Appellants

vs.

BOARD OF EDUCATION OF TOPEKA, SHAWNEE COUNTY, KANSAS, ET AL
Appellees.

Case No. 8

Washington, D.C.
Tuesday, December 9, 1952.

The above-entitled cause came on for oral argument at 1:35 p.m.

PRESENT:

The Chief Justice, Honorable Fred M. Vinson, and Associate Justices Black, Reed,
Frankfurter, Douglas, Jackson, Burton, Clark, and Minton.

APPEARANCES:

On behalf of the Appellants:
ROBERT L. CARTER, ESQ.

On behalf of the Appellees:
PAUL E. WILSON, ESQ.

THE CHIEF JUSTICE: Case No. 8, Oliver Brown and others versus the Board of Education of Topeka, Shawnee County, Kansas.

THE CLERK: Counsel are present.

THE CHIEF JUSTICE: Mr. Carter.

ARGUMENT ON BEHALF OF THE APPELLANTS

by MR. CARTER

MR. CARTER: This case is here on direct appeal pursuant to Title 28, section 1253, 2101(b), from the final judgment of a statutory three-judge court, District Court, for the District of Kansas, denying appellants' motion, application for a permanent injunction to restrain the enforcement of Chapter 72–1724 of the General Statutes of Kansas, on the grounds of that statute's fatal conflict with the requirements and guarantees of the Fourteenth Amendment.

The statute in question empowers boards of education in cities of the first class in Kansas to maintain and operate public elementary schools on a segregated basis, with the exception of Kansas City, Kansas, which is empowered to maintain segregated public high schools also.

The law of Kansas is clear, as construed by the highest court of that state, that except for this statutory authority, the appellees in this instance would have no power to make any distinction whatsoever in public schools among children on the basis of race and color; or, to put it another way, the law of Kansas is this: that it is a violation of state law for any state officer to use race as a factor in affording educational opportunities unless that authority is specifically, clearly, and expressly granted by the legislature.

The state cases, which are set forth and would set this out, are cited at page 2 of our brief.[1]

Now, it is to be noted that this statute prohibits any type of color discrimination in high schools, with the exception of Kansas City, Kansas.

The Topeka school system is operated on a six-three-three plan: elementary schools going through the sixth grade, thereafter junior high schools through the ninth grade, and thereafter senior high schools.

So that in this instance, appellants are required to attend segregated elementary schools through the sixth grade, but thereafter they go to high schools without any determination being made as to which school they will attend on the basis of race.

If appellants are of Negro origin, they are minors who are not eligible at the present time to attend the public elementary schools in Topeka.

The appellees are empowered by state law to maintain the public school system in Topeka, Kansas. The City of Topeka has been divided into eighteen territorial divisions for public school purposes. In each of these divisions appellees maintain one school for white residents; in addition, they maintain four segregated schools for Negroes.

It is the gravamen of our complaint—it was the gravamen of our complaint below, and it is the gravamen of our appeal here—that the appellees have deprived—we have been deprived of the equal protection of the laws where the statute requires appellants to attend public elementary schools on a segregated basis, because the act of separation and the act of segregation in and of itself denies them equal educational opportunities which the Fourteenth Amendment secures.

In the answer below, the appellees, the school board, defended this action on the ground that they were acting pursuant to the statute; that appellants were not entitled to attend the elementary schools in Kansas, the eighteen elementary schools, which they maintained for white children, solely because of race and color, and that they wouldn't be admitted into those schools because they were Negroes.

The State of Kansas in the court below, and in its brief filed here, defends the constitutionality of the statute in question, and affirmatively asserts that the state has the power to authorize the imposition of racial distinction for public school purposes.

The only state or federal constitutional limitation which the State of Kansas concedes on that power is that when these distinctions are imposed the school physical facilities for Negro children must be equal.

With that limitation, they say that there can be no constitutional limitation on their power to impose racial distinctions.

[1]The briefs and records of all cases argued before the Supreme Court are deposited in approximately twenty law libraries throughout the country, including Harvard, Columbia, Yale, the New York Bar Association library as well as at the Supreme Court library.

A three-judge court was convened in the court below, pursuant to title 28 of the United States Code, section 2281 and 2284, and there a trial on the merits took place.

At the trial, appellants introduced evidence designed to conclusively demonstrate that the act of segregation in and of itself made the educational opportunities which were provided in the four schools maintained for Negroes inferior to those in the eighteen schools which were maintained for white children, because of racial segregation imposed which severely handicapped Negro children in their pursuit of knowledge, and made it impossible for them to secure equal education.

In the course of the development of this uncontroverted testimony, appellants showed that they and other Negro children similarly situated were placed at a serious disadvantage with respect to their opportunity to develop citizenship skills, and that they were denied the opportunity to learn to adjust personally and socially in a setting comprising a cross section of the dominant population of the city.

It was testified that racial segregation, as practiced in the City of Topeka, tended to relegate appellants and their group to an inferior caste; that it lowered their level of aspiration; that it instilled feelings of insecurity and inferiority with them, and that it retarded their mental and educational development, and for these reasons, the testimony said, it was impossible for the Negro children who were set off in these four schools to secure, in fact or in law, an education which was equal to that available to white children in the eighteen elementary schools maintained for them.

On August 3, the District Court filed its opinion, its findings of fact and its conclusions of law, and a final decree, all of which are set out at page 238 of the record.[2]

We accept and adopt as our own all of the findings of fact of the court below, and I wish specifically to call to the Court's attention the findings which are findings 4, 5, and 6, which are set out at page 245, in which the court found that there was no material difference between the four schools maintained for Negroes, and the eighteen schools maintained for white children with respect to physical facilities, the educational qualifications of teachers, and the courses of study prescribed.

Here we abondon any claim, in pressing our attack on the unconstitutionality of this statute—we abandon any claim— of any constitutional inequality which comes from anything other than the act of segregation itself.

In short, the sole basis for our appeal here on the constitutionality of the statute of Kansas is that it empowers the maintenance and operation of racially segregated schools, and under that basis we say, on the basis of the fact that the schools are segregated, that Negro children are denied equal protection of the laws, and they cannot secure equality in educational opportunity.

This the court found as a fact, and I will go into that finding, which is also set out on page 25 of the brief, later in the development of my argument.

But suffice it to say for this purpose, that although the court found that racial segregation created educational inequality in fact, it concluded, as a matter of law,

[2]The District Court decision is reported at 98 F. Supp. 797 and appears at p. 539 of this volume.

that the only type of educational inequality which was cognizable under the Constitution was an educational inequality which stems from material and physical factors; and absent any inequality of that level, the court said:

> We are bound by *Plessy* v. *Ferguson,* and *Gong Lum* v. *Rice* to hold in appellees' favor and uphold the constitutionality of that statute.[3]

We have one fundamental contention which we will seek to develop in the course of this argument, and that contention is that no state has any authority under the equal protection clause of the Fourteenth Amendment to use race as a factor in affording educational opportunities among its citizens.

We say that for two reasons: First, we say that a division of citizens by the states for public school purposes on the basis of race and color effect an unlawful and an unconstitutional classification within the meaning of the equal-protection clause; and, secondly, we say that where public school attendance is determined on the basis of race and color, that it is impossible for Negro children to secure equal educational opportunities within the meaning of the equal protection of the laws.

With regard to the first basis of our attack on the statute, Kansas has authorized, under certain conditions, certain boards of education to divide its schools at the elementary school level for the purpose of giving them education opportunities.

It is our position that any legislative or governmental classification must fall with an even hand on all persons similarly situated.

This Court has long held that this is the law with respect to a lawful classification, and in order to assure that this evenhandedness of the law in terms of classification exists, this Court has set standards which say that where the legislature of a state seeks to make a classification or distinction among persons, that that classification and those distinctions must rest upon some differentiation fairly related to the object which the state seeks to regulate.

Now, in this case the Negro children are—and other Negro children similarly situated are—put in one category for public school purposes, solely on the basis of race and color, and white children are put in another category for the purpose of determining what schools they will attend.

JUSTICE MINTON: Mr. Carter, I do not know whether I have followed you or all the facts on this. Was there a finding that the only basis of classification was race or color?

MR. CARTER: It was admitted—the appellees admitted in their answer—that the only reason that they would not permit Negro children to attend the eighteen white schools was because they were Negroes.

---

[3]Plessy v. Ferguson, 163 U.S. 537 (1896), held that a Lousiana state law providing for separate but equal accomodations on railroads for Negroes and whites did not violate the Constitution. It was thereafter cited as the source of the "separate but equal" doctrine. In Gong Lum v. Rice, 275 U.S. 78 (1927), a young Chinese girl sought admittance to a white public school in Mississippi. The authorities refused to admit her, saying she was classified as part of the colored race for the purpose of school attendance. The Supreme Court refused to intervene.

JUSTICE MINTON: Then we accept on this record that the only showing is that the classification here was solely on race and color?

MR. CARTER: Yes, sir. I think the state itself concedes this is so in its brief.

Now, we say that the only basis for this division is race, and that under the decisions of this Court that no state can use race, and race alone, as a basis upon which to ground any legislative, any lawful constitutional authority and, particularly this Court has indicated in a number of opinions that this is so because it is not felt that race is a reasonable basis upon which to ground acts; it is not a real differentiation, and it is not relevant and, in fact, this Court has indicated that race is arbitrary and an irrational standard, so that I would also like to point out, if I may, going to and quoting the statute, that the statute itself shows that this is so.

I am reading from the quote of the statute from page 3 of our brief. The statute says:

[The Board of Education may] organize and maintain separate schools for the education of white and colored children, including the high schools in Kansas City, Kansas; no discrimination on account of color shall be made in high schools except as provided herein.

We say that on the face of the statute this is explicit recognition of the fact that the authorization which the state gave to cities of the first class, and so forth, to make this segregation on the basis of race, carried with it the necessary fact that they were permitted to discriminate on the basis of race and color, and that the statute recognizes that these two things are interchangeable and cannot be separated.

Now, without further belaboring our classification argument, our theory is that if the normal rules of classification, the equal protection doctrine of classification, apply to this case—and we say they should be applied—that this statute is fatally defective, and that on this ground, and this ground alone, the statute should be struck down.

We also contend, as I indicated, a second ground for the unconstitutionality of the statute, a second part of the main contention, is that this type of segregation makes it impossible for Negro children and appellants in this case to receive equal educational opportunities, and that in this case, the court below found this to be so as a fact; and I would turn again to quote on page 245 of the record, finding No. 8, where the court in its finding said, and I quote:

Segregation of white and colored children in public schools has a detrimental effect upon the colored children. The impact is greater when it has the sanction of the law; for the policy of separating the races is usually interpreted as denoting the inferiority of the Negro group. A sense of inferiority affects the motivation of a child to learn. Segregation with the sanction of law, therefore, has a tendency to [restrain] the edutional and mental development of Negro children and to deprive them of some of the benefits they would receive in a racial integrated school system.

Now, as we had indicated before, this finding is amply supported by the uncontroverted testimony, and we feel that what the court did in this case in approaching this finding was that it made the same approach on a factual basis that this Court made in the McLaurin and Sweatt cases.[1]

It is our contention, our view, that when this Court was confronted with the question of whether McLaurin and Sweatt were afforded equal educational opportunities that it looked at the restrictions imposed to find out whether or not they in any way impaired the quality of education which was offered and, upon finding that the quality of education that had been offered under the segregated conditions, that this Court held in both instances that those racial restrictions could not stand.

The court below, based on this finding, starts its examination in this same way. It finds that the restrictions which the appellants complained of place them and other Negro children in the class at a disadvantage with respect to the quality of education which they would receive, and that as a result of these restrictions, Negro children are—the development of their minds, and the learning process is impaired and damaged.

We take the position that where there exists educational inequality, in fact, that is necessarily follows that educational inequality in the law is also present.

But the court below felt, as I indicated before, that the only concern of the Constitution with the question of educational equality, was that the physical facilities afforded had to be equal; and absent any inequality with regard to physical facilities, they say, "We are bound by *Plessy* v. *Ferguson* and *Gong Lum* v. *Rice*."

It is also clear from the court's opinion that it was in a great deal of confusion and doubt and, perhaps, even in torture in reaching these results.

I would again like to quote from the record the court's opinion, on page 243, and the court says:

> If segregation within a school as in the McLaurin case is a denial of due process, it is difficult to see why segregation in separate schools would not result in the same denial. Or if the denial of the right to commingle with the majority group in higher institutions of learning as in the Sweatt case and gain the educational advantages resulting therefrom, is lack of due process, it is difficult to see why such denial would not result in the same lack of due process if practiced in the lower grades.

We say that but for the constraint which the court feels was imposed upon it by the McLaurin case—

THE CHIEF JUSTICE: We will recess for lunch.

(A short recess was taken.)

THE CHIEF JUSTICE: Mr. Carter?

MR. CARTER: Just before the recess, I was attempting to show that in the opinion of the court below that it was clear from the opinion that the court felt

[1]In McLaurin v. Oklahoma State Regents, 339 U.S. 637 (1950), the Court ordered a Negro graduate student at the University of Oklahoma to be treated exactly as the white students and required the special seats and tables to which he was assigned in the classroom, library, and cafeteria removed. In Sweatt v. Painter, 339 U.S. 629 (1950), the Court found a new Negro law school opened by the State of Texas to be inferior to the University of Texas Law School and therefore required the University to admit a qualified Negro applicant.

that the rule of law applicable in the McLaurin and Sweatt cases should apply here, but felt that it was constrained and prevented from doing that by virtue of *Plessy* v. *Ferguson* and *Gong Lum* v. *Rice.*

We believe that the court below was wrong in this conclusion. We think that the rules of law applicable to McLaurin and Sweatt do apply, and that there are no decisions of this Court which require a contrary result.

JUSTICE REED: Was there any evidence in the record to show the inability, the lesser ability, of the child in the segregated schools?

MR. CARTER: Yes, sir, there was a great deal of testimony on the impact of racial distinctions and segregation, on the emotional and mental development of a child.

Now, this is, in summary, Finding 8 of the court, a summarization of the evidence that we introduced on that.

JUSTICE REED: And the findings go to the ability to learn or merely on the emotional reaction?

MR. CARTER: The finding says that—

JUSTICE REED: I know about the finding, but the evidence?

MR. CARTER: The evidence, yes, sir. The evidence went to the fact that in the segregated school, because of these emotional impacts that segregation has, that it does impair the ability to learn, that you are not able to learn as well as you do if you were in a mixed school, and that further than that, you are barred from contact with members of the dominant group and, therefore, your total educational content is somewhat lower than it would be ordinarily.

JUSTICE REED: Would those citations be in your brief on page 9?

MR. CARTER: Yes, sir. In fact, what we attempted to do was to pick up in summary and refer the Court to the record of the various disabilities to which our witnesses testified, and we covered the question of the content of education. They are all set out on page 9 of our brief as citations.

JUSTICE BURTON: It is your position that there is a great deal more to the educational process even in the elementary school than what you read in the books?

MR. CARTER: Yes, sir, that is precisely the point.

JUSTICE BURTON: And it is on that basis which makes a real difference whether it is segregated or not?

MR. CARTER: Yes, sir. We say that the question of your physical facilities is not enough. The Constitution does not, in terms of protecting, giving equal protection of the laws with regard to equal educational opportunities, does not stop with the fact that you have equal physical facilities, but it covers the whole educational process.

THE CHIEF JUSTICE: The findings in this case did not stop with equal physical facilities, did they?

MR. CARTER: No, sir, the findings did not stop, but went beyond that. But, as I indicated, the Court did not feel that it could go in the law beyond physical facilities.

Of the two cases which the court below indicates have kept it from ruling as a matter of law in this case that educational, equal educational, opportunities were not afforded, the first is the *Plessy* v. *Ferguson* case.

It is our position that *Plessy* v. *Ferguson* is not in point here; that it had nothing to do with educational opportunities whatsoever.

We further take the position that whatever the court below may have felt about the reach of the Plessy case, that this Court in the Sweatt case made it absolutely clear that *Plessy* v. *Ferguson* had nothing to do with the question of education.

The Court, in its opinion, after discussing the Sipuel case, the Fisher case, and the Gaines case[5], in the Sweatt opinion said that these are the only cases in this Court which control the issue of racial distinction in state-supported graduate and professional education.

We think this was a pointed and deliberate omission in *Plessy,* and that the Court is saying the *Plessy* v. *Ferguson* certainly has nothing to do with the validity of racial distinctions in graduate and professional schools.

By the same logic, we say that since *Plessy* had nothing to do with the higher level of education, it certainly has nothing to do with equal educational opportunities in the elementary grades.

For that reason we think that *Plessy* need not be considered; that it has nothing to do with this case, and it is out of the case entirely.

THE CHIEF JUSTICE: Well, in regard to the findings, it was found that the physical facilities, curricula, courses of study, qualifications and quality of teachers, as well as other educational facilities in the two sets of schools are comparable?

MR. CARTER: Yes, sir.

THE CHIEF JUSTICE: And the only item of discrimination, an item of discrimination, was transportation by bus for the colored students without that facility for the white students.

MR. CARTER: That is true. But the court—these are the physical factors that the court found, and then the court went on to show how segregation made the educational opportunities inferior, and this, we think, is the heart of our case.

[5]In Sipuel v. Board of Regents, 332 U.S. 631 (1948), the Court ordered the state authorities to admit a Negro to the University of Oklahoma Law School. In Fisher v. Hurst, 333 U.S. 147 (1948) a further order of the district court in the Sipuel case was affirmed. Missouri ex rel. Gaines v. Canada, 305 U.S. 337 (1938), was the first decision requiring a state (Missouri) to admit qualified Negro students to a graduate school (in that case a law school) where equal facilities were not available elsewhere in the state. The state could not discharge its duty under the equal protection clause by paying the student's tuition to go to another school in another state.

THE CHIEF JUSTICE: That is all that you really have here to base your segregation issue upon.

MR. CARTER: That is right.

THE CHIEF JUSTICE: I mean, of course, you could have the issue as to equal facilities on the other, but so far as all the other physical facilities, curricula, teachers, and transportation and all that, and so forth, there is a finding that they are equal?

MR. CARTER: Yes, sir, and we do not controvert that finding.

The other case that the court below cited was the *Gong Lum* v. *Rice* case. We do not think that that case is controlling here either.

In that case it is true that what was involved was racial distinction in the elementary grades.

JUSTICE DOUGLAS: Was that a Chinese student?

MR. CARTER: That was the Chinese student. But we think that case is so different from our case that it cannot control the decision in this case, because there the issue which was raised by petitioner of Chinese origin was that she did not at all contest the state's power to enforce a racial classification.

She conceded that the state had such power. What petitioner was objecting to was the fact that, as a Chinese, a child of Chinese origin, that she was required to have contact with Negroes for school purposes which, under the segregation laws of Mississippi, white children were protected against.

She said that if—her contention was, that if there were some benefits or harms that would flow to white children from being forced to have contacts with Negroes, that she had an equal right to benefit or to be free of that harm from such contact, and that to require her to be classified among Negroes for school purposes was a denial to her of the equal protection of the laws.

Our contention is that in that instance that case cannot control a decision when here we are contesting the power of the state to make any classification whatsoever, and we think that what the court did below, this Court, in defining what was the issue in this case, said that the question was whether an American citizen of Chinese origin is denied equal protection and classed among the colored races for public school purposes, and furnished equal educational opportunities.

It said that were this a new question:

> We would think it would need our full consideration, and it would be necessary for full argument, but it is not a new question. It is the same question that we have many times decided to be within the purview of the States, without the intervention of the Federal Constitution.

Now, we do not believe that *Gong Lum* can be considered as a precedent contrary to the position we take here. Certainly it cannot be conceded as such a precedent until this Court, when the issue is squarely presented to it, on the question of the power of the state, examines the question and makes a determination in the state's favor; and only in that instance do we feel that *Gong Lum* can be any authority on this question.

JUSTICE FRANKFURTER: Mr. Carter, while what you say may be so, nevertheless, in its opinion, the Court, in *Gong Lum,* did rest on the fact that this issue had been settled by a large body of adjudications going back to what was or might fairly have been called an abolitionist state, the Commonwealth of Massachusetts.

Going back to the Roberts case[6]—

MR. CARTER: Yes, sir.

JUSTICE FRANKFURTER: —I want to ask you—and, may I say, particularly in a case of this sort, a question does not imply an answer; a question merely implies an eager desire for information—I want to ask you whether in the light of that fact, this was a unanimous opinion of the Court which, at the time, had on its membership Justice Holmes, Justice Brandeis, Justice Stone—and I am picking those out not invidiously, but as judges who gave great evidence of being very sensitive and alert to questions of so-called civil liberties—and I should like to ask you whether you think that decision rested on the concession by the petitioner in that case, and the problem of segregation was not involved and, in fact, that underlay the whole decision, the whole adjudication—whether you think a man like Justice Brandeis would have been foreclosed by the concession of the parties?

MR. CARTER: Well, Your Honor, in all honesty, I would say that only partially would I consider that to be true. I think that what the Court did in *Gong Lum,* the Court was presented with the issue or the question, and it assumed that facilities were equal; and the Court at that time, with regard to this issue which was raised, although they conceded the power and did not have to make any full examination, it felt after reviewing those other decisions that the only question that they would have to consider or settle was the question of equal facilities.

JUSTICE FRANKFURTER: Yes. But the Court took as settled by a long course of decisions that this question was many times decided that this power was within the constitutional power of the state legislatures, this power of segregation.

MR. CARTER: Yes, sir.

JUSTICE FRANKFURTER: The more specific question I would like to put to you is this: Do we not have to face the fact that what you are challenging is something that was written into the public law and adjudications of courts, including this Court, by a large body of decisions and, therefore, the question arises whether, and under what circumstances, this Court should now upset so long a course of decisions?

Don't we have to face that, instead of chipping away and saying, "This was dictum," and "This was a mild dictum," and "This was a strong dictum," and is anything to be gained by concealing that central fact, that central issue?

[6]Roberts v. City of Boston, 59 Mass. 198 (1850). School segregation in Boston was upheld despite a Massachusetts constitutional provision that all persons were equal before the law. In 1855 segregation was eliminated in Boston's public schools.

MR. CARTER: Well, I do not think, Your Honor, that you have to face that issue.

My view is that with regard to this particular question this Court decided with *Sweatt* v. *Painter*—

In *Sweatt* v. *Painter* in this Court, the only decision here which was decided on the question of "separate but equal " was a dictum coming out from *Plessy* v. *Ferguson*, and this Court in the Sweatt case, it seems to me very carefully to have decided that it did not have to face the question because *Plessy* v. *Ferguson* was not involved.

I think in this particular case the only decision of this Court which can be said to have decided a question of the validity of racial distinction in elementary schools is this case that I am discussing.

Now, I think that in view of the concession, in view of the fact that the Court felt this was not a case of first impression, although I think it was and is a case of first impression in this Court at the time it came here, that this Court did not give the arguments at all a full consideration which we think that they require.

JUSTICE FRANKFURTER: You are quite right in suggesting that this question explicitly as to segregation in the primary grades has not been adjudicated by this Court.

This question is in that frame, in that explicitness, unembarrassed by physical inequalities, and so on before the Court for the first time. But a long course of legislation by the states, and a long course of utterances by this Court and other courts in dealing with the subject, from the point of view of relevance as to whether a thing is or is not within the prohibition of the Fourteenth Amendment, is from my point of view almost as impressive as a single decision, which does not mean that I would be controlled in a constitutional case by a direct adjudication; but I do think we have to face in this case the fact that we are dealing with a long-established historical practice by the states, and the assumption of the exercise of power which not only was written on the statute books, but has been confirmed and adjudicated by state courts, as well as by the expressions of this Court.

MR. CARTER: Well, Mr. Justice Frankfurter, I would say on that that I was attempting here to take the narrow position with regard to this case, and to approach it in a way that I thought the Court approached the decision in *Sweatt* and *McLaurin*.

I have no hesitancy in saying to the Court that if they do not agree that the decision can be handed down in our favor on this basis of this approach, that I have no hesitancy in saying that the issue of "separate but equal" should be faced and ought to be faced, and that in our view the "separate but equal" doctrine should be overruled.

But as I said before, as the Court apparently approached *Sweatt* and *McLaurin*, it did not feel it had to meet that issue, and we do not feel it has to meet it here, but if the Court has reached a contrary conclusion in regard to it, then we, of course, take the position that the "separate but equal" doctrine should squarely be overruled.

JUSTICE FRANKFURTER: May I trouble you to clarify that? Do I understand from what you have just said that you think this Kansas law is bad on the record, is bad in the Kansas case, on the "separate but equal" doctrine, and that even by that test this law must fall?

MR. CARTER: No, sir, I think—

JUSTICE FRANKFURTER: Then why do we not have to face the "separate but equal" doctrine?

MR. CARTER: Because in so far as this Court is concerned, as I have indicated before, this Court, with the exception of *Gong Lum,* has not at the elementary level adopted the "separate but equal" doctrine.

There is no decision in this Court, unless the Court feels that *Gong Lum* v. *Rice* is that decision.

As I attempted to indicate before, that was a case of first impression, although the Court did not seem to think it was, and that here actually we are now being presented—the Court is now being presented—with a case of first impression, when it has a full record, which you can give full consideration to, and that *Gong Lum,* which did not squarely raise the issue, ought not to be controlling.

All I am saying is that you do not have to overrule "separate but equal" at the elementary school level in deciding the Kansas case because you have never decided the "separate but equal" applied at the elementary school level.

JUSTICE FRANKFURTER: Are you saying that we can say that "separate but equal" is not a doctrine that is relevant at the primary school level? Is that what you are saying?

JUSTICE DOUGLAS: I think you are saying that segregation may be all right in street cars and railroad cars and restaurants, but that is all that we have decided.

MR. CARTER: That is the only place that you have decided that it is all right.

JUSTICE DOUGLAS: And that education is different, education is different from that.

MR. CARTER: Yes, sir.

JUSTICE DOUGLAS: That is your argument, is it not? Isn't that your argument in this case?

MR. CARTER: Yes.

JUSTICE FRANKFURTER: But how can that be your argument when the whole basis of dealing with education thus far has been to find out whether it, the "separate but equal" doctrine is satisfied?

JUSTICE DOUGLAS: You are talking about the gist of the cases in this Court?

JUSTICE FRANKFURTER: I am talking about the cases in this Court.

MR. CARTER: As I interpret the cases in this Court, Your Honor, as I interpret the Sweatt case and the McLaurin case, the question of "separate and equal," as to whether the separate and equal doctrine was satisfied, I do not believe that that test was applied there. In *McLaurin* there was no separation.

JUSTICE FRANKFURTER: But take the Gaines case, take the beginning of the "separate but equal," and unless I completely misconceive the cases I have read before I came here and those in which I have participated, the test in each one of these cases was whether "separate and equal" is relevant or whether it was satisfied, and we have held in some of the cases that it was not satisfied, and that in a constitutional case we do not have to go beyond the immediate necessities of the record, and we have said as to others that for purposes of training in the law you have a mixed situation; you cannot draw that line.

MR. CARTER: Well, take the Gaines case, Your Honor; the only thing that I would say on the Gaines case is that what the Court decided in the Gaines case was that since there were no facilities available to Negroes, that the petitioner Gaines had to be admitted to the white school.

Now, it is true that there is certain language in the Gaines case which would appear to give support to *Plessy* v. *Ferguson,* but the language in terms of the decision—you have to take the language in regard to what the decision stated in the Sipuel case—I think it is the same thing, and when we get over to *Sweatt* and *McLaurin,* we have a situation in which this Court went beyond certain physical facilities and said, "These are not as important as these other things that we cannot name," and it decided then to set standards so high that it certainly would seem to me to be impossible for a state to validly maintain segregation in law schools.

In the McLaurin case, without any question of separation, what the Court did was that you have the same teachers, and so forth, so there could have been no question of his being set apart, except in the classroom, and so forth—there could be no question of the quality of instruction not being the same.

This Court held that those restrictions were sufficient in and of themselves to impair McLaurin's ability to study and, therefore, to deprive him of the equal protection of the law.

So, in my view, although the Gaines case is a case where you have the language, the decisions really do not hinge on that.

JUSTICE REED: In the Gaines case it offered what they called equal facilities, did it not?

MR. CARTER: They offered facilities out of state, out-of-state facilities.

JUSTICE REED: But which they said were equal.

MR. CARTER: Yes.

JUSTICE REED: The Court said that they were not equal.

MR. CARTER: Yes, sir; this Court said not only were they not equal, but that the state had the obligation of furnishing whatever facilities it was going to offer within the state.

JUSTICE REED; Well, we did have before us in the Gaines case the problem of "separate and equal." We determined that they were not equal because they were out of the state.

MR. CARTER: Well, Your Honor, I do not conceive of "separate and equal" as being the type of offering that the State of Missouri offered when they attempted to give out-of-state aid.

JUSTICE REED: Neither did this Court; but Missouri claimed that they were equal.

MR. CARTER: I am sorry, I do not think you have understood my answer. I do not conceive of the out-of-state aid which Missouri offered to petitioner Gaines to go to some institution outside of the state as being within the purview of a "separate but equal" doctrine.

I think that in terms of the "separate but equal" doctrine, that there must be the segregation. The "separate but equal" doctrine, I think, concerns itself with segregation within the state and the setting up of two institutions, one for Negroes and one for whites.

All the state was doing, I think there, was that it knew that it had the obligation of furnishing some facilities to Negroes, and so it offered them this out-of-state aid. But I do not believe that actually it can be—I mean, my understanding is that this cannot be classified as a part of the "separate but equal" doctrine.

JUSTICE REED: No. This Court did not classify it that way. They said it is not separate and equal to give education in another state and, therefore, "You must admit him to the University of Missouri."

MR. CARTER: The University of Missouri, yes.

JUSTICE REED: Yes.

JUSTICE FRANKFURTER: But there is another aspect of my question, namely, that we are dealing here with a challenge to the constitutionality of legislation which is not just one legislative responsibility, not just an episodic piece of legislation in one state.

But we are dealing with a body of enactments by numerous states, whatever they are—eighteen or twenty—not only the South but border states and northern states, and legislation which has a long history.

Now, unless you say that this legislation merely represents man's inhumanity to man, what is the root of this legislation? What is it based on? Why was there such legislation, and was there any consideration that the states were warranted in dealing with—maybe not this way—but was there anything in life to which this legislation responds?

MR. CARTER: Well, Your Honor, I think that this legislation is clear—certain of this legislation in Kansas—that the sole basis for it is race.

JUSTICE FRANKFURTER: Is race?

MR. CARTER: Is race.

JUSTICE FRANKFURTER: Yes, I understand that. I understand all this legislation. But I want to know why this legislation, the sole basis of which is race—is there just some wilfulness of man in the states or some, as I say, of man's inhumanity to man, some ruthless disregard of the facts of life?

MR. CARTER: As I understand the state's position in Kansas, the State of Kansas said that the reason for this legislation to be applicable in urban centers, is that although Negroes compose 4 per cent of the population in Kansas, 90 per cent of them are concentrated in the urban areas, in the cities of the first class, and that Kansas has people from the North and the South with conflicting views about the question of the treatment of Negroes and about the separation and segregation, and that, therefore, what they did was that they authorized, with the power that they had, they authorized these large cities where Negroes appeared in large numbers to have segregated public elementary schools.

THE CHIEF JUSTICE: When did that first appear in the Kansas law?

MR. CARTER: I am not sure, but I believe in 1862.

THE CHIEF JUSTICE: In 1862, and the next amendment was 1868?

MR. CARTER: 1862, Mr. Wilson tells me. The legislation on which this statute arose was first enacted in 1862.

THE CHIEF JUSTICE: That was amended in 1868.

MR. CARTER: That is right. But our feeling on the reach of equal protection, the equal protection clause, is that as these appellants, as members of a minority group, whatever the majority may feel that they can do with their rights for whatever purpose, that the equal protection clause was intended to protect them against the whims, as they come and go.

JUSTICE FRANKFURTER: How would you establish the fact that it was intended to protect them against them? How would I find out if I liked to follow your scent; that is, what the amendment is intended to accomplish, how would I go about finding that out?

MR. CARTER: I think that this Court in, certainly since, *Plessy* v. *Ferguson*—this Court, and in *Shelley* v. *Kraemer,*[7] has repeatedly said this was the basis for the amendment. The amendment was intended to protect Negroes in civil and political equality with whites.

JUSTICE FRANKFURTER: Impliedly it prohibited the doctrine of classification, I take it?

MR. CARTER: I would think, Your Honor, that without regard to the question of its effect on Negroes, that this business of classification, this Court has dealt with it time and time again.

[7]334 U.S. 1 (1948). Attempts to enforce restrictive covenants excluding Negroes from owning or occupying real property were declared unconstitutional since judicial enforcement of the agreements amounted to state action within the meaning of the Fourteenth Amendment.

For example, in regard to a question of equal treatment between a foreign corporation admitted to the state, and a domestic corporation, where the only basis for the inequality is the question of the residence of the foreign corporation, this Court has held under its classification doctrine that there is a denial of equal protection.[8]

JUSTICE FRANKFURTER: Meaning by that that there was no rational basis for the classification?

MR. CARTER: Well, I think that our position is that there is no rational basis for classification based on that.

JUSTICE FRANKFURTER: But do you think that you can argue that or do you think that we can justify this case by some abstract declaration?

MR. CARTER: Well, I have attempted before lunch, Your Honor, to address myself to that point, and that was one of the bases for our attack; that this was a classification, an instance of a classification, based upon race which, under these decisions of this Court do not form a valid basis for the legislation.

JUSTICE REED: Mr. Carter, you speak of equal protection. Do you make a distinction between equal protection and classification, on the one side, and due process on the other? Is that your contention, that this violates due process?

MR. CARTER: We do not contend it in our complaint. We think that it could, but we thought that equal protection was sufficient to protect us.

JUSTICE REED: And do you find a distinction between equal protection and due process in this case?

MR. CARTER: I do not. I think that the Court would, in terms of equal protection and due process, decide that under the equal protection clause and, therefore, do not consider due process. But so far as my understanding of the law, I would see that there would be no real distinction between the two.

I would like to reserve the next few minutes for rebuttal.

THE CHIEF JUSTICE: General Wilson.

ARGUMENT ON BEHALF OF THE APPELLEES

by MR. WILSON

MR. WILSON: May it please the Court, I represent the State of Kansas, who was an intervening defendant in this proceeding.

The issue raised by the pleadings filed by the state in the court below was restricted solely to the matter of the constitutionality of this statute, and I want to limit my remarks to that particular phase of the subject.

[8]See Hanover Ins. Co. v. Harding, 272 U.S. 494 (1926); Southern Railway Co. v. Greene, 216 U.S. 400 (1910); Wheeling Steel Corp. v. Glander, 337 U.S. 562 (1948); Terral v. Burke Construction Co., 257 U.S. 529 (1922).

This Court heretofore noted an apparent reluctance on the part of the State of Kansas to appear in this case and participate actively in these proceedings. Because of that fact I would like to digress for a moment and explain to you the position that the state takes with regard to this litigation.

As my adversary pointed out, the effect of the Kansas statute is local only; it is not statewide.

Furthermore, the statute permits, and does not require, boards of education in designated cities to maintain segregated school systems.

Pursuant to that statute, the Board of Education of the City of Topeka set up and does operate a segregated school system affecting students in the elementary grades.

Now, this lawsuit in the court below was directed at the Topeka Board of Education.

The school system set up and maintained by that board was under attack. The Attorney General, therefore, took the position that this action was local in nature and not of statewide concern. We did not participate actively in the trial of the case.

However, after the trial in the court below there was a change in personnel and a change in attitude on the part of the Board of Education. The Board of Education determined then that it would not resist this appeal.

The Attorney General thereupon determined that he should be governed, his attitude should be governed, by the attitude taken on the local level. Consequently we did not appear.

I mention this to emphasize the fact that we have never at any time entertained any doubt about the constitutionality of our statute.

THE CHIEF JUSTICE: General Wilson, may I state to you that we were informed that the Board of Education would not be represented here in argument, and would not file a brief, and it being a very important question, and this case having facets that other cases did not, we wanted to hear from the State of Kansas.

MR. WILSON: We are very glad to comply with the Court's request. I was simply attempting to emphasize that we did not intentionally disregard our duty to this Court.

THE CHIEF JUSTICE: I understand it.

As I understand it, you had turned it over to the Board of Education and expected them to appear here, is that right?

MR. WILSON: That is correct, sir.

THE CHIEF JUSTICE: And when we found out that they were not going to, we did not want the State of Kansas and its viewpoint to be silent.

MR. WILSON: Now, the views of the State of Kansas can be stated very simply and very briefly: We believe that our statute is constitutional. We did not believe it violates the Fourteenth Amendment.

We believe so because our Supreme Court, the Supreme Court of Kansas, has specifically said so. We believe that the decisions of the Supreme Court of

Kansas follow and are supported by the decisions of this Court, and the decisions of many, many appellate courts in other jurisdictions.

In order to complete the perspective of the Court with respect to the Kansas school system, I should like to allude briefly to the general statutes of Kansas which provide for elementary school education.

There are three types of municipal corporations in Kansas authorized to maintain public elementary schools. There is the city of the first class, cities consisting of 15,000 or more persons, of which there are twelve in the state; then, there are cities of the second class, and cities of the third class, which are included within the common school districts.

Now, this statute, I want to emphasize, applies only to cities of the first class, to those cities which have populations of more than 15,000.

It does authorize separate schools to be maintained for the Negro and white races in the elementary grades in those cities, with the exception of Kansas City, where a separate junior high school and high school is authorized.

My adversary has conceded, and the court below has found, that there was no substantial inequality in the educational facilities afforded by the City of Topeka to these appellants. The physical facilities were found to be the same, or substantially alike.

Not only was that finding made with regard to physical facilities, but the course of study was found to be that subscribed by state law and followed in both systems of schools.

The instructional facilities were determined to be substantially equal. There was the item of distinction wherein transportation was supplied to the Negro students and not to the white students. That certainly was not an item which constituted one of discrimination against the Negro students.

Therefore, it is our theory that this case resolves itself simply to this: whether the "separate but equal" doctrine is still the law, and whether it is to be followed in this case by this Court.

My adversary has mentioned—again I want to emphasize that the Negro population in Kansas is slight. Less than 4 per cent of the total population belong to the Negro race.

JUSTICE FRANKFURTER: What is that number?

MR. WILSON: Sir?

JUSTICE FRANKFURTER: What is that number?

MR. WILSON: The population of the State, the total population, is approximately 2\million. The total Negro population is approximately 73,000.

JUSTICE FRANKFURTER: And of those, how many are in the cities of 15,000, about nine-tenths, would you say?

MR. WILSON: Our brief says that nine-tenths of the Negro population lived in cities classified as urban.

The urban classification includes those of 2,500 or more. I should say that two-thirds of the Negro population lived in cities of the first class.

JUSTICE FRANKFURTER: And this, according to your brief, as I remember—the present situation in Kansas is that this segregated class of primary schools are in only nine of those cities?

MR. WILSON: In only nine of our cities.

As I recall, there are eighteen separate elementary schools maintained in the State under and by virtue of the statute. There is one separate junior high school and one separate high school.

In other communities we do have voluntary segregation, but that does not exist with the sanction or the force of law.

JUSTICE BLACK: Do you have any Indians in Kansas?

MR. WILSON: We have a few, Your Honor.

JUSTICE BLACK: Where do they go to school?

MR. WILSON: I know of no instances where Indians live in cities of the first class. Most of our Indians live on the reservation. The Indians who do live in cities of the first class would attend the schools maintained for the white race.

JUSTICE BLACK: Those who live on the reservations go to Indian schools?

MR. WILSON: Yes, sir; attend schools maintained by the Government.

JUSTICE BLACK: Do any people go to them besides the Indians?

MR. WILSON: I do not believe so, sir.

JUSTICE FRANKFURTER: May I trouble you before you conclude your argument, to deal with this aspect of the case, in the light of the incident of the problems in Kansas, namely, what would be the consequences, as you see them, for this Court to reverse this decree relating to the Kansas law, or to put it another way, suppose this Court reversed the case, and the case went back to the District Court for the entry of a proper decree. What would Kansas be urging should be the nature of that decree in order to carry out the direction of this Court?

MR. WILSON: As I understand your question, you are asking me what practical difficulties would be encountered in the administration of the school system?

JUSTICE FRANKFURTER: Suppose there would be some difficulties? I want to know what the consequences of the reversal of the decree would be, and what Kansas would be urging us the most for dealing with those consequences of the decree?

MR. WILSON: In perfect candor, I must say to the Court that the consequences would probably not be serious.

As I pointed out, our Negro population is small. We do have in our Negro schools Negro teachers, Negro administrators, that would necessarily be assimilated in the school system at large. That might produce some administrative difficulties. I can imagine no serious difficulty beyond that.

Now, the question of the segregation of the Negro race in our schools has frequently been before the Supreme Court of Kansas, and at the outset I should say that our Court has consistently held that segregation can be practiced only where authorized by the statutes.

The rationale of all those cases is simply this: The municipal corporation maintaining the school district is a creature of statute. It can do only what the statute authorizes. Therefore, unless there is a specific power conferred, the municipal corporation maintaining the school district cannot classify students on the basis of color.

JUSTICE REED: Have there been efforts made to remove the act permitting segregation or authorizing segregation in Kansas?

MR. WILSON: I recall, I think I mentioned in my brief, in 1876 in a general codification of the school laws, the provision authorizing the maintenance of separate schools was apparently, through inadvertence, omitted by the legislature. It was nevertheless deemed to be repealed by implication.

But thereafter, in 1879, substantially the same statute was again enacted. Since that time, to my knowledge, there have been no considered efforts made in the legislature to repeal that statute.

JUSTICE JACKSON: Mr. Attorney General, you emphasized the 4 per cent, and the smallness of the population. Would that affect your problem if there were heavier concentrations?

MR. WILSON: It is most difficult for me to answer that question. It might. I am not acquainted with the situation where there is a heavier concentration, in other words.

JUSTICE JACKSON: I mean, your statute adapts itself to different localities. What are the variables that the statute was designed to take care of, if any, if you know, at this late date?

MR. WILSON: My theory of the justification of the statute is this: The state of Kansas was born out of the struggle between the North and the South prior to the war between the states, and our state was populated by squatters from the North and from the South.

Those squatters settled in communities. The proslavery elements settled in Leavenworth, in Atchison, and Lecompton. The Free Soil elements settled in Topeka, in Lawrence, and in Wyandotte. The Negroes who came to the state during and immediately subsequent to the war also settled in communities.

Consequently, our early legislatures were faced with this situation: In some communities the attitudes of the people were such that it was deemed best that the Negro race live apart. In other communitites a different attitude was reflected. Also in some communities there was a substantial Negro population. In other communities there were few Negroes.

Therefore, the legislature sought by this type of legislation to provide a means whereby the community could adjust its plan to suit local conditions, and we believe they succeeded.

JUSTICE JACKSON: You mentioned Topeka as one of the three state settlements, and that seems to be the subject that is involved here with the segregation ordinances. Is there any explanation for that?

MR. WILSON: As I explained these matters—I am speculating—we have in Kansas—

JUSTICE JACKSON: Your speculation ought to be worth more than mine.

MR. WILSON: We have in Kansas history a period of migration of the Negro race to Kansas which we call the exodus, the black exodus, as spoken of in the history books.

At that time, which was in the '80s, large numbers of Negro people came from the South and settled in Kansas communities. A large number of those people settled in Topeka and, for the first time, I presume, and again I am speculating, there was created there the problem of the racial adjustment within the community.

The record in this case infers that segregation was established in Topeka about fifty years ago.

I am assuming that in my speculation for the Court that segregation began to be practiced in Topeka after the exodus had given Topeka a substantial colored population.

JUSTICE REED: You spoke of the density of the Negro population, of about 4 per cent covering the State as a whole. Have you in mind what city has the largest concentration of residents by percentage?

MR. WILSON: The city with the largest concentration of Negro population is Kansas City, Kansas.

JUSTICE REED: That is by percentage?

MR. WILSON: By percentage, as well as in absolute numbers.

JUSTICE REED: How high is it there?

MR. WILSON: The Negro population, I should say—perhaps Mr. Scott can help me with this—I should say not more than 10 per cent, is that correct?

MR. SCOTT: That is about right, yes.

MR. WILSON: This statute has been squarely challenged in our Kansas Supreme Court and has been upheld, and I cite in my case the leading case of *Reynolds* v. *The School Board*[9] where in 1903 the Court held flatly that the Kansas statute does not violate the Fourteenth Amendment to the Constitituion of the United States.

That opinion is an exhaustive one wherein the Court drew on the Roberts case in Massachusetts, and numerous other cases cited in the appellate courts of the state, and the Court followed specifically the rule laid down in the Plessy case.

---

[9]Reynolds v. Board of Education, 66 Kans. 672, 72 Pac. 274 (1903).

It is our position that the principle announced in the Plessy case and the specific rule announced in the Gong Lum case are absolutely controlling here.

We think it is sheer sophistry to attempt to distinguish those cases from the case that is here presented, and we think the question before this Court is simply this: Is the Plessy case and the Gong Lum case and the "separate but equal" doctrine still the law of this land?

We think if you decide in favor of these appellants, the Court will necessarily overrule the doctrines expressed in those cases and, at the same time, will say that the legislatures of the seventeen or twenty-one states, that the Congress of the United States, that dozens of appellate courts have been wrong for a period of more than seventy-five years, when they have believed and have manifested a belief that facilities equal though separate were within the meaning of the Fourteenth Amendment.

JUSTICE FRANKFURTER: There is a third one—

JUSTICE BURTON: Don't you recognize it as possible that within seventy-five years the social and economic conditions and the personal relations of the nation may have changed so that what may have been a valid interpretation of them seventy-five years ago would not be a valid interpretation of them constitutionally today?

MR. WILSON: We recognize that as a possibility. We do not believe that this record discloses any such change.

JUSTICE BURTON: But that might be a difference between saying that these courts of appeals and state supreme courts have been wrong for seventy-five years.

MR. WILSON: Yes, sir.

We concede that this Court can overrule the Gong Lum doctrine, the Plessy doctrine, but nevertheless until those cases are overruled they are the best guide we have.

JUSTICE FRANKFURTER: As I understood my brother Burton's question or as I got the implication of his question, it was not that the Court would have to overrule those cases; the Court would simply have to recognize that laws are kinetic, and some new things have happened, not deeming those decisions wrong, but bringing into play new situations toward a new decision. I do not know whether he would disown me, but that is what I got out of it.

MR. WILSON: We agree with that proposition. But I repeat, we do not think that there is anything in the record here that would justify such a conclusion.

Now, something has been said about Finding of Fact No. 8 in the District Court, and I would like to comment briefly upon that finding of fact.

The Court will recall that that is the finding of fact wherein the lower court determined generally that segregation of white and colored children in the public schools has a detrimental effect upon the colored children.

It may be significant that this finding of fact was based upon the uncontroverted testimony of witnesses produced by the appellants in this case.

I should also like to point out that that finding of fact was based upon the uncontested evidence presented by the case.

We think it is obvious, however, that the District Court regarded Finding of Fact No. 8 as being legally insignificant because having made a finding of fact, Finding of Fact No. 8, wherein the general statement is made that Negro children might be benefited by attendance at an integrated school system, the District Court concluded in its conclusion of law simply this: The court has heretofore filed its finding of fact and conclusions of law, together with an opinion, and has held that, as a matter of law, the plaintiffs have failed to prove that they were entitled to the relief demanded.

In other words, Finding of Fact No. 8 is immaterial, we believe, so far as the issues of this case are concerned.

The court did find, and we have mentioned the finding specifically, that physical facilities were equal; the court found that instructional facilities were equal, the court found that courses of study were equal. Those are the items that the state and the school districts have within their power to confer.

This additional item, the psychological reaction, is something which is something apart from the objective components of the school system, and something that the state does not have within its power to confer upon the pupils therein.

Therefore, the District Court, and we believe rightly, regarded it as something that is inconsequential, immaterial, not governing in this case.

We make one further point in our brief that may be significant, and that is that Finding of Fact No. 8 is a general finding. It does not relate to these specific appellants.

As we understand the law, in order to obtain an injunction, obtain injunctive relief, which is prayed for here, it is necessary that these appellants show in the court below, first, that they have actually suffered personal harm from attending segregated schools in Topeka, Kansas; they must show that either they have been deprived of some benefit that is conferred on the rest of the population or they must show that they are being subjected to some detriment that the rest of the population does not suffer.

Now, we submit that there is nothing in the Finding of Fact No. 8 which indicates that these appellants specifically have suffered any harm by reason of being compelled to attend an integrated school system in the City of Topeka.

I think it is significant that all of the other findings of fact relate specifically to the Topeka school system. They use the definite article when describing "the" system, until Finding of Fact No. 8, and there the general statement is made indicating that the court believes that Negro children generally would be better off if they were attending an integrated school system.

Now, we submit on the basis of that finding of fact the plaintiffs below and the appellants here have not shown their right to injunctive relief because they have not shown the injury that the decisions of this Court seem to require.

The position of the State of Kansas, to emphasize again, is simply this: Our statute is constitutional; it does not violate the Fourteenth Amendment, and that position is supported by all of the decisions of the Kansas courts. That position, we think, is supported by the decisions of this Court.

Thank you.

REBUTTAL ARGUMENT ON BEHALF OF APPELLANTS

by MR. CARTER

MR. CARTER: We think that finding of fact of the court below makes necessary a reversal of its judgment.

Without regard to any other consideration, the court below found that inequality flowed from segregation, and our position, as stated previously, is if there are facilities, educational opportunities, in fact, that educational opportunities can not be equal in law.

JUSTICE BLACK: Why do you think that would apply?

MR. CARTER: Because of the fact, sir—

JUSTICE BLACK: Suppose it had been found differently?

MR. CARTER: If it had been found or I should say if the Court agrees that the findings are correct—

JUSTICE BLACK: Suppose another court finds strictly to the contrary with reference to the general principle, what would you say?

MR. CARTER: Well, this Court, of course, in a question like that reexamines the findings or the basis for the findings and can reach its own conclusion in that regard.

JUSTICE BLACK: Do you think the Court can make a finding independent of the basis of fact?

MR. CARTER: No, sir, they do not. What I meant to say was that this Court, if they agreed with the findings on an examination of this record, agreed with the findings of fact of the court below, and came to the conclusion that the court below had correctly found the facts on its own independent examination, that this Court would—it would necessitate a reversal of that court's judgment. I do not mean that the findings of the court below come here and that you have to accept them. Of course, I do not agree with that.

JUSTICE BLACK: Do you think that there should be a different holding here with reference to the question involved, according to the place where the segregation might occur, and if not, why do you say it depends—why do you say that it depends on the findings of fact at all?

MR. CARTER: I say about the findings of fact because what I think the court below did was in approaching this question it followed the example of this Court in *McLaurin* and *Sweatt* and, I think, it approached the question correctly; so that it found that inequality in educational opportunity existed as a result of the racial restrictions.

JUSTICE BLACK: Is that a general finding or do you state that for the State of Kansas, City of Topeka?

MR. CARTER: I think I agree with the fact that the finding refers to the State of Kansas and to these appellants and to Topeka, Kansas. I think that the findings were made in this specific case referring to this specific case.

JUSTICE BLACK: In other words, if you are going to go on the findings, then you would have different rulings with respect to the places to which this applies, is that true?

MR. CARTER: Well, the only thing that I think the findings do when this Court reached the question and held this finding, it seems to me that the only thing that the findings would do is that—without regard to the question, the court below, examining the facilities found that they were unequal.

Now, of course, under our theory, you do not have to reach the finding of fact or a fact at all in reaching the decision because of the fact that we maintain that this is an unconstitutional classification being based upon race and, therefore, it is arbitrary.

But all I was attempting to address myself to was to the specific examination by the court below on the impact of segregation on the equality of educational opportunities afforded.

JUSTICE BLACK: Are you planning to attach relevance to anything except the question of whether they are separate but equal?

MR. CARTER: I think that they are relevant to the question of whether there are equal educational opportunities that are being afforded. I think whether, in fact, you have equal education in the opinion of the court below, that the findings are relevant, and I think that the court below found that the educational facilities were unequal as a result of segregation, but it felt that it could not reach the legal conclusion that they were unequal because of two decisions we have discussed.

Now, to conclude, our feeling is that this case could be decided on the question of the illegality of the classification itself.

This case also could be decided on the question of equal educational opportunities as they are examined by the approach of *McLaurin* and *Sweatt*.

We think that the court below did the same thing. The court below did what this Court did in *McLaurin* and in *Sweatt,* and we think that in the examination of the equality of education offered, that what it did was it found that these restrictions imposed disabilitities on Negro children and prevented them from having educational opportunities equal to white, and for these reasons we think that the judgment of the court below should be reversed and the Kansas statute should be struck down.

(Whereupon, at 3:15 p.m., the argument was concluded.)

HARRY BRIGGS, JR., et al.,
Appellants,

vs.

R. W. ELLIOTT, CHAIRMAN, J. D. CARSON, et al.,
MEMBERS OF BOARD OF TRUSTEES OF SCHOOL DISTRICT NO. 22,
CLARENDON COUNTY, S.C., et al.
Appellees.

Case No. 101

Tuesday, December 9, 1952.

The above-entitled cause came on for oral argument at 3:15 p.m.

APPEARANCES:
On behalf of the Appellants:
THURGOOD MARSHALL, ESQ.

On behalf of Appellees:
JOHN W. DAVIS, ESQ.

THE CHIEF JUSTICE: Case No. 101, Harry Briggs, Jr., et al., against Roger W. Elliott, Chairman, J. D. Carson, et al., Members of Board of Trustees of School District No. 22, Clarendon County, South Carolina, et al.

THE CLERK: Counsel are present.

ARGUMENT ON BEHALF OF APPELLANTS

by MR. MARSHALL

MR. MARSHALL: May it please the Court, this case is here on direct appeal from the United States District Court for the Eastern District of South Carolina. The issue raised in this case was clearly raised in the pleadings, and was clearly raised throughout the first hearing. After the first hearing, on appeal to this Court, it was raised prior to the second hearing. It was raised on motion for judgment, and there can be no question that from the beginning of this case, the filing of the initial complaint, up until the present time, the appellants have raised and have preserved their attack on the validity of the provision of the South Carolina Constitution and the South Carolina statute.

The specific provision of the South Carolina Code is set forth in our brief at page 10, and it appears in appellees' brief at page 14, and reads as follows:

It shall be unlawful for pupils of one race to attend the schools provided by boards of trustees for persons of another race.

That is the Code provision.

The constitutional provision is, again, on page 10 of our brief, and is:

Separate schools shall be provided for children of the white races—

This is the significant language—

and no child of either race shall ever be permitted to attend a school provided for children of the other race.

Those are the two provisions of the law of the State of South Carolina under attack in this particular case.

At the first hearing, before the trial got under way, counsel for the appellees, in open court, read a statement in which he admitted that although prior to that time they had decided that the physical facilities of the separate schools were equal, they had concluded finally that they were not equal, and they admitted in open court that they did not have equality, and at the suggestion of senior Judge Parker,[10] this was made as an amendment to the answer, and the question as to physical facilities from that stage on was not in dispute.

At that time, counsel for the appellants, however, made the position clear that the attack was not being made on the "separate but equal" basis as to physical facilities, but the position we were taking was that these statutes were unconstitutional in their enforcement because they not only produced these inevitable inequalities in physical facilities, but that evidence would be produced by expert witnesses to show that the governmentally imposed racial segregation in and of itself was also a denial of equality.

I want to point out that our position is not that we are denied equality in these cases. I think there has been a considerable misunderstanding on that point. We are saying that there is a denial of equal protection of the laws, the legal phraseology of the clause in the Fourteenth Amendment, and not just this point as to equality, and I say that because I think most of the cases in the past have gone off on the point of whether or not you have substantial equality. It is a type of provision that, we think, tends to get us into trouble.

So pursuing that line, we produced expert witnesses, who had surveyed the school situation to show the full extent of the physical inequalities, and then we produced expert witnesses. Appellees, in their brief comment, say that they do not think too much of them. I do not think that the District Court thought too much of them. But they stand in the record as unchallenged as experts in their field, and I think we have arrived at the stage where the courts do give credence to the testimony of people who are experts in their fields.

On the question that was raised a minute ago in the other case about whether or not there is any relevancy to this classification on a racial basis or not, in the case of the testimony of Dr. Robert Redfield[11]—I am sure the Court will remember his testimony in the Sweatt case—the District Court was unwilling to carry the case over an extra day. Dr. Redfield was stuck with the usual air travel from one

[10]Judge John J. Parker (1885–1958) was appointed to the Fourth Circuit Court of Appeals by President Coolidge in 1925 and became Chief Judge in 1931. He was nominated as a Justice of the Supreme Court by President Hoover in 1930 but not confirmed by the Senate because of allegedly anti-labor decisions and anti-Negro remarks. He also acted as alternate member of the International Military Tribunal at Nuremburg after World War II.

[11]Dr. Robert Redfield (1897–1960), noted anthropologist, taught at the University of Chicago and Cornell University. Among his many books are *The Folk Culture of Yucatan* (1941) and *The Primitive World and its Transformations* (1953).

city to another. And by agreement of counsel and with approval of the court, we placed into the record Dr. Redfield's testimony.

If you will remember, Dr. Redfield's testimony was to this effect, that there were no recognizable differences from a racial standpoint between children, and that if there could be such a difference that would be recognizable and connected with education, it would be so insignificant as to be unworthy of anybody's consideration.

In substance, he said, on page 161 of the record—I think it is page 161—that given a similar learning situation, a Negro child and a white child would tend to do about the same thing. I think I have it here. It is on page 161:

> Question: As a result of your studies that you have made, the training that you have had in your specialized field over some twenty years, given a similar learning situation, what, if any differences, is there between the accomplishment of a white and a Negro student, given a similar learning situation?
> Answer: I understand, if I may say so, a similar learning situation to include a similar degree of preparation?
> Question: Yes.
> Answer: Then I would say that my conclusion is that the one does as well as the other on the average.

He has considerable testimony along the lines. But we produced testimony to show what we considered to be the normal attack on a classification statute, that this Court has laid down the rule in many cases set out in our brief, that in the case of the object or persons being classified, it must be shown, (1) that there is a difference in the two, (2) that the state must show that the difference has a significance with the subject matter being legislated, and the state has made no effort up to this date to show any basis for that classification other than that it would be unwise to do otherwise.

Witnesses testified that segregation deterred the development of the personalities of these children. Two witnesses testified that it deprives them of equal status in the school community, that it destroys their self-respect. Two other witnesses testified that it denies them full opportunity for democratic social development. Another witness said that it stamps him with a badge of inferiority.

The summation of that testimony is that the Negro children have road blocks put up in their minds as a result of this segregation, so that the amount of education that they take in is much less than other students take in.

The other significant point in this case is that one witness, Dr. Kenneth Clark,[12] examined the appellants in this very case and found that they were injured as a result of this segregation. The court completely disregarded that.

I do not know what clearer testimony we could produce in an attack on a specific statute as applied to a specific group of appellants.

The only evidence produced by the appellees in this case was one witness who testified as to, in general, the running of the school system and the difference between rural schools and consolidated schools, which had no basis whatsoever on the constitutional question.

[12]Dr. Kenneth Clark, distinguished educator and psychologist, is the author of *Desegregation: An Appraisal of the Evidence* (1953), *Prejudice and Your Child* (1955), and *Dark Ghetto* (1965).

Another witness, E. R. Crow, was produced to testify as to the new bond issue that was to go into effect after the hearing this case, at which time they would build more schools as a result of that money. That testimony was admitted into the record over objection of the appellants. The appellants took the position that anything that was to be talked about in the future was irrelevant to a constitutional issue where a personal and present right was asserted. However, the court overruled the objection. Mr. Crow testified.

Then he was asked as to whether or not it would not be "unwise" to break down segregation in South Carolina. Then Mr. Crow proceeded to testify as an expert. He had six years of experience, I think, as superintendent of schools, and prior to that time he was principal of a high school in Columbia. He testified that it would be unwise. He also testified that he did not know but what the legislature would not appropriate the money.

On cross-examination he was asked as to whether or not he meant by the first statement that if relief was granted as prayed, the appellees might not conform to the relief, and Judge Parker made a very significant statement which appears in the record, that if we issue an order in this case, it will be obeyed, and I do not think there is any question about it.

On this second question on examination, when he was asked, who did he use as the basis for his information that this thing would not work in the South, he said he talked to gangs of people, white and colored, and he was giving the sum total of their testimony, or rather their statements to him. And again on cross-examination he was asked to name at least one of the Negroes he talked to, and he could not recall the name of a single Negro he had ever talked to. I think the basis of his testimony on that point should be weighed by that statement on cross-examination.

He also said that there was a difference between what happened in northern states, because they had a larger number of Negroes in the South, and they had a larger problem because the percentage of Negroes was so high. And again on cross-examination, he was asked the specific question: "Well, assuming that in South Carolina the population was 95 per cent white and 5 per cent colored, would your answer be any different?" And he said, no, he would make the same answer regardless.

That is the only evidence in the record for the appellees here. They wanted to put on the speech of Professor Odom,[13] and they were refused the right to put the speech in, because, after all, Professor Odom was right across, in North Carolina, and could have been called as a witness.

So here we have a record that has made no effort whatsoever—no effort whatsoever—to support the legislative determinations of the State of South Carolina. And this Court is being asked to uphold those statutes, the statute and the constitutional provision because of two reasons. One is that these matters are legislative matters, as to whether or not we are going to have segregation. For example, the majority of the court in the first hearing said, speaking of equality under the Fourteenth Amendment, "How this shall be done is a matter for the school

[13]Prof. Howard Odom of the University of North Carolina delivered a speech in Atlanta entitled "The Mid-Century South Looking Both Ways" which the defendants sought unsuccessfully to introduce into evidence.

authorities and not for the court, so long as it is done in good faith and equality of facilities is offered."

Again the court said, in Chief Judge Parker's opinion:

> We think, however, that segregation of the races in the public schools, so long as equality of rights is preserved, is a matter of legislative policy for the several states, with which the Federal courts are powerless to interfere.

So here we have the unique situation of an asserted federal right which has been declared several times by this Court to be personal and present, being set aside on the theory that it is a matter for the state legislature to decide, and it is not for this Court. And that is directly contrary to every opinion of this Court.

In each instance where these matters come up in what, if I say "sensitive" field, or whatever I am talking about, civil rights, freedom of speech, et cetera—at all times they have this position. The majority of the people wanted the statute; that is how it was passed.

There are always respectable people who can be quoted as in support of a statute. But in each case, this Court has made its own independent determination as to whether that statute is valid. Yet in this case, the Court is urged to give blanket approval that this field of segregation, and if I may say, this field of racial segregation, is purely to be left to the states, the direct opposite of what the Fourteenth Amendment was passed for, the direct opposite of the intent of the Fourteenth Amendment and the framers of it.

On this question of the sensitiveness of this field, and to leave it to the legislature, I know lawyers at times have a hard time finding a case in point. But in the reply brief, I think that we have a case in point that is persuasive to this Court. It is the case of *Elkison* v. *Deliesseline*,[14] a decision by Mr. Justice William Johnson, appointed to this Court, if I remember, from South Carolina. The decision was rendered in 1823. And in 1823, Mr. Justice Johnson, in a case involving the State of South Carolina, which provided that where free Negroes came in on a ship into Charleston, they had to put them in jail as long as the ship was there and then put them back on the ship—and it was argued by people arguing for the statute that this was necessary, it was necessary to protect the people of South Carolina, and the majority must have wanted it and it was adopted— Mr. Justice Johnson made an answer to that argument in 1823, which I think is pretty good law as of today. Mr. Justice Johnson said:

> But to all this the plea of necessity is urged; and of the existence of that necessity we are told the state alone is to judge. Where is this to land us? Is it not asserting the right in each state to throw off the federal constitution at its will and pleasure? If it can be done as to any particular article it may be done as to all; and, like the old confederation, the Union becomes a mere rope of sand.

There is a lot of other language and other opinions, but I think that this is very significant.

---

[14] 8 Fed. Cases 493 (No. 4,366) (C.C.D.S.C. 1823). Justice Johnson sitting on circuit held unconstitutional the South Carolina Negro Seaman Act (requiring all Negro sailors from foreign ships to be housed in jail while their ships were in port). Johnson served on the Supreme Court from 1804 to 1834.

THE CHIEF JUSTICE: Mr. Marshall, what emphasis do you give to the words, "So long as equality of rights is preserved"?

MR. MARSHALL: In Judge Parker's opinion—

THE CHIEF JUSTICE: Yes.

MR. MARSHALL:—of physical facilities, because he ends up in this statement, and makes it, I think, very clear. On the second hearing, on three or four occasions, he made it clear that segregation was not involved in the case any longer.

JUSTICE REED: Segregation or equality of rights?

MR. MARSHALL: He said that segregation was out of the case, and that we had disposed of it. And page 279—I think I marked it—yes, sir, the question was asked of me about building the schools overnight, and down near the end of the page he mentions the fact of segregation:

Well, I understand you do not admit that any conditions exist that require segregation. I understand that.

MR. MARSHALL: Yes, sir, that is right.

JUDGE PARKER: But that has been ruled on by the Court. What we are considering now is the question: Whether the physical facilities, curricula—"

THE CHIEF JUSTICE: (Interposing)—"and the other things that can be made equal, without the segregation issue, are being made equal?"

MR. MARSHALL: He is talking about physical facilities.

THE CHIEF JUSTICE: He is also talking about the curricula, "and the other things that can be made equal."

MR. MARSHALL: I am sorry I mentioned that, sir. I considered curricula in the physical facilities.

THE CHIEF JUSTICE: That is a shorthanded question.

MR. MARSHALL: Yes, sir. But again on page 281, they asked the question of whether something can be done, and I said that they could break down segregation. Judge Dobie[15] said, "Let that alone."

Judge Parker said, "That is the same question."

So I think for all intents and purposes, the District Court ruled out the question of all of this argument that segregation had the effect on these children to deny the children their rights under the Constitution, and they passed upon curricula, transportation, faculty, and schools. At the second hearing, the report

[15]Judge Armistead M. Dobie (1881–1956), one of the three judges on the Fourth Circuit panel which upheld the South Carolina segregation laws, was a former dean of the University of Virginia Law School (1932–1939) and served on the Fourth Circuit from 1940 to 1956.

showed that they were making progress. The schools still were not equal. But the question was that if they proceeded the way they were as of March of last year, they would be equal as of the September just past.

But in this case in the trial we conceived ourselves as conforming to the rule set out in the McLaurin and the Sweatt cases, where this Court held that the only question to be decided was the question as to whether or not the action of the state in maintaining its segregation was denying to the students the equal protection of the laws.

Of course, those decisions were limited to the graduate and professional schools. But we took the position that the rationale, if you please, or the principle, to be stronger, set out in those cases would apply just as well down the line provided evidence could be introduced which would show the same type of injury.

That is the type of evidence we produced, and we believed that on the basis of that testimony, the District Court should properly have held that in the area of elementary and high schools, the same type of injury was present as would be present in the McLaurin or the Sweatt case.

However, the District Court held just to the contrary, and said that there was a significant difference between the two. That is, in the Sweatt case it was a matter of inequality, and in the McLaurin case, McLaurin was subject to such humiliation, et cetera, that nobody should put up with it, whereas in this case, we have positive testimony from Dr. Clark that the humiliation that these children have been going through is the type of injury to the minds that will be permanent as long as they are in segregated schools, not theoretical injury, but actual injury.

We believe that on the basis of that, on that narrow point of Sweatt and McLaurin—on that I say, sir, that we do not have to get to *Plessy* v. *Ferguson;* we do not have to get to any other case, if we lean right on these two cases—we believe that there is a broader issue involved in these two cases, and despite the body of the law, *Plessy* v. *Ferguson, Gong Lum* v. *Rice,* the statement of Chief Justice Hughes in the Gaines case, some of the language in the Cumming case,[16] even though not applicable as to here—we also believe that there is another body of law, and that is the body of law on the Fifth Amendment cases, on the Japanese exclusion cases, and the Fourth Amendment cases, language that was in *Nixon* v. *Herndon,*[17] where Mr. Justice Holmes said that the states can do a lot of classifying that nobody can see any reason for, but certainly it cannot go contrary to the Fourteenth Amendment; then the language in the Skinner[18] case, the language of Mr. Justice Jackson in his concurring opinion in the Edwards[19] case.

[16]Cumming v. County Board of Education, 175 U.S. 528 (1899). The Court decided that a Georgia school board could legally close down a Negro high school when it had sufficient funds only for the white schools and a Negro primary school. The Court refused to divest funds from the white schools or order them closed until money was made available, as requested by the plaintiffs.

[17]The Japanese exclusion cases are Hirabayashi v. United States, 320 U.S. 81 (1943) and Korematsu v. United States, 323 U.S. 214 (1944), described in n. 56 and n. 58 *infra.,* In Nixon v. Herndon, 273 U.S. 536 (1927), Justice Holmes held for a unanimous court that a Texas law barring Negroes from participating in a state primary election violated the Fourteenth Amendment.

[18]Skinner v. Oklahoma, 316 U.S. 535 (1942). A law providing for sterilization of habitual criminals was found to violate the equal protection clause.

So on both the Fourteenth Amendment and the Fifteenth Amendment, this Court has repeatedly said that these distinctions on a racial basis or on a basis of ancestry are odious and invidious, and those decisions, I think, are entitled to just as much weight as *Plessy* v. *Ferguson* or *Gong Lum* v. *Rice.*

THE CHIEF JUSTICE: Mr. Marshall, in *Plessy* v. *Ferguson,* in the Harlan[20] dissent—

MR. MARSHALL: Yes, sir.

THE CHIEF JUSTICE: Do you attach any significance when he is dealing with illustrations of the absence of education?

MR. MARSHALL: Yes, sir. I do not know, sir. I tried to study his opinions all along. But I think that he was trying to take the position of the narrow issue involved in this case, and not touch on schools, because of the fact that at that time—and this is pure speculation—at that time the public school system was in such bad shape, when people were fighting compulsory attendance laws, they were fighting the money to be put in schools, and it was in a state of flux, but on the other hand, in the majority opinion, the significant thing, the case that they relied on, was the Roberts case, which was decided before the Fourteenth Amendment was even passed.

JUSTICE FRANKFURTER: But that does not do away with a consideration of the Roberts case, does it?

MR. MARSHALL: No, sir, it does not.

JUSTICE FRANKFURTER: The significance of the Roberts case is that that should be considered by the Supreme Court at a time when that issue was rampant in the United States.

MR. MARSHALL: Well, sir, I do not know about those days. But I can not conceive of the Roberts case being good for anything except that the legislatures of the states at those times were trying to work out their problems as they best could understand. And it could be that up in Massachusetts at that time they thought that Negroes—some of them were escaping from slavery, and all—but I still say that the considerations for the passage of any legislation before the Civil War and up to 1900, certainly, could not apply at the present time. I think that every race has made progress, but I do not believe that those considerations have any bearing at this time. The question today is—

---

[19]Edwards v. California, 314 U.S. 160, 181 (1941). The majority opinion held that a California law making it a crime to assist in bringing into the state an indigent person was an unconstitutional burden on interstate commerce. Justice Jackson would have invalidated the law as a violation of the privileges and immunities clause.

[20]Justice John M. Harlan, (1833–1911), the only dissenter in Plessy, served on the Supreme Court from 1877 to 1911. He was the only voice for Negro rights in that period, dissenting in many anti-civil rights decisions, such as the Civil Rights Cases, 109 U.S. 3 (1883) and Berea College v. Kentucky, 211 U.S. 45 (1908).

JUSTICE FRANKFURTER: They do not study these cases. But may I call your attention to what Mr. Justice Holmes said about the Fourteenth Amendment?

The Fourteenth Amendment itself as an historical product did not destroy history for the state and substitute mechanical departments of law . . .[20a]

MR. MARSHALL: I agree, sir.

JUSTICE FRANKFURTER: Then you have to face the fact that this is not a question to be decided by an abstract starting point of natural law, that you cannot have segregation. If we start with that, of course, we will end with that.

MR. MARSHALL: I do not know of any other proposition, sir, that we could consider that would say that because a person who is as white as snow with blue eyes and blond hair has to be set aside.

JUSTICE FRANKFURTER: Do you think that is the case?

MR. MARSHALL: Yes, sir. The law of South Carolina applies that way.

JUSTICE FRANKFURTER: Do you think that this law was passed for the same reason that a law would be passed prohibiting blue-eyed children from attending public schools? You would permit all blue-eyed children to go to separate schools? You think that this is the case?

MR. MARSHALL: No, sir, because the blue-eyed people in the United States never had the badge of slavery which was perpetuated in the statutes.

JUSTICE FRANKFURTER: If it is perpetuated as slavery, then the Thirteenth Amendment would apply.

MR. MARSHALL: But at the time—

JUSTICE FRANKFURTER: Do you really think it helps us not to recognize that behind this are certain facts of life, and the question is whether a legislature can address itself to those facts of life in despite of or within the Fourteenth Amendment, or whether, whatever the facts of life might be, where there is a vast congregation of Negro population as against the states where there is not, whether that is an irrelevant consideration? Can you escape facing those sociological facts, Mr. Marshall?

MR. MARSHALL: No, I cannot escape it. But if I did fail to escape it, I would have to throw completely aside the personal and present rights of those individuals.

JUSTICE FRANKFURTER: No, you would not. It does not follow because you cannot make certain classifications, you cannot make some classifications.

[20a]Jackman v. Rosenbaum Co., 260 U.S. 22, 31 (1922).

MR. MARSHALL: But the personal and present right that I have to consider like any other citizen of Clarendon County, South Carolina, is a right that has been recognized by this Court over and over again. And so far as the appellants in this case are concerned, I cannot consider it sufficient to be relegated to the legislature of South Carolina where the record in this Court shows their consideration of Negroes, and I speak specifically of the primary cases.

JUSTICE FRANKFURTER: If you would refer to the record of the case, there they said that the doctrine of classification is not excluded by the Fourteenth Amendment, but its employment by state legislatures has no justifiable foundation.

MR. MARSHALL: I think that when an attack is made on a statute on the ground that it is an unreasonable classification, and competent, recognized testimony is produced, I think then the least that the state has to do is to produce something to defend their statutes.

JUSTICE FRANKFURTER: I follow you when you talk that way.

MR. MARSHALL: That is part of the argument, sir.

JUSTICE FRANKFURTER: But when you start, as I say, with the conclusion that you cannot have segregation, then there is no problem. If you start with the conclusion of a problem, there is no problem.

MR. MARSHALL: But Mr. Justice Frankfurter, I was trying to make three different points. I said that the first one was peculiarly narrow, under the McLaurin and the Sweatt decisions.

The second point was that on a classification basis, these statutes were bad.
The third point was the broader point, that racial distinctions in and of themselves are invidious. I consider it as a three-pronged attack. Any one of the three would be sufficient for reversal.

JUSTICE FRANKFURTER: You may recall that this Court not so many years ago decided that the legislature of Louisiana could restrict the calling of pilots on the Mississippi to the question of who your father was.[21]

MR. MARSHALL: Yes, sir.

JUSTICE FRANKFURTER: And there were those of us who sustained that legislation, not because we thought it was admirable or because we thought it comported with human notions or because we believed in primogeniture, but for different reasons, that it was so imbedded in the conflict of the history of that problem in Louisiana that we thought on the whole that was an allowable justification.

MR. MARSHALL: I say, sir, that I do not think—

[21]Kotch v. Pilot Commissioners, 330 U.S. 552 (1947).

JUSTICE FRANKFURTER: I am not taking that beside this case. I am not meaning to intimate any of that, as you well know, on this subject. I am just saying how the subjects are to be dealt with.

MR. MARSHALL: But Mr. Justice Frankfurter, I do not think that segregation in public schools is any more ingrained in the South than segregation in transportation, and this Court upset it in the Morgan case.[22] I do not think it is any more ingrained.

JUSTICE FRANKFURTER: It upset it in the Morgan case on the ground that it was none of the business of the state; it was an interstate problem.

MR. MARSHALL: That is a different problem. But a minute ago the very question was raised that we have to deal with realities, and it did upset that. Take the primary case. There is no more ingrained rule than there were in the cases of McLaurin and Sweatt, the graduate school cases.

JUSTICE FRANKFURTER: I am willing to suggest that this problem is more complicated than the simple recognition of an absolute *non possumus*.

MR. MARSHALL: I agree that it is not only complicated. I agree that it is a tough problem. But I think that it is a problem that has to be faced.

JUSTICE FRANKFURTER: That is why we are here.

MR. MARSHALL: That is what I appreciate, Your Honor. But I say, sir, that most of my time is spent down in the South, and despite all these predictions as to what might happen, I do not think that anything is going to happen any more except on the graduate and professional level. And this Court can take notice of the reports that have been in papers such as the New York *Times*. But it seems to me on that question, this Court should go back to the case of *Buchanan* v. *Warley*,[23] where on the question as to whether or not there was this great problem, this Court in *Buchanan* v. *Warley* said:

> That there exists a serious and difficult problem arising from a feeling of race hostility which the law is powerless to control, and to which it must give a measure of consideration, may be freely admitted. But its solution cannot be promoted by depriving citizens of their constitutional rights and privileges.

In this case, granting that there is a feeling of race hostility in South Carolina, if there be such a thing, or granting that there is that problem, we cannot have the individual rights subjected to this consideration of what the groups might do; for example, it was even argued that it will be better for both the Negro and the so-called white group. This record is not quite clear as to who is in the white group, because the superintendent of schools said that he did not know; all he knew was that Negroes were excluded. So I imagine that the other schools take in everybody.

[22]Morgan v. Virginia, 328 U.S. 373 (1946). A Virginia law requiring segregation on buses was declared unconstitutional as an improper burden on interstate commerce.

[23]245 U.S. 60, 80 (1917). A Louisiana ordinance forbidding Negroes from occupying residences on a block inhabited by a majority of whites was declared invalid.

So it seems to me that insofar as this case is concerned, whereas in the Kansas case there was a finding of fact that was favorable to the appellants—in this case the opinion of the court mentions the fact that the findings are embodied in the opinion, and the court in that case decided that the only issue would be these facilities, the curriculum, transportation, et cetera.

In the brief for the appellees in this case and the argument in the lower court, I have yet to hear any one say that they denied that these children are harmed by reason of this segregation. Nobody denies that, at least up to now. So there is a grant, I should assume, that segregation in and of itself harms these children.

Now, the argument is made that because we are drawn into a broader problem down in South Carolina, because of a situation down there, that this statute should be upheld.

So there we have a direct cleavage from one side to the other side. I do not think any of that is significant. As a matter of fact, I think all of that argument is made without foundation. I do not believe that in the case of the sworn testimony of the witnesses, statements and briefs and quotations from magazine articles will counteract what is actually in the brief.

So what do we have in the record? We have testimony of physical inequality. It is admitted. We have the testimony of experts as to the exact harm which is inherent in segregation wherever it occurs. That I would assume is too broad for the immediate decision, because after all, the only point before this Court is the statute as it was applied in Clarendon County. But if this Court would reverse and the case would be sent back, we are not asking for affirmative relief. That will not put anybody in any school. The only thing that we ask for is that the state-imposed racial segregation be taken off, and to leave the county school board, the county people, the district people, to work out their own solution of the problem to assign children on any reasonable basis they want to assign them on.

JUSTICE FRANKFURTER: You mean, if we reverse, it will not entitle every mother to have her child go to a nonsegregated school in Clarendon County?

MR. MARSHALL: No, sir.

JUSTICE FRANKFURTER: What will it do? Would you mind spelling this out? What would happen?

MR. MARSHALL: Yes, sir. The school board, I assume, would find some other method of distributing the children, a recognizable method, by drawing district lines.

JUSTICE FRANKFURTER: What would that mean?

MR. MARSHALL: The usual procedure—

JUSTICE FRANKFURTER: You mean that geographically the colored people all live in one district?

MR. MARSHALL: No, sir, they do not. They are mixed up somewhat.

JUSTICE FRANKFURTER: Then why would not the children be mixed.

MR. MARSHALL: If they are in the district, they would be. But there might possibly be areas—

JUSTICE FRANKFURTER: You mean we would have gerrymandering of school districts?

MR. MARSHALL: Not gerrymandering, sir. The lines could be equal.

JUSTICE FRANKFURTER: I think that nothing would be worse than for this Court—I am expressing my own opinion—nothing would be worse, from my point of view, than for this Court to make an abstract declaration that segregation is bad and then have it evaded by tricks.

MR. MARSHALL: No, sir. As a matter of fact, sir, we have had cases where we have taken care of that. But the point is that it is my assumption that where this is done, it will work out, if I might leave the record, by statute in some states.

JUSTICE FRANKFURTER: It would be more important information in my mind, to have you spell out in concrete what would happen if this Court reverses and the case goes back to the district court for the entry of a decree.

MR. MARSHALL: I think, sir, that the decree would be entered which would enjoin the school officials from, one, enforcing the statute; two, from segregating on the basis of race or color. Then I think whatever district lines they draw, if it can be shown that those lines are drawn on the basis of race or color, then I think they would violate the injunction. If the lines are drawn on a natural basis, without regard to race or color, then I think that nobody would have any complaint.

For example, the colored child that is over here in this school would not be able to go to that school. But the only thing that would come down would be the decision that whatever rule you set in, if you set in, it shall not be on race, either actually or by any other way. It would violate the injunction, in my opinion.

JUSTICE FRANKFURTER: There is a thing that I do not understand. Why would not that inevitably involve—unless you have Negro ghettoes, or if you find that language offensive, unless you have concentrations of Negroes, so that only Negro children would go there, and there would be no white children mixed with them, or vice versa—why would it not involve Negro children saying, "I want to go to this school instead of that school"?

MR. MARSHALL: That is the interesting thing in this procedure. They could move over into that district, if necessary. Even if you get stuck in one district, there is always an out, as long as this statute is gone.

There are several ways that can be done. But we have instances, if I might, sir, where they have been able to draw a line and to enclose—this is in the North—to enclose the Negroes, and in New York those lines have on every occasion been declared unreasonably drawn, because it is obvious that they were drawn for that purpose.

JUSTICE FRANKFURTER: Gerrymandering?

MR. MARSHALL: Yes, sir. As a matter of fact, they used the word "gerrymander."

So in South Carolina, if the decree was entered as we have requested, then the school district would have to decide a means other than race, and if it ended up that the Negroes were all in one school, because of race, they would be violating the injunction just as bad as they are by violating what we consider to be the Fourteenth Amendment now.

JUSTICE FRANKFURTER: Now, I think it is important to know, before one starts, where he is going. As to available schools, how would that cut across this problem? If everything was done that you wanted done, would there be physical facilities within such drawing of lines as you would regard as not evasive of the decree?

MR. MARSHALL: Most of the school buildings are now assigned to Negroes, so that the Negro buildings are scattered around in that county. Now, as to whether or not lines could be properly drawn, I say quite frankly, sir, I do not know. But I do know that in most of the southern areas—it might be news to the Court—there are very few areas that are predominately one race or the other.

JUSTICE FRANKFURTER: Are you going to argue the District of Columbia case?

MR. MARSHALL: No, sir.
If you have any questions, I would try, but I cannot bind the other side.

JUSTICE FRANKFURTER: I just wondered, in regard to this question that we are discussing, how what you are indicating or contemplating would work out in the District if tomorrow there were the requirement that there must be mixed groups.

MR. MARSHALL: Most of the schools in the District of Columbia would be integrated. There might possibly be some in the concentrated areas up in the northwest section. There might be. But I doubt it. But I think the question as to what would happen if such decree was entered—I again point out that it is actually a matter that is for the school authorities to decide, and it is not a matter for us, it seems to me, as lawyers, to recommend except where there is racial discrimination or discrimination on one side or the other.

But my emphasis is that all we are asking for is to take off this state-imposed segregation. It is the state-imposed part of it that affects the individual children. And the testimony in many instances is along that line.

So in South Carolina, if the District Court issued a decree—and I hasten to add that in the second hearing when we were prevented from arguing segregation, the argument was made that on the basis of the fact that the schools were still unequal, we should get relief on the basis of the Sipuel decision—the court said in that case, no, that the only relief we could get would be this relief as of September, and in that case the court took the position that it would be impossible to break into the middle of the year. If I might anticipate a question on that, the point would come up as to, if a decree in this case should happen to be issued by the District Court, or in a case similar to this, as to whether or not there would be a time given for the actual enrollment of the children, et cetera, and changing of children from school to school. It would be my position in a case like that, which is very much in answer to the brief filed by the United States in this case—it would be my position that the important thing is to get the principle established, and if a decree were entered saying that facilities are declared to be unequal and that the appellants are entitled to an injunction, and then the District Court issues the injunction, it would seem to me that it would go without saying that the local school board had the time to do it. But obviously it could not do it over night, and it might take six months to do it one place and two months to do it another place.

Again, I say it is not a matter for judicial determination. That would be a matter for legislative determination.

I would like to save my fifteen minutes for rebuttal.

JUSTICE JACKSON: Coming back to the question that Justice Black asked you, could I ask you what, if any, effect does your argument have on the Indian policy, the segregation of the Indians. How do you deal with that?

MR. MARSHALL: I think that again that we are in a position of having grown up. Indians are no longer wards of the Government. I do not think that they stand in any special category. And in all of the southern states that I know of, the Indians are in a preferred position so far as Negroes are concerned, and I do not know of any place where they are excluded.

JUSTICE JACKSON: In some respects, in taxes, at least, I wish I could claim to have a little Indian blood.

MR. MARSHALL: But the only time it ever came up was in the—

JUSTICE JACKSON: But on the historical argument, the philosophy of the Fourteenth Amendment which you contended for does not seem to have been applied by the people who adopted the Fourteenth Amendment, at least in the Indian case.

MR. MARSHALL: I think, sir, that if we go back even as far as *Slaughter-House* and come up through *Strauder,*[24] where the Fourteenth Amendment was passed for the specific purpose of raising the newly freed slaves up, et cetera, I do not know.

JUSTICE JACKSON: Do you think that might not apply to the Indians?

MR. MARSHALL: I think it would. But I think that the biggest trouble with the Indians is that they just have not had the judgment or the wherewithal to bring lawsuits.

[24] In the Slaughter-House Cases, 16 Wall. 36 (1873), the Court refused to strike down a Lousiana law granting a monopoly to certain white butchers in New Orleans. The decision gave a narrow reading to the privileges and immunities clause of the recently passed Fourteenth Amendment. Strauder v. West Virginia, 100 U.S. 303 (1880), held a West Virginia law forbidding Negroes from serving on juries unconstitutional.

JUSTICE JACKSON: Maybe you should bring some up.

MR. MARSHALL: I have a full load now, Mr. Justice.

THE CHIEF JUSTICE: Mr. Davis.

ARGUMENT ON BEHALF OF THE APPELLEES

by MR. DAVIS

MR. DAVIS: May it please the Court, I think if the appellants' construction of the Fourteenth Amendment should prevail here, there is no doubt in my mind that it would catch the Indian within its grasp just as much as the Negro. If it should prevail, I am unable to see why a state would have any further right to segregate its pupils on the ground of sex or on the ground of age or on the ground of mental capacity. If it may classify it for one purpose on the basis of admitted facts, it may, according to my contention, classify it for other.

Now, I want to address myself during the course of this argument to three propositions, and I will utilize the remaining minutes of the afternoon to state them.

The first thing which I want to contend for before the Court is that the mandate of the court below, which I quote, "Required the defendants to proceed at once to furnish plaintiffs and other Negro pupils of said district educational facilities, equipment, curricula, and opportunities equal to those furnished white pupils."

That mandate has been fully complied with. We have been found to have obeyed the court's injunction. The question is no longer in the case, and the complaint which is made by the appellants in their brief that the school doors should have been immediately thrown open instead of taking the time necessary to readjust the physical facilities, is a moot question at this stage of the case.

The second question to which I wish to address myself is that Article XIV, section 7, of the Constitution of South Carolina, and section 5377 of the Code, both making the separation of schools between white and colored mandatory, do not offend the Fourteenth Amendment of the Constitution of the United States or deny equal protection.

The right of a state to classify the pupils in its public schools on the basis of sex or age or mental capacity, or race, is not impaired or affected by that amendment.

Third, I want to say something about the evidence offered by the plaintiffs upon which counsel so confidently relied.

I see that the evidence offered by the plaintiffs, be its merit what it may, deals entirely with legislative policy, and does not tread on constitutional right. Whether it does or not, it would be difficult for me to conceal my opinion that that evidence in and of itself is of slight weight and in conflict with the opinion of other and better informed sources.

I hope I have not laid out too much territory for the time that is allotted to me. Let me attack it seriatim.

I want to put this case in its proper frame, by reciting what has transpired up to this time, so that Your Honors may be sure that my assertion of full performance is not an idle boast.

When the first hearing was at an end, the court entered its decree, demanding us to proceed forthwith to furnish, not merely physical facilities, as my friend would have it, but educational facilities, equipment, curricula, and opportunities equal on the part of the state for the Negro as for the white pupil.

Now, the court could have stopped there, and for the enforcement of its decree it could have awaited the moment when some complainant would have come in and invoked process of contempt against the delinquent defendants. That would have satisfied the duty of the chancellor. He would have retained in its own hand the powers of enforcement which the rules of equity give him, and perhaps his conscience might have been at rest with the feeling that he had done all that judicially he was called upon to do.

But the court below went further. In order to ensure the obedience to its decree, it required the defendants within the period of six months, not later than six months, to report what progress they were making in the execution of the court's order. The court might have said, "You must do this tomorrow"; I gather from counsel that not even counsel for the appellants here contends so much.

Insofar as the equality, equalization required the building of buildings and, of course, the court knew, as every sensible man knew, that you do not get buildings by rubbing an Aladdin's lamp, and you cannot create them by court decree. To say that the day following this decree, all this should have been done would have been *brutus fulmen,* and no credit to the court or anybody else.

In December, within the allotted time, the defendants made report of progress. At that time; the case was on Your Honor's docket. Because of the fact that an appeal had been taken from so much of the decree below, they refused to strike down the constitution and the statute.

Thereupon, the District Court sent that report to you, and you, not desiring to pass upon it, remanded the case to the District Court, and called upon them to pass upon their report which had been made to them, and to free their hands entirely for such action as they might see fit. You vacated the order entered below.

The District Court thereupon resumed control of the case. It set it down for a hearing in March of 1952, at which time the defendants filed a supplemental report showing the progress up to that precise day and minute. Thereupon, the court declared that the defendants had made every possible effort to comply with the decree of the court, that they had done all that was humanly possible, and that by the month of September, 1952, equality between the races in this area would have been achieved.

So the record reads.

Now, I should just like briefly to summarize what the situation was that those reports exposed. They showed that in the State of South Carolina, under the leadership of its present Governor,[25] there was a surge for educational reform and improvement, which I suspect has not been exceeded in any state in this Union. It began with the legislature which adopted the act providing for the issuance of a maximum of $75,000,000 in bonds for school purposes, not an ultimate of $75,

[25]James F. Byrnes (1879–   ) was Governor of South Carolina from 1951 to 1955. He also served as United States Senator (1931–1941), Associate Justice of the Supreme Court (1941–42), and Secretary of State of the United States (1945–1947).

000,000, but a maximum at any one time of $75,000,000, and that to be supported and serviced by a 3 per cent sales tax. Speaking from some slight personal experience, I can assert that it escapes very few transactions in that state.

That being done, the legislature set up an educational finance commission, with power to survey the educational system of the state, to consolidate districts for better finance, to allot funds to the districts all over the state in such manner as this commission might find to be appropriate. Thereupon, the commission goes to Clarendon County, which is the seat of the present drama. It finds that in Clarendon County there are thirty-four educational districts, so-called, each with its separate body of officers and administrators, and all of them bogged down, I take it, by similar poverty.

It directed that that county be readjusted, redistricted, into three districts, one, District No. 1 to contain the contentious District No.22, with which the litigation began, and six others. I gather that counsel wants to reverse that process. Having brought these districts into unity and strength, he has some plan, the mathematics of which I do not entirely grasp, by which the districts will be redistricted again with resulting benefit to all concerned.

District No. 1 was created. Its officers entered this litigation, and agreed to be bound by the decree, and are here present.

The first thing that the district did was to provide for the building of a new Negro high school at Scott's Branch, and for the repair of the secondary school at Scott's Branch, for which it expended the sum of $261,000 on a contract that they should be completed and put into use by September of 1952.

I speak outside the record, but that has been accomplished.

It was also provided that it should purchase the site for some two Negro secondary schools, which should be serviced by this fund.

$21,000 was appropriated immediately for additional equipment, and those secondary schools are now on the verge of completion.

But what could be done immediately—and with this I shall close for the afternoon—what could be done immediately by this school board was done. Salaries of teachers were equalized. Curricula were made uniform, and the State of South Carolina appropriated money to furnish school buses for black and white. Of course, in these days, the schoolboy no longer walks. The figure of the schoolboy trudging four miles in the morning and back four in the afternoon swinging his books as he went is as much a figure of myth as the presidential candidate born in a log cabin. Both of these characters have disappeared.

THE CHIEF JUSTICE: The Court will adjourn.
(Whereupon, at 4:30 p.m., the Court arose.)
(Oral argument was resumed at 12:10 p.m., December 10, 1952.)

THE CHIEF JUSTICE: Case No. 101, Harry Briggs, Jr., et al against R. W. Elliott, Chairman, et al.

THE CLERK: Counsel are present.

THE CHIEF JUSTICE: Proceed.

ARGUMENT ON BEHALF OF APPELLEES—Resumed

by MR. DAVIS

MR. DAVIS: If the Court please, when the Court arose on yesterday, I was reciting the progress that had been made in the public school system in South Carolina, and with particular reference to the improvement of the facilities, equipment curricular, and opportunities accorded to the colored students.

I might go further on that subject, but I am content to read two sentences from the opinion of the court below. This is the opinion of Judge Parker:

> The reports of December 21 and March 3 filed by defendants, which are admitted by plaintiffs to be true and correct and which are so found by the Court, show beyond question that defendants have proceeded promptly and in good faith to comply with the Court's decree.

They add:

> There can be no doubt that as a result of the program in which defendants are engaged the educational facilities and opportunities afforded Negroes within the district will, by the beginning of the next school year beginning in September, 1952, be made equal to those afforded white persons.

The only additional fact which I want to mention, aside from leaving the remainder to my brief of the opinion of the court below is a fact of which I think Mr. Marshall should take cognizance when he proceeds to his redistricting program, and that is the fact that in District No. 1, the district here in controversy, there are now, speaking of the report of last March, 2,799 registered Negro students and 295 registered white students. In other words, the proportion between the Negroes and the whites is about in the ratio of ten to one. And whether discrimination is to be abolished by introducing 2,800 Negro students in the schools now occupied by the whites, or conversely introducing 295 whites into the schools now occupied by 2,800 Negroes, the result in either event is one which one cannot contemplate with entire equanimity.

I come, then, to what is really the crux of the case. That is the meaning and interpretation of the Fourteenth Amendment to the Constitution of the United States. We devote to that important subject but five pages of our brief. We trust the Court will not treat that summary disposition of it as due to any lack of earnestness on our part.

We have endeavored to compress the outline of the argument for two reasons. The first is that the opinion of Judge Parker rendered below is so cogent and complete that it seems impossible to add anything to his reasoning. The second is, perhaps more compelling at the moment, that Your Honors have so often and so recently dealt with this subject that it would be a work of supererogation to remind you of the cases in which you have dealt with it or to argue with you, the authors, the meaning and scope of the opinions you have emitted.

But if, as lawyers or judges, we have ascertained the scope and bearing of the equal protection clause of the Fourteenth Amendment, our duty is done. The rest must be left to those who dictate public policy, and not to courts.

How should we approach it? I use the language of the Court: An amendment to the Constitution should be read, you have said,

"in a sense most obvious to the common understanding at the time of its adoption." For it was for public adoption that it was proposed.[25a]

Still earlier you have said it is the duty of the interpreters,

to place ourselves as nearly as possible in the condition of the men who framed the instrument.[25b]

What was the condition of those who framed the instrument? The resolution proposing the Fourteenth Amendment was proffered by Congress in June, 1866. In the succeeding month of July, the same Congress proceeded to establish, or to continue separate schools in the District of Columbia, and from that good day to this, Congress has not waivered in that policy. It has confronted the attack upon it repeatedly. During the life of Charles Sumner,[26] over and over again, he undertook to amend the law of the District so as to provide for mixed and not for separate schools, and again and again he was defeated.

JUSTICE BURTON: What is your answer, Mr. Davis, to the suggestion mentioned yesterday that at that time the conditions and relations between the two races were such that what might have been unconstitutional then would not be unconstitutional now?

MR. DAVIS: My answer to that is that changed conditions may affect policy, but changed conditions cannot broaden the terminology of the Constitution, the thought is an administrative or a political question, and not a judicial one.

JUSTICE BURTON: But the Constitution is a living document that must be interpreted in relation to the facts of the time in which it is interpreted. Did we not go through with that in connection with child labor cases, and so forth?

MR. DAVIS: Oh, well, of course, changed conditions may bring things within the scope of the Constitution which were not originally contemplated, and of that perhaps the aptest illustration is the interstate commerce clause. Many things have been found to be interstate commerce which at the time of the writing of the Constitution were not contemplated at all. Many of them did not even exist. But when they come within the field of interstate commerce, then they become subject to congressional power, which is defined in the terms of the Constitution itself. So circumstances may bring new facts within the purview of the constitutional provision, but they do not alter, expand, or change the language that the framers of the Constitution have employed.

[25a] Eisner v. Macomber, 252 U.S. 189, 220 (1920) (Holmes, J., dissenting).

[25b] Ex parte Bain, 121 U.S. 1, 12 (1887).

[26] Charles Sumner (1811–1874) was a leading anti-slavery Senator from Massachusetts from 1851 to 1874. He was assaulted in the Senate by Representative Preston Brooks of South Carolina for his anti-slavery remarks, sustaining severe injuries. He continued his fight for Negro rights after the Civil War.

JUSTICE FRANKFURTER: Mr. Davis, do you think that "equal" is a less fluid term than "commerce between the states"?

MR. DAVIS: Less fluid?

JUSTICE FRANKFURTER: Yes.

MR. DAVIS: I have not compared the two on the point of fluidity.

JUSTICE FRANKFURTER: Suppose you do it now.

MR. DAVIS: I am not sure that I can approach it in just that sense.

JUSTICE FRANKFURTER: The problem behind my question is whatever the phrasing of it would be.

MR. DAVIS: That what is unequal today may be equal tomorrow, or vice versa?

JUSTICE FRANKFURTER: That is it.

MR. DAVIS: That might be. I should not philosophize about it. But the effort in which I am now engaged is to show how those who submitted this amendment and those who adopted it conceded it to be, and what their conduct by way of interpretation has been since its ratification in 1868.

JUSTICE FRANKFURTER: What you are saying is, that as a matter of history, history puts a gloss upon "equal" which does not permit elimination or admixture of white and colored in this aspect to be introduced?

MR. DAVIS: Yes, I am saying that.

JUSTICE FRANKFURTER: That is what you are saying?

MR. DAVIS: Yes, I am saying that. I am saying that equal protection in the minds of the Congress of the United States did not contemplate mixed schools as a necessity. I am saying that, and I rest on it, though I shall not go further into the congressional history on this subject, because my brother Korman speaking for the District of Columbia will enter that phase of it.

It is true that in the Constitution of the United States there is no equal protection clause. It is true that the Fourteenth Amendment was addressed primarily to the states. But it is inconceivable that the Congress which submitted it would have forbidden the states to employ an educational scheme which Congress itself was persistent in employing in the District of Columbia.

I therefore urge that the action of Congress is a legislative interpretation of the meaning and scope of this amendment, and a legislative interpretation of a legislative act, no court, I respectfully submit is justified in ignoring.

What did the states think about this at the time of the ratification? At the time the amendment was submitted, there were 37 states in the Union. Thirty of them had ratified the amendment at the time it was proclaimed in 1868. Of those 30 ratifying states, 23 either then had, or immediately installed separate schools for white and colored children under their public school systems. Were they violating the amendment which they had solemnly accepted? Were they conceiving of it in any other sense than that it did not touch their power over their public schools?

How do they stand today? Seventeen states in the Union today provide for separate schools for white and colored children, and 4 others make it permissive with their school board. Those 4 are Wyoming, Kansas, of which we heard yesterday, New Mexico, and Arizona, so that you have 21 states today which conceive it their power and right to maintain separate schools if it suits their policy.

When we turn to the judicial branch, it has spoken on this question, perhaps with more repetition and in more cases than any other single separate constitutional question that now occurs to me. We have not larded our brief with quotations from the courts of last resort of the several states. It would be easy to do so, but we have assembled in our appendix a list of cases which the highest courts in the states have decided on this question. I am not sure that that list is exhaustive. In fact, I am inclined to think that it is not exhaustive. But certainly it is impressive, and they speak with a single voice that their separate school system is not a violation of the Constitution of the United States.

What does this Court say? I repeat, I shall not undertake to interpret for Your Honors the scope and weight of your own opinions. In *Plessy* v. *Ferguson, Cumming* v. *Richmond County Board of Education, Gong Lum* v. *Rice, Berea College* v. *Kentucky,*[27] *Sipuel* v. *Board of Regents, Gaines* v. *Canada, Sweatt* v. *Painter,* and *McLaurin* v. *Oklahoma,* and there may be others for all I know, certainly this Court has spoken in the most clear and unmistakable terms to the effect that this segregation is not unlawful. I am speaking for those with whom I am associated.

We find nothing in the latest cases that modified that doctrine of "separate but equal" in the least. *Sweatt* v. *Painter* and similar cases were decided solely on the basis of inequality, as we think, and as we believe the Court intended.

It is a little late, said the court below, after this question has been presumed to be settled for ninety years—it is a little late to argue that the question is still at large.

I want to read just one of Judge Parker's sentences on that. Said he:

It is hardly reasonable to suppose that legislative bodies over so wide a territory, including the Congress of the United States, and great judges of high courts have knowingly defied the Constitution for so long a period or that they have acted in ignorance of the meaning of its provisions. The constitutional principle is the same now that it has been throughout this period, and if conditions have changed so that segregation is no longer wise, this is a matter for the legislatures and not for the courts. The members of the judiciary [it goes on to say] have no more right to read their ideas of sociology into the Constitution than their ideas of economics.

It would be an interesting, though perhaps entirely useless, undertaking to enumerate the numbers of men charged with official duty in the legislative and the judicial branches of the Government who have declared that segregation is not per se unlawful. The members of Congress, year after year, and session after session, the members of state constitutional conventions, the members of state legislatures, year after year and session after session, the members of the higher courts of the states, the members of the inferior federal judiciary, and the members of this

[27] 211 U.S. 45 (1908). A Kentucky law forbidding colleges to enroll both white and Negro students was upheld. Justice John M. Harlan dissented.

tribunal—what their number may be, I do not know, but I think it reasonably certain that it must mount well into the thousands, and to this I stress for Your Honors that every one of that vast group was bound by oath to support the Constitution of the United States and any of its amendments—is it conceivable that all that body of concurrent opinion was recreant to its duty or misunderstood the constitutional mandate, or was ignorant of the history which gave to the mandate its scope and meaning? I submit not.

Now, what are we told here that has made all that body of activity and learning of no consequence? Says counsel for the plaintiffs, or appellants, we have the uncontradicted testimony of expert witnesses that segregation is hurtful, and in their opinion hurtful to the children of both races, both colored and white. These witnesses severally described themselves as professors, associate professors, assistant professors, and one describes herself as a lecturer and adviser on curricular. I am not sure exactly what that means.

I did not impugn the sincerity of these learned gentlemen and lady. I am quite sure that they believe that they are expressing valid opinions on their subject. But there are two things notable about them. Not a one of them is under any official duty in the premises whatever; not a one of them has had to consider the welfare of the people for whom they are legislating or whose rights they were called on to adjudicate. And only one of them professes to have the slightest knowledge of conditions in the states where separate schools are now being maintained. Only one of them professes any knowledge of the condition within the seventeen segregating states.

I want to refer just a moment to that particular witness, Dr. Clark. Dr. Clark professed to speak as an expert and an informed investigator on this subject. His investigation consisted of visits to the Scott's Branch primary and secondary school, at Scott's Branch, which he undertook at the request of counsel for the plaintiffs. He called for the presentation to him of some sixteen pupils between the ages of six and nine years, and he applied to them what he devised and what he was pleased to call an objective test. That consisted of offering to them sixteen white and colored dolls, and inviting them to select the doll they would prefer, the doll they thought was nice, the doll that looked bad, or the doll that looked most like themselves. He ascertained that ten out of his battery of sixteen preferred the white doll. Nine thought the white doll was nice, and seven thought it looked most like themselves. Eleven said that the colored doll was bad, and one that the white doll was bad. And out of that intensive investigation and that application of that thoroughly scientific test, he deduced the sound conclusion that segregation there had produced confusion in the individuals—I use his language— "and their concepts about themselves conflicting in their personalities, that they have been definitely harmed in the development of their personalities."

That is a sad result, and we are invited to accept it as a scientific conclusion. But I am reminded of the scriptural saying, "Oh, that mine adversary had written a book." And Professor Clark, with the assistance of his wife, has written on this subject and has described a similar test which he submitted to colored pupils in the northern and nonsegregated schools.[28] He found that 62 per cent of the colored

[28]The article referred to was "Racial Identifications and Preferences in Negro Children" appearing in *Readings in Social Psychology* (Newcomb & Hartley, ed. New York, 1947).

children in the South chose a white doll; 72 per cent in the North chose the white doll; 52 per cent of the children in the South thought the white doll was nice; 68 per cent of the children in the North thought the white doll was nice; 49 per cent of the children in the South thought the colored doll was bad; 71 per cent of the children in the North thought the colored doll was bad.

Now, these latter scientific tests were conducted in nonsegregating states, and with those results compared, what becomes of the blasting influence of segregation to which Dr. Clark so eloquently testifies?

The witness Trager,[29] who is the lecturer and consultant on curricular, had never been in the South except when she visited her husband who was stationed at an Army post in Charleston during the war. And I gather that the visit was of somewhat brief character. She also was in search of scientific wisdom, and she submitted that same scientific test to a collection of children in the schools of Philadelphia, where segregation has been absent for many years. She made as a result of that what seems to have been surprising to her, the fact that in children from five to eight years of age, they were already aware, both white and colored, of racial differences between them.

Now, that may be a scientific conclusion. It would be rather surprising, if the children were possessed of their normal senses, if they were ignorant of some racial differences between them, even at that early age.

I am tempted to digress, because I am discussing the weight and pith of this testimony, which is the reliance of the plaintiffs here to turn back this enormous weight of legislative and judicial precedent on this subject. I may have been unfortunate, or I may have been careless, but it seems to me that much of that which is handed around under the name of social science is an effort on the part of the scientist to rationalize his own preconceptions. They find usually, in my limited observation, what they go out to find.

One of these witnesses, Dr. Krech,[30] speaks of a colored school, gives, as he says, "what we call in our lingo environmental support for the belief that Negroes are in some way different from and inferior to white people, and that in turn, of course, supports and strengthens beliefs of racial differences, of racial inferiority."

I ran across a sentence the other day which somebody said who was equally as expert as Dr. Krech in the "lingo" of the craft. He described much of the social science as "fragmentary expertise based on an examined presupposition," which is about as scientific language as you can use, I suppose, but seems to be entirely descriptive.

Now, South Carolina is unique among the states in one particular. You have often heard it said that an ounce of experience is worth a pound of theory. South Carolina does not come to this policy as a stranger. She had mixed schools for twelve years, from 1865 to 1877. She had them as a result of the Constitutional Convention of 1865, which was led by a preacher of the Negro race, against whom

---

[29]Mrs. Helen Trager taught at Vassar and acted as educational consultant to city schools in New York, Philadelphia, Denver, San Diego, and Detroit.

[30]Dr. David Krech taught social psychology at Harvard and the University of California.

I know nothing, who bore the somewhat distinguished name of Cardozo, and he forced through that convention the provision for mixed schools.[31]

The then Governor of South Carolina, whose term was expiring, was the war governor, Governor Orr, who denounced the provision. He was succeeded by—I hope the term has lost its invidiousness—a carpetbagger from Maine, named Scott, and Scott denounced the provision. And Dr. Knight, the Professor of Education at the University of North Carolina, who has written on the subject, declares that it was the most unwise action of the period, and that that is a certainty.[32]

When South Carolina moved from mixed to segregated schools, it did so in the light of experience, and in the light of the further fact, these authorities state, that it had been destructive to the public school system of South Carolina for fifty years after it was abolished.

Now, these learned witnesses do not have the whole field to themselves. They do not speak without contradiction from other sources. We quote in our brief—I suppose it is not testimony, but it is quotable material, and we are content to adopt it—Dr. Odum, of North Carolina, who is perhaps the foremost investigator of educational questions in the entire South; Dr. Frank Graham, former president of the University of North Carolina; ex-Governor Darden, president of the University of Virginia; Hodding Carter, whose recent works on Southern conditions have become classic; Gunnar Myrdal, Swedish scientist employed to investigate the race question for the Rockefeller Foundation; W.E.B. DuBois; Ambrose Caliver; and the witness Crow, who testified in this case, all of them opposing the item that there should be an immediate abolition of segregated schools.[33]

Let me read a sentence or two from Dr. DuBois. I may be wrong about this,

[31]F. L. Cardozo was the son of a Charleston economist, J. N. Cardozo, and a half-Negro, half-Indian mother. He was Secretary of State of South Carolina (1868-1872) and Treasurer of the State (1872-1876).

[32]James L. Orr (1822-1873) served as a member of the House of Representatives (1849-1859), Speaker (1857-1859), Republican Governor of South Carolina (1866-1868). He was succeeded by Robert K. Scott of Ohio (not Maine) who served as Republican Governor from 1868 to 1872. The book referred to is Edgar W. Knight, *Public Education in the South* (Chapel Hill, 1922).

[33]Frank Graham served as United States Senator (1949-1950), President of the University of North Carolina (1930-1949), member of the Civil Rights Commission (1946-1949), and special envoy to Pakistan for the United Nations. Hodding Carter is editor and publisher of the Delta *Democrat-Times,* Greenville, Miss., winner of a Pulitzer Prize in 1946, author of many books including *Southern Legacy* (1950) and *Robert E. Lee and the Road of Honor* (1954). Gunnar Myrdal, the distinguished Swedish economist, is the author of *An American Dilemma* (1941), one of the most thorough examinations of the Negro problem in America. W. E. B. DuBois (1868-1963) was the noted Negro educator and author. A founder of the NAACP in 1909, leader of the Niagara Movement (1906), an early attempt by Negro leaders to end discrimination, and teacher at Atlanta University. He was the author of *The Philadelphia Negro* (1899), *The Souls of Black Folks* (1903), *Black Reconstruction* (1935). He moved to Ghana in 1961 where he became director of the Encyclopedia Africana. Ambrose Caliver was senior specialist on Negro Education in the United States Office of Education from 1930 to 1945.

but I should think that he has been perhaps the most constant and vocal opponent of Negro oppression of any of his race in the country. Says he:

> It is difficult to think of anything more important for the development of a people than proper training for their children; and yet I have repeatedly seen wise and loving colored parents take infinite pains to force their little children into schools where the white children, white teachers, and white parents despised and resented the dark child, make mock of it, neglected or bullied it, and literally rendered its life a living hell. Such parents want their children to "fight" this thing out—but, dear God, at what a cost!

He goes on:

> We shall get a finer, better balance of spirit; an infinitely more capable and rounded personality by putting children in schools where they are wanted, and where they are happy and inspired, than in thrusting them into hells where they are ridiculed and hated.

If this question is a judicial question, if it is to be decided on the varying opinions of scholars, students, writers, authorities, and what you will, certainly it cannot be said that the testimony will be all one way. Certainly it cannot be said that a legislature conducting its public schools in accordance with the wishes of its people—it cannot be said that they are acting merely by caprice or by racial prejudice.

Says Judge Parker again:

> The questions thus presented are not questions of constitutional right but of legislative policy, which must be formulated, not in vacuo or with doctrinaire disregard of existing conditions, but in realistic approach to the situations to which it is to be applied.

Once more, Your Honors, I might say, What underlied this whole question? What is the great national and federal policy on this matter? Is it not a fact that the very strength and fiber of our federal system is local self-government in those matters for which local action is competent? Is it not of all the activities of government the one which most nearly approaches the hearts and minds of people, the question of the education of their young?

Is it not the height of wisdom that the manner in which that shall be conducted should be left to those most immediately affected by it, and that the wishes of the parents, both white and colored, should be ascertained before their children are forced into what may be an unwelcome contact?

I respectfully submit to the Court, there is no reason assigned here why this Court or any other should reverse the findings of ninety years.

THE CHIEF JUSTICE: Mr. Marshall.

REBUTTAL ARGUMENT ON BEHALF OF APPELLANTS

by MR. MARSHALL

MR. MARSHALL: May it please the Court, so far as the appellants are concerned in this case, at this point it seems to me that the significant factor running through all these arguments up to this point is that for some reason, which is still unexplained, Negroes are taken out of the main stream of American life in these states.

There is nothing involved in this case other than race and color, and I do not need to go to the background of the statutes or anything else. I just read the statutes, and they say, "White and colored."

While we are talking about the feeling of the people in South Carolina, I think we must once again emphasize that under our form of government, these individual rights of minority people are not to be left to even the most mature judgment of the majority of the people, and that the only testing ground as to whether or not individual rights are concerned is in this Court.

If I might digress just for a moment, on this question of the will of the people of South Carolina, if Ralph Bunche were assigned to South Carolina, his children would have to go to a Jim Crow school. No matter how great anyone becomes, if he happens to have been born a Negro, regardless of his color, he is relegated to that school.

Now, when we talk of the reasonableness of this legislation, the reasonableness, the reasonableness of the Constitution of South Carolina, and when we talk about the large body of judicial opinion in this case, I respectfully remind the Court that the exact same argument was made in the Sweatt case, and the brief in the Sweatt case contained, not only the same form, but the exact same type of appendix showing all the ramifications of the several decisions which had repeatedly upheld segregated education.

I also respectfully remind the Court that in the Sweatt case, as the public policy of the State of Texas, they also filed a public opinion poll of Texas showing that by far the majority of the people of Texas at this late date wanted segregation.

I do not believe that that body of law has any more place in this case than it had in the Sweatt case.

I think we should also point out in this regard that when we talk about reasonableness, what I think the appellees mean is reasonable insofar as the Legislature of South Carolina decided it to be reasonable, and reasonable [to the] people of South Carolina. But what we are arguing in this case is as to whether or not it is reasonableness within the decided cases of this Court on the Fourteenth Amendment. As to this particular law involved in South Carolina, the constitutional provision and the statute—the Constitution, I think, was in 1895—I do not know what this Court would have done if that statute had been brought before it at that time, but I am sure that this Court, regardless of its ultimate decision, would have tested the reasonableness of that classification, not by what the State of South Carolina wanted, but as to what the Fourteenth Amendment meant.

In the year 1952, when a statute is tested, it is not tested as to what is reasonable insofar as South Carolina is concerned; it must be tested as to what is reasonable as to this Court.

That is why we consider the case that Mr. Justice Johnson decided, cited in our reply brief, that even if this case had been tested back in those days, this Court would have felt a responsibility to weigh it against the applicable decisions of the Fourteenth Amendment, not on the question as to what is good for South Carolina.

Insofar as the argument about the states having a right to classify students on the basis of sex, learning ability, et cetera, I do not know whether they do or not, but I do believe that if it could be shown that they were unreasonable, they would feel, too, that any of the actions of the state administrative officials that affect any classification must be tested by the regular rules set up by this Court.

So we in truth and in fact have what I consider to be the main issue in this case. They claim that our expert witnesses and all that we have produced are a legislative argument at best; that the witnesses were not too accurate, and were the run-of-the-mill scientific witnesses.

But I think if it is true that there is a large body of scientific evidence on the other side, the place to have produced that was in the District Court, and I do not believe that the State of South Carolina is unable to produce such witnesses for financial or other reasons.

JUSTICE FRANKFURTER: Can we not take judicial notice of writings by people who competently deal with these problems? Can I not take judicial notice of Myrdal's book without having him called as a witness?

MR. MARSHALL: Yes, sir. But I think when you take judicial notice of Gunnar Myrdal's book, we have to read the matter, and not take portions out of context. Gunnar Myrdal's whole book is against the argument.

JUSTICE FRANKFURTER: That is a different point. I am merely going to the point that in these matters this Court takes judicial notice of accredited writings, and it does not have to call the writers as witnesses. How to inform the judicial mind, as you know, is one of the most complicated problems. It is better to have witnesses, but I did not know that we could not read the works of competent writers.

MR. MARSHALL: Mr. Justice Frankfurter, I did not say that it was bad. I said that it would have been better if they had produced the witnesses so that we would have had an opportunity to cross-examine and test their conclusions.

For example, the authority of Hodding Carter, the particular article quoted, was a magazine article of a newspaperman answering another newspaperman, and I know of nothing further removed from scientific work than one newspaperman answering another.

I am not trying—

JUSTICE FRANKFURTER: I am not going to take issue with you on that.

MR. MARSHALL: No, sir. But it seems to me that in a case like this that the only way that South Carolina, under the test set forth in this case, can sustain that statute is to show that Negroes as Negroes—all Negroes—are different from everybody else.

JUSTICE FRANKFURTER: Do you think it would make any difference to our problem if this record also contained the testimony of six professors from other institutions who gave contrary or qualifying testimony? Do you think we would be a different situation?

MR. MARSHALL: You would, sir, but I do not believe that there are any experts in the country who would so testify. And the body of law is that—even the witnesses, for example, who testified in the next case coming up, the Virginia case, all of them, admitted that segregation in and of itself was harmful. They said that the relief would not be to break down segregation. But I know of no scientist that has made any study, whether he be anthropologist or sociologist, who does not admit that segregation harms the child.

JUSTICE FRANKFURTER: Yes. But what the consequences of the proposed remedy are, is relevant to the problem.

MR. MARSHALL: I think, sir, that the consequences of the removal of the remedy are a legislative and not a judicial argument, sir. I rely on *Buchanan* v. *Warley,* where this Court said that insofar as this is a tough problem, it was tough, but the solution was not to deprive people of their constitutional rights.

JUSTICE FRANKFURTER: Then the testimony is irrelevant to the question.

MR. MARSHALL: I think the testimony is relevant as to whether or not it is a valid classification. That is on the classification point.

JUSTICE FRANKFURTER: But the consequences of how you remedy a conceded wrong bear on the question of whether it is a fair classification.

MR. MARSHALL: I do not know. But it seems to me that the only way that we as lawyers could argue before this Court, and the only way that this Court could take judicial notice of what would happen, would be that the Attorney General or some responsible individual officer of the State of South Carolina would come to this Court and say that they could not control their own state.

JUSTICE FRANKFURTER: No, that is not what I have in mind. I want to know from you whether I am entitled to take into account, in finally striking this judgment, whether I am entitled to take into account the reservation that Dr. Graham and two others, I believe, made in their report to the President.[34] May I take that into account?

MR. MARSHALL Yes, sir.

JUSTICE FRANKFURTER: May I weigh that?

MR. MARSHALL: Yes, sir.

JUSTICE FRANKFURTER: Then you have competent consideration without any testimony.

MR. MARSHALL: Yes, sir. But it is a policy matter. And that type of information, I do not believe, is more than persuasive when we consider constitutionally protected rights.

---

[34]Frank Graham (see n. 33, *supra*) was a member of the President's Committee on Civil Rights which in 1947 issued a comprehensive report on minority rights, entitled *To Secure These Rights.* Graham dissented from certain of the proposals recommended by the full committee.

JUSTICE FRANKFURTER: Of course, if it is written into the Constitution, then I do not care about the evidence. If it is in the Constitution, then all the testimony that you introduced is beside the point, in general.

MR. MARSHALL: I think, sir, that so far as the decisions of this Court, this Court has repeatedly said that you cannot use race as a basis of classification.

JUSTICE FRANKFURTER: Very well. If that is a settled constitutional doctrine, then I do not care what any associate or full professor in sociology tells me. If it is in the Constitution, I do not care about what they say. But the question is, is it in the Constitution?

MR. MARSHALL: This Court has said just that on other occasions. They said it in the Fifth Amendment cases, and they also said it in some of the Fourteenth Amendment cases, going back to Mr. Justice Holmes in the first primary case in *Nixon* v. *Herndon*. And I also think—I have no doubt in my mind—that this Court has said that these rights are present, and if all of the people in the State of South Carolina and most of the Negroes still wanted segregated schools, I understand the decision of this Court to be that any individual Negro has a right, if it is a constitutional right, to assert it, and he has a right to relief at the time he asserts that right.

JUSTICE FRANKFURTER: Certainly. Any single individual, just one, if his constitutional rights are interfered with, can come to the bar of this Court and claim it.

MR. MARSHALL: Yes, sir.

JUSTICE FRANKFURTER: But what we are considering and what you are considering is a question that is here for the very first time.

MR. MARSHALL: I agree, sir. And I think that the only issue is to consider as to whether or not that individual or small group, as we have here, of appellants, that their constitutionally protected rights have to be weighed over against what is considered to be the public policy of the State of South Carolina, and if what is considered to be the public policy of the State of South Carolina runs contrary to the rights of that individual, then the public policy of South Carolina, this Court, reluctantly or otherwise is obliged to say that this policy has run up against the Fourteenth Amendment, and for that reason his rights have to be affirmed.

But I for one think—and the record shows, and there is some material cited in some of the amicus briefs in the Kansas case—that all of these predictions of things that were going to happen, they have never happened. And I for one do not believe that the people in South Carolina or those southern states are lawless people.

Every single time that this Court has ruled, they have obeyed it, and I for one believe that rank and file people in the South will support whatever decision in this case is handed down.

JUSTICE FRANKFURTER: I have not heard that the bar of this case has suggested that South Carolina or Kansas will not obey whatever decree this Court hands down.

MR. MARSHALL: There was only one witness, and he was corrected by Judge Parker. That was in this particular case. So it seems to me, and I in closing would like to emphasize to the Court, if I may, that this question, the ultimate question of segregation at the elementary and high school levels, has come to this Court through the logical procedure of case after case, going all the way back to the Gaines case, and coming up to the present time.

We had hoped that we had put in the evidence into the record, the type of evidence which we considered this Court to have considered in the Sweatt and McLaurin cases, to demonstrate that at the elementary and high school levels, the same resulting evil which was struck down in the Sweatt and McLaurin cases exists, for the same reason, at the elementary and high school levels, and I say at this moment that none of that has been disputed.

The only thing put up against it is a legislative argument which would ultimately relegate the Negro appellants in this case to pleas with the Legislature of South Carolina to do what they have never done in the past, to recognize their pleas.

We therefore respectfully urge that the judgment of the United States District Court be reversed.

JUSTICE REED: Is there anything in the record which shows the purpose of the passage of the legislation of South Carolina?

MR. MARSHALL: No, sir. We did considerable research, and we had help on it. There is so much confusion and there are so many blank spots in between that we did not believe that it was in shape to give to anyone.

As a matter of fact, at that time there was a terrific objection to public education, one; and, two, an objection to the compulsory attendance laws.

So the three things got wound up together, the segregation and those two points.

JUSTICE REED: Is it fair to assume that the legislation involving South Carolina, as these cases do, was passed for the purpose of avoiding racial friction?

MR. MARSHALL: I think that the people who wrote on it would say that. You bear in mind in South Carolina—I hate to mention it—but that was right in the middle of the Klan period, and I cannot ignore that point. Considerable research in other states has shown that there were varying statements made in the debates, some of which could be interpreted as just plain race prejudice. But I think that the arguments back and forth in South Carolina, at least, you could draw no conclusion from them.

But we do know, and the authorities cited in the Government's brief in the Henderson case,[35] and, if you will remember, in the law professor's brief in the

[35]Henderson v. United States, 339 U.S. 816 (1950). The practice of a southern railroad permitting only one dining car table to be used by Negroes was held to violate the Interstate Commerce Act.

Sweatt case—the authorities were collected to show that the effect of this has been to place upon the Negroes this badge of inferiority.

JUSTICE REED: In the legislatures, I suppose there is a group of people, at least in the South, who would say that segregation in the schools was to avoid racial friction.

MR. MARSHALL: Yes, sir. Until today, there is a good-sized body of public opinion that would say that, and I would say respectable public opinion.

JUSTICE REED: Even in that situation, assuming, then, that there is a disadvantage ot the segregated group, the Negro group, does the legislature have to weigh as between the disadvantage of the segregated group and the advantage of the maintenance of law and order?

MR. MARSHALL: I think that the legislature should, sir. But I think, considering the legislatures, that we have to bear in mind that I know of no Negro legislator in any of these states, and I do not know whether they consider the Negro's side or not. It is just a fact. But I assume that there are people who will say that it was and is necessary, and my answer to that is, even if the concession is made that it was necessary in 1895, it is not necessary now because people have grown up and understand each other.

They are fighting together and living together. For example, today they are working together in other places. As a result of the ruling of this Court, they are going together on the higher level. Just how far it goes—I think when we predict what might happen, I know in the South where I spent most of my time, you will see white and colored kids going down the road together to school. They separate and go to different schools, and they come out and they play together. I do not see why there would necessarily be any trouble if they went to school together.

JUSTICE REED: I am not thinking of trouble. I am thinking of whether it is a problem of legislation or of the judiciary.

MR. MARSHALL: I think, sir, that the ultimate authority for the asserted right by an individual in a minority group is in a body set aside to interpret our Constitution, which is our Court.

JUSTICE REED: Undoubtedly that passes on the litigation.

MR. MARSHALL: Yes, sir.

JUSTICE REED: But where there are disadvantages and advantages, to be weighed, I take it that it is a legislative problem.

MR. MARSHALL: In so far as the state is concerned, in so far as the majority of the people are concerned. But in so far as the minority—

JUSTICE REED: The states have the right to weigh the advantages and the disadvantages or segregation, and to require equality of employment, for instance?

MR. MARSHALL: Yes, sir.

JUSTICE REED: I think that each state has been given that authority by decisions of this Court.

MR. MARSHALL: And some states have, and others have not. I think that is the main point in this case, as to what is best for the majority of the people in the states. I have no doubt—I think I am correct—that that is a legislative policy for the state legislature.

But the rights of the minorities, as has been our whole form of government, have been protected by our Constitution, and the ultimate authority for determining that is this Court. I think that is the real difference.

As to whether or not I, as an individual, am being deprived of my right is not legislative, but judicial.

THE CHIEF JUSTICE: Thank you.

MR. MARSHALL: Thank you, sir.

DOROTHY E. DAVIS, BERTHA M. DAVIS AND INEZ D. DAVIS, ETC., ET. AL.,
Appellants,

vs.

COUNTY SCHOOL BOARD OF PRINCE EDWARD COUNTY, VIRGINIA, ET AL.,
Appellees.

Case No. 191

Washington, D.C.,
Wednesday, December 10, 1952

The above-entitled cause came on for oral argument at 1:15 p.m.

APPEARANCES:

On behalf of the Appellants:
SPOTTSWOOD W. ROBINSON, III, ESQ.

On behalf of the Appellees:
T. JUSTIN MOORE, ESQ.

THE CHIEF JUSTICE: Case No. 191, Davis, et al, against County School Board of Prince Edward County, Virginia, et al.

THE CLERK: Counsel are present.

ARGUMENT ON BEHALF OF APPELLANTS

by MR. ROBINSON

MR. ROBINSON: May it please the Court, this case comes before this Court upon appeal from the final decree of the United States District Court for the Eastern District of Virginia, denying an injunction against the enforcement of section 140 of the Constitution of Virginia, and section 22-221 of the Code of Virginia, each requiring that white and colored children be taught in separate schools.

The appellants, who were the plaintiffs below, are infant high school students residing in Prince Edward County, Virginia, and their respective parents and guardians. The appellees are the County School Board of Prince Edward County and the Division Superintendent of Schools of the County, who were the original defendants below, and who as officers of the State of Virginia enforce its segregation laws, and the Commonwealth of Virginia, which intervenes as a party defendant after the filing of the action.

The complaint in this case alleged that the original defendants maintain separate schools for white and Negro high school students residing in the county, but the public high schools maintained for Negroes was unequal to the public high schools maintained for white students in plant, equipment, curricula, and other opportunities, advantages, and facilities, and that it was impossible for the infant appellants to secure public high school opportunities, advantages, and facilities equal to those afforded white children so long as the segregation laws are in force.

The complaint therefore sought a judgment declaratory of the invalidity of the laws as a denial of appellant's rights secured by the due process and equal protection clauses of the Fourteenth Amendment, and an injunction restraining the appellees from enforcing these laws or from making any distinction based upon race of color among the children attending the high schools of Prince Edward County.

In their answer, the original defendants admitted that they were enforcing the segregation laws of the State, admitted that the Negro high school was inferior in plant and equipment to the two white high schools, but denied that it was otherwise unequal and denied that segregation in the public schools contravened any provision of the federal Constitution.

After intervention by the commonwealth in its answer it made the same admissions and asserted the same defenses as did the original defendants.

There are three high schools in Prince Edward County, which are the Farmville High School and the Worsham High School, which are maintained for white students, and the Moton High School, which is maintained for Negro students.

Attendance of white children at the Farmville High School or the Worsham High School is largely determined according to the area in which the child lives. But the segregation laws of the state, so it was testified to in this record by the Division Superintendent of Schools, determine whether the child attends the Moton School, on the one side, or one of the other two schools on the other.

A three-judge District Court was convened pursuant to sections 2281 and 2284 of Title 28 of the United State Code, and at the trial both the appellants and the appellees introduced evidence, including expert testimony, first as to the extent of the existing inequalities in the Negro high school as compared with the two white high schools with respect to physical facilities and curricula, and secondly, on the issue as to whether equality of educational opportunities and benefits can ever be afforded Negro children in a racially segregated public school system.

The evidence on the second score will be summarized in a later portion of this argument.

At the conclusion of the trial, the District Court found that the Moton High School for Negroes was inferior to the white schools, not only in plant and equipment, but also in curricula and means of transportation. It ordered the appellees to forthwith provide the appellants with curricula and transportation facilities substantially equal to those afforded to white students, and to proceed with all reasonable diligence and dispatch to remove the existing inequalities by building, furnishing, and providing a high school building and facilities for Negro students in accordance with the program which the evidence for the appellees indicated would result in the availability for Negro students of a new Negro high school in September, 1953.

At the same time, the District Court refused to enjoin the enforcement of the segregation laws or to restrain the appellees from assigning school space in the county on the basis of race or color, and in its opinion it asserted the following grounds:

First, it said that on the issue of the effects of segregation in education, it accepted the decision in *Briggs* v. *Elliott*, the District Court's decision, and the decision of the Court of Appeals for the District of Columbia in *Carr* v. *Corning*,[36] cases which, as the court said, had upheld segregation and had refused to decree that it should be abolished.

Additionally, the court said that on the issue of the effects of segregation, of the effects upon the pupil resulting from the fact of segregation itself, the court could not see that the plaintiffs' evidence overbalances the defendants!

It further felt that nullification of the segregation laws was unwarranted in view of the evidence of the appellees that the segregation laws declare what the court called one of the two ways of life in Virginia, having an existence of more than eighty years, evidence that segregation had begotten greater opportunities for the Negro, including employment in Virginia alone of more Negro public-school teachers than in all thirty-one nonsegregating states, in view of evidence which was offered by the appellees that in 63 of Virginia's 127 cities and counties, the high school facilities are equal to those for whites, and in 30 of these 63 cities and counties, they are or soon will be better than those for whites, in view of the evidence, or testimony submitted by the appellees' witnesses that the involuntary elimination of segregation would lessen public interest in and support of the public schools, and would injure both races, which the court felt was, in the language of the court, "a weighted practical factor to be considered in determining whether a reasonable basis had been shown to exist for the continuation of the school segregation."

The court further felt that having found no hurt or harm to either race, that ended its inquiry, stating that it was not for the court to adjudicate the policy as right or wrong, but that the Commonwealth of Virginia must determine for itself.

An appeal was duly taken to this Court from this decision under the provisions of sections 1253 and 2101(b) of Title 28 of the United States Code.

Probable jurisdiction was noted by this Court on October 8, 1952, and presented for decision in this case are the following questions:

First, whether the segregation laws of Virginia are invalid because violative of rights secured by the due process and equal protection clauses of the Fourteenth Amendment;

Secondly, whether after finding that the buildings, facilities, curricula, and means of transportation afforded appellants were equal to those afforded whites, the court should have issued a decree forthwith restraining the appellees from excluding the infant appellants from the superior secondary school facilities of the county on the basis of race or color, and whether or not under the due process and equal protection clauses, the appellants are entitled to equality in all aspects of the public secondary educational process, including all educationally significant factors affecting the development of skills, mind, and character, in addition to equality merely in physical facilities and curricula, and whether the District Court should have so found on the evidence presented.

At the outset, I would like to place the Virginia case in what I consider to be its proper setting. Unlike *Gebhart* v. *Belton,* the Delaware case, this case does not

---

[36]Carr v. Corning, 182 F.2d 14 (D.C. Cir. 1950). The Court of Appeals for the District of Columbia upheld the validity of the District's segregated school system over the dissent of Judge Henry Edgerton.

present the situation of a finding of inequality of physical facilities and curricula coupled with an injunction against the continuance of segregation in these circumstances.

In this case, the District Court made a finding of inequality of physical facilities and curricula and still refused to enjoin the segregation practice in the school system in question.

Unlike *Brown* v. *Board of Education,* the Kansas case, this case does not present the situation of equal physical facilities and curricula coupled with a finding of injury resulting from the fact of segregation itself.

In this case, the facilities and curricula were found to be unequal, and the District Court erroneously, in our view, made a finding that no harm resulted to the student from the fact of segregation.

Unlike *Bolling* v. *Sharpe,* the District of Columbia case, the appellants in this case did not concede an equality of physical facilities and curricula. But like in *Bolling* v. *Sharpe* and unlike the other state cases, we urge that state-imposed educational segregation is a denial of due process, as well as a denial of the equal protection of the laws.

I submit that it is important to distinguish between two dissimilar approaches to the basic problem in this case. It has been urged that the segregation laws derive validity as a consequence of a long duration supported and made possible by a long line of judicial decisions, including expressions in some of the decisions of this Court.

At the same time, it is urged that these laws are valid as a matter of constitutionally permissible social experimentation by the states. On the matter of stare decisis, I submit that the duration of the challenged practice, while it is persuasive, is not controlling.

This Court has not hesitated to change the course of its decision, although of long standing, when error has been demonstrated, and courts are even less reluctant to examine their decisions when it is plain that the conditions of the present are substantially different from those of the past.

No court has ever considered itself irrevocably bound into the future by its prior determinations. As a matter of social experimentation, the laws in question must satisfy the requirements of the Constitution. While this Court has permitted the states to legislate or otherwise officially act experimentally in the social and economic fields, it has always recognized and held that this power is subject to the limitations of the Constitution, and that the tests of the Constitution must be met.

Upon examination in the past, it has found such experimentation to be constitutionally wanting when predicated solely on the facts of race.

JUSTICE FRANKFURTER: Mr. Robinson, if I heard you right—and I was looking at your brief to clarify my impression—if you are right, this injunction is reversible because it violates the Gaines doctrine?

MR. ROBINSON: I would submit, Mr. Justice Frankfurter, for the additional reason—that is correct, sir.

JUSTICE FRANKFURTER: Not for the additional reason. I should say it is for the prior reason. This Court ought not to pass on constitutional issues bigger than the record calls for.

MR. ROBINSON: Let me answer Your Honor's question this way. I believe, and I intend to argue, that by reason of the physical inequalities and the inequalities in curricula which the District Court found and which were supported largely by uncontradicted testimony, that alone should have justified the issuance of an injunction which would have admitted these appellants to share the high school facilities of the county without regard to race, in other words, would have unsegregated the schools at that point.

JUSTICE FRANKFURTER: We have specific appellants here, specific plaintiffs, and particular children, boys and girls, I take it—

MR. ROBINSON: That is correct, sir.

JUSTICE FRANKFURTER: —who want to get to a high school.

MR. ROBINSON: That is correct, sir.

JUSTICE FRANKFURTER: And you say that they ought to be allowed because they do not have adequate high schools with equal facilities?

MR. ROBINSON: I would answer the question this way. I do not know where they will go, sir. I do not mean to imply that all of them can get in a white high school, because I know that they cannot.

JUSTICE FRANKFURTER: I am talking about your clients.

MR. ROBINSON: That is correct, sir.

JUSTICE FRANKFURTER: And if you are right, then, any decree should have been issued according to *Gaines* v. *Canada*?

MR. ROBINSON: That is one of our decisions here. But we feel that the other question is also necessarily involved for additional reasons.

If we got that decree, I take it that it would unsegregate the schools and keep them in that fashion only so long as there would be a showing, or we would be able to maintain a showing, of physical inequality.

Now, the appellants in this case say that they will have a new Negro high school available in September of 1953.

But be that as it may, if their right to enjoy the superior facilities of public education depends upon the existence or the nonexistence of inequality, then it seems very fair to me that there is no permanency in the administration of the schools, and there is no permanency in the status of these appellants. Any way we look at the situation, it means that if the facilities are unequal, you cannot segregate. If the scope of the decision is limited to that, if the facilities are equal, you can segregate; consequently, as the facilities change in that regard, as equilibrium is disturbed by the variety of facts and circumstances present in any educational system, then under those circumstances we could have segregated or we have nonsegregated education.

JUSTICE FRANKFURTER: But this Court, constituted as it is at this moment, has faced that problem in several cases, and has decided that with inequality, the order will be issued on that basis, and we shall not borrow trouble in 1953 or 1954 or whenever it is.

MR. ROBINSON: I agree with Your Honor entirely. My understanding of the past cases has been that the basis of the decision under those circumstances has been one upon which it was pretty nearly impossible to resume segregation at some future time.

Looking at the Gaines case, for example, the factors which this Court enumerated in its opinion, in order to make out the showing of inequality, not merely inequality of physical facilities and curricula—they were there—but this Court considered, and it based its opinion upon what it termed the more important considerations which were involved in a situation of that sort. And I certainly take it that after the decision in the Sweatt case, it is no longer possible for any state to have hope of establishing a separate segregated law school for Negro students.

JUSTICE FRANKFURTER: But if Mr. Marshall is right, and your clients are going to go to present white schools, things might turn out to be so happy and so congenial and so desirable that you do not know what the result may be.

MR. ROBINSON: I am fully aware of that, if Your Honor please. But it seems to me that there should be more in the way of stability, in the disposition of a situation of this sort.

We have the matter of the administration of the schools, and also, I submit, we have the matter of the right of the pupils who are involved. And I just do not see how, if we simply rest the decision upon a narrow ground which will not afford any reasonable expectation, or let me put it this way, any sound assurance that whatever changes will occur in the system at the present time, as a consequence of those inequalities, will continue, but we might revert back to the situation where we are once the facilities are made physically equal and the same courses of instruction are put in, under those circumstances it seems to me that the normal disinclination to base a decision upon a broader ground—

JUSTICE FRANKFURTER: It is not disinclination. It is not a restriction of that order. It is not just a personal preference.

MR. ROBINSON: I understand that in the historical context, of course, considering the whole history of this nation, it is a fact that the legislation of a state should not be disturbed unless it is fatally in collision with the Constitution.

I should like to urge upon Your Honors in this connection that what we sought in this case was a permanent injunction. It seems to me that we do not get it. If we are simply limited to that particular phase of the matter, it means, as I have tried to emphasize here, that we are in a situation where we cannot depend on anything.

The schools may be unequal, if Your Honor please, tomorrow, and consequently we are shunted right on out.

JUSTICE REED: Assuming that you would be admitted by decree to the high schools that you seek to enter, would it not be necessary to admit them on a segregated basis as the law stands now?

MR. ROBINSON: Yes, I suppose so.

JUSTICE REED: As the law stands now, you will be admitted on a segregated basis?

MR. ROBINSON: That is correct, sir.

JUSTICE REED: Because you have not had a decision that below the grade of colleges you are required to have an association of students.

MR. ROBINSON: Then, of course, if Your Honor please, we might have the other situation where they will take the white students and put them into bad schools. So consequently, I think any way we look at it, I agree with Your Honor's suggestion in that regard.

I submit that at least we get to the point, it seems to me, where the basis of decision must be something more than a basis which would permit of a shuttling of pupils back and forth into segregated schools and into an unsegregated system, something which would have no assurance, and something which I cannot conduce will be helpful, either to the school authorities or to the pupils involved.

JUSTICE REED: This is not a class suit, is it?

MR. ROBINSON: Yes, it is; yes, Your Honor. We brought it as a class suit on behalf of all Negroes similarly involved.

I might say for the benefit of the Court that I do not intend to unduly consume the Court's time on behalf of the question of constitutionality per se. But in view of the fact that I do feel that the question is in the Virginia case, I would like to be indulged for just a moment to make reference to a few things that I think are particularly important.

I have just said that on examination this Court had in the past found that legislation or other types of state activity, official activity, which were predicated solely on the fact of race were unconstitutional. I was going to make reference to the decisions of this Court in the area of the ownership and occupancy of real property, the Buchanan and Shelley cases, specially.

The Takahashi case[37] opened the field of employment or occupation. Restrictions on the right to vote were *Nixon* v. *Herndon,* based solely on the question of race, and in the Court's decision, having no relationship whatsoever to the end which the legislation sought to attain; and in the area of professional and graduate education, *McLaurin* v. *the Oklahoma State Regents,* which, incidentally, was a case in which there was no inequality present at all, but quite on the grounds of other factors which the Court found to exist in the situation in which it was concluded that there was a violation of the Fourteenth Amendment.

[37]Takahashi v. Fish and Game Commission,334 U.S.410 (1948),held unconstitutional a California law prohibiting the issuance of fishing licenses to persons ineligible to citizenship.

JUSTICE REED: What do you conceive to be the purpose of the Virginia enactment of the statute?

MR. ROBINSON: If Your Honor please, I am in very much the same situation that counsel in the South Carolina case are. The only thing which appears in the record which might be helpful to the Court in that regard is the testimony of Doctor Colgate W. Darden, the present president of the University of Virginia, and a former Governor of the State.

That testimony commences in the record at page 451. Doctor Darden went into an examination—he gave rather an outline of the historical development of public education in Virginia, and he said, according to his testimony—and it is a fact as a check of the statutes will show—that segregation came into Virginia in pretty much the same way as it did in South Carolina, at the time when the public school system of Virginia was just getting under way.

Virginia embarked upon a broad program of public education about 1870, and the first provision with respect to the segregation of white and colored pupils appeared on the statute books of Virginia in that particular year. It did not appear in the Consitution of Virginia until about 1900.

On page 462 of the record, Doctor Darden characterized the problem before the court as a by-product, and a fearful by-product, of human slavery, and he went on to say that we are the inheritors of that system.

I think from the historical viewpoint, there is much to sustain the position that the original notion behind the school segregation laws was to impose upon Negroes disabilities which prior to the time of the adoption of the Thirteenth, Fourteenth, and Fifteenth Amendments they labored under. That is the only thing that I can offer to this Court in the way of a justification.

JUSTICE REED: You say, to impose disabilities?

MR. ROBINSON: I beg your pardon. I meant, the Thirteenth, Fourteenth, and Fifteenth Amendments were passed to eliminate disabilities which were upon the Negro prior to the time of the adoption of the Thirteenth, Fourteenth, and Fifteenth Amendments, which had as their purpose the elimination of those disabilities.

In so far as the statute is concerned, Doctor Darden speaks of it here, in his very words, as a by-product, and a fearful by-product, of human slavery.

Before moving to the next point I would like to urge upon the Court that the reasonableness or the unreasonableness of educational segregation per se at the elementary and high school levels has never been tested.

Its validity in the previous decisions of this Court has been assumed to follow from its duration and acceptance over a long period of time.

As Mr. Marshall made reference, the duration of the particular practice has not been considered by this Court in the past to prevent reexamination of the problem. We had the same thing, for example, to come before the Court in the cases dealing with this problem at the graduate and professional levels, where it came here with a history of long duration; yet the mere fact that the practice had existed for many years, the mere fact that it had become a part of the community life, did not, in the judgment of the Court, establish its validity.

The same thing is true with respect to the restrictive covenant area, the area of exclusion of Negroes from jury service, segregation of passengers in interstate commerce, all instances where there were practices of long duration, yet they were found to be constitutionally fatal, and this Court so held.

So it is our position in Virginia, on this particular score, that it should now be determined by the application of the normal constitutional standards, whether the legislation here involved meets the challenge of the Fourteenth Amendment, and we respectfully submit that upon such examination, they will be found to be lacking.

On the second point, as I have already said, the District Court found that there was physical inequality and inequality of curricula.

In these circumstances, we submit that the action which the District Court should have taken at that particular time was to have enjoined the enforcement of segregation under those circumstances.

I should also like to point out that in addition to the finding of the District Court, which is found on page 622 of the record, in which the court goes into some small amount of discussion of the extent of the inequality, our record is pretty well loaded with evidence, most of which was uncontradicted, showing physical inequalities in the various areas.

As a matter of fact, the appellees did not even bother to cross-examine the chief witness that we put on the stand, whose testimony established these inequalities.

I should like to request the attention of the Court to the fact that the Farmville High School, one of the two white high schools, is a school which is accredited by the Southern Association of Colleges and Secondary Schools, while the Moton School for Negroes is not.

As a consequence of this accreditation, the white graduate of Farmville will generally be admitted to institutions of higher learning outside the state on his record alone, while Negro graduates of Moton will generally be required to take examinations to get in, or, if admitted without examination, will be accorded only a probationary status.

Farmville also offers to its students the opportunity of membership in the National Honor Society, which creates educational motivation and affords preferences in college acceptance and employment.

Our evidence in this case shows not only these inequalities, but clearly demonstrated that these inequalities in themselves handicap Negro students in their educational endeavors and make it impossible for Negro students to obtain educational opportunities and advantages equal to those afforded white students.

While the District Court did forthwith enjoin the continuation of discrimination in curricula offerings, I think it is important to note—and this is uncontradicted on this record—that lack of, inferiority of proper facilities for teaching many of the courses prevents advantageous instruction in some of these courses, and in some instances prevents those courses from being taught at all.

Going back for just a moment, the Court will recall that the District Court here did enter an injunction requiring forthwith the elimination of discrimination with respect to transportation means and curricula, but while that is true, we are faced with the situation where, absent the particular facilities essential for teaching the course, or, if not that, the inferiority of the facilities for teaching the course, it simply is not possible, even though we have a decree which purports to forthwith equalize curricular offerings—

THE CHIEF JUSTICE: What is your solution to that problem?

MR. ROBINSON: The solution, we submit, was not the solution taken by the District Court—

THE CHIEF JUSTICE: I say, what is your solution?

MR. ROBINSON: That, under the circumstances, the Court should have immediately entered an injunction which would have prevented the school authorities from assigning school space in the county on the basis of race, would have removed—

THE CHIEF JUSTICE: If you did not have the facilities, and if you did not have the teachers, how would you take care of them, regardless of what kind of curricula you had?

MR. ROBINSON: There are a sufficient number of teachers in the county, Mr. Chief Justice, to take care of all of the students. There is a sufficient amount of school space in the county to take care of all the students.

The differences here are —

THE CHIEF JUSTICE: You mean, to take them out of this particular locality and transport them over to some other part of the county?

MR. ROBINSON: No. At the present time, if Your Honor please, we have the situation where the white children are getting these courses; Negro children are getting, not all of them, but they are getting some of these courses, anyway. But the trouble is that over in the Negro school you have these inferiorities.

Now, we submit that you cannot continue to discriminate against Negroes, or these Negro students; under the circumstances, what you do is, you simply make all the facilities in the county available to all the pupils, without restriction or assignment to particular schools on the basis of race.

THE CHIEF JUSTICE: What was the order of the District Court?

MR. ROBINSON: The District Court did not order—

THE CHIEF JUSTICE: I did not ask you what they did not do; what did they do?

MR. ROBINSON: The District Court on the matter of courses forthwith enjoined discrimination in the curricular offerings. That was the order of the District Court. I was trying to make the distinction, if the Chief Justice please, between the so-called equalization decree and what I would call an antisegregation decree.

In this regard—and I think that I have already pretty well indicated our position—we feel that in view of the fact that in this particular area we are dealing with an exercise of state power which has been shown to affect rights which are secured by the Fourteenth Amendment, an area in which the authority of the state is subordinate to the mandate of the Amendment, that whatever the fate of educational segregation may be under other circumstances, it is perfectly plain that it cannot obtain in the face of these inequalities.

As this Court has on several occasions said, the rights which are involved are personal and present, and the Constitution does not countenance any moratorium upon the satisfaction of these particular rights.

So under the line of decisions of this Court, commencing with *Gaines* and going right straight through with *Sweatt,* we feel that the relief which I have suggested in arguing here today should have been granted by the District Court.

I should also like to point out that we feel that there are additional reasons why this equalization decree should not have been entered, and I think I can be brief in this regard, because Mr. Marshall in his argument touched upon this yesterday.

We feel that any undertaking by a court to establish or maintain constitutional equality by judicial decree simply means that the court is in the business of supervising the school system and is in there indefinitely.

We are not dealing with a physical thing. We are not dealing with a static thing. We are dealing with an educational system that has a number of variables and a number of dissimilarities. We have schools that are different in size, location, and environment, and we have teachers who differ in ability, personality, and effectiveness, and consequently their teachings vary in value.

So consequently, all up and down the educational system we are going to find points of difference. Additionally, education is an ever-growing and progressing field, and facilities and methods are constantly changing.

They get better as experience and need demonstrate the way. As a matter of fact, several of the witnesses for the appellees testified that notwithstanding an effort to provide equal buildings and facilities and equally well prepared teachers, identity of educational opportunity could not be afforded under any circumstances, and at the very best the facilities could only be made comparable or approximately equal.

Consequently, we submit that this is a task for which the Court's machinery is not entirely suited, and consequently the regulation or maintenance of constitutional equality by an equalization decree embracing, as it does, the necessity that pupils and school authorities almost constantly stay in court, should be avoided, if possible.

We have also set forth in our brief something of the history of the equalization decree in Virginia. There have been four cases in which permanent injunctions against discrimination upon a finding that there was inequality of curricula or inequality of physical facilities, have been forthcoming.

Nevertheless, in each instance it was necessary, after the decree, to have further proceedings in the court with respect to efforts to obtain that sort of educational equality.

On the final point, I should like to say this. As I indicated earlier in the argument, the evidence in Virginia was conflicting—I should put in this way. There was evidence on both sides, evidence offered by both sides on the question of harm or the effect resulting from segregation itself. The witness for the appellees—

THE CHIEF JUSTICE: What did the court say about that?

MR. ROBINSON: The court concluded that, first, it found no hurt or harm resulting from segregation to the pupils of either race.

Secondly, the court said that on the fact issue as to whether Negroes could obtain in a separate school an equal education, the court could not say that the evidence for the plaintiffs overbalanced the evidence for the defendants.

Our testimony went quite fully into the matter, and I will not bother at the present time—we set it forth in pretty good summary, I think, in our brief—to summarize it here.

But I should like to make these comments addressed to the disposition which was made of this evidence by the District Court.

Notwithstanding the fact that the District Court concluded that there was no harm or hurt to any student, upon the examination of the evidence submitted by the appellees, the situation actually is that all of their experts who testified except one admitted that there was either harm, or that there was a possibility of harm.

Additionally, on the question as to whether separate education can ever afford equal educational opportunity, the witnesses who expressed the opinion for the appellees that it was possible that there might be equality in a separate school based their conclusion upon the conditions existent in Virginia at the present time.

They were influenced by what the situation would be in the event race should be removed as a factor in the educational system, and consequently predicated the opinions under those circumstances.

We submit that under these conditions, a reexamination of this evidence will demonstrate that the conclusion of the District Court in this particular regard is without foundation and consequently it should not be held binding upon this Court.

I would like to reserve the remainder of my time for rebuttal.

JUSTICE REED: You spoke of the fact that you depended, not only on equal protection, but due process.

MR. ROBINSON: Yes, sir.

JUSTICE REED: Did I hear you make a distinction between the two?

MR. ROBINSON: I would be glad to do so at the present time.

JUSTICE REED: Is there a distinction, in your mind?

Mr. ROBINSON: I think that I can say this: Anything that due process will catch, I think equal protection will catch, in this area. But certainly a legislative enactment which makes a distinction based solely on race in the enjoyment of the educational program offered by the state, I think would be that type of arbitrary and unreasonable legislation which would be in violation of the due process clause.

JUSTICE REED: You could have a valid classification under equal protection; you could have a classification under due process?

MR. ROBINSON: That is correct, sir.

JUSTICE REED: You do not make any point on that?

MR. ROBINSON: It is also conceivable to me that you might have the other situation, though, by reason of the fact that I feel in this particular instance certainly the legislation is caught by the one or by the other.

THE CHIEF JUSTICE: Mr. Moore.

ARGUMENT ON BEHALF OF APPELLEES

by MR. MOORE

MR. MOORE: May it please the Court, we believe it to be particularly fortunate that the Court concluded to assume for argument all five of these cases together because while in theory each case stands on its own record, there is, of course, one main stream which runs through all of the cases, and it is obvious from the arguments already made by counsel for the appellants that that is the real question with which they are concerned, namely, to test finally, if possible, the issue as to whether the mere fact of segregation by law is a denial of equal protection.

Now, the Virginia case is one which is equally helpful, I believe not only in respect of its own setting, but in its bearing on these other cases.

I am going to undertake in the discussion of this case to deal with it in that sort of way, not merely from the standpoint of our case, but also in its bearing on the other.

There are several distinctive features of this Virginia case that I want to call to Your Honors' attention at the outset. The first is the nature of the record that you find here. You were impressed, I am sure, with the fact that you have a much larger record. We believe that was not unnecessarily made large. When we were requested to represent this little county of Prince Edward and also to be associated with the Attorney General in the representation of the commonwealth, we found that there had been these four or five cases in the federal court where the question of inequality of facilities had been the issue, and that was the only issue. Where the courts had found that to exist, they promptly made decrees requiring equalization.

We also found that the state had undertaken an amazing program of expenditures of money and expansion of the public school system, particularly over the last twenty years, with the view to making the facilities equal for Negroes and whites, so that perhaps with the exception of the State of North Carolina, Virginia stands probably at the top among all these southern states in that program, which I am going to refer to more fully a little later.

But we also found in comparing and getting the benefit of the Kansas and the South Carolina case, which has just been heard, that these appellants had laid all this great stress on what they call the psychological issue. But we also found that there was quite a conflict of opinion among the experts on that matter.

So we undertook to prepare a full record, and Your Honors would find, when you browse through this record that you have, instead of, as in the Kansas case where all of these teachers and educators and psychologists testified on one side, and in the South Carolina case on the appellant's side—you find a great array of very distinguished persons who testified in the Virginia case in direct conflict on this crucial question of fact.

So the first distinctive feature is the fuller record.

The second distinctive feature is the difference in the findings of the court.

The court, in contrast to the Kansas case, based upon the historical background in Virginia and upon all this evidence, found on the crucial questions which these gentlemen had stressed so much that they failed to prove their case, even on that point.

That is one of the main distinctive features in this case.

There also will be presented the difference as compared to, with the Kansas case, as to the great impact that would result in Virginia from a sudden elimination of segregation.

Now, those are among the issues. There is this other distinctive feature, which I should mention at the outset. This case on this point is similar to the South Carolina case, in large degree, because when the case of South Carolina was tried, the facilities were not yet completed on the first trial, and were not completed on the second hearing. But when the case reaches this Court, they have been completed.

Now, Virginia is just a little bit behind South Carolina in that respect. But there is no doubt about it, no question from this record, that the funds are in hand, the buildings are going up, and the facilities will be equal by next September.

Those are the four principal distinctive features.

Now, may it please the Court, in undertaking to make a very brief statement of the case, as to how the issues come here, there are several facts that I believe should be brought to your attention at the outset. This case arises in a comparatively small county of the 100 counties of Virginia, Prince Edward County. It has only about 15,000 population. It has one town of any size, much, in it the town of Farmville, where the old Hampden-Sydney College is located.

The population is divided about 52 per cent Negro and 48 per cent white in the county. The school population is higher among the Negroes than that figure. There is about 60 per cent of the school population that is Negro and 40 per cent white.

So, roughly, you may regard the situation as being one where the ratio is about three to one, whites three to one. Now, these appellants are high school students. This case relates entirely to high school students. The South Carolina case was elementary and high school. These cases vary. But this is strictly a high school.

JUSTICE BLACK: What did you say about the three to one?

MR. MOORE: I said that the ratio is about three whites to one Negro.

JUSTICE BLACK: Where?

MR. MOORE: Throughout the state. I am sorry, I did not clear that up.

JUSTICE BLACK: I thought you were referring to the county. That is quite different.

MR. MOORE: That is right. I am sorry.

Now, in the county, I should mention that this is a rather poor county financially, in the state. It has an assessed value of only about $9,500,000. The total assessed property, on the ratio of assessment of about 50 per cent—the total real and personal property value is about $18,500,000.

Now, there are three high schools in the county, two for white and one for Negro. As might be expected, they are not identical. In the three high schools in 1951, there were 400 white children and 460 Negro children.

In standing, the Farmville High School was shown to be the best high school. That is, the white high school in Farmville. The next is the Moton School, the Negro school at Farmville, and the worst is the Worsham, which is a white school, a small combination high school and elementary school.

Now, one of the principal reasons why the Moton School, which, as Your Honors will realize, is named for the distinguished colored educator,[38] who, by the way, was educated largely in Virginia, where there was segregation—one of the main reasons why Farmville is ranked first is because of the unequal growth in school population in the last ten years, particularly among the Negroes. The record shows that the Negro pupils increased in the last ten years 225 per cent, but unfortunately whites have declined about 25 per cent.

The school authorities, in view of that increase in Negro attendance, particularly in view of that, made a survey in 1947 as to school requirements, approval, and so on. And they finally have approved a program which the record shows will cost about $2,500,000 in all to carry out, with about $2 million of that being allocated for Negro schools, and about $500,000 for white schools.

Now, among other things, one of the main things in the financing program was a new Negro high school in place of the existing Moton School. They were trying to arrange a bond issue for that, but unfortunately, in April and May, there was a two week strike called in the Negro school, which the Negro principal claimed that he could not control. The record indicates—and the matter was argued in the District Court—that the strike was really inspired by outsiders.

However that may be, the strike came at a very unfortunate time. It lasted two weeks. But that absolutely put an end to any bond issue.

The school authorities then undertook to raise the money for the new school from the state, and the state, which does have ample funds in Virginia, I am glad to say, through two sources, provided all the funds required. We have what is called a Battle Fund in Virginia, which is named after our present Governor, Governor Battle, and I am going to refer to that a little later after lunch. But it is a great source of money for these purposes, and about $250,000 out of the $900,000 required for the new Negro school was granted from that fund, and the remaining $600,000 was made in the way of a loan from the Literary Fund at two per cent.

Now, this suit was filed in May of last year, shortly after the strike, and as I said, it broke up the bond issue, but the state provided the funds, so that we are in the fortunate position of having the cash, the building is right under way, there is no question about the fact from the record and from the decree of the court that it is going to be completed.

[38]Robert R. Moton (1867–1940), educator and teacher, succeeded Booker T. Washington as head of the Tuskegee Institute.

THE CHIEF JUSTICE: Has that money been obtained, and firm commitments made?

MR. MOORE: Yes, sir, all that has gone in the record.

THE CHIEF JUSTICE: When?

MR. MOORE: The money was obtained finally in June of 1951. You see, they were on the program of the bond issue when the strike created such a public sentiment that it was felt that they could not carry that through.

THE CHIEF JUSTICE: What is the present situation in regard to the building program?

MR. MOORE: The building is under way.

THE CHIEF JUSTICE: What do you mean by "under way," Mr. Moore?

MR. MOORE: It is about 25 to 30 per cent complete. A firm contract is made. The funds are available to be drawn on from the state, just as the funds are needed, and the record shows that there is no reason why the school should not be in operation, a better school than any school in the county or that whole area, by next September.

Now, the challenge which was presented in this trial, which required five days—the case was very fully heard—was on two grounds:

First, it was said that on the basis of the federal precedent the segregation in the schools at the high school level violated constitutional standards. On that issue, the court held, "We cannot say that Virginia's separation of white and colored children in the public schools is without substance in fact or reason. We have found no hurt or harm to either race."

I was astonished at the statement that my friend—I will defer that until we come back.

(Whereupon, at 2:00 o'clock p.m., the Court recessed to reconvene at 2:30 o'clock p.m.)

MR. MOORE: May it please the Court, when the Court rose for its luncheon recess, I had just mentioned the first of two very important findings that we feel the trial court made here.

The first was that on the basis of the record made, they found that the separation scheme that had been in effect in Virginia through these eighty years—we cannot say that it was without foundation in fact or reason, and there was no hurt or harm to either race.

Now, there is another finding. These are set out at great length there in the record at pages 19 through 21, and the facts proved in our case presently demonstrate or potently demonstrate, why nullification of the cited sections is not warranted.

In those pages of the opinion Judge Bryan, sitting with Judge Dobie and Judge Hutcheson,[39] had given a very much more adequate answer, may it please

[39]Judge Albert V. Bryan (1899–   ) served on the Eastern District Court of Virginia from 1947 to 1961 when he was appointed to the Fourth Circuit Court of Appeals. Judge C. Sterling Hutcheson (1894–   ) sat in the Virginia District Court from 1944.

Your Honor, Justice Reed, than our friends on the other side did to your question as to what was the real basis and, therefore, I was about to comment when we adjourned for lunch that I was very astonished at the comment that had just been made that there was such a scanty record.

Judge Bryan, in the opinion, went back and traced the history of this scheme to the acts of 1869 and 1870 in Virginia, with the various changes in those laws that were passed right during the reconstruction period when, as everyone knows, there was this zeal involved in protecting the Negroes' rights, but stemming right from the first Act of 1869-1870, the law has been substantially the way it is today.

Instead of President Darden of the University leaving the matter, as our friend on the other side suggested, if Your Honors would look at page 456 of the record, you will see a very much more illuminating comment, where he goes on to show quite a bit about this history.

Of course, this system did spring out of the system which was in effect in the South before the war, but because it sprang out of that system it does not follow that there was any intent to continue a form of slavery or form of servitude such as here argued.

He goes ahead and points out there that actually in the consideration of the Underwood constitution, [40] there were twenty-two Negroes in the convention, and they were split eleven to eleven—eleven voting against the proposal to include a prohibition against segregation. That was obviously because of the friction that was involved arising out of that period.

Now, there is another set of facts here that I believe to be very pertinent. We observe that during the argument of our opponents, there was distributed among the Justices of the Court, two very interesting sheets, which we were not able to obtain until a few days ago, from the Census, and you will see from those sheets that the problem, as exists in these seventeen states that have segregation, and the District of Columbia, is a very different problem from many of the other states.

You will observe on that first sheet entitled, "Relationship of White and Negro Population," that there is a factor of 10 per cent of the total population of the country today that is Negro, about 15 million, it is very interesting to see how that is distributed.

In the seventeen states and in the District of Columbia, the total population in those states that is Negro is 20.5 per cent; in all these other states it is 4.6 per cent. But there is a concentration of the Negro population in those seventeen states and the District to the extent of approximately 70 per cent.

In the second sheet you will observe that there is a variation all the way from about one tenth of one percent in Vermont to 45 per cent in Mississippi, with about 22 per cent in Virginia, Justice Black—that is where I was confused just a moment ago, as you will see right there.

It is perfectly clear that that situation is a very pertinent thing in the consideration of this matter.

[40] John C. Underwood (1809-1873) was a judge for the federal Circuit Court for Virginia in the Reconstruction years (1864-1873). He presided over the constitutional convention of 1868 which drafted a new Virginia constitution ratified in modified form in 1869.

JUSTICE REED: Have you carried it out into the counties?

MR. MOORE: We do not have it in the counties. As a matter of fact, we had much difficulty getting it from the Census people to this extent. We have got it for the county that is in question here. I gave that just before we adjourned for lunch.

Sixty per cent of the school population is Negro in this county to 40 per cent white, and the total population is 52 per cent Negro and 48 per cent white.

May I just undertake in my remaining time to address myself very briefly to four questions which we believe are the controlling questions in this case: First, while we know that Your Honors are so familiar with the precedents that are here talked about so much, we do not feel we could do justice to this case without referring to them, at least briefly, and I then want to refer briefly to what we call the Virginia situation as shown on these facts and, third, I want to mention briefly the expert evidence that became so important in this case and, fourthly, I wish to talk briefly about the point that Justice Frankfurter mentioned a moment ago as to what is the kind of decree or remedy that should be granted in a situation like this where, as distinguished from South Carolina, we have not quite got our facilities in shape, although they have been able to do that in South Carolina. I am going to take up those four matters in that order just as briefly as I can.

Mr. Davis stressed in his argument so far as background for the issue, the main issue in all these cases, the question as to whether separation by law is per se a violation of equal protection. He stressed the legislative history primarily.

There is an equally important area, we believe, involving the legal precedents.

Of course, all these cases come down finally to the question as to whether this type of case falls over into the category of *Gong Lum* —really that is the closest case; *Plessy* v. *Ferguson* is, of course, its forerunner, but do they fall under the doctrine of *Gong Lum* or do they fall under the *Sweatt* v. *Painter,* and *McLaurin;* that is the real crucial question.

I am not going to labor the point. Judge Parker has worked it out better than any of these other courts have. He has done that better, more fully, but you have got not only these statutes that have been passed, but this large body of decisions which certainly over a period of eighty years has recognized that the thing that is existing here in the South, particularly, as you saw from those sheets, is a thing that has become a part of a way of life, as our court said in our case, in the South.

It is plainly based on real reason, and if that is so, then there is no reason why the equal facilities, equal but separate facilities, doctrine should not apply.

What the court held in *Sweatt* v. *Painter,* and in *McLaurin,* was that on the facts, that at that level equality could not be provided.

Now, we took the trouble here to obtain—there are three very distinguished experts that testified in our case, right on that point, that there are great differences at the high school level on this question as to whether equality of not only facilities and curricula and all can be afforded as compared with the graduate and professional schools.

We did not have to rely simply upon what the Court might take notice of, but Your Honors will find the testimony of Dr. Lindley Stiles, who is the head of the Department of Education of the University of Virginia, a man with wide experience all over the country, teaching and supervising segregated schools and nonsegregated schools, who stressed that there was a difference in that level at adolescent age; you find Dr. Henry E. Garrett, head of the Department of Psychology of Columbia University, who testified at great length on this subject; and then Dr. Dabney L. Lancaster, the president of Longwood College in Virginia, stresses that situation.

Now, there the gist of their testimony was that equality of opportunity really could be provided and, possibly better provided, at the high school level with separate schools provided you had equal facilities, just as good teachers, just as good curricula, and all the facilities that go along with it.

On that basis there is no occasion to approach this matter from the standpoint of *Sweatt* v. *Painter,* and *McLaurin.*

It is shown right here definitely—and that is what Judge Bryan's opinion rests on—it is shown by evidence that at this level you have not got the problem that exists at the graduate and professional school level.

These gentlemen on the other side at great length, cite a long line of cases in this Court which they say are pertinent, and which we contend are not pertinent, and I just list them and state our position.

They mention cases like these: The Jury Duty case,[41] the Right to Vote case,[42] the Right to the Fishing License,[43] the Florida Shepherd case,[44] the Right to Participate in Primary Elections,[45] the Right to Own Property,[46] *Shelley* v. *Kraemer,* and then they rely upon these commerce cases, *Morgan* v. *Virginia,* and the recent Chance case.[47]

Those cases are not comparable here. There you had a complete denial of a right. The question of separation but with equal facilities and equal opportunities really did not exist in those cases; there was a denial, a complete denial.

What really happened, as we see it, in the appellants' theory is that we believe they are quite confused. They come here and they first make their attack in this way: They say that the doctrine, the separate but equal doctrine, just per se amounts to an offense to the Constitution, the Fourteenth Amendment.

Now that, of course, as was pointed out in the first case, the Kansas case

[41]Strauder v. West Virginia, 100 U.S. 308 (1880), see n. 24, *supra.* See also Cassell v. Texas, 339 U.S. 282 (1950). A murder conviction was reversed when it appeared Negroes had been systematically excluded from a grand jury panel that had returned the indictment.

[42]Nixon v. Condon, 286 U.S. 73 (1932). The Court invalidated a resolution of the Executive Committee of the Democratic Party in Texas allowing only whites to participate in a primary election.

[43]Takahashi v. Fish and Game Commission, 334 U.S. 410 (1948), see n. 37, *supra.*

[44]Shepherd v. Florida, 341 U.S. 50 (1951). A conviction for rape was reversed on the authority of Cassell v. Texas, 339 U.S. 282 (1950), since Negroes had been systematically excluded from the grand jury that indicted the Negro defendants.

[45]Nixon v. Herndon, 273 U.S. 536 (1927), Smith v.Allwright, 321 U.S. 649 (1944), and Terry v. Adams, 345 U.S. 461 (1953).

[46]Buchanan v. Warley, 245 U.S. 60 (1917), see n. 23, *supra.* See also Oyama v. California, 332 U.S. 633 (1948).

[47]Chance v. Lambeth, 186 F.2d 879 (4th Cir. 1951). The Court of Appeals for the Fourth Circuit declared invalid a private railroad regulation attempting to segregate passengers in its trains.

yesterday, is just a direct attack on *Plessy* v. *Ferguson,* and the *Gong Lum* doctrine.

But then they come along and make a second contention. They say that as long as there is separation then, as a matter of fact, there cannot be equality, and the only basis they have for urging that is to draw on this so-called expert testimony of the psychologists, and they say that because of that line of testimony you can never attain equality as a fact.

Now, in the Virginia case, we meet head-on on that issue. It may be, as some of the questions from Your Honors have indicated, that, perhaps, all of that testimony may be irrelevant. If we are right in our first proposition that *Gong Lum* is still the law then, perhaps, all that testimony may be irrelevant. But we did not want to take any chances in the Virginia case. We knew that there was this great body of expert opinion which was in conflict with that which had been presented without conflict in Kansas and in South Carolina, and we presented it. So that if, as a fact, that issue becomes important, we have met it head-on, and we have a finding of the court in our favor.

May I just refer very briefly to what, for short, I may call the Virginia scene in which this whole problem arises?

Of course, it is obvious that it is not just Prince Edward County that is involved or Clarendon County, South Carolina, it is a state-wide question, and this record abounds with information that shows that over the last twenty years there has been a tremendous movement springing largely with the position that Dr. Lancaster, now the head of Longwood College, at Farmville, Virginia, right where this controversy arose, while he was the head of the Department of Education, he saw ahead that this problem was going to arise in the way in which it has, and the state, under his sponsorship, and his successors, put on this tremendous program which, perhaps, except for North Carolina, is the greatest program in the South, of expending these huge sums for building up these facilities.

You have a situation today where the State of Virginia has every reason to be proud of what has been accomplished, although complete perfection has not yet been attained in every one of the counties and cities of the state.

Let me give you just a few figures. As Dr. Darden pointed out, public education somewhat dragged in Virginia until about 1920. At that time there were only 31,000 high school students in the state. Today there are 155,000.

During these last ten years the state, according to this record, has reached the point where the Negro salaries have been equalized with the whites throughout; there are actually more four-year college graduates among the Negro teachers in Virginia than there are white teachers.

The Negro expenditures in this state have increased 161 per cent as compared with 123 per cent.

According to a survey that was put in evidence in our case, it appeared that approximately one-half of the counties and cities in the state are now or within a very short time will be carrying out programs now in effect—will be on the basis of as good as or better than the whites.

As a matter of fact, in the city of Richmond, the finest high school in the city is a Negro high school, and at Charlottesville there has just been completed the finest high school for Negroes that there is in all that area.

Now, as an indication of what has been accomplished—I sound as if we are trying to brag in comparison with South Carolina, and we do not mean it that way, but we believe these figures are very pertinent, Your Honors. We are telling that to you because we have no other way of getting these facts to you except by telling them to you.

In Virginia we have put on this program that I referred to as the Battle Fund. It is $60 million as compared with the $75 million in South Carolina.

Of that amount, $10 million have already been allocated for the Negroes, and $18 million for the whites. They are getting much more than their share.

We have this tremendous Literary Fund, as it is called in Virginia. We are more fortunate in Virginia financially than many of the states, and through that fund, loans are being made to these schools, with the Negroes greatly benefiting in proportion.

Of the $48 million that have been loaned out of—comparing the $48 million loaned for whites, are $16.5 million loaned for the Negroes at 2 per cent interest, at a 2 per cent interest rate.

THE CHIEF JUSTICE: Are those loans made to the boards of education?

MR. MOORE: That is right, sir, at 2 per cent and that was the $600,000 in this $900,000 program for this very high school. So you see the funds are really right there in hand. There is no trouble about going out with a sales tax like our friends have to do in South Carolina.

We have got the money, and we have got a contract, and we have got a court decree which tells us that we have got to go ahead as quickly as possible.

Now, there is just one more fact in this connection, and I am through with this point. It is very striking that in the four-year plan that the board of education has adopted there are 168 projects for whites, with 73 projects for Negroes, involving for whites $189 million, may it please Your Honors.

Just think of what that means in taxation and in burdens to the people of Virginia in carrying out this program, with $74.5 million for Negroes. In other words, they are sharing in all this huge program in a ratio of about two to one, although their ratio in the state is only about 22 per cent.

In view of all that, the court could not find that this program, so important to the welfare of the people of Virginia, rested on prejudice, but it represented a way of life, and it represented a firm determination on the part of the people of Virginia, because they were able to bear the burden better than many of the Southern states, but they were fully committed in good faith to provide for the Negro child just as good education as a white child could get, and they were doing it and, therefore, the court found that they could not find that that program rested on prejudice.

Now, isn't that of some importance in this matter when this matter reaches the stage of this Court? The trial court said that they found that the program rested neither upon prejudice nor caprice nor upon any nebulous foundation but rather the proof is that it declares one of the ways of life in Virginia.

May I just very briefly refer to this expert testimony because, perhaps that, together with the difference in findings of the court, is the most distinctive thing about this case.

We are glad to get the benefit among our brethren involved in the other cases, if that be appropriate, with their testimony.

We were able to profit by the trials in these other cases. They could have gotten the experts if they had deemed it essential or relevant to do it. They, proceeding in their own way, considered in the light of the decisions of this Court and the numerous decisions of the state courts that all that line of expert testimony presumably was irrelevant.

Now, the statement is made here that time after time there is consensus of opinion among social scientists that segregation is bad.

I was interested in the appendix which is signed by some thirty-two alleged social scientists who say that appendix is out on the frontiers of scientific knowledge; that is the way they describe it.

When you examine that appendix you find that five of the persons who signed that appendix were cross-examined in our case, and the appendix is really just an effort—I say this without any lack of respect—but it is just an effort to try to rehabilitate those gentlemen and add to it with some other persons.

Now, it is our view that when you consider the expert evidence on the two sides in this case, it is perfectly clear that the trial court was justified in finding as they did.

Let me just briefly give you a description as to the kind of expert testimony that was presented in the Virginia case. Some of these witnesses apparently travel around over the country quite a bit testifying in these cases.

There were four principal experts for the plaintiffs in our case: A man named Dr. John J. Brooks, who runs an experimental school in New York where about three hundred students attend, and he tries to get a cross section of the population, a certain number of whites, a certain number of Negroes, and a certain number of others.

He has had practically—he had no experience in Virginia. He had a little experience in Georgia. He testified, in effect, that he felt that segregation was bad.

The next was Dr. Brewster Smith, who was a professor of psychology at Vassar. His chief contribution was that he considered that as a matter of principle segregation in the abstract was an official insult. That is about what his testimony finally boiled down to.

One of the most interesting witnesses was Dr. Isidor Chein. He has written a great deal on this subject, and he testified as to a questionnaire that he had sent out to some 850 social scientists, he said, asking them two main questions: First, as to whether or not in their view segregation was harmful to those segregated; secondly, was it harmful to those who did not segregate, and he said that the replies he got were some 500, and that some 90 per cent of the people who answered said that it was bad on both groups.[48]

We showed on cross-examination and otherwise that there were some six or eight thousand persons who were eligible to have that questionnaire sent to them;

[48]Dr. Isidor Chein was Director of Research of the Commission on Community Relations of the American Jewish Congress. The article referred to is Deutscher and Chein, "The Psychological Effect of Enforced Segregation: A Survey of Social Science Opinion," 26 Journal of Psychology 259 (1948).

we showed that only thirty-two came from south of the Mason and Dixon line, and he was unable to show a single one from Virginia, and what you wind up with is that you get a statement in the air as sort of a moral principle—it is kind of a religious statement that you get—that, in principle or in theory, in the abstract that segregation is a bad thing to have.

JUSTICE FRANKFURTER: Mr. Moore, of what would the six or eight thousand people be specialists in or of?

MR. MOORE: Well, there is a great line—

JUSTICE FRANKFURTER: Who are these specialists in that field?

MR. MOORE: Well, they described them as sociologists, anthropologists, psychologists, and variations of those groups, principally, Your Honor.

JUSTICE FRANKFURTER: Everybody in the sociological field is an expert in his domain?

MR. MOORE: That is right, Your Honor.

We say it does not mean a thing except as a matter of starting something in the abstract. You might as well be talking about the Sermon on the Mount or something like that, that it would be better—

JUSTICE FRANKFURTER: It is supposed to be a good document.

MR. MOORE: Well, I say you might as well be asking people whether it is desirable for everybody to try to live according to the Sermon on the Mount as to ask them the kind of questions that they had put to them.

Now, let us look for a moment at the experts we called. We had eight people who testified, who were especially familiar with conditions in Virginia and in the South.

We started at the lower level with the superintendent of education, Mr. J. I. McIlwaine, who had been the superintendent for over thirty years in that very area.

We then moved up to the next level. We took the present superintendent of education of the state, Dr. Dowell J. Howard: we took the ex-superintendent, Dr. Lancaster.

Then we moved up to the university level. We took Dr. Stiles, who has had this broad knowledge and experience all over the country, as the head of the Department of Education, and then took Dr. Darden, and took them, and then we followed through with three other kinds of experts. We called a leading child psychiatrist, Dr. William H. Kelly, a leading man in all our area, who testified and who had wide experience all over the country; as a matter of fact, in the war among the soldiers and what not, he had such experience.

We then called a clinical psychologist, Mr. John N. Buck, who had had wide experience, and then—our friends like to chide us with the fact that our star witness was Dr. Garrett—they would have given their right eye to have gotten Dr. Garrett. He happened to be the teacher in Columbia of two of their experts, this very Dr. Clark who made these doll tests, and who studied under Dr. Garrett.

Dr. Garrett, it so happened, was born and raised very near this very place where this controversy arose in Virginia. He was educated in the Richmond public schools and at the University of Richmond, and then he went on to Columbia, and finished his graduate work, and for years has been a leading professor of psychology, years the head of the department of psychology, with some twenty-five professors and assistant professors under him, with wide experience as an adviser to the War Department in connection with the psychological tests among soldiers during the war.

I have not time—my time is going by so fast, I see it is almost gone—and I must read you one or two things about what Dr. Garrett said about this thing.

He said this. He said:

> What I have said was that in the State of Virginia, in the year 1952, given equal facilities, that I thought, at the high school level, the Negro child and the white child—who seem to be forgotten most of the time—could get better education at the high school level in separate schools, given those two qualifications; equal facilities and the state of mind in Virginia at the present time.
> If a Negro child goes to a school as well equipped as that of his white neighbor, if he had teachers of his own race and friends of his own race, it seems to me he is much less likely to develop tensions, animosities, and hostilities, than if you put him into a mixed school where, in Virginia, inevitably he will be a minority group.

Then he says again:

> It seems to me that in the State of Virginia today, taking into account the temper of its people, its mores, and its customs and background, that the Negro student at the high school level will get a better education in a separate school than he will in mixed schools.

It is a better education he is talking about because of this friction that would arise and these eighty years of history in Virginia.

Is all that to be ignored? Is that not, Your Honor, Justice Frankfurter, a basis for classification with eighty years in this background, just as in the pilot case you mentioned yesterday—I was not familiar with it yesterday until you mentioned it, but I read it this morning, but it is very important, the historical background in the light of this testimony.

JUSTICE REED: What am I to draw from this argument that you are making now?

MR. MOORE: I think you are to draw—evidently I have not been successful, as successful as I had hoped.

JUSTICE REED: Perhaps I should express my question a little more fully.

MR. MOORE: Yes.

JUSTICE REED: What if they had decided to the contrary?

MR. MOORE: You mean the trial court?

JUSTICE REED: The trial court; and your experts had not been so persuasive as they were, and there were other experts, and the trial court had accepted their conclusion that this was detrimental and was injurious to the ability of the Negro child to learn or of the white child to learn, and created great difficulties, what difference does it make which way they decided this particular question?

MR. MOORE: I think you can argue the matter two ways, Your Honor. I think, in the first place, you can argue that the difference, for instance, in the Kansas finding and the Virginia finding point up how important is the legislative policy that is involved, that Mr. Davis talked about so much this morning. It just illustrates how it really is a policy question.

JUSTICE REED: I can understand that. But is it your argument that there are two sides to it?

MR. MOORE: It illustrates there are two sides to it, and it points up that the real crux of the whole matter is that there is involved fundamentally a policy question for legislative bodies to pass on, and not for courts.

Now, in the second place, it emphasizes, I hope, that the historical background that exists, certainly in this Virginia situation, with all the strife and the history that we have shown in this record, shows a basis, a real basis, for the classification that has been made.

JUSTICE REED: There has been a legislative determination in Virginia?

MR. MOORE: That is right, sir.

JUSTICE REED: That the greatest good for the greatest number is found in segregation?

MR. MOORE: That is right; with these lawmakers continuously since 1870 doing their job to do their best in the general welfare.

It is significant that the Virginia statutes since 1870 have contained straight through a requirement that there should not only be a separation, but there should be treatment with equality and with efficiency all the way through; that is the policy.

My time is almost up.

JUSTICE JACKSON: Suppose Congress should enact a statute, pursuant to the enabling clause of the Fourteenth Amendment, which nobody seems to attach any importance to here, as far as I have heard, that segregation was contrary to national policy, to the national welfare, and so on, what would happen?

MR. MOORE: Your Honor, we thought of that in here, and that is a big question, as you realize.

JUSTICE JACKSON: That is why I asked it.

MR. MOORE: Our view of the matter is that it should not be held valid in this Court; that the only effective way to accomplish that is to be done through an act of Congress, which would be by amending the Constitution.

JUSTICE JACKSON: You think that the Fourteenth Amendment would not be adequate to do that?

MR. MOORE: We do not believe so, and I have not the time and I have no desire to engage in this very interesting discussion that Justice Burton and Justice Frankfurter engaged in, as to whether there is any difference through the passage of time and through progress which has been made between the commerce clause and the Fourteenth Amendment.

But I would suggest in that connection that it certainly is much more easy to find facts that demonstrate that as progress has gone on, such as in *Morgan* v. *Virginia,* where the separation of race on the interstate buses is involved, it is much easier to find facts which will show, as time has gone on, that there should be a different application than there is where a question of equal protection is involved.

We believe, as Mr. Davis pointed out this morning, I think touching this same point, although very slightly, that the Fourteenth Amendment here should be viewed in the light of what was really intended, and what was understood by Congress and by the legislatures at that time.

JUSTICE FRANKFURTER: But Justice Jackson's question brings into play different questions and different considerations, Mr. Moore, because the enabling act of the Fourteenth Amendment is itself a provision of the Fourteenth Amendment; patently Congress looked forward to implementing legislation; implementing legislation patently looked forward to the future, and if Congress passed a statute doing that which is asked of us to be done through judicial decree, the case would come here with a pronouncement by Congress in its legislative capacity that in its view of its powers, this was within the Fourteenth Amendment and, therefore, it would come with all the heavy authority, with the momentum and validity that a congressional enactment has.

Mr. MOORE: That may be so, your Honor, but that is another case.

JUSTICE FRANKFURTER: That is a good answer.

MR. MOORE: Yes, it is another case.

JUSTICE JACKSON: I wonder if it is. I should suppose that your argument that this was a legislative question might have been addressed to the proposition that the enforcement of the Fourteenth Amendment, if this were deemed conflicting, might be for the Congress rather than for this Court. I would rather expect and I had rather expected to hear that question discussed. But you apparently are in the position that no federal agency can supersede the state's authority in this matter which, I say, you have good precedents for arguing.

MR. MOORE: Your Honor will appreciate that you have asked a question that to try to answer adequately requires a lot more time than I have got.

JUSTICE FRANKFURTER: I understood you to say that that is a different case—

MR. MOORE: That is right.

JUSTICE FRANKFURTER: (Continuing)—meaning that you do not have an act of Congress.

MR. MOORE: That is right, sir. Now, of course, in the District—

JUSTICE JACKSON: What I am trying to get at is, do you attach any importance to the fact that there is not any act of Congress? Apparently you do not, because there could not be one.

MR. MOORE: I am very glad there is not; yes, sir, I am very pleased with that anyway.

May I just take one more minute or two? I wanted to take a couple of minutes on this last question that Justice Frankfurter asked, because it is a very important point in our case, and I would like to take a moment.

The question is posed as to whether or not we are in a different position in Virginia rather than that in the South Carolina case because our building is not yet finished.

I do not think so. In line with the doctrine that Your Honor, Justice Frankfurter, saw this Court declare in *Eccles* v. *Peoples Bank*,[49] there certainly must be some leeway here in a court of equity and in a declaratory judgment proceeding.

Our friend on the other side, Mr. Marshall, said yesterday he realized there must be a transition period. We are operating under a court decree which says, "Do that thing right now."

THE CHIEF JUSTICE: He was talking then, was he not, about segregation, and if it should be held that segregation per se was invalid, then he would be willing to let some time pass.

But as I have understood him here, he says it is of the present, and it should be here admitted presently.

Mr. MOORE: Well, the short answer here really is that as a practical matter in the situation we are in with the building under construction, under the court decree, with our knowing it is going to be ready in September, all we could really do practically would be to close the schools down until June, and then come along with equality.

Now, we do not believe that is in the interest of anybody.

I am sorry, I have encroached a little bit on Judge Almond's time. Judge Almond, the Attorney General, desires the remainder of the time.

ARGUMENT ON BEHALF OF THE APPELLEES

by MR. ALMOND

MR. ALMOND: May it please the Court, just a few minutes are available to our side in which I would like to discuss with the Court what we conceive to be the historical background of this question in Virginia.

The question posed yesterday, or the remark made by Mr. Justice Frankfurter, is whether or not in the minds of some it may represent man's inhumanity to man or whether or not Virginia and the other Southern states made these provi-

[49]333 U.S. 426 (1948). The Court dismissed an action under the Declaratory Judgment Act by a bank against the Board of Governors of the Federal Reserve Board on the ground that the bank's grievance was too remote and speculative.

sions in its law, its statute, and its constitution, for the separation of the races in the field of education because she had the power to do it or, as answered by our worthy opponent, Mr. Robinson, this morning, that it was placed there to place disabilities upon the Negro.

Prior to 1865 there were no public free schools in Virginia supported by any government, state or local.

In 1865 kind missionaries from New England came into Virginia and established schools on a separate basis for the Negro children of former slaves.

The people were impoverished, and the poor white people—and nearly all of them were poor because the land was ravaged as a result of that unfortunate conflict, and they had no place to send their children to school except to do the very best they could through private tutorship.

So that arrangement lasted until 1870, when the public free school system of Virginia came into being virtue of the enactment of the Legislature of Virginia found here in substantially the same language that it was put into the Constitution of Virginia in 1902.

THE CHIEF JUSTICE: In 1865, General, you say there were missionaries who came down from the North?

MR. ALMOND: Yes, sir.

THE CHIEF JUSTICE: What funds did they have?

MR. ALMOND: They were private funds.

THE CHIEF JUSTICE: Private funds; and private schools, I take it?

MR. ALMOND: They were private schools.

THE CHIEF JUSTICE: For the Negro?

MR. ALMOND: For the Negro children.

But when the state took over or decided after a terrific conflict as to whether or not it should go into the field of public education, because it was the custom and tradition of our people prior to that time that every family should educate its own children—they were opposed to the expending of public funds for the education of the children of our people.

But a distinguished Virginian, a Dr. William H. Ruffing, became the first superintendent of schools in Virginia, and he wrote that statute which we have before us today, providing that white and colored children shall not be taught in the same schools, but under the same general regulations as to usefulness and efficiency.

As has been pointed out here, in the Underwood Convention of 1870, when the Underwood Constitution was adopted that Convention was presided over by an individual distinctly hostile to the great majority of the white people in Virginia, and the question came before that Convention as to whether or not a provision would be written into the Constitution requiring that the schools be mixed and operated by the state and the localities jointly on a mixed basis.

An amendment was offered by an eminent Negro doctor from the city of

Norfolk to bring that about and, to use an expression that is frequently used in my state today, I may say to the Court that the fur flew; but, as Mr. Moore has pointed out, there were twenty-two Negro members of the Convention, and on the vote, eleven of them voted not to have mixed schools in Virginia.

The debates in that Convention reflect what have been said here today relative to the mixed school which prevailed in the State of South Carolina for a period of twelve years, and that was discussed.

That was adopted in the light of the fact that they knew then that in 1862 the Congress of the United States provided for separate schools in the District of Columbia. That was adopted because they knew then, and discussed that when the Fourteenth Amendment was submitted to the people or proposed on June 16, 1867, and in the great debate raging in Congress relative to the adoption of the enabling Civil Rights Act, that Congress itself had established the policy of separation of schools, because of the feeling that had grown as an aftermath of that great struggle between the States, and because of the bitterness that ensued, unfortunately—it was determined in Virginia, not as a badge of inferiority, not to place the Negro man or the Negro child in the position where he could never rise to take his place in a free society, but the only way that we could have a free public school system was on a separate basis.

And then during the readjuster period, when impoverished as our public treasury and our peoples were, it became necessary to use tax funds for other purposes, and the public treasury and provisions for school purposes were raided to this extent, or diverted; and Dr. Ruffing made a big fight on that. But throughout the readjuster period, and not until 1920 did the people of Virginia awaken to the necessity of improvement of their public schools.

Sad to relate, I am ashamed to say, that during many of those years of the past we have been grossly neglectful of our responsibility in bringing about equal facilities for the Negro race in Virginia.

In 1920 there were only 31,000 children of high school age in Virginia going to school, and today there are something like 155,000 of them.

With that undertaking, our people have come to believe and to know and to feel as a moral proposition, if Your Honors please, that the only position we can take, the one that is morally defensible is that they are entitled to equal facilities, and there has been launched this great program in Virginia, appropriating millions of dollars and, Mr. Moore has pointed out, at this time we are spending more for facilities for Negro children than we are for whites, and we should do it because we were laggards in the years past in doing what we should have done.

THE CHIEF JUSTICE: General, I understood Mr. Moore to say that it was a legal responsibility for Virginia to have the equal facilities in the statute itself.

MR. ALMOND: In the statute itself there is a legal responsibility, and in the years past has not been discharged as it should have been discharged.

What I said about it is independently of his right that we should do it, it is our policy and it is our determination; we are irrevocably dedicated and our people are enthusiastically in support of equal facilities for Negroes at the secondary level in Virginia. That is our program today, and that is the program that we want to go forward with, and that we are going forward with.

The Legislature of 1950, on the recommendation of the Governor, almost without a dissenting voice, appropriated $50 million for school construction.

The Legislature of 1952 appropriated another $15 million, making a total of $60 million that have been appropriated in those two sessions of the Legislature of Virginia to be dedicated almost solely toward the improvement of facilities at the secondary level in Virginia.

THE CHIEF JUSTICE: Are those $60 million what you call the Battle Fund?

MR. ALMOND: That is right, Mr. Chief Justice.

THE CHIEF JUSTICE: What is the Literary Fund, for what purpose and in what amount? Is it temporary or permanent?

MR. ALMOND: No, sir. Written into the Constitution of Virginia are provisions for what we call a Literary Fund, and there goes into that Fund the collections of all fines that are paid in Virginia; they go permanently into that Fund, and that is a revolving fund from which the school boards of the various localities may make application for moneys for school purposes, principally for school construction, and meet certain minimum requirements laid down by the State Board of Education, and then they issue their bonds which are held at 2 per cent interest by the State Board of Education; and as the interest comes in and the funds are paid in, it revolves, and it self-perpetuates itself. Then it has been aug- mented from time to time by direct appropriations from the Legislature into that Literary Fund.

Today, as I cite from memory, and I think the record bears it out, there are loans either in actual operations or applications approved for in excess of $48 million from the Literary Fund, which have been applied to the construction of white schools, and something over $12 million which have been applied to the construction of the Negro schools.

If I may have just another moment—

THE CHIEF JUSTICE: All right, General, you may have five additional minutes, and you may have five minutes for rebuttal.

MR. ALMOND: Thank you, sir.
I just want to say a word—

THE CHIEF JUSTICE: I do not want to penalize you by my questions.

MR. ALMOND: I just want to say a word, if Your Honors please, relative to the impact of a decision that would strike down, contrary to the customs, the traditions and the mores of what we might claim to be a great people, established through generations, who themselves are fiercely and irrevocably dedicated to the preservation of the white and colored races.

We have had a struggle in Virginia, particularly from 1920 on, to educate our people, white and colored, to the necessity of promoting the cause of secondary education.

We think we have had great leaders to develop in that field. One, Dr. Dabney Lancaster, now president of Longwood College, I think, made himself very unpopular because he advocated and fought tooth and nail for the equalization of salaries between white and Negro teachers.

That has been accomplished. The curricula have been accomplished; facilities are rapidly being accomplished, and our people, deeply ingrained within them, feel that it is their custom, their use and their wont, and their traditions, if destroyed, as this record shows, will make it impossible to raise public funds through the process of taxation, either at the state or the local level, to support the public school system of Virginia, and it would destroy the public school system of Virginia as we know it today. That is not an idle threat.

Then, too, a thing that concerns us—

THE CHIEF JUSTICE: General, in what way will it destroy it?

MR. ALMOND: It would destroy it, Mr. Chief Justice, because we must have—it is a costly proposition—money with which to operate the public school system at both the state level and the local level, and the only source of income, of course, is the source of taxation at the state and local level, and bond issues at the local level, and the people would not vote bond issues through their resentment to it.

I say that not as a threat.

Then, another thing, we have 5,243 Negro teachers in the public school system of Virginia on an average of splendid qualification. That 5,243 exceed the Negro teachers in all of the thirty-one States of this Union, where there is not segregation by law.

They would not, as a hard fact of realism, and not in a spirit of recrimination do I say this, but simply as hard stark reality—those Negro teachers would not be employed to teach white children in a tax-supported system in Virginia.

Now, I know they tell us "Why didn't you raise that voice when the Negro was admitted to the University of Virginia?"

I did not raise it. I advised the University of Virginia that they had no defense, and I sat down with distinguished counsel in this case and agreed to the stipulations and helped prepare the decree that was entered by the court, and there was no evidence taken on it.

But here there is distinction, if Your Honor please, with 22.7 per cent of our population, the Negro population, with 59 per cent of the school population of Prince Edward County Negro population, to make such a transition, would undo what we have been doing, and which we propose to continue to do for the uplift and advancement of the education of both races. It would stop this march of progress, this onward sweep.

I thank you.

THE CHIEF JUSTICE: Mr. Robinson, you understand that you have five additional minutes.

REBUTTAL ARGUMENT ON BEHALF OF APPELLANTS

by MR. ROBINSON

MR. ROBINSON: In addition to the time that was reserved to me, yes.

May it please the Court, in addition to the evidence in the record to which I have referred the Court to answer a question put to me by Mr. Justice Reed upon the opening argument, I should also like to request the attention of the Court directly to our statement as to jurisdiction, pages 9 to 11, where we did undertake to incorporate some historical evidence which we thought would be of value on the question of the basis, the original basis, of the segregation legislation, data which are not contained in the record in the case.

Examination of this material will indicate that prior to the time of the Civil War, as a consequence of the Dred Scott decision, the Negro did not enjoy citizenship rights equal to those enjoyed by a white person.

As a matter of fact, in that case the Court had decided that he possessed no rights which a white person was bound to respect at all.

And so it goes that after the Civil War, and even after the Negro was affirmatively ganted full and equal citizenship by the Thirteenth and Fourteenth Amendments, and even though his right to suffrage was given protection by the provisions of the Fifteenth Amendment, the white South was not content with this constitutional change. Consequently, we had the so-called period of the "Black Codes", which were a body of laws which were expressly intended and indeed did accomplish the disability of the Negro.

Examination of the records of the constitutional conventions of the Southern states during the period that legislative education of segregation had its beginning, gives, as I stated this morning, a reliable indication that the real basis of this legislation was not what it has been stated to this Court it is, but rather that the segregation laws themselves were intended to, and have, in fact, in Virginia accomplished, a matter which I shall get to in just a few minutes—were intended to limit the educational opportunities of the Negro, and place him in a position where he could not obtain in the state's educational system opportunities and benefits from the public educational program equal to those which flowed to white students.

We have incorporated in our statement as to jurisdiction as one piece of evidence specifically referable to Virginia, the report of the proceedings during the debates at the 1902 Constitutional Convention over one of the provisions which was then up for discussion, a resolution that state funds for schools must be used to maintain the primary schools for a certain period of time before these funds could be used for the establishment of high schools or indeed grades beyond the higher grades.

The question was then asked as to whether or not the effect of this provision would be to tend to prevent the establishment of schools in sections of the country where such schools ought to be prevented, and the eminent Mr. Carter Glass[50] answered the question by pointing out that this provision had been considered, that there was a discussion of this demand, stating as he did—and these are his words:

> Certainly, in my judgement, a very reasonable demand, that the white people of the black sections of Virginia should be permitted to tax themselves, and after a certain point has been passed which would safeguard the poorer classes in these communities, divert that fund to the exclusive use of the white children.

[50]Representative from Virginia (1902–1918), Secretary of the Treasury (1918–1922), Senator from Virginia (1920–1946).

It was at the same Constitutional Convention that Senator Glass made the statement that discrimination was one of the purposes for which the convention was called—I am speaking about discrimination over in the area of suffrage—and it was at this very same convention that he said that one of the purposes of the convention was to discriminate to the very extremity of permissible action under the limitations of the federal Constitution, with a view to the elimination of every Negro voter who can be gotten rid of legally without materially impairing the numerical strength of the white electorate. The so-called Virginia picture bears out this purpose.

I would like to ask the Court's attention—invite the Court's attention—to the data which we have incorporated in our reply brief commencing at page 11, the data pertaining to the present and the future educational system in Virginia.

Although Negroes constitute or they did constitute in 1950–51, 26 per cent of the total number of pupils enrolled in the schools of the commonwealth, they did not receive, when measured on a dollars and cents basis, anything like their fair share of the educational funds, anything like their fair share of the school property employed by the commonwealth in its educational program.

We have set forth there data to demonstrate that for each dollar invested in each category per Negro student, the investment for the 1950–51 school session per Negro student was 61 cents in sites and buildings, 50 cents in furniture and equipment, 67 cents in buses, and 61 cents in total school property. That is the situation in Virginia.

It was a situation in Virginia as we were able to present it up to the latest possible point at the time of the trial of this case.

JUSTICE JACKSON: I hope you will take time enough before you finish to tell me what your position is about the provision of the Fourteenth Amendment, that Congress pass appropriate legislation to enforce it, and what effect, if any, it has on these cases.

MR. ROBINSON: That are now before the Court, sir?

JUSTICE JACKSON: Yes, cases of this character.

MR. ROBINSON: I will be glad to do that, Mr. Justice Jackson, right now.

I disagree with counsel for the appellees that Congress does not have full power under section 5 of the Fourteenth Amendment to enact legislation that would outlaw segregation in state public schools.

But I do feel that insofar as the present cases are concerned that has relatively little merit.

We come before this Court presenting what we consider to be justiciable questions, questions that are not essentially different in character from those which have been presented in cases which in the past have been brought here.

In other words, I do not feel that the mere fact that under the authority of section 5 of the Fourteenth Amendment Congress could enact legislation which would settle this problem would in any way encroach upon the jurisdiction of this Court, if, as a matter of fact, a violation of the Constitution has been shown.

JUSTICE JACKSON: Of course, in the jury cases you have legislation by Congress; in the interstate commerce cases you have legislation by Congress.

MR. ROBINSON: That is correct, sir.

JUSTICE JACKSON: In a good many of our cases, but not all, you are quite right, that some do have them. But in a number of cases they rest on specific statutory implementation of this amendment.

MR. ROBINSON: Yes. I would like to make—

JUSTICE DOUGLAS: What statute of Congress regulates juries?

MR. ROBINSON: I think it is section 47 of Title 8 of the United States Code, I think it is; I have forgotten. [Now 42 U.S.C., section 1985 (2)]

JUSTICE JACKSON: I pointed it out in a dissenting opinion some time ago, but Justice Douglas apparently did not read my dissent.[51]

MR. ROBINSON: I do not remember the exact number, Mr. Justice Douglas, but it is up in Title 8, and, as I recall, it is somewhere in the forties; it is in the forties section.

I would like to make reference to this—

JUSTICE DOUGLAS: Has the Court ever held that the Fourteenth Amendment is not executed unless Congress acts?

MR. ROBINSON: No, I do not think so.

There is a large area of law which has been developed by this Court in which the decision has rested upon the provisions of the due process and equal protection clauses, and in a few instances of the privileges and immunities clause where there was not any implementing legislation by Congress.

As I understand the theory, particularly as it came as a consequence of the civil rights cases, that authority was there that Congress could exercise, if it desired to do so, but the position which we urge upon the Court is the mere fact that if Congress has not done it, it will not preclude this Court from deciding constitutional questions.

I can make reference, for example, to the situation which was recently presented to this Court in he so-called restrictive covenant cases,[52] and in those cases we had a piece of legislation involved that was section 42 of Title 8 of the United States Code. [Now 42 U.S.C., section 1981 et seq.]

This Court nevertheless held that a state court enforcement of those restrictions resulted in the denial of the equal protection of the laws, notwithstanding the fact in that situation we did have a case in which Congress, under its authority conferred by section 5 of the Fourteenth Amendment, might have outlawed the thing, to start off with, so that the question might never have gotten to this Court.

[51]Frazier v. United States, 335 U.S. 497, 514 (1948). The selection of federal juries is now governed by 28 U.S.C., section 1861 et seq. Interfering with jurors is made a crime by 42 U.S.C., section 1875 (2).

[52]Shelley v. Kraemer, 334 U.S. 1 (1948), see n. 7, supra.

JUSTICE REED: But if segregation is not a denial of equal protection or due process, legislation by Congress could do nothing more except to express congressional views, and wouldn't that be decisive?

MR. ROBINSON: Yes, I am inclined to—

JUSTICE REED: So you would be forced to decide whether or not segregation per se comes under that question.

MR. ROBINSON: Of course, that is our position here, sir.

JUSTICE FRANKFURTER: The Fourteenth Amendment is not unlike, in some aspect, the commerce clause. There are many things that the states cannot do merely because the commerce clause exists. There are many things that a state can do until Congress steps in.

MR. ROBINSON: That is right, sir. Under those circumstances—

JUSTICE REED: The state cannot violate the Fourteenth Amendment.

MR. ROBINSON: I beg pardon?

JUSTICE REED: The state cannot violate the Fourteenth Amendment.

MR. ROBINSON: That is right, and I was just about to observe that it cannot violate the commerce clause either.

JUSTICE FRANKFURTER: We would not be arguing for ten hours if it is clear that this is a violation of it. We do not argue for ten hours a question that is self-evident.

MR. ROBINSON: I understand, sir.

Now, going back to the so-called Virginia picture, reference was made and questions were asked concerning the Literary Fund allocations, the approximately $60 million allocated by the state Literary Fund for school construction in the state.

We have pointed out in our reply brief, and we have demonstrated statistically, that even with this large expenditure, when you add it to the present value of buildings and sites the ratio of investment in school property in Virginia will be increased from the present 61 cents to only 74 cents per Negro student.

I should like to also emphasize the fact that no time has been set for the completion of these projects and, consequently, we do not even know when the ratio is going to be realized; but even if all of the Negro projects which are proposed are completed, and even though no additional money whatsoever is invested in white schools, the amount of money invested in buildings and sites per Negro student over the entire state would only be $343.30 as compared with $366.73 that are already invested in school property per white student.

So, consequently, the Literary Fund program, the construction which is expected to develop out of the Literary Fund allocations would not seem to bring about this equality even of physical facilities within any point in the near future.

Reference was made in this case also to the so-called four-year program.

That is a program that has been developed, and that contemplates the expenditure of some $263 million for new construction and improvements, and it has been emphasized that 77.7 per cent of this money will be spent on white projects, and 23.3 per cent on Negro projects, and the emphasis is placed there by reason of the fact that the percentages of expenditures are slightly in excess of the percentages of school population.

The money for this program, as the record clearly shows, is not now available, and even if the money were available, and the entire program were completed by 1956, the amount invested in sites and buildings would only be 79 cents per Negro student for each dollar per white student, and thus, I urge the Court this is a very vast program.

Virginia does not have the money for it now. Even though Virginia could spend $263 million—an enormous sum by Virginia standards—all that we succeed in doing is moving from a present 61 cents to 79 cents per Negro student for each dollar that is invested in buildings and sites for white students.

THE CHIEF JUSTICE: Have you got any breakdown as to the number of school buildings that have been constructed in the last, say, five years? I heard about the high school of Richmond and Charlottesville. I am fearful that this percentage business does not make it very clear to me because it is a question of the number of schools, it is a question of how the students are grouped, as to whether they are getting the fair "divvy," I might say.

MR. ROBINSON: Yes, Mr. Chief Justice.

Now, maybe I can help. On the Literary Fund allocations that I was talking about just a few minutes ago, the evidence at the time of the trial showed that there had been projects—no, it does not give the number of schools. It simply shows the scope of the program, that is, the number of cities and counties over which the construction would extend.

If Your Honor will indulge me just a moment, I will look at the exhibit. If we have it in the record at all, might I make this suggestion: There are a large number of exhibits in this case, and all of this statistical information is contained in those exhibits.

Those exhibits are before the Court. If the information is available at all it will be found there.

We have in our reply brief a specific pointed and detailed reference in each case where we get to one of these particular things. I do not recall that the precise information concerning which Your Honor has asked me does appear in the record.

THE CHIEF JUSTICE: It would seem to me that if it did appear it would either show a stepped-up program or maybe retrogression in respect of the—if you had the breakdown it would show something.

MR. ROBINSON: Well, the appellees do insist that this is, in other words, a stepped-up program.

THE CHIEF JUSTICE: Do I understand that you take the same position that Mr. Marshall would take if we were to hold that segregation per se was unconstitutional in regard to the time element?

MR. ROBINSON: On the matter of necessity of the administrative problem in these segregated—oh, yes.

THE CHIEF JUSTICE: Then why, if you take that position there—and I assume you take it as a matter of necessity—why do you not take that position here under the equal facilities doctrine?

MR. ROBINSON: If Your Honor please, I think that there is a difference between a postponement of a right and a delay which is incidental to affording the remedies that we asked for.

I do not think that it would be possible without encroaching upon the previous decisions of this Court, to take the position that notwithstanding a present denial of the constitutional rights of the appellants, that notwithstanding that they must wait until the state gets around to fixing the schools.

THE CHIEF JUSTICE: Of course, I take it, that you recognize the distinction in the cases in regard to the number of students affected, and all that sort of thing, but if you agree that a reasonable period of time should be granted if we held segregation was unconstitutional, I just wonder why you take the position you do in regard to the equal facilities, unless you say that the stepped-up program is just not sufficient to meet the situation.

MR. ROBINSON: We do take the latter position, if Your Honor please, and we have set forth—and since my time is just about up—I can only now refer the Court to the data which we have set forth in our reply brief in that connection, in which we point out that this stepped-up program of this state is not going to produce even physical equality on a state-wide basis at any time in the near future, and we tried to calculate that time as best we could from the available information.

Now, with respect to the other portion of Your Honor's question, our position on it is simply this: I appreciate the fact that even though there has been a violation of legal right, in affording a remedy it may be necessary and it may be entirely necessary for there to be some delay incidental to the affording of that remedy.

A case that I can think of is if a court should decree specific performance of a contract to tear down a house, the man has got to have a reasonable opportunity to get the house down.

But I do not think in that particular case if the man is entitled to that decree—

THE CHIEF JUSTICE: A man might have to have a reasonable opportunity to get out of the house before it is torn down.

MR. ROBINSON: I agree with that, too.

In other words, we have the administrative practical problem arising from the affording of the remedy, and to that particular situation and to that particular extent, of course, we readily recognize some lapse of time. I am not in a position to suggest what it should be.

I think it is an administrative problem initially, at least, for the school authorities to work out. We appreciate that, but I do not see how we can, without encroaching upon the body of decisions of this Court which have established the rights involved in these cases, as present and personal, as to how we can say that notwithstanding that, we may delay the right; in other words, that a person must be compelled before he can get satisfaction of his rights—he may be postponed at some time into the future before he can get what the Constitution entitled him to, and what his white counterparts are getting already.

THE CHIEF JUSTICE: Now, take the South Carolina case. Would you say that, assuming the equal facilities rule will still continue, would you say that the lapse of time in their construction program was not fully justified by the lower court?

MR. ROBINSON: Well, I would have to answer that question, if Your Honor please, this way: I do not personally feel, and I could not urge upon the Court that suspension of the satisfaction of a constitutional right is ever justified.
In other words, I would—

THE CHIEF JUSTICE: But you realize you are in equity; you realize that you have got the rights of other people involved in regard to dislocation?

MR. ROBINSON: I appreciate that.

THE CHIEF JUSTICE: And in the South Carolina case there was some delay, but we are told here that when the new buildings were constructed and occupied in September—I recall there was some effort, special effort, made to get the material to build the gymnasium—at one time they thought they would not get it, but they worked around and got it for the gymnasium.

MR. ROBINSON: Yes. As I understand the "separate but equal" rule, even under that, at that particular time, at the time of the first hearing when the facilities were—

THE CHIEF JUSTICE: All right, go ahead.

MR. ROBINSON: —unequal, the court should, instead of entering an equalization decree, should have removed the segregation. That is what this Court said in the Gaines case is the consequence of trying to maintain segregation where you do not have equal physcial facilities.

THE CHIEF JUSTICE: Well, the Court did not—

MR. ROBINSON: The Court did not under those circumstances, and I say that at that particular point what the Court there was doing, the Court was not simply delaying the thing for purposes which would be incidental to giving to the plaintiffs the relief which, under that doctrine, they were then entitled to.
The Court was delaying it until conditions could be remedied in such a way that under the "separate but equal" doctrine, if limited to that particular point, they would not be entitled to any relief at all.

THE CHIEF JUSTICE: Well, now, what is your view in regard to the way it was handled by the lower court?

MR. ROBINSON: In the Virginia case?

THE CHIEF JUSTICE: No, in the South Carolina case, considering that they ruled segregation per se not unconstitutional? Do you have objection to that method of handling it?

MR. ROBINSON: Well, if the Court should rule—I want to make certain—

THE CHIEF JUSTICE: Well, they did rule. I say so far as they are concerned, they did so rule.

MR. ROBINSON: Yes. I am just trying to understand Your Honor's question.

THE CHIEF JUSTICE: Would you say that under the circumstances in the South Carolina case, having ruled on the segregation question as they did, that immediately, *eo instanti,* they should have said, "entry into white schools" or seeing the imminent construction that they should continue as they did?

MR. ROBINSON: Not the latter, if you please; the former, taking into consideration that immediately would not mean five minutes from now.

THE CHIEF JUSTICE: Well, now, how many minutes, how many days? That is the point.

MR. ROBINSON: I would not be able—I have tried to make plain that I consider that that is an administrative problem, and that gets into things that, frankly, I do not think that I am able to answer.

THE CHIEF JUSTICE: What about the courts?

MR. ROBINSON: I do not think that courts are, either. In other words, my position in that particular regard is that they are entitled to the relief immediately which should be afforded them just as soon as expeditious administrative arrangements can be made to unsegregate the schools, as I understand the Gaines and the subsequent cases, the doctrine of those cases, requires.

For these reasons, we respectfully submit that the decree of the District Court should be reversed.

(Thereupon, the argument in the above-entitled cause was concluded.)

SPOTTSWOOD THOMAS BOLLING, ET AL.,

Petitioners,

vs.

C. MELVIN SHARPE, ET AL.,

Respondents.

Case No. 413

Washington, D.C.

Wednesday, December 10, 1952.

The above-entitled cause came on for argument at 3:30 p.m.

APPEARANCES:

On behalf of the Petitioners:

GEORGE E. C. HAYES, ESQ., and JAMES M. NABRIT, JR., ESQ.

On behalf of the Respondents:

MILTON D. KORMAN, ESQ.

THE CHIEF JUSTICE: Number 413, Bolling, et al., versus C. Melvin Sharpe, and others.

All right, Mr. Hayes.

ARGUMENT ON BEHALF OF PETITIONERS

by MR. HAYES

MR. HAYES: May it please the Court, this case is here on a petition for a writ of certiorari addressed to the United States Court of Appeals for the District of Columbia Circuit.

The jurisdiction of this Court to review by writ of certiorari is conferred by Title 28, United States Code, section 1254 (1) and section 2101 (e).

This case was on appeal to the United States Court of Appeals for the District of Columbia, where no judgment had been rendered, and no order had been entered, and the matter came up under the rule, as I have stated.

This case came before the court on a complaint and on a motion to dismiss, and the facts are, therefore, not controverted.

The minor petitioners, Negroes, fully qualified to attend a junior high school in the District of Columbia, accompanied by their parents, made application to the Sousa Junior High School for admission, and they were denied admission to the Sousa Junior High School solely on the ground of race or color.

Thereafter, through their attorneys, to each echelon in the administrative setup of the schools of the District of Columbia, they made application for admission, and finally to the Board of Education, and in each of these areas they were denied admission solely because of their race or color.

Thereafter, and having exhausted their administrative remedies, a suit was filed asking for a declaratory judgment and for injunctive relief.

A motion was filed to dismiss. That motion was granted, and an appeal was taken. Certiorari was granted in this case on November 10, 1952.

Your Honors have listened for a number of hours to discussions with respect to this matter of segregation.

In the case of the District of Columbia, in our opinion it presents an entirely novel question, one which this Court has not been called upon to pass upon, and in which we specifically and solely present the question as to whether segregation is unconstitutional per se.

There are no factual questions as to facilities; we raise no issue with respect to facilities.

Our proposition is baldly as to whether or not the respondents have the power, the statutory or constitutional power, to deny to these pupils admission to the Sousa Junior High School.

JUSTICE DOUGLAS: Where is the statute that is relied upon?

MR. HAYES: If Your Honor please, the statutes that are relied upon are in our brief beginning at page 23.

I want to call Your Honors' attention to the fact, at the very outset, that these statutes, contrary to the statutes to which Your Honors have listened for the last two days, nowhere, in and of themselves, require segregation. It, to our mind, is a matter solely of interpretation of these statutes as to whether or not segregation is required.

Our opponents take the position that these statutes do require it.

JUSTICE FRANKFURTER: Suppose we do not agree with your construction of the statute? Is that the end of the case?

MR. HAYES: No, Your Honor, that is not, because, if Your Honors were to determine that our construction of the statute was incorrect, and that by so much these statutes require segregation, we would then take the position that any such requirement is beyond the power of the Government to announce, and we would rely upon that for decisions of this Court as making that an impossibility.

JUSTICE FRANKFURTER: So your argument is that as a matter of construction this is not mandatory, but just exercising discretion by the educational authorities?

MR. HAYES: That is right, sir.

JUSTICE FRANKFURTER: And that in construing it, I suppose, that we should take into account that possibly a serious constitutional question is involved, even if on the face of it it does not yield to the construction that you argue; but you argue, in the third place, that if one cannot escape the constitutional question, then you assail it?

MR. HAYES: That is correct, sir; that is exactly our position, Mr. Justice Frankfurter.

JUSTICE DOUGLAS: Has this statute that you refer to consistently been interpreted by the Board of Education as requiring segregation?

MR. HAYES: Yes, sir; Mr. Justice Douglas, it has.

JUSTICE DOUGLAS: This is an old statute?

MR. HAYES: Yes, Mr. Justice Douglas; again, it has been in since 1864; originally there were the Acts of 1862, but the Acts here relied on go from 1864 forward.

JUSTICE REED: Why do you say an interpretation requiring segregation?

MR. HAYES: When I say interpreting as requiring, I mean by that, at any rate, they have required it.

JUSTICE REED: That may be permissive.

MR. HAYES: From our point of view, yes. They take the position, as I understand it, that they are required. From our point of view it could be purely permissive, and from our point of view, they are, if anything at all, simply permissive because they are in no sense—we take the position—mandatory.

JUSTICE DOUGLAS: Do you set forth the legislative history of this statute?

MR. HAYES: No, Your Honor, we do not set it forth in any—

JUSTICE DOUGLAS: Does it throw any light upon this?

MR. HAYES: I beg your pardon?

JUSTICE DOUGLAS: Does it throw any light upon this?

MR. HAYES: I am sorry.

JUSTICE DOUGLAS: Does it throw any light on this subject as to whether or not Congress intended there be segregation?

MR. HAYES: From our point of view it does not.
We say that because it is our belief that Congress, by the statutes, have indicated that it did not intend it because had they so intended, certainly the legislature would have been competent to have spelled it out in a manner so entirely different from the statute that we face because, as Your Honors well know, we have, for instance, the South Carolina statutes saying that these children shall never be educated together; we have the Virginia statute saying that they shall not be in the same schools.
There is no language in any of these which say any such thing, and so we say that Congress has never said that.

THE CHIEF JUSTICE: In seeking appropriations, the estimates that are put in, are they for the different schools in the city?

MR. HAYES: Yes, Your Honor.

THE CHIEF JUSTICE: Does that show that the schools are for Negroes and schools for whites?

MR. HAYES: It shows that, and we do not pretend that the legislature is not mindful of it.

THE CHIEF JUSTICE: And Congress throughout the period of years has been mindful of it?

MR. HAYES: Yes, Your Honor. We take the position that being mindful or being mandatory or being constitutional are entirely different propositions.

JUSTICE BLACK: What provisions of the Constitution do you assert this violates?

MR. HAYES: It violates, we will say, a number of them. I shall outline to you the manner in which we think they do violate it.

JUSTICE BLACK: Which?

MR. HAYES: It violates the due process clause of the Fifth Amendment; it violates, as we conceive it, the civil rights statutes; it is in violation of the public policy that this Government has just seen fit to announce in the Charter of the United Nations; all of them, we think, are violated by any attempts to deny to these people, the petitioners, admission into the Sousa Junior High School.

JUSTICE FRANKFURTER: Mr. Hayes, may I ask one other question?

MR. HAYES: Yes, Mr. Justice Frankfurter.

JUSTICE FRANKFURTER: Do I understand you to say that this legislation is not mandatory, but permissive?

MR. HAYES: If at all, it would be nothing but permissive.

JUSTICE FRANKFURTER: Wouldn't you, in your point of view, be attacking the constitutionality of legislation even if Congress authorizes it?

MR. HAYES: No, Your Honor, because from our point of view we take the position—if I stated it was permissive, then I am in error, we take the position—that this language is neither mandatory nor permissive.

JUSTICE FRANKFURTER: You say this does not even authorize it?

MR. HAYES: That is right, sir.

JUSTICE FRANKFURTER: And you say for how many years has the District been acting without authority?

MR. HAYES: We do not say without authority; we say that the fact that they acted with knowledge does not mean that the statute gives the authority.

JUSTICE FRANKFURTER: If the statute does not give the authority, then it was ultra vires for the District to have been doing what they have been doing; is that right?

MR. HAYES: No, if Your Honor please, because our position is that when the District recognizes that a situation exists, and when they appropriate for the sake of the statement, to an existing situation, that that does not mean that they themselves are given the authority nor does it mean that they are holding that it is mandatory, and this Court—

JUSTICE FRANKFURTER: Still somebody must have been doing something lawlessly for a good many years; is that it?

MR. HAYES: If Your Honor says lawlessly, perhaps, I cannot go along with the idea of lawlessness, but it has been done without constitutional authority, I do say that.

JUSTICE FRANKFURTER: Somebody has been asleep as to the illegality of what has been done?

MR. HAYES: No, I would not say asleep as to the illegality. I say rather—

JUSTICE FRANKFURTER: If I may say so, I am in deep sympathy with you in not trying to invalidate legislation if it can be dealt with otherwise. But I find a little difficulty in seeing how we can fail to reach the validity of this legislation unless you say that what has been done by the District authorities has been done, if not lawlessly, then without authority of law. How about that, would you accept that?

MR. HAYES: We would say, sir, if this Court were to determine that what has been done up to this time has been done validly, that then for the first time this Court has had the opportunity to say, "No, this is not the proper way."

We say that this is the opportunity for this Court to say that any such attempt as this, based solely on the question of race or color, is not within the Constitution.

JUSTICE FRANKFURTER: "Hereafter you have no lawful authority to do this, but we do not care about the past."

MR. HAYES: I would not want Your Honors' statement to indicate that we do not care about the past, but for the first time we have had the opportunity to pass upon it, and we frown upon it.

If Your Honor please, as I have indicated, these three propositions I have outlined are as follows:

We take the position, of course, that the court was wrong in having denied the relief sought, and in having granted the motion to dismiss.

This Government—and this is the point which seems to us so fundamental—that in these other situations where the question of these states has been involved, and where the question of equal facilities has been involved, that is one thing.

But in our case, this Government of ours is being asked to support a statute having as its basis nothing other than race or color, and we say that this Government cannot afford to do just that.

As I have said, the question of the right of this Government to legislate for the District of Columbia is without question because they expressly have been authorized to legislate for the District of Columbia. But this Court, with respect to that, acting for the District of Columbia, has said that they cannot do it and violate one's constitutional rights.

You have said so in *Capital Traction* v. *Hof,* and you said in *Callen* v. *Wilson*[53] that, as a matter of fact, the right to administer for the District of Columbia is restricted by the fact that you cannot violate the constitutional rights of persons in so doing.

This Court has seen fit to pass upon rights which come within the purview of the due process clause of the Fifth Amendment, and have explained and expressed what the word "liberty" means, and this Court has seen fit to indicate and incorporate in that word "liberty" things which we believe point out the way as to what should be done in this instance.

Governmental restrictions on the right to teach a foreign language, the right of a parent to send his child to a private school, the right for them to acquire knowledge, the right of parents and pupils to a reasonable choice with respect to teachers, curricula, and text books, the right of parents to secure for their children the type of education which they think best, and which is not harmful, have been held by this Court to be fundamental educational rights protected from arbitrary government action by the due process clause of the Fifth Amendment.

That language is found in *Meyer* v. *Nebraska, Bartels* v. *Iowa, Pierce* v. *Society of Sisters.*[54]

JUSTICE BLACK: Were those cases decided under the Fifth Amendment?

MR. HAYES: They were decided under the Fourteenth Amendment, if Your Honor please, but under the due process clause of the Fourteenth Amendment, and this Court, however, in the case of *Farrington* v. *Tokushige*[55] has seen fit to refer specifically to those three cases, indicating that the due process clause of the Fourteenth Amendment, as referred to in those cases, is incorporated and is taken over and assumed as being part of the Fifth Amendment.

As far as the Fifth Amendment cases are concerned, and so in the Takahashi case, this Court, it seems to us, has embraced these educational cases that might be referred to as coming within the Fourteenth Amendment, and has said that the Fifth Amendment applies in instances where due process of law is concerned and that, if Your Honor please, is the exact situation that we have here.

I would not pretend, because it would not be candid to pretend, that in those cases there was not something having to do with economic situations, with the question of ownership, that there was not a question of it being brought by owners

[53]Capital Traction Co. v. Hof, 174 U.S. 1 (1899); Callan v. Wilson, 127 U.S. 540 (1888). Both cases required the District of Columbia to follow the Constitutional requirements of trial by jury.

[54]Meyer v. Nebraska, 262 U.S. 390 (1923). A state law forbidding the teaching of a modern language other than English below the eighth grade was held invalid. Bartels v. Iowa, 262 U.S. 404 (1923) (same holding); Pierce v. Society of Sisters,268 U.S. 510(1925), upset an Oregon law requiring every parent to send his child to a public school.

[55]273 U.S. 284 (1927). Hawaii was not permitted to require a fee and a permit before a foreign language school could begin operation. The case discussed the relation between the Fourteenth and Fifth Amendments.

114

and teachers rather than by parents and children, so that for the sake of the statement someone might say it is dicta.

But I call the Court's attention to the fact that what you said in the Farrington case so entirely, as we conceive it, gave the concept of what this Court has in mind with respect to this question of liberty under this due process clause, and that there was no need to inquire whether or not it was in any sense any other than what this Court was embracing as being its doctrine.

JUSTICE REED: Do you take the same position that the Virginia counsel did, that this legislation was intended to be inimical to the interests of Negroes?

MR. HAYES: That this legislation was, if Your Honor means by inimical, the question of putting them in—simply segregating them?

JUSTICE REED: As I understood previous counsel, they urged that Virginia had passed these laws in order to deprive Negroes of educational opportunities.

MR. HAYES: I think, if Your Honor please, that unquestionably the answer must be that legislation of this character was pointed solely at the Negro, and that it was done purely and for no other reason than because of the fact that it pretended to keep for him this place of secondary citizenship.

I think it could have no other conceivable purpose. I have been concerned—

JUSTICE REED: You do not think that it had any relation to these prior considerations?

MR. HAYES: I do not think it had the slightest relationship to that, if Your Honor please; I do not think anyone can pretend in this jurisdiction that it has any such purpose because this question of the schools, if Your Honor please—this is the only governmentally constructed situation that has as its basis segregation in the District of Columbia, the only one, and to us it is entirely inconceivable and inconsistent that under those circumstances for any conceivable reason, that the argument can be had that it is necessary on account of any alleged difficulties that might arise.

This Court has seen fit to say that any legislation based on racism is immediately suspect. That is what this Court has said.

In the Hirabayashi[56] case this Court said that legislation of this character is suspect, and immediately that it is suspect we take the position that the burden then comes upon the Government to show as to why under those conditions any such thing should be allowed. We throw down that challenge to our friends on the other side, to indicate why this should be done if there be any purpose other than pure racism.

If there be any answer other than it is purely on account of color, then we ask them to indicate to us what that situation is.

THE CHIEF JUSTICE: Mr. Hayes, if it was solely due to racism, you mean that after the adoption of the amendments—of course, they would not affect

[56]Hirabayashi v. United States, 320 U.S. 81 (1943). The Court upheld wartime curfews restricting the movement of Japanese-Americans on the West Coast.

this particular area—that segregation continued solely for racism and, therefore, the Fourteenth Amendment should now declare that under such circumstances the resultant relationships were invalid as unconstitutional?

MR. HAYES: If Your Honor please, I say again—and this is said on something that I hope is not based on obsession because of the fact that I am a Negro—I said to you that I believe that any of the facts—the Fourteenth Amendment, which had in it the question of the equal protection clause—the equal protection clause, as I conceive it, was put into the Fourteenth Amendment not because of the fact that there was any attempt at segregation at that time, but it was the question of getting segregation for Negroes, not of administering it. It was a question of getting it, and I think that the Fourteenth Amendment, when it provided for citizenship, mindful of the situation, and saying that they should have full citizenship, I think that they could not consistently have had that in mind and passed that and, at the same time, had in mind the question of that we shall segregate in schools.

THE CHIEF JUSTICE: The point, to me, coming so close to the end of the war between the states, so far as the District of Columbia is concerned—

MR. HAYES: Yes, sir.

THE CHIEF JUSTICE: —were the people who were there in the Congress at the time the amendments were passed, and were there when ratified, and were there when this legislation was passed, and it is hard for me to understand that if it is racism, that it was not done deliberately, and the constitutional amendments were so interpreted, and I assume that you would not go that far, would you, in regard to the war amendments.

MR. HAYES: Mr. Chief Justice, I think that what was done was a matter of politics, was a matter of doing the thing which, at that time, was to them the opportune thing to do; it was the question of giving away this with the idea of pressing this which was the stronger thing.

It was the idea of putting through this act and giving up this, because of the fact that this was the expedient thing to do, and I think that that very situation was what occasioned them not writing into any of these acts anything specific with regard to it, because in the same vein in which Your Honor indicates that this was an allowable circumstance, if they had intended that it should be a matter of segregation they could have written into this this, that Your Honor has indicated.

THE CHIEF JUSTICE: I was just merely asking your view relative to the frame of mind in which the people who passed the amendments had in this situation in the District of Columbia to have separate schools at the time when the amendments—the Fourteenth Amendment was being ratified by the states, if they did this for the purpose of just punishing the Negro or was it their interpretation of what the Fourteenth Amendment meant?

MR. HAYES: I have attempted to indicate to Your Honor that in my opinion it was not given as punishment; it was given as an expedient. It was done as an expedient; it was done because, as a matter of fact, at that time it seemed for them, I presume, an expedient thing not to press for this particular thing, but rather to allow the amendment to go through and, as I say, I think it is for that reason expressly that they put nothing into it other than what they did.

May I make just this one additional suggestion, because my time has already gone, and my associate, Mr. Nabrit, is going to argue the other points, but I do want to say in these Japanese war cases, where the Court took the position, as I said, that any segregated thing based upon race alone was suspect, they took the position that the only justification for the denial of constitutional rights can be found where there is pressing public necessity such as the severity of war, and even there the Court must be satisfied in sustaining such restrictions that (1) the purpose of the restriction is within the competency of the Government to effect—we say that this is not within the competency of the Government to effect; (2) the restriction must be clearly authorized, and we call atention to the fact that this Government of the United States, with express powers and implied powers only to carry those express powers, has no such indication as to such clear authorization, and that they must, restrictions must have a reasonable relation to a proper purpose.

JUSTICE FRANKFURTER: Mr. Hayes, before you sit down I would like to put to you a question because of the candor with which I know you will answer. I do not suppose that anybody could deny that this legislation, all these enactments, concern drawing a line, drawing a color line. I suppose that is what this this is all about. As to motives, the devil himself, as some one wise man said some time ago, "Knoweth not the mind of man."

But I must want to ask you whether it is your position that the Fourteenth Amendment or the Fifth, for your purposes, automatically invalidates all legislation which draws a line determined because of race?

I do not want to have trouble tomorrow or the day after tomorrow, but one has to look ahead these days.

I wonder whether you would say, right off from your analysis of the Constitution, that marriage laws relating to race are ipso facto on the face of things, unconstitutional?

MR. HAYES: I would say to Your Honor, in answer to the first question as to whether or not in my opinion—

JUSTICE FRANKFURTER: Because I need hardly tell you there is a good deal of legislation in this country drawing the line in connection with it.[56a]

MR. HAYES: Oh, yes, I am aware of that, sir. But I think that the problem is an entirely different one. With respect to the first part of your query as to whether or not I think automatically it becomes—

JUSTICE FRANKFURTER: I mean that that denial to the states and to the Congress of the United States and to the District is written in by plain implication of the Fourteenth and the Fifth Amendment, that is what I want to know.

[56a]Miscegenation laws were finally declared unconstitutional in Loving v.Virginia, 388 U.S. 1 (1967).

MR. HAYES: I want to say my answer to that is this, if Your Honor please: I think that the very purpose of this Court is the very answer to that question. I think that this Court is called upon with that question now properly posed to ꞮΠake the answer.

JUSTICE FRANKFURTER: You mean as to schools?

MR. HAYES: Yes, sir; that is what your first question, I thought, was addressed to.

JUSTICE FRANKFURTER: Yes.

MR. HAYES: I answered that by saying as to schools this Court is called upon to say that this sort of thing cannot happen because it is a violation of the due process clause of the Fifth Amendment, and the due process clause of the Fifth Amendment does not lend itself to any substantial proposition. You can have substantial equality but you cannot have substantial liberty.

JUSTICE FRANKFURTER: Is that because no legislation which draws any line with reference to race is automatically outlawed by the Fifth and the Fourteenth Amendment? So that takes you over—I am violating my own rule against posing hypothetical cases and, particularly, one that is as full of implications as the laws relating to the marriage laws involved, but I think one has to test these things to see what is the principle which you are invoking before this Court.

Is it all-embracing, is it the all-embracing principle, that no legislation which is based on differentiation of race is valid?

MR. HAYES: I am invoking rather the principle which I think this Court involved in the Hirabayashi case when this Court said that legislation based upon race is immediately suspect; that is what I am invoking.

JUSTICE FRANKFURTER: Well, that is a very candid and logical answer. That simply means that it can be valid. It is not an absolute prohibition, that good cause must be shown or great cause must be shown for the rule.

MR. HAYES: That is right, sir; and it is for that reason that I move to the next position of public necessity that was pointed out in those cases, and of the fact that even with the public necessity you must meet the three requirements.

JUSTICE BLACK: Why do you have to equate the Fourteenth Amendment and the Fifth Amendment provisions on that score?

MR. HAYES: I am not attempting to equate them, if Your Honor please. I am attempting rather to say that as far as the Fifth Amendment is concerned there is no possibility of equating. You cannot make a quantum with respect to one's liberty.

JUSTICE BLACK: You have just referred to the fact that we said that under the Fifth Amendment such laws are suspect, which means that we look at them very carefully to see if they can discriminate on account of race or distinguish on account of race. Do you think the same rule applies with reference to the

Fourteenth Amendment which was passed under entirely different circumstances and for entirely different purposes?

MR. HAYES: Yes. I think the Fourteenth Amendment has within it inherent those possibilities. They have inherent within it the due process clause as well as the equal protection clause.

JUSTICE FRANKFURTER: But you have got to stand on the due process clause?

MR. HAYES: Yes. I am standing on due process.

JUSTICE FRANKFURTER: I take it that was what Justice Black had in mind, and which was behind Justice Black's question.

MR. HAYES: If that be the answer, that is what I was attempting to say. I was not attempting to equate them. We are relying on due process.

JUSTICE DOUGLAS: Your closest case in point so far as decisions go is Farrington?

MR. HAYES: Yes, Your Honor, and in fact, the Farrington case embraced the Meyer, Bartels, and the Pierce case. And that brings them into this.

ARGUMENT ON BEHALF OF PETITIONERS

by MR. NABRIT

MR. NABRIT: If the Court please, it would appear necessary that petitioners make clear the position which they take in the midst of these five cases.

It is our position, simply stated, that the respondents, the public school board officials, in the District of Columbia do not possess either the constitutional power or the statutory power to deny these minor petitioners admission to Sousa Junior High School solely because of race or color. Now, that, as we take it, is the sole question to be considered by this Court.

In considering that question, we would urge upon the Court that it consider whether these respondents possess that power under the due process clause, whether they possess it because these acts of Congress compel it or authorize it, either, whether they possess it in the face of sections 41 and 43 of Title 8 of the United States Code, known as the Civil Rights Act of 1866, or whether they possess it in light of the pledge which this Government has given towards the implementation of human freedoms and rights without any distinction on the basis of race or color; in other words, not as a requirement of the charge but as a policy which is enunciated by the charge.

Now, it would appear to petitioners that it is necessary also for this Court to consider the fact that we are not dealing with the State of South Carolina, we are not dealing with the State of Virginia, the State of Delaware, or the State of Kansas. We are not here concerned with those over-sensitive areas of state and federal relation. That is not involved in this case. We are not involved in this case with the question of the sensitiveness of states with the projection of federal power.

We are concerned here solely with the question of the relationship of the federal government to its citizens. It might be assumed as the basis for our approach to this problem that we go back and look at something of the history of our Constitution. We know that when the Constitution was adopted, there were provisions in there which made it possible for us to have an institution of slavery.

We also know that the juristic concepts were such, in *Dred Scott* v. *Sandford*,[57] that it was decided that a Negro could not be a citizen.

But along came the Thirteenth, Fourteenth and Fifteenth Amendments. The Thirteenth Amendment removed slavery as a condition, as a status. The Fourteenth, so far as the federal citizens are concerned, gave citizenship to those born or naturalized in the United States.

Now, those things together would appear to us to have removed from the federal government any power to impose racial distinctions in dealing with its citizens.

Now, we know that this is a government of limited powers, and we know that it has express powers, and one of these is to deal with the District of Columbia.

JUSTICE MINTON: Is it your thought that the adoption of the Fourteenth Amendment's due process clause changed the meaning of the Fifth Amendment's due process clause?

MR. NABRIT: No, Mr. Justice. I thought, with the abolition of slavery and the federal citizenship conferred in the first section of the Fourteenth Amendment, that those two things robbed any dubious power which the federal government may have had prior to that time to deal with people solely on the basis of race or color.

JUSTICE BLACK: Do you think that there is any doubt that they had complete power before that?

MR. NABRIT: No, not in the light of *Dred Scott* v. *Sandford*, I do not doubt it, because in the light of *Dred Scott* v. *Sandford*, they simply said that no matter whether you went to Missouri, or where you went, you are a Negro and you cannot be a citizen, and as soon as you cannot be a citizen, you cannot come within the purview of these things about which we are talking.

JUSTICE FRANKFURTER: We are talking about the District.

MR. NABRIT: That is right.

JUSTICE FRANKFURTER: We are talking about the District.

MR. NABRIT: Yes, I am saying the District, because if you could not be a federal citizen—and that is what *Dred Scott* held—it was for jurisdictional purposes, but everybody in the country took it as a finding of a lack of status as far as Negroes were concerned in 1856.

----

[57]19 How. 393 (1857). The famous Dred Scott case declared that even if a Negro slave settled in free territory he was still a slave and could never attain the rights of United States citizenship.

JUSTICE FRANKFURTER: You could not be a citizen merely by going to Missouri.

MR. NABRIT: Yes, I agree with you, Mr. Justice Frankfurter, if you say that the Court went further than it should have or had to. But I would say this, that after the citizenship that was conferred under the first clause of the Fourteenth Amendment, and after the abolition of slavery, that we would seriously question, as this Court questioned, the power of the federal government to deal with a federal citizen solely on the basis of his race. The only two cases that I can recall in the history of this Court where it is held that they could be done were in two cases where the Court said that there was an express power to wage war, that that was one of the all-embracing powers, and that as an implied power necessary to prevent sabotage and espionage, this Court said, under those circumstances, that a citizen of the United States might, one, be detained in his home overnight, and the other, be removed to a relocation center and there detained.[58]

So this Court itself, even when it recognized the all-inclusiveness of the war power, when the security of the nation was at stake—this Court has said, "We must test this detention, first, to see if it is authorized and see if the statute authorizes it." If it is a case like *Ex parte Endo*,[59] or it is not authorized, it is not good. Even if it is authorized, there must be a relationship between the purpose and the statute, and when we find that, as the Court said, we are not satisfied. There must also be some purpose which it is within the competency of this Government to effect.

JUSTICE REED: Who is to determine that?

MR. NABRIT: This Court.

JUSTICE REED: And Congress cannot determine it for itself?

MR. NABRIT: No, sir. Never in the history of this country have the individual liberties of the citizen been entrusted in the hands of the legislators. The very founders of the Government refused to agree to the Constitution itself until they could be satisfied, Jefferson and others, that they had a Bill of Rights, so as to protect individual liberties.

JUSTICE REED: That would mean that we would examine the basis, the foundation of Congressional enactments relating to race, such as the Japanese cases?

MR. NABRIT: It is my position—

JUSTICE REED: Who is going to make that determination as to whether it is necessary or proper or desirable? This Court?

[58]Hirabayashi v. United States, *supra*, n. 56 and Korematsu v. United States, 323 U.S. 214 (1944), where the Court upheld the exclusion of all Japanese from a West Coast military area during World War II.

[59]323 U.S. 283 (1944). The Court interpreted the law under which Japanese were relocated on the West Coast as not permitting indefinite detention of loyal Japanese-Americans.

MR. NABRIT: I would say this, that this Court, faced with a piece of legislation by Congress which did that, or an act under a piece of legislation which did that, would in my opinion test it by the same type of test that it used in *Korematsu* and in *Hirabayashi* and in *Endo*. This Court tested it by that same method and found that it had no such authority and released Mitsye Endo. In other words, we ask nothing different than that we be given the same type of protection in peace that these Japanese were given in time of war. We are not asking anything different.

We are simply saying that liberty to us is just as precious, and that the same way in which the Court measures out liberty to others, it measures to us, and Congress itself has nothing to do with it, except that in the exercise of a power which Congress has, if Congress determines that it has something that it must do as an implied necessity in order to carry out that power, and then we say it does not and we bring the question to this Court, this Court would decide it.

I cannot make the statement that there is no situation in which Congress might not use race. I do not know of one right now, except the war powers. But that certainly leaves it open for determination by this Court.

But at the same time, I assert that there is absolutely no basis that can be produced that would be accepted in our country in 1952 that would justify Congress making it such a racial basis for the exclusion of a student from a high school in the District of Columbia.

JUSTICE REED: Would that same test apply on it for Congress under the commerce clause?

MR. NABRIT: Under the commerce clause?

JUSTICE REED: I just happened to choose that.

MR. NABRIT: I was trying to think of one under the commerce clause.

JUSTICE REED: Or any of the other clauses?

MR. NABRIT: Or any of the other clauses, where the only purpose was the purpose of making a racial distinction, in affording it.

For instance, if they say that no Negro can ride the trains, the answer is yes; it would apply precisely.

JUSTICE REED: Could we examine the reasonableness of that decision?

MR. NABRIT: Because you have said already, Mr. Justice Reed, or this Court, that as soon as we see that, we suspect it. It is not to say that it is unconstitutional, but it is to say that it is suspect, and you have said in so many cases, race is invidious; race is irrelevant. So when we get over in the federal government where there is nobody to deal with, but just us, the federal government, we do not have to worry. We know it is irrelevant, invidious, odious and suspect. So this Court should examine it.

(Whereupon, at 4:30 p.m., the Court arose.)

(Oral argument was resumed at 12:10 p.m., December 11, 1952.)

THE CHIEF JUSTICE: Number 413, Bolling, et al., versus C. Melvin Sharpe, et al.

Mr. Nabrit.

ARGUMENT ON BEHALF OF PETITIONERS—Resumed

by MR. NABRIT

MR. NABRIT: If it please the Court, at the close of the Court's session yesterday, we were attempting to outline the basic arguments of the petitioners. Unfortunately, we only have ten minutes left, and probably we can barely outline it.

We would like to address ourselves, however, to some of the questions which seem to be of concern to the Court in these cases.

JUSTICE FRANKFURTER: Before you sit down, I hope you will include in your answers the answer to this question, whether during the life of this statute there came before Congress periodically or at such periods as there did come, if any, the requirement to make appropriations for the enforcement of this statute, or, since you question whether they had the duty to enforce it the way they did, for the things that the District authorities did, and whether during that period there was any legislative effort to stop these appropriations or to prohibit the authorities from doing what I understand you and your colleagues said was not authorized by this legislation.

MR. NABRIT: I would be very happy to address myself to that at this moment, Mr. Justice Frankfurter.

In looking at these statutes enacted by Congress governing the schools in the District, I should like to preface my answer by saying that the first statute passed with respect to public education in the District of Columbia was passed in 1862.

Now, at the time petitioners drafted their briefs in support of our proposition, we had taken the position that the statutes did require it, and we did set out the history. However, if the Court is interested in the history, there is in the brief filed in this case amicus curiae for the eighteen organizations, on pages 20 and 21, some historical analysis of these statutes, which may be of help to the Court.

The Court may also take judicial notice of the Barnard Report, which is in the special report of the Commissioner of Education of the Public Schools of the District of Columbia in 1871, and in that volume at page 49 and page 267, they give the history of the public schools of the District of Columbia up to that time, and they also discuss the Act of 1864, to which I shall advert in just a moment.

JUSTICE FRANKFURTER: Is that report referred to in your brief or in the amici brief?

MR. NABRIT: No.

JUSTICE FRANKFURTER: What is the name of that report?

MR. NABRIT: The District of Columbia, the Barnard Special Report, Commissioner of Education on the Public Schools in the District of Columbia, 1871.

JUSTICE FRANKFURTER: Thank you.

MR. NABRIT: That is the Government Printing Office. It does not give any other name. It is the House of Representatives.

Now, if the Court please, in 1862, this was the situation in the District of Columbia. There were a number of private schools for whites and a number of private schools for Negroes in Georgetown, Washington, and the District of Columbia. As you recall, we had not yet combined all of those into what is now the District. But for purposes of this discussion I think that the Court may take those as one.

At that time, these private schools were supported by private philanthropy. In 1862, Congress, as discussions in Congress indicated—about that there is no dispute—being concerned about the support of the schools which existed in the District for the Negroes, enacted a measure which provided that these schools should be supported by tax funds derived from taxes levied upon free Negroes.

That did not appear either to produce revenue or to be satisfactory. So Congress then enacted a statute the latter part of that year in which Congress said that these schools should be supported by funds derived from the general revenue, that is, from the taxes of all of the inhabitants of the District.

Now, this, as you recall, was in 1862, before the Fourteenth Amendment and before the actual effect of the Emancipation Proclamation.

Now, at this time, the members of the legislature stated that they were concerned about what should be done for the Negroes who would be free. I think it is also fair to say to the Court that in the Barnard Report, to which I referred, the Congressmen, in presenting this to the House, and stating that there had been no printed report of the proceedings, stated that they were providing no separate schools for Negroes because they had no adequate financial support, and they were concerned about the educational situation.

In 1864, the basic acts out of which grow the present acts governing the schools in the District of Columbia were enacted. They provided in substance that suitable rooms and schools should be provided for the training of the colored pupils, and in addition to that they provided mandatory legislation to ensure that a proportionate share of the funds secured from revenue in the District should be allotted to these schools.

I might say to the Court that they did this because experience had shown that there was some diversion of funds that Congress had intended for these schools to the white schools.

Now, all of this is uncontroverted. There is no dispute about this.

Then, after the proposal of the Fourteenth Amendment in 1866, and after its adoption in 1868, there was, in 1874, a re-enactment of these statutes, in substance as they are found in our brief.

Now, it appears to petitioners that it is the contention of the respondents that that re-enactment after the adoption of the Fourteenth Amendment was a congressional construction of these acts that they permitted separate schools, and I think that it was the issue which underlies the question of Mr. Justice Frankfurter, as to re-enactment of these statutes and as to the appropriations in respect to these acts over all these years.

THE CHIEF JUSTICE: Do I understand that the schools were separate prior to the adoption of the Fourteenth Amendment?

MR. NABRIT: Yes, sir, they were.

THE CHIEF JUSTICE: And at one time they taxed property separately; they taxed colored property for the maintenance of colored schools and white property for the maintenance of white schools?

MR. NABRIT: No. They did not say anything about the white schools. I should say this—

THE CHIEF JUSTICE: The white schools were run out of general revenues?

MR. NABRIT: I presume so. I did not find that phrase. But I would answer your question by saying that they must have been supported out of the general revenue, since this special provision was made.

But I should say this, Mr. Chief Justice. At this time, public education—this is the first public education attempt in the District of Columbia—public education itself was suspect in the country, especially with these compulsory features that were attached to it, so that the least we can say is that at the beginning of public education, Congress indicated before the Fourteenth Amendment, by its support to these separate schools, that at that time separate schools existed, and could exist.

THE CHIEF JUSTICE: And in the District of Columbia, they did exist at the time of the passage and the adoption of the Fourteenth Amendment?

MR. NABRIT: That is correct.

Now, it is the petitioners' position at that stage in the history of these statutes that prior to the adoption of the Fourteenth Amendment, respondents can get no support from whatever Congress did with these schools; that they must gain their support by reason of the action of Congress thereafter. I think they joined in that position. It is therefore the position of petitioners that the action of Congress in 1874, in re-enacting these statutes, is not persuasive on this Court as to whether or not either (1) Congress intended compulsory or authorized segregation in the District, or (2) whether that is constitutional.

THE CHIEF JUSTICE: Mr. Nabrit, in view of the questions from the bench, you may have five minutes' more time, and the District may have similar time.

MR. NABRIT: Thank you.
As to the re-enactment of these statutes—

JUSTICE FRANKFURTER: I did not mean to divert you on any legal implication. I wanted to know what the facts were, whether from year to year appropriations had to be made, or whether the question was raised, and whether it got through without anybody's thinking about it.

MR. NABRIT: Yes, sir. I wanted to address myself to that, but I thought you were entitled to have some background for it.

Now, specifically addressing myself—

JUSTICE REED: Apparently there is no reference in the briefs to legislative history. Was there a discussion of the desirability or the undesirability of segregation in 1874?

MR. NABRIT: I do not know about 1874, but there was a discussion of it prior to 1874, in 1866 and 1864.

JUSTICE REED: Was it directed toward the adoption of segregation?

MR. NABRIT: That is right. And there was considerable difference of opinion among the Negroes in the District of Columbia on that question.

JUSTICE REED: I meant on the floor of the Congress.

MR. NABRIT: It was not printed, you see. So we just have to suppose that there was some discussion. I would say for the purpose of the Court, it might be assumed that there was discussions. But it was not printed.

THE CHIEF JUSTICE: But that was prior to the adoption of the Amendment?

MR. NABRIT: That is right. And we take the position that on this particular problem, it is not persuasive to the Court.

Now, as to your specific question, Mr. Justice Frankfurter, there have been acts in support of these schools, appropriation acts, directed to the support of this separate system in the District of Columbia each year, and also in 1906 a group of citizens went before Congress to urge in the appropriation bill the adoption of more powers for the then assistant Negro superintendent.

Also, subsequent to that, there was agitation for the creation of another first assistant superintendent for the white schools and for the Negro schools, and in each of those two instances, Congress provided the money and the position, and as to the first assistant, white and colored, they wrote that into the legislation, in addition to the appropriation.

Now, as to whether or not—

JUSTICE FRANKFURTER: You say they wrote into the legislation that there was to be an assistant, or deputy, superintendent for colored schools and for white schools?

MR. NABRIT: Precisely, in language as clear as that.

JUSTICE FRANKFURTER: That goes back to when, you say? 1906?

MR. NABRIT: Nineteen hundred six was when they enlarged the powers. This last act, I believe, was in 1947. I mean, this first assistant.

JUSTICE FRANKFURTER: But it was in 1906 that there was explicit legislative recognition that there is such a person as a superintendent for colored schools?

MR. NABRIT: This is correct.

There is no question so far as petitioners are concerned that that type of language has persisted in the District of Columbia. And as to the enforcement, there is no question about it, the Congress has done it.

It is petitioners' position (1) that there is nothing in this language that anybody can find that compels segregation. This is clear. There is language which may be said to permit it, or authorize it. About that, men may differ. Some may think that the differences are unreasonable, in view of the language. It is petitioners' position that it does not authorize it. But if it does authorize it, to the extent that it is implemented by these respondents, it is unconstitutional action on the part of respondents.

JUSTICE FRANKFURTER: You would say that providing whatever it is, X thousand dollars' salary, for an assistant superintendent for Negro schools is merely a provision that if there are to be Negro schools, and if there is to be the assistant superintendent, he is to get $6,000; is that it?

MR. NABRIT: I would go further than that. I would say, since there is in the District of Columbia a system of Negro schools—I mean, I would recognize the fact that they are.

JUSTICE FRANKFURTER: If you say that—

MR. NABRIT: I would.

JUSTICE FRANKFURTER: I wonder if you are not saying, since there is, and Congress appropriated for it, that it recognized the right, at least, under the statute, that there should be Negro schools?

MR. NABRIT: Now, the reason I do not say that, Mr. Justice Frankfurter, is that the language of this Court in *Ex parte Endo,* when they said that wherever there is implied legislation which restricts the individual, or curtails, to use the Court's language, the individual rights of citizens, that curtailment has to be explicitly stated in clear and unmistakable language.

JUSTICE FRANKFURTER: It does not touch on a constitutional point.

MR. NABRIT: Yes.

JUSTICE FRANKFURTER: I wonder if it does not carry permissiveness into a clear recognition by Congress here in the situation where they provide money, because the alternative is that Congress was providing money for something that they did not authorize.

MR. NABRIT: I would say yes, and I would say that that would not change petitioners' position. In other words, I agree to that.

Now, with this other principle, I want to say—

JUSTICE FRANKFURTER: In the course of these years, was there opposition to this legislation, or were there voices raised to the Congress, or objections to this? Did the issue ever come to discussion or to challenge?

MR. NABRIT: As to whether or not this system should be changed?

JUSTICE FRANKFURTER: Yes.

MR. NABRIT: In the early years—

JUSTICE FRANKFURTER: I am not meaning to draw any inference. I just want the facts.

MR. NABRIT: In the early years, there was such discussion. And I am also of the opinion that we may, on an exhaustive study of that question, find such language even later, and it is petitioners' position that, as this Court has said, Congress does not enact statutes, or does not deal with things in many instances for political or other reasons, so that petitioners would not consider that persuasive.

Now, I would like to say this final thing before my time runs out, that if the Court disagrees with us, which it may, and says that these statutes compelled and authorized, and therefore this action may be constitutional, we urge the Court not to do it, because, as this Court has said, where a possible interpretation might lead into the danger of declaring a statute unconstitutional, the Court will avoid that construction.

It is our opinion that if you do hold that these statutes compelled and authorized, they would then be unconstitutional under the due process clause of the Fifth Amendment, but more than that, we suggest to the Court that they would be in violation of Article I, section 9, clause 3, as bills of attainder, not under the classical concept of a bill of attainder, but under the concept of a bill of attainder as enunciated by this Court in *United States* v. *Lovett*,[60] and it would appear to us that denial of admission solely on the basis of race or color of petitioners to Sousa fits precisely the formula set forth by this Court in *United States* v. *Lovett*.

Now, if I have time, I will explain it. That is, in *United States* v. *Lovett*, this Court said that where Congress had named Lovett and two others in an appropriation bill and said that they should not receive funds from that until they had been recommended by the President and approved by Congress, that that was a permanent ban on employment. This Court went to the congressional discussion to find out whether they were trying to get them for disloyalty and subversive activities.

Now, we say that if this Court decides that these statutes prohibit Negroes from ever associating with whites or ever studying with whites in a white school, they have placed the same ban upon them, and they have done it without a trial, as in the other, merely because for some undisclosed crime, some status, some position, some matter of birth, appropriation, or something else in the past, these Negroes are unfit to associate with whites, and under the definition of a bill of attainder as laid down by this Court in *United States* v. *Lovett*, we suggest that there would be another danger that these acts would be unconstitutional.

Therefore, we urge upon this Court not to adopt that construction, and we

[60]328 U.S. 303 (1946). A law forbidding the payment of compensation to certain named government employees charged with subversive activities was held to be an unconstitutional bill of attainder.

say this to the Court: You would not reach the constitutionality, because if you find these statutes do not require it and do not authorize it, then the action of respondents is unlawful, and you may direct admission into Sousa Junior High School.

THE CHIEF JUSTICE: Mr. Korman.

ARGUMENT ON BEHALF OF RESPONDENTS

by MR. KORMAN

MR. KORMAN: May it please the Court, questions have been asked by the Court concerning the history of this legislation, and my distinguished opponent, Mr. Hayes, has thrown the gauntlet down to us to show the real reason for this type of legislation setting up a dual school system in the District of Columbia.

I shall endeavor to point out to the Court the history of this legislation, and I accept the challenge of Mr. Hayes to show what the real reason for this legislation was.

In 1862, there was slavery in the District of Columbia. In April of 1862, by an Act of April 16, the Congress abolished slavery in the District. That was three and one-half years before the Thirteenth Amendment abolished it in the States.

There was a problem of doing something for these emancipated people. Up to that point, they had had no schools except some few private schools for the free Negroes.

So the first enactment of Congress on May 20, 1862, was to set up a system of schools in the County of Washington. At that time, the District of Columbia consisted of three parts: the City of Georgetown, the City of Washington, and the County of Washington. They were distinct entities.

The City of Georgetown had its own council, mayor, and board of aldermen; the City of Washington had the same setup; the county was governed by a levy court.

It appears that there were no schools of any kind, white or colored, in the county. There apparently were schools for white children, publicly supported, in the cities.

On May 20, 1862, the Congress passed an enactment which established a system of schools in the county, white and colored. It was a long act, with some thirty-six sections to it, and in section 35 they provided that the levy court in its discretion—apparently there were not many Negroes in the county at that time—but the levy court in its discretion might levy a tax of 1/8 of 1 per cent on property owned by persons of color for the purpose of initiating a system of education of colored children in said county.

But I remind you that in that same act, they set up for the first time a system of white schools in the county. Now, in that same paragraph 35, they said this:

And said trustees are authorized to receive any donations or contributions that may be made for the benefit of said schools —

that is, the schools for colored children—

by persons disposed to aid in the elevation of the colored population in the District of Columbia.

That was the purpose of these acts, to aid in the elevation of the colored population of the District of Columbia, and not to stamp them, as Mr. Hayes says, with a badge of inferiority, this pure racism that he speaks of.

They were trying to elevate these people.

It goes on to say that:

Said trustees shall account for those funds.

Then the next day, May 21, the Congress passed another act for the Cities of Washington and Georgetown, and with your permission I should like to read that entire act, which is not lengthy, because to me it shows what the purpose of this legislation was:

BE IT ENACTED, [and so forth]
That from and after the passage of this Act it shall be the duty of the municipal authorities of the Cities of Washington and Georgetown in the District of Columbia to set apart ten per-centum of the amount received from taxes levied on the real and personal property in said Cities owned by persons of color, which sum received from taxes as aforesaid shall be appropriated for the purpose of initiating a system of primary schools for the education of colored children residing in said Cities.
BE IT FURTHER ENACTED that the board of trustees of the public schools in said Cities shall have sole control of the fund arising from the tax aforesaid as well as from contributions by persons disposed to aid in the education of the colored race, or from any other source which shall be kept as a distinct fund from the general school fund.

which I believe answers Mr. Justice Frankfurter's question.

It is made their duty to provide suitable rooms and teachers for the number of schools as in their opinion will best accommodate the colored children in the various portions of said Cities.

Section 3 deals with the setting up of boards of trustees, which says that they shall have equal supervision over both the white and colored schools.

Section 4—this is the same Act, I remind Your Honors—

That all persons of color in the District of Columbia or in the corporate limits of the Cities of Washington and Georgetown shall be subject and amenable to the same laws and ordinances to which free white persons are or may be subject or amenable; that they shall be tried for any offenses against the laws in the same manner as free white persons are or may be tried for the same offenses, and that upon being legally convicted of any crime or offense against any law or ordinance, such persons of color shall be liable to the same penalty or punishment, and no other, as would be imposed on or inflicted upon white persons for the same crime or offense and all acts or parts of acts inconsistent with the provisions of this Act are hereby repealed.

Now, when we find those provisions in the same Act setting up schools for colored children and saying that they may receive funds from those who may want to help the colored race, and setting up these provisions for equal treatment of both races before the law, there can be no question of what the intention of the Congress was at that time.

On July 11, 1862, a few months later, Congress transferred to the board of trustees of the schools for colored children—of the schools for colored children—thereby created the powers with respect to such schools vested by the Act of May 21 in the board of trustees for public schools in the cities.

By an Act of June 25, 1864, Congress established the Board of Commissioners of Primary Schools of Washington County, District of Columbia, and in section 9 thereof authorized that Board to purchase sites, erect schools, regulate the number of children to be taught in each school, and the price of tuition, and so on, and said this:

> That any white resident might place his or her child in the schools provided for the education of white children in said county, and any colored resident should have the same rights with respect to the colored schools.

It seems to me that that definitely established an intent to set up separate schools.

Then in the Act of May 21, 1862, in section 18 of that Act, they authorized the municipal authorities of the Cities of Washington and Georgetown to set apart each year from the whole fund received from all sources applicable to public education such proportionate part thereof as the number of colored children between the ages of sixteen and seventeen in the respective cities bears to the total number of children to help support these colored schools.

Then in 1871, the Congress enacted the Legislative Assembly Act, which combined the Cities of Washington and Georgetown and the county into one unit, and they transferred all these schools to the combined board of education which governed all of the schools in the two cities and the county.

A question was asked by Mr. Justice Frankfurter, I believe, as to whether or not there were any specific attacks upon this system of separate schools, and it was intimated that while there were some before the adoption of the Fourteenth Amendment, there were none thereafter.

I specifically call the Court's attention to the fact, which is mentioned in our brief, that in the 41st, 42nd, and 43rd Congresses, between 1870 and 1874, there were three separate bills introduced by Senator Sumner of Massachusetts to strike down the dual school system in the District of Columbia, and they all failed of passage.

The Fourteenth Amendment was adopted in 1868, and all three of these things came after that.

Specifically, I call the Court's attention to the fact that the Civil Rights Act of 1875 was debated over a considerable period during the 42nd and 43rd Congresses, although that Act is not now constitutional, having been so declared on other grounds. But the bill which became the Civil Rights Act of 1875, as originally drawn, specifically provided for the abolition of separation in the schools of the United States, in and out of the District of Columbia, but as finally enacted, the word "schools" was stricken from that Act.

So it seems to me that as late as 1875, you have a specific declaration by Congress that there shall be a dual school system in the District of Columbia.

Now, what transpired thereafter? In 1900, Congress set up a new school board, a paid school board, of seven persons, and they provided at that time for a board of education, a superintendent, and two assistant superintendents, one of whom under the direction of the superintendent shall have charge of the schools for colored children.

That was the Act of June 6, 1900.

Then, in 1906, the Congress reorganized the whole school system here, and they established the present Board of Education as it exists today. The organic Act of 1906 was debated at some length, and there were lengthy hearings on that before a subcommittee of the Congress.

In our brief, I set forth some of the expressions of Negro leaders at that time, and I should ask the Court to please bear with me while I read some of them to you, because it seems to me that they go to the very heart of this question.

We find Professor William A. Joiner—

JUSTICE REED: What page is that?

MR. KORMAN: This is on page 25 of respondents' brief.

We find Professor William A. Joiner, of Howard University, addressing the committee, and I did not include the letter which he had presented to the committee, but I should like to read you one sentence from the letter, which he handed to the committee prior to making this statement. He says this, and this is found on page 199 of the hearings on that bill:

Experience in the past dating back to the first organization of the schools for colored children in the District has tended to prove that the interests of these schools are most carefully guarded by those who are most deeply interested in the children who attend them.

Then he said this:

I think, Mr. Chairman, that that embodies the main sentiment as expressed by that organization, an organization composed of those whose minds have led them into literary pursuits and those who have given attention to the best welfare and interest of their people. It may seem strange that this particular word 'colored' or the idea of colored schools thrusts itself into this argument. I would it were not so. Facts are stubborn things, and when we deal with facts we must deal with them as they exist and not as we would they were; and so, Mr. Chairman, it becomes our province and our duty to do what we can to see that in the administration of school affairs in that most precious birthright of equality of opportunity spoken to us by President Eliot (of Harvard) that there will not be the slightest divergence from the division, 'unto him who needs and most unto him who needs most.'

Then Professor Lewis B. Moore, of Howard University, said this at the same hearings, and I am reading from page 26 of our brief:

Give us what is being asked for here by the colored citizens, give us that, and we shall conduct under the guidance of the Board of Education the colored schools of the District of Columbia in such a way as to produce just as good results as are produced anywhere else in this country.

As the result of those sorts of expressions, we find this in the report on the bill, which became the Act of 1906 setting up the school board: The bill does not change the number of assistant superintendents, merely enlarging the power of the colored superintendent so that he shall, besides having jurisdiction over the colored grade schools, also have entire jurisdiction over the colored normal, high, and manual-training schools. This was done at the earnest solicitation of the colored educators who appeared before the committee and was heartily endorsed by the superintendent of Howard University. The hearings developed that a great deal of friction had arisen between the director of high schools and the teachers in the colored high school, and to avoid this it was the unanimous opinion and desire of all who testified that not only should the colored superintendent have control, but that the colored schools in every instance should be designated as colored schools, so that no possible mistake could arise in that regard.

So in the Act of 1906, the Congress provided for a superintendent of schools and for two assistant superintendents of schools, one of whom, a colored man, should have charge of the colored schools.

That is not, however, the last expression by the Congress upon this point. As has been intimated, every year for practically ninety years there have been applications to the Congress for funds to operate these schools, and every year the justification for the appropriations has contained statements that so much is needed for colored schools, so much is needed for colored teachers, so much is needed for white schools, so much is needed for white teachers, so much is needed for new construction because the colored population has increased and we need another colored school, and so forth, and so forth.

In addition, in the Teachers' Salary Act of 1945, we find these expressions by the Congress:

There shall be two first assistant superintendents of schools

—they are now first assistant superintendents—

one white first assistant superintendent for the white schools, who under the direction of the superintendent of schools shall have general supervision over the white schools, and one colored first assistant superintendent for the colored schools who under the direction of the superintendent of schools shall have sole charge of all employees, classes, and schools in which colored children are taught

—not the colored schools, but the schools, classes, and employees under which colored children are taught.

The next section of that Act is:

Boards of examiners for carrying out the provisions of the statutes with reference to the examination of teachers shall consist of the superintendent of schools and not less than four or more than six members of the supervisory or teaching staff of the white schools for the white schools, and of the superintendent of schools and not less than four nor more than six members of the supervisory or teaching staff of the colored schools for the colored schools.

Then in the next section:

There shall be appointed a board of education on the recommendation of the superintendent of schools, a chief examiner for the board of examiners for white schools, and an associate superintendent in the colored schools shall be designated by the superintendent as chief examiner for the board of examiners for the colored schools.

and so on, almost identical language in the Teachers' Salary Act of 1947, two years later, and the latest expression by the Congress on that score was the Act of October 24, 1951, amending the Teachers' Salary Act, where we find in section 13—and this was one year ago, if the Court please:

is court was not created by the Constitution for such purposes. Higher and graver
sts have been confided to it, and it must not falter in the path of duty.

That, Your Honors, was from *Dred Scott* v. *Sandford,* oh, almost one
red years ago.

But it is equally applicable today.

They speak there of the civilized nations and how we look to them, just as my
ls say to us here today that we must be careful; as the Attorney General says,
ust be careful because the Iron Curtain countries talk about us. But he
ts that they tell some lies about us. Would the change in this system stop
from telling lies if they want to tell them?

As regards the question of the applicability of the Fifth Amendment, even the
ney General concedes that it raises a grave constitutional question when we
Does the Fifth Amendment control the situation?"

o some extent, I am indebted to the Attorney General for some of the things
s said in his brief amicus curiae. He speaks of "vexing problems which may
n eliminating segregation," and he suggests to the Court that if you should
to the point where you should strike down separate schools in the United
, then you should do it gradually over a period, which he suggests as much
en years, class-by-class, starting in the kindergarten and going on up.

Vhy? Because I say to the Court, he recognizes that "vexing problems would
n many places."

efore I leave the Fifth Amendment, there was a suggestion by Mr. Justice
n that there might be effect upon the Indians if this Court should hold that
te schools may not be maintained under the Fifth Amendment. And I sug-
at there are whole chapters of the United States Code which are entitled
ction of the Indians," and under which Congress has legislated especially
m, because it is recognized that there is a people that needs protection. You
an go out and buy a bottle of liquor if we want. The Indian cannot, nowhere
United States. And he is a citizen. Why? Because it is recognized that it is
d for him, and he needs protection.

at assumes, I know, that it is good for us.

JSTICE JACKSON: I live very close to the Seneca Reservation, in New
nd I would just as soon deal with a drunken Indian as with a drunken white
yself, under modern conditions. It may have been different in the days of
knives.

R. KORMAN: Possibly so.

STICE DOUGLAS: Referring to the educational system in the part of
ntry I come from, the Indians are not barred from the public schools, but
ols on the reservations are open only to Indians, and the white man would
d from those schools.

R. KORMAN: That is quite a different problem, Mr. Justice. In anticipa-
that question, I talked to representative of the Indian Bureau, and I was
them that there are some 230 schools on reservations which are restricted
ns, and there are nineteen schools off reservations which are restricted to

There shall be appointed by the Board of Education on the recommendation of the
superintendent of schools a chief examiner for the board of examiners for white
schools and a chief examiner for the board of examiners for colored schools. All
members of the respective boards of examiners shall serve without additional compensation.

It seems to me that that should dispose of this question of whether or not
Congress intended that there should be separate schools for white and colored
children.

In addition, however, twice in the history of these acts, the United States
Court of Appeals for the District of Columbia Circuit has passed upon the question. In the case of *Wall* v. *Oyster,*[61] in 1910, the court specifically said that these
acts of 1862 and 1864, and so on, that I read to the Court, and which were carried
over into the revised statutes in 1874—the court said that they "manifest an intention by Congress that these schools shall be separate.

In the case of *Carr* v. *Corning,* and *Browne* v. *Magdeburger,* decided on a
joint opinion in 1950,[62] the court came to exactly the same conclusion, the court
saying:

These various enactments by the Congress cannot be read with any meaning except
that the schools for white and colored children were then intended to be separate.

Now, in the light of those decisions by the highest court of the District of
Columbia—and I remind the Court that this Court has said many times that it
accepts the construction of purely locally applicable statutes as decided by the
highest court of the jurisdiction—in the case of the states, the interpretation by
the highest court of the state is, it has been said, completely binding on this
Court, and in the case of the Court of Appeals of the District of Columbia, this
Court has said several times that in most instances, and generally, you accept the
interpretation of that court of locally applicable statutes.

I might read to you further from the expressions of leaders at the time the bill
which became the Act of 1906 was being considered. There were expressions by
Dr. Kelly Miller, one of the leaders of his people in this city, one of the foremost
fighters for rights for the colored people. Indeed, one of the newest junior high
schools for colored in the District is named after him, and he says essentially the
same things that I have read to Your Honors in support of that Act of 1906.

What, then, is the situation? I say to the Court, and I say to my distinguished
adversary, Mr. Hayes, these acts were not passed, this dual school system was not
set up to stamp these people with a badge of inferiority. There was not this racial
feeling that he speaks of with such fervor behind these acts. There was behind
these acts a kindly feeling; there was behind these acts an intention to help these
people who had been in bondage. And there was and there still is an intention by
the Congress to see that these children shall be educated in a healthful atmosphere, in a wholesome atmosphere, in a place where they are wanted, in a place
where they will not be looked upon with hostility, in a place where there will

[61]36 App. D.C. 60.
[62]See n. 36, *supra.*

be a receptive atmosphere for learning for both races without the hostility that undoubtedly Congress thought might creep into these situations.

We cannot hide our faces and our minds from the fact that there is feeling between races in these United States. It is a deplorable situation. Would that it were not so. But we must face these facts.

We know that there have been outbursts between races north of here where there are not separate schools for white and colored. We know that these things exist, and constitutionally, if there be a question as to which is better, to throw these people together into the schools and perhaps bring that hostile atmosphere, if it exists, into the schoolroom and harm the ability to learn of both the races, or to give them completely adequate, separate, full educational opportunities on both sides, where they will be instructed on the white side by white teachers, who are sympathetic to them, and on the colored side by colored teachers, who are sympathetic to them, and where they will receive from the lips of their own people education in colored folklore, which is important to a people—if that is to be decided, who else shall decide it but the legislature, who decides things for each jurisdiction?

And I say that the Constitution does not inveigh against such a determination by the legislature.

The Fifth Amendment contains a due process clause, as does the Fourteenth Amendment. It does not, however, contain an equal protection clause. It has been said by this Court that the Congress is not bound not to pass discriminatory laws. It can pass discriminatory laws, because there is no equal protection clause in the Fifth Amendment. This Court has likewise over a long period of time, some ninety years, said that under the Fourteenth Amendment separate schools for white and colored children may be retained.

If, therefore, this Court has said that such schools may be maintained under the Fourteenth Amendment where there is an equal protection clause, how can my friends here argue to the Court that there may not be a dual school system in the District of Columbia for such fine reasons as I have demonstrated to the Court, when there is no equal protection clause binding on the Congress of the United States?

And if there be questions concerning the long line of decisions leading up to this point where this Court has said that separation in schools is proper and constitutional, there can be no clearer statement than there was in the case of *Gaines* v. *Canada,* decided scarcely fourteen years ago, where this Court said, through Mr. Chief Justice Hughes:

The state has sought to fulfill that obligation by furnishing equal facilities in separate schools, a method the validity of which has been sustained by our decisions.

That was the language, "a method the validity of which has been sustained by our decisions."

But then they went on to say that you cannot do it in this case because those equal facilities have to be within the borders of the state and not outside the state.

That is all that case said. But it established the principle that if there were separate but equal facilities within the state, then it was constitutional. And I say to the Court that it is conceded here by my distinguished opponents that there is no question of equality here.

You live here in the District of Columbia or in its have a complete system of schools here. I invite your a so complete that we have two side-by-side complete s and colored, autonomous each in every respect, with tendent over them and a board of education laying d tems. But from the janitor up to the first assistant schools are completely autonomous, and if we need a they turn out, I will turn to my friend here, a product c

What has changed the Constitution in fourteen What changes have occurred? What policy announce Congress?

Questions were directed to counsel all throug conditions. Mr. Justice Burton asked counsel if it v cases could be disposed of as being proper law at th not now in the light of changed conditions.

I ask the rhetorical question, What changed c in fourteen years that we did not know in 1938 wher What is there now?

I submit to the Court that the answer is, noth the same today as it was in 1938 at the time all th the lips of this Court.

It has been said here by our distinguished op by the Attorney General of the United States th Columbia in which we live, is the window through It does not seem to me that is a constitutional argu something to the Court, if I may, with the Court this Court. After I have read it, I will tell you the c

No one, we presume, supposes that any change in tion to this unfortunate race, in the civilized natio should induce the court to give to the words of the struction in their favor than they were intended t framed and adopted.

—or, if I may paraphrase by saying, that they we each amendment of it—

Such an argument would be altogether inadmissibl pret it. If any of its provisions are deemed unjust, instrument itself by which it may be amended; but be construed now as it was understood at the time c

—or, if I may paraphrase, at the time of its amer

It is not only the same in words, but the same ir powers to the Government and reserves and secur the citizen; and as long as it continues to exist in in the same words but with the same meaning and came from the hands of its framers, and was voted United States. Any other rule of construction wo of this court and make it the mere reflex of the po

JUSTICE DOUGLAS: That merely keeps the white man out. The public school systems of the West, at least, are open to Indians.

MR. KORMAN: That may be. But that is a state proposition, left up to the states in the individual case. If the states want to let them in and think that it will not cause a problem, that is up to the legislation of the states.

JUSTICE DOUGLAS: Some of these cases are state questions.

MR. KORMAN: Perhaps.

JUSTICE DOUGLAS: Not yours?

MR. KORMAN: Perhaps.
I call your attention to the fact that there is separation, I have learned, by sexes in many of the large cities of the country, not in all the schools, apparently, but in some, perhaps for some special reason. I find from the National Education Association that they have separate schools for the sexes in San Francisco, Louisville, New Orleans, Baltimore, Boston, Elizabeth, Buffalo, New York City, even, Cleveland, Portland, Philadelphia. Such cities as those separate by sexes. Those are the things which are left to the decision of the decision of the legislature, the competent authority in each case to decide what is best for that community.

Of course, this Court has said many times that it is not concerned with the wisdom of legislation or the policy except as it is expressed in acts of Congress.

Mention has been made that there is violation of the Civil Rights Act. The two sections of the Civil Rights Act that are set forth in the complaint and in the brief for the appellants are sections 41 and 43, and in the case which first had to deal with that, a case for Indiana, the Court reviewed the Civil Rights statute at some length, and said, after reading the language of the statute:

In this, nothing is left to inference. Every right intended is specified.[62a]

The Court of Appeals of the District of Columbia, in *Carr* v. *Corning,* came to exactly the same conclusion.

I should like to point out with reference to the Civil Rights Act that Mr. Justice Vinson in the case of *Hurd* v. *Hodge,*[63] pointed out the fact that the Civil Rights Act of 1866, as amended in 1870, was passed by the same Congress that submitted the Fourteenth Amendment to the States, and that that same Congress, as was pointed out in *Carr* v. *Corning,* as I pointed out to the Court earlier—that same Congress is the one which passed some of these laws setting up separate schools in the District of Columbia for the two races.

How, then, can it be said that the contemporaneous thought on this by the people who made these enactments had any idea that schools were to be included in the Civil Rights Act.

In *Hurd* v. *Hodge,* there was another section of the Civil Rights Act involved, section 42 of Title 8 of the United States Code, [now 42 U.S.C., section 1982] and

[62a] Cory v. Carter, 48 Ind. 327 (1874).

[63] 334 U.S. 24 (1948). Enforcement of restrictive covenants in the District of Columbia was forbidden under a provision of the Civil Rights Act of 1866.

that dealt only with the right to hold and own real property and to transfer it and lease it and contract for it, and so on. That has no bearing on the question of the right to integrate the schools in the District of Columbia.

My distinguished opponents have taken a different tack here than they have in their brief and than they took in their petition and in the argument in the District Court with regard to the provisions of the United Nations Charter. In their petition and in their brief they have said that these laws violate the provisions of the United Nations Charter. Apparently they recede from that position now, and they say only that the United Nations Charter expresses the policy of the United States. If it expresses the policy of the United States, it expresses the policy of the United States to enact legislation upon a particular subject, and that is all that it expresses.

It has been demonstrated rather clearly that the United Nations Charter is not a self-executing treaty. It is a non-self-executing treaty which must be implemented by Acts of Congress.

In Article 55 of the Charter it is said:

With a view to the creation of conditions of stability and well-being which are necessary for peaceful and friendly relations among nations based on respect for the principle of equal rights and self-determination of peoples, the United Nations shall promote:
A. higher standards of living, full employment, and conditions of economic and social progress and development;
B. solutions of international economic, social, health, and related problems; and international cultural and educational cooperation; and
C. universal respect for, and observance of, human rights and fundamental freedoms for all with distinction as to race, sex, language, or religion.

All that we say in there is that we pledge ourselves in future legislation to keep these things in mind. And as set forth in our brief, the framers of that Article 55 intended only that it was to give to the rest of the world those constitutional rights which we have here in America and which they are denied. That was the purpose of it. That was the purpose expressed to the Senate of the United States when they presented this charter to them for ratification. That was the purpose expressed to the President of the United States in the report on the charter as it came out of San Francisco.

What is the meaning of "human rights and fundamental freedoms"? It is not defined in the charter anywhere. "Fundamental freedom" is not defined. No one knows what it means. There has been set up a separate organization, an organization which I think is called the Council on Human Rights, which has attempted to define that term, but it has been stated specifically by Mrs. Roosevelt, who heads that, that that has no binding effect even on the General Assembly of the United Nations, much less on the signatory powers.

We bar people into this country on grounds of polygamy. Polygamy is a fundamental right and freedom in some nations. How can these things be justified together?

They cannot be.

My distinguished friend, Mr. Nabrit, has said that these laws constitute a bill of attainder. As I read the law of a bill of attainder, I shall give the definition as it comes from the leading case in the United States, *Cummings* against *Missouri,* 4 Wall. 277. At page 323 of that opinion, the court said:

> A bill of attainder is a legislative act, which inflicts punishment without a judicial trial. If the punishment be less than death, the act is termed a bill of pains and penalties. Within the meaning of the Constitution, bills of attainder include bills of pains and penalties. In these cases the legislative body, in addition to its legitimate functions, exercises the powers and office of judge; it assumes, in the language of the textbooks, judicial magistracy; it pronounces upon the guilt of the party, without any of the form or safeguards of trial; it determines the sufficiency of the proofs produced, whether conformable to the rules of evidence or otherwise; and it fixes the degree of punishment in accordance with its own notions of the enormity of the offense.

This Court has said that when it speaks of punishment, it may mean deprivation of rights, but it mean deprivation of rights, civil or political, previously enjoyed which may be punishment.

These people have never enjoyed anything which has been taken away from them. These laws which set up these schools for them were to give them something, and not to take something away from them. These laws which set up the dual school system in the District of Columbia are not to take anything from my friends and they are not to take anything from the white children. They are set up so that there will be schools which have an atmosphere wholesome to the reception of education by both races. That is the only thing that Congress has said is right for them in the District of Columbia.

They attempt to twist this word "punishment" in some way to say that they have punishment inflicted upon them by being required to go to schools to which white children are not admitted and by being denied the right to go to schools in which white children are taught.

I cannot really get their reasoning. Before that, they cite some of these sociologists, some of these psychologists that have been mentioned in earlier arguments. In this brief, I have set forth a list of publications, monographs, psychological treatises, and what-not that oppose the views of the psychologists that have been named by my friends and by those in other cases.

I do not say that either one or the other is right. I take no position on that. I do not know. I am not a sociologist. Frankly, I think the effect of that psychological testimony has been already demolished here in this Court by Mr. Davis and Mr. Moore.

I might say more upon it, but I do not think that the issue justifies further argument.

I leave with the Court the citations, however, if the Court thinks that they have any merit at all.

It seems to me, Your Honors, that I have answered specifically the points which have been raised by my adversaries, and I have answered, I believe, most of the questions which the Court has put to other counsel.

It seems to me, as I have listened to seven hours of argument that preceded my addressing the Court, this is the situation, that my friends say, "This is the time for a change."

JUSTICE BLACK: Does that have anything to do with the law in the case?

MR. KORMAN: I do not think so, sir.

JUSTICE BLACK: You do not.

JUSTICE JACKSON: There has been a promise of change.

MR. KORMAN: Sir, if there has been a promise of change and it comes through the proper channels, I certainly, and the respondents certainly, have no objection to it, if it comes in the proper way by the judgment of the Congress that should pass upon it. We do not object to it. But if they decide that there is no need further for separation of the children of white and colored people in the schools so that the two may benefit from being separated because of the receptive air, the wholesome atmosphere that pervades those schools, we do not object.

Perhaps this is the time. I do not know. But I say that this is not the forum for such arguments. I say that these arguments should be made in the halls of Congress, and not in this chamber.

Incidentally, while there has been talk about breaking down segregation in all fields, I note that it has not been completely broken down in the armed forces, where it could be done by executive order, where we do not have to go to the Court and we do not have to go to the Congress. There have been some moves in that direction, and incidentally, while we are talking about progress in that direction, I should like to call the attention of the Court—and I am indebted to my friends in the amici briefs for this, because they have pointed to those fields wherein there has been advancement, where there is no longer segregation, and I thank them for suggesting it to me, and I have looked into it myself and I find that here in the District of Columbia Negroes are admitted to all the legitimate theaters, that they are admitted to a number of downtown moving pictures, that they are admitted to a number of the fine restaurants, including the famous Harvey's Restaurant, that there is a gradual integration on the playgrounds, that they are admitted onto all the recreation areas, that they are accepted into many of our larger and better hotels, that they serve on the staffs of the hospitals—particularly I call your attention to the Gallinger Hospital, which is conducted by the District of Columbia—that they take part in entertainment and in athletic contests along with white people. I say to you that even in the school system there has been a movement toward the betterment, or a breaking down, let us say, a breaking down of any of the possible feeling of hostility, the possible thought that these races cannot get along together.

It has recently been ruled that mixed groups of entertainers may come into the schools and put on performances, which was denied them previously.

This is not generally known, but in the southwest section there have been joint meetings called of teachers, parents and pupils where they confer together for the betterment of their neighborhood. Those are steps which have been accomplished without the intervention of courts, without the intervention of legislative bodies, and if those things have been accomplished, pray God the day will come when all things will be merged and the white and colored men will meet together in every place, even in the school, and it will not require even arguments from my friends before the halls of Congress, because there will be a general acceptance of the proposition that these two races can live side by side without friction, without hostility, without any occurrences.

If that be so, then there will be a general movement without their taking any action to help it, without their seeking it, to bring those things about.

This legislation is now in the place where it can be handled by the Congress, and not where it will be cut off completely by this Court without power of change.

I should like to read to Your Honors what Judge Prettyman of the United States Court of Appeals said in 1950 in the Carr case:

> Since the beginning of human history, no circumstance has given rise to more diffi-cult and delicate problems than has the coexistence of different races in the same area. Centuries of bitter experience in all parts of the world have proved that the problem is insoluble by force of any sort. The same history shows that it is soluble by the patient processes of community experience. Such problems lie naturally in the field of legislation, a method susceptible of experimentation, of development, of adjustment to the current necessities in a variety of community circumstances.

That is what I urge upon this Court, to leave this issue where constitutionally it belongs, in the body that can legislate one way or another as it finds the situation to be and as it finds the needs to be in each community. Particularly I speak for the District of Columbia. But I say it is true in all areas. And these allusions to the Japanese cases and the other cases that they have said to Your Honors control this situation, I say they do not. In those cases, there were complete denials. Hirabayshi, Korematsu, and Endo were kept in their homes as prisoners. They were taken from their homes and put in concentration camps. Takahashi was denied the right to fish, and in the Farrington case, which they say is the nearest approach to their problem, there was an attempt to legislate out of existence by regulation the foreign language schools of Hawaii.

In each of these cases, there was either denial or an attempt to completely deny. These people are denied nothing. They have a complete system of education, which they admit is equal in all respects. They do not raise that issue.

I say to the Court that this issue should be left to the Congress where it belongs. There is no constitutional issue here. It has been decided by this Court. It should be left where it now is.

REBUTTAL ARGUMENT ON BEHALF OF APPELLANTS

by MR. NABRIT

MR. NABRIT: If the Court please, I would like to adopt for the petitioners the complete argument of Mr. Korman with respect to changed conditions and to urge the Court that those changed conditions that he suggests are the very condi-tions that we have been saying to the Court should have a bearing upon the con-struction of these acts of respondents.

In the District of Columbia, contrary to the situation in the states, he has explained that the whole situation is one in which this action will create no prob-lems, so that the question of "vexatious problems" which he mentioned does not exist in the District, and we adopt his answers to that.

Now, with respect to his statement that there is no constitutional issue, we think our brief deals with this whole argument. It appears that he does not believe that there is a constitutional issue, and refuses to meet it. Giving to his argument the full meaning of it, that is, that these statutes give the authority, he has failed to deal with the question as to whether or not, conceding that they are authorized by the statutes, that is a constitutional delegation of power, and he has not addressed himself to that.

Rather he has dwelt in the past upon the white man's burden, and he has seemed to feel that for some reason that exists today.

It would appear to me that in 1952, the Negro should not be viewed as anybody's burden. He is a citizen. He is performing his duties in peace and in war, and today, on the bloody hills of Korea, he is serving in an unsegregated war.

All we ask of this Court is that it say that under the Constitution he is entitled to live and send his children to school in the District of Columbia unsegregated, with the children of his war comrades. That is simple. The Constitution gives him that right.

The basic question here is one of liberty, and under liberty, under the due process clause, you cannot deal with it as you deal with equal protection of laws, because there you deal with it as a quantum of treatment, substantially equal.

You either have liberty or you do not. When liberty is interfered with by the state, it has to be justified, and you cannot justify it by saying that we only took a little liberty. You justify it by the reasonableness of the taking.

We submit that in this case, in the heart of the nation's capital, in the capital of democracy, in the capital of the free world, there is no place for a segregated school system. This country cannot afford it, and the Constitution does not permit it, and the statutes of Congress do not authorize it.

(Whereupon, at 1:27 p.m., the argument was concluded.)

FRANCIS B. GEBHART, ET AL.,
Petitioners,

vs.

ETHEL LOUISE BELTON, ET AL.,
Respondents.

Case No. 448

FRANCIS B. GEBHART, ET AL.,
Petitioners,

vs.

SHIRLEY BARBARA BULAH, ET. AL.,
Respondents.

Washington, D.C.,
December 11, 1952.

The above-entitled cause came on for oral argument at 1:27 p.m.

APPEARANCES:

On behalf of the Petitioners:
H. ALBERT YOUNG, ESQ.

On behalf of the Respondents:
LOUIS L. REDDING, ESQ., and JACK GREENBERG, ESQ.

THE CHIEF JUSTICE: Case No. 448, Francis B. Gebhart, and others, versus Ethel Louise Belton, and others.

THE CLERK: Counsel are present.

ARGUMENT ON BEHALF OF PETITIONERS

by MR. YOUNG

MR. YOUNG: May it please the Court, it seems that I have a Herculean task to perform in attempting to add to what has already been presented for some eight hours of argument before this Court. But there are some points which I will only touch upon briefly since it has been so ably presented by counsel in all of the other cases that preceded mine for argument.

In this case, involving the State of Delaware, a petition for writ of certiorari and supporting brief was filed on November 13 of this year.

The Delaware Supreme Court handed down its mandate on September 9, 1952, and certiorari was granted on November 24, 1952, the Court advising me that I would be permitted to file my brief not later than three weeks after argument, and I can assure the Court that the brief will be in before the three weeks are out.

Jurisdiction in this case is invoked under 28 United States Code, section 1257, paragraph 3.

The validity of the Delaware constitutional provisions and the statutes invoked was challenged by the respondents. The pertinent provisions of the Delaware constitution and statute are as follows, section 1, Article 10, of the Constitution of the State of Delaware being as follows:

> The General Assembly shall provide for the establishment and maintenance of a general and efficient system of free public schools, and may require by law that every child, not physically or mentally disabled, shall attend the public schools, unless educated by other means.
> Section 2. In addition to the income of the investments of the Public School Fund, the General Assembly shall make provision for the annual payment of not less than one hundred thousand dollars for the benefit of the free public schools which, with the income of the investments of the Public School Fund shall be equitably apportioned among the school districts of the State as the General Assembly shall provide; and the money so apportioned shall be used exclusively for the payment of teachers' salaries and for furnishing free textbooks; provided, however, that in such apportionment, no distinction shall be made on account of race or color, and separate schools for white and colored children shall be maintained.

The statutory counterpart provides:

> The State Board of Education is authorized, empowered, directed and required to maintain a uniform, equal and effective system of public schools throughout the State, and shall cause the provisions of this Chapter, the by-laws or rules and regulations and the policies of the State Board of Education to be carried into effect. The schools provided shall be of two kinds: those for white children and those for colored children.

The State contended that under our constitution and statutes, segregation in the public schools was lawful and not in violation of the equal protection clause of the Fourteenth Amendment, and that if inequalities were found to exist, any judgment in favor of the plaintiffs should be limited to an injunction directing the defendants to equalize the facilities within a reasonable time.

The Delaware Court of Chancery and the Delaware Supreme Court held that these provisions insofar as they require segregation in the public schools, based on race or color, do not offend against the provisions of the Fourteenth Amendment forbidding any state to deny any citizen the equal protection of the laws, so that the Delaware Supreme Court did sustain the State's position that segregation per se is valid in the State of Delaware.

The cases of *Plessy* v. *Ferguson,* and *Gong Lum* v. *Rice,* the Delaware Supreme Court said are decisive of the question.

It is important in the approach to the question in our case, which is a very narrow one with respect to the form of the decree, if Your Honors please, that I read from portions of the opinion in order to demonstrate to this Court how the Delaware Supreme Court arrived at its decision.

On page 43—and I am sorry that I cannot refer to a brief, but I can assure the Court that it will be fully covered—

JUSTICE BLACK: Page 43 of what?

MR. YOUNG: Page 43 of the opinion, which will be found in the supplementary appendix of appellees—it is the blue-covered book—at the bottom of page 43, the Supreme Court said:

A detailed review of these cases is unnecessary, since we are cited to no case holding to the contrary. They establish the principle that the constitutional guarantee of equal protection of the laws does not prevent the establishment by the state of separate schools for whites and Negroes, provided that the facilities afforded by the state to the one class are substantially equal to those afforded to the other (often referred to as the 'separate but equal' doctrine). The question of segregation in the schools, under these authorities, is one of policy, and it is for the people of our state, through their duly chosen representatives, to determine what that policy shall be. When so determined, it must be given effect by our courts, subject always to the rule enjoined both by the Constitution of the United States and our own statute, that substantially equal treatment must be accorded. . . .

The refusal of the Chancellor to enter the declaratory judgment prayed for was therefore, in our opinion, correct.

The Delaware Supreme Court, however, held that an injunction where an inequality is found to exist commanding the defendants to admit plaintiffs to the designated schools maintained for white children was required by the equal protection clause of the Fourteenth Amendment.

The asserted conflict, the court held, of our constitutional and statutory provision with the equal protection clause of the Fourteenth Amendment was the sole basis for the judgment of the Delaware court upholding the type of relief that was granted.

JUSTICE FRANKFURTER: Mr. Attorney General, may I ask you whether I am to assume that the finding of the Chancellor on page 193a of your blue appendix, Folio 579—

MR. YOUNG: What page is that?

JUSTICE FRANKFURTER: 193a, Folio 579.

MR. YOUNG: If Your Honor please, the reason for the confusion in these things—

JUSTICE FRANKFURTER: I will hand you mine.

Am I to assume that that is a finding which persisted through the decision of the Supreme Court of Delaware? I marked it.

MR. YOUNG: I see, Your Honor.

No, Your Honor, because the Supreme Court held that that was not—if it was a finding, it was an irrelevant finding, and that it had—as a matter of fact, the decision was that segregation per se is valid in the State of Delaware, and that had no relevancy to the finding or the conclusion.

JUSTICE FRANKFURTER: To the finding. But that paragraph is in terms of a finding on the evidence as to what factors, whether any legal inference is to be drawn from it or not. You will notice the terms in which your Chancellor stated that on the evidence—doesn't he say something about "on the evidence I find this is a fact"? Does that survive his modification of the decree by the Supreme Court?

MR. YOUNG: It does not.

JUSTICE FRANKFURTER: It does not?

MR. YOUNG: It does not, Your Honor, and I will come to that in the course of my argument.

The Delaware Supreme Court held that the right to equal opportunity is a personal right; that the rights under the equal protection clause are personal and present, and for its authority relied on the cases about which so much was said during the course of the arguments here, the Gaines case, the Sipuel case, and the Sweatt case.

Those cases, however, did not involve a constitutional provision of a state. Furthermore, there was no showing in those cases that equal facilities could be provided in a reasonable time.

There is quite a difference, I submit, between not being able to afford any facilities, and correcting certain disparities that exist, which would equalize the existing facilities and educational opportunities; and for that reason, I submit, that the Chancellor and the Supreme Court. which affirmed the decree of the Chancellor, were in error.

These cases, the Gaines case, the Sipuel case, and the Sweatt case, were not considered by the three-judge court in the Davis and Briggs cases as requiring any relief other than an injunction compelling the defendants to equalize the facilities, and giving them a reasonable time to do so.

Now, this case involved two school districts. One is known as the Claymont School District, and the other the Hockessin School District.

In the Claymont School District, there is one high school, the Claymont High School, for white children only. There is also a high school in the city of Wilmington, some nine miles away, the Howard High School for Negro children.

The plaintiff Belton, fifteen years of age, and of high school age, attending the tenth grade, and living in Claymont, was required to go to the Howard High School in the city of Wilmington.

There are about 404 pupils in the Claymont High School and there are 1274 pupils in the Howard High School.

I would like to point out that with the Howard High School there is an annex some nine blocks away known as the Carver School, which is devoted primarily to vocational study.

This particular plaintiff, who went to Howard High School, took up typing and shorthand, and two afternoons a week would be required to go from Howard High School to Carver in order to take up those studies.

The plaintiffs contended that there was inequality. The state took the position that there was no inequality; that the curricula were the same or substantially the same; that the physical facilities were the same, that the teacher preparation was the same, and many other factors to show that there was equality.

We also pointed out, if the Court please, that the Carver Annex, which was some nine blocks away from the Howard School, was to be abandoned, and that there were plans for its abandonment before the suit was even started, and that there was to be a consolidation at the Howard High School for Negro students with respect to its academic studies and vocational work.

The court found that there was disparity between the two schools, and they found that the disparity existed in some items, some factors, one being the gymnasium—not that the gymnasium at Howard High was not a good gymnasium—it was a fine gymnasium, but that it was overcrowded, and would be overcrowded because of the number of students attending.

They found that travel, not because of distance itself, made for inequality, but because the petitioner or the plaintiff had to go to Howard High, and then from Howard High had to walk the nine blocks to Carver which, we contended, would be abandoned, and the court also found that the physical education classes were larger than they should be in order to afford proper and adequate instruction.

They also found disparity with respect to the playground at Carver—Carver, the annex that we said was going to be abandoned, and that we had admitted was inadequate, but because Carver had no playground, although Howard High had the opportunity to permit its pupils to go to a park which adjoined Howard High consisting of some ten acres, the fact that Carver had no playground was considered as one of the factors making for inequality, and, of course, it was held that the Carver building itself was wholly inadequate.

We contested these questions but, nevertheless, we showed the court that the state had embarked upon a plan and program of improving the conditions in Howard High School, and we showed that Howard High School was going to be enlarged. We also showed that there was going to be a school built in the county, another school in Middletown for Negroes, which is not in the record, but I would like to say to the Court is about to be completed at a cost of $1,350,000, and we were going to show that the students at the Howard High School in the junior high grades were going to be transferred to another school known as the Bancroft School, which is presently occupied and attended by white children, and that will be a school primarily for Negroes, so that the tension of overcrowding will be relieved at the Howard High School.

The court, in finding these items of disparity with respect to the Carver building, which it was not going to ignore, the fact that this was a building that we said we were going to abandon, and the fact that the gym was overcrowded, and the fact that there was this travel required by the plaintiff from Howard High to Carver, found that as to the allocation of public funds, there was equality of treatment; that as to the buildings proper they were the same; that as to accreditation, they were equal; that as to equipment and instruction material, they were equal; that the libraries were the same, with the library of Howard being larger; that the physical and mental health and nursing services at Howard, the colored school, were superior; and the court went on to say that the other differences were too insubstantial to find—to support a finding of inequality.

The other case had to do with an elementary school in what is known as Hockessin, School 107, is the school for colored children, a two-room school, having forty-four pupils.

Number 29 is a four-room school having 111 pupils.

There are two teachers in 107; there are four teachers in 29.

In that case, travel, with respect to travel, no bus transportation was provided the plaintiff, although there was bus transportation provided for white children.

In that case it was held that 107 receives equal or greater support now, and it did receive equal and greater support at the time of the hearing, although there was evidence that prior thereto the colored school did not receive equal support, which, perhaps, made for the disparity in the maintenance and upkeep of that particular school.

Both buildings—both are brick buildings; both are substantially constructed, so that the court in the case involving the elementary schools which have classes from the first grade to the sixth grade, held there was disparity in value, in upkeep, in exterior painting and floors, in toilet facilities, fire hazard, auditorium and custodial services.

We contend that these items making for disparity, as was found in the Delaware case, are such as can be readily corrected, and that the state should have been given the time, or the Board of Education should have been given the time, where there was this recognition of the "separate but equal" doctrine, in order to correct the inequalities that exist.

The defendants show the court that there was under way in the City of Wilmington, as I stated before, a far-reaching program for the improvement of facilities in the Negro schools.

As I said, the Carver School was to be abandoned. The junior high school pupils at the Howard School, that is, the Negro high school, were to be transferred to the Bancroft School so as to relieve it from crowding, and the Howard School was to be enlarged.

There were to be new shops; the laboratories would be added, and the Bancroft School is to be a completely modern junior high school.

All of these things were to be equalized, and will be equalized, by September of 1953, and the Middletown High School, as I indicated before, will be completed at a cost of $1,350,000.

As to the form of the decree, the court enjoined the defendants from denying plaintiffs admittance to the two schools, retaining—

JUSTICE REED: Your objection here, Mr. Attorney General, is as to the fitness of the decree with respect to immediacy?

MR. YOUNG: Correct.

JUSTICE REED: Your contention is that it should wait until later?

MR. YOUNG: That is correct.

JUSTICE REED: Will you address yourself as to why we should overrule the findings of the Chancellor?

MR. YOUNG: Yes.

The contention is that based on the ground of the Chancellor and the Delaware Supreme Court, in affirming the Chancellor, did not interpret the cases upon which they relied, the Sipuel case and the Gaines case and the Sweatt case, in making a finding that unless they grant immediate relief it would be in violation of the equal protection clause of the Fourteenth Amendment.

May I refer to the portion of the opinion of the Supreme Court, on page 63:

In affirming the Chancellor's order we have not overlooked the fact that the defendants may at some future date apply for a modification of the order if, in their judgment, the inequalities as between the Howard and Claymont schools or as between School No.29 and School No. 107 have then been removed. As to Howard, the defendants, as above stated, assert that when the Howard-Carver changes are completed, equality will exist. The Chancellor apparently thought the contrary. We do not concur in his conclusion, since we think that that question, if it arises, is one which will have to be decided in the light of the facts then existing and applicable principles of the law.

The Chancellor properly reserved jurisdiction of the cause to grant such further and additional relief as might appear appropriate in the future, and we construe this reservation to be a general reservation to any party to the cause to make an application to modify the order in any respect if and when changed conditions are believed to warrant such action.

JUSTICE FRANKFURTER: Has this litigation had any effect upon other school districts in your state, Mr. Attorney General?

MR. YOUNG: Well, I must speak outside the record.

JUSTICE FRANKFURTER: Yes, that is my question.

MR. YOUNG: As a matter of fact, that is the reason I am here now, because of the terrific impact upon the rest of the state by this decision.

JUSTICE FRANKFURTER: Would not each district, whatever the units may be, call for a separate assessment of the conditions in that district, the way your court did here?

MR. YOUNG: What it would mean, Your Honor, is that each case might involve litigation.

JUSTICE FRANKFURTER: That is right.

MR. YOUNG: And it would also prevent, perhaps, the legislators from voting for particular allotments for particular school districts, not knowing whether they can maintain the "separate but equal" phase of it or not.

JUSTICE FRANKFURTER: I may be wrong, but I should assume that it is almost inevitable that the conditions in the various districts would not be identical, and therefore differentiation would be almost inevitable, and the claim that the two colored and white schools are not the same would almost inevitably be made, and it would have to be decided with proper reference to each set of circumstances.

MR. YOUNG: I absolutely agree with you, sir; I absolutely agree, but what I contend is this: that in a state which recognizes the "separate but equal" doctrine, where inequalities exist, and it can be shown that those inequalities can be corrected, let us say overnight or within a week, to make an order that the Negro children shall be admitted into the white school is indirectly saying—abolishing segregation.

JUSTICE FRANKFURTER: Am I to infer that you think that the thrust of the decision of the Supreme Court is that if inequality is shown, and this whole litigation is unlike the litigation in all the other records—that if inequality is shown, a decree must be issued at once, although it might be corrected overnight?

MR. YOUNG: That is correct. That seems to be my feeling about it and my understanding of that opinion—that as long as inequality—

JUSTICE FRANKFURTER: In other words, you are arguing on the assumption that that is what the opinion of your Supreme Court means?

MR. YOUNG: Exactly.

JUSTICE REED: How can you say that when you yourself, as I understood it, said that it would not be corrected until September 1, 1953?

MR. YOUNG: That, Your Honor, went as far as the Claymont School, the high school, was concerned, where we said a new building had to be constructed.

But in the Hockessin situation, a two-room school, where we could, perhaps, within ten days put on an additional room or improve the toilet facilities or those other things that Your Honor will note in the opinion, we feel that they can be corrected with dispatch.

JUSTICE REED: So it is a problem of weighing the time it would take to make the corrections?

MR. YOUNG: That is correct.

JUSTICE REED: Even in the one that is not to be ready until 1953?

MR. YOUNG: That is correct.

JUSTICE REED: You take the position that that is an adequate time?

MR. YOUNG: We think that is a reasonable time, as long as we have shown—

JUSTICE REED: As long as there are facilities and institutions afforded?

MR. YOUNG: Precisely; and as long as it is shown that we are willing and able to do it, and that there is every reason to believe that it will be done, the "separate but equal" doctrine being recognized by the court—there should be no immediacy for the entrance of those Negro pupils into the white schools.

JUSTICE REED: Has litigation of this type reached your Supreme Court in the last five or ten years?

MR. YOUNG: This is the first in the history of the state.

JUSTICE JACKSON: Do I understand that the inequality is largely a matter of overcrowding, relative overcrowding?

MR. YOUNG: I want to differentiate between the two cases.

JUSTICE JACKSON: Yes.

MR. YOUNG: In the Claymont High School, they claimed it was due to overcrowding, not in the school entirely, but only in physical education classes.

JUSTICE JACKSON: Has there been a shift or population? That is, have you had a migration which has occurred since the war, with war industries?

MR. YOUNG: Well, we have some, yes.

JUSTICE JACKSON: You have some.

MR. YOUNG: But I do not know whether we can attribute too much to that. But the fact is that the Howard High School had both the junior and the senior pupils there, and the fact that we are taking those pupils away from the Howard High School into this other school will certainly correct this situation.

But apparently the Delaware Supreme Court seemed to term this inequality only as to the overcrowding in a particular class, which did not make for proper instruction in physical education, but it seemed to hold that as to all other classes the difference in size between twenty-five pupils in white schools, and thirty or thirty-one or thirty-two in classes in the colored schools did not make for inequality so as to effect educational opportunity or instruction.

The State contends that where disparity exists under the equal protection clause of the Fourteenth Amendment, the rights of Negro children are protected by a decree compelling school administrators to equalize the facilities in the segregated schools involved where a state constitutional provision makes mandatory the maintenance of separate schools for white and colored children, and where school administrators have reasonably shown that the existing inequality can and probably will be corrected within a reasonable time.

So the Court of Chancery, of course, sat as a court of equity, and the form of the decree, we contend, violates the fundamental equitable principles as laid down in *Eccles* v. *Peoples Bank*.

In that case the court said:

It is always the duty of a court of equity to strike a proper balance between the needs of the plaintiff and the consequences of giving the desired relief.

There was no showing that the state could not equalize or that it was unwilling to equalize, and the effect of the decree is demoralizing to the Negro pupils as well as to the white pupils, to the teachers, to the State Board of Education.

There is no permanency, there is no stability, as one of the counsel mentioned during the course of the argument in the Virginia case.

The decree in its present form, which says that the Negro children shall be permitted to go to the white school and that the Board of Education may come in next week, next month, and modify the decree would result in shunting those Negro children back and forth.

There would be no stability, there would be no permanency. I would rather if the court had said that segregation per se is bad; "Let the Negro children go the white schools."

(Whereupon, a luncheon recess was taken.)

AFTER RECESS

MR. YOUNG: Mr. Justice Frankfurter, you asked me whether the Chancellor's finding on the evidence that segregation produces detrimental results so far as educational opportunities are concerned, if it is applied—and I call the Court's attention to the opinion of the Supreme Court of Delaware on page 44, beginning with the third paragraph:

> it is said that the uncontradicted evidence adduced by the plaintiffs shows that state-imposed segregation in the public schools and equality of educational opportunity are inherently incompatible, and that the Chancellor so held. The Chancellor indeed found on the evidence that segregation itself results in the Negro's receiving inferior educational opportunities, and expressed the opinion that the 'separate but equal' doctrine should be rejected. He nevertheless recognized that his finding was immaterial to the legal conclusion drawn from the authorities above cited. We agree that it is immaterial, and hence see no occasion to review it.

JUSTICE FRANKFURTER: Therefore, it is not before us.

MR. YOUNG: That is right.

JUSTICE BLACK: But does that necessarily follow? They did not set it aside, so that you have a finding of your Chancellor so far as segregation is concerned in Delaware that the result of it is the affording of an inferior opportunity of education and your Supreme Court says that nevertheless the Supreme Court of the United States, in effect, has held that that can never be a constitutional ground.

MR. YOUNG: So did the Chancellor, Your Honor.

JUSTICE BLACK: But you still have your finding that, so far as Delaware is concerned—and I presume he was not looking at evidence anywhere but Delaware, that the system of segregation there, even though the facilities, physical facilities, are equal, results in inferior education for them.

MR. YOUNG: He did so state.

JUSTICE BLACK: We have that finding without its being set aside.

MR. YOUNG: Well, I think we have it, in effect, set aside when the Supreme Court says that he considered it immaterial to the conclusion in his case and the decision in his case.

JUSTICE BLACK: That is right. He considered it immaterial, but nevertheless are we not faced with this situation: Do you conceive that segregation might be held on evidence in some places to supply equal opportunities for education, while in others it might be held that the situation was such that it gave an inferior opportunity for education?

MR. YOUNG: Depending on the facilities offered, and the educational opportunities.

JUSTICE BLACK: I mean, assuming that the facilities are the same—

MR. YOUNG: Yes.

JUSTICE BLACK: —do you conceive that it is impossible for segregation in one place to result in an equality of opportunity of education, while in another it might result in inequality of opportunity for education?

MR. YOUNG: No, I cannot conceive of that myself.
Now, it may be that—

JUSTICE BLACK: There might be many things involved, might there not?

MR. YOUNG: That is true, but I am not prepared to say whether, all factors being equal, mere segregation of and by itself will bring about inferiority so far as educational opportunities are concerned.

JUSTICE BLACK: Well, assuming that you had facts, and that your court found on the facts that in Delaware, where your two schools functioned, and with the general conditions of education in Delaware and the relationship between the races and all of that was such that even though the facilities were identical—physical facilities—nevertheless, in Delaware, the results of segregation were to give an unequal opportunity of education to the colored people.
Would you say that, assuming that finding on local facts, and it is accepted, that the separate but equal doctrine would not make it necessary to state that?

MR. YOUNG: I would not, if Your Honor please, under our Constitution and its statutory counterpart—we are required to maintain separate schools for white and colored as long as we afford them equal opportunities and equal facilities and I think that that would merely be an oblique way of striking down segregation, and desegregating schools.

JUSTICE BLACK: If you assume that the facts are correctly found. Suppose I asked you to assume that the court found those facts, and assume that he is right, and you had no way to overturn them. He would say that conditions in Delaware—given consideration on the facts—require him to see whether or not the colored people get an equal opportunity for education.
Now, I find that they do so far as the physical results are concerned, but I am led to the conclusion from the evidence and find from the evidence that they do not because the relationship that exists here, and by reason of the manner of going to school, and the mixture in other places, and so forth, I find that the effect on the children is that they get an inferior opportunity for education. Would you say that that would still not bring them within the "separate but equal" doctrine?

MR. YOUNG: I would, Your Honor. I would because I say that would be violative of the equal protection clause of the Fourteenth Amendment, and would also be violative of our own constitutional provisions, because we are assuming now facilities being equal, educational opportunities being equal; I would like to say I do not know what evidence Your Honor is referring to that the chancellor could rely on other than the sociologists and anthropologists and psychologists.

JUSTICE BLACK: I just read the findings, and I asked you the question at the beginning of these arguments, you may remember.

MR. YOUNG: I remember.

JUSTICE BLACK: About the difference in findings, and I wondered—both sides seem to be relying on the findings so much, and I wondered if the assumption we must make from that is that both sides believe that it could be found in one state and one locality by reason of a different situation that opportunities were unequal, even though the facilities were equal, while in another state that would not be the case.

MR. YOUNG: I do not subscribe to that, Your Honor.

JUSTICE FRANKFURTER: Mr. Attorney General, since I got you into this trouble, perhaps I might help straighten out the way the matter lies in my mind.

I had not read that sentence to which you called attention in the opinion of the Supreme Court. I think for myself this situation is very different from the Kansas situation.

In the Kansas situation we have a finding of fact similar to the finding made by your Chancellor, and the court said that finding does not bear on the legal question, namely, that the state has power to segregate, no matter what the psychological consequences may be, and that is what your Chancellor found.

As I understand it myself, when your Supreme Court came to review the decision of the Chancellor, it said that inasmuch as his finding of fact is irrelevant, it was not going to review it. Therefore, we have a finding of an inferior court specifically not reviewed by the highest court of the state.

The Chancellor found that on his appraisal of the evidence—insofar as I am concerned it may well be that your Supreme Court might not have reached that conclusion, and might not have weighed the evidence that the Chancellor did and, therefore, we have not got, for myself in this case, what we have in the Kansas case, a finding of fact which binds us, because for all I know your Supreme Court might have disagreed with your Chancellor, and then we would be in a position where the highest court said that the evidence does not yield to the conclusions that the Chancellor thought it yielded.

MR. YOUNG: That is precisely the point, Your Honor, and what is more, a review of the opinion would show that the Delaware Supreme Court did not agree with many things that the Chancellor said in his opinion in the lower court.

JUSTICE FRANKFURTER: Yes. The legal position that you take is on the assumption that was presented by the Kansas case. I think that your record presents a different set of facts.

MR. YOUNG: Exactly. There was no finding of fact that was considered at all. It was considered immaterial to the issue.

JUSTICE FRANKFURTER: A very powerful finding by the Chancellor.

MR. YOUNG: Oh, yes.

JUSTICE BLACK: I do not like to interrupt again, but taking that as true, if we assume and admit such a finding is relevant, you would be in a situation of having a finding by your Chancellor which is relevant, which might cause the case to turn one way or the other, which has not been reviewed by your highest court.

MR. YOUNG: That is right. But there is one thing I want to make plain: That notwithstanding that finding, and notwithstanding the fact that it was disregarded by the Supreme Court, I nevertheless address Your Honor's attention to the point that the shape of the decree, in any event, was not a proper decree under the circumstances, even if that were so.

Let us assume that were so, and it just desegregated the schools; nevertheless, the form of the decree being in conflict with the other jurisdiction, was not a proper decree, taking into account the needs and the relief to be granted, and the public interest involved.

This Court, as I contend, is not exercising—it was not a question of abuse of discretion, and it is not a matter of administration nor a matter of enforcing the injunction.

Both courts, my position is, said that under and only by reason of the Fourteenth Amendment was it justified to make the kind of decree it did.

The decree in the court below, while asserting that the plaintiffs were entitled to relief, made no attempt to assess the effect of its decree on the defendants, on the children and their parents, both white and colored, in the school districts affected.

No consideration was given to the ability of the defendants to equalize the facilities involved within a reasonable time; no consideration was given to the effect of a possible later decree based on changing circumstances; no consideration was given to the effect of the decree on the school administrators who would be faced with the problem of determining how and where to enroll children in the various school districts in the state.

No consideration was given to the effect of the decree on the public, generally, and on the legislature in planning for the future, in allocating funds for the maintenance and construction of school facilities.

The court below stated that the plaintiffs' rights were personal and present, and this does not necessarily mean that they are entitled immediately to admittance to the schools maintained for white children only.

The plaintiffs' rights are given full consideration when the court orders the defendants to proceed forthwith to make the facilities of the respective schools equal.

In this case, too, I am grateful to the Attorney General for his brief, and in his amicus curiae brief. On page 28 I would like the Court to take note of what he said:

> If, in any of the present cases, the Court should hold that to compel colored children to attend 'separate but equal' public schools is unconstitutional, the Government would suggest that in shaping the relief the Court should take into account the need, not only for prompt vindication of the constitutional rights violated, but also for orderly and reasonable solution of the vexing problems which may arise in eliminating such segregation. The public interest plainly would be served by avoidance of needless dislocation and confusion in the administration of the school systems affected. It must be recognized that racial segregation in public schools has been in effect in many states for a long time. Its roots go deep in the history and traditions of these states. The practical difficulties which may be met in making progressive adjustments to a nonsegregated system cannot be ignored or minimized.

JUSTICE REED: I asked a question similar to this before. Why do you contend that that is a problem here? Is it a violation of the federal law or a violation of the federal Constitution that the Delaware Supreme Court has acted somewhat precipitately, from your point of view?

MR. YOUNG It is because, Your Honor, we contend that the Supreme Court, affirming the Chancellor who acted in this matter, in shaping the form of the decree, said that he was compelled to make that kind of a decree under the equal protection clause of the Fourteenth Amendment. It was not a question of exercising discretion; in fact, it negated that proposition.

If, for example he would reach the same result by saying that he is exercising his discretion, perhaps we would have another matter. But he said he was compelled to issue that kind of a decree under the equal protection clause of the Fourteenth Amendment.

JUSTICE DOUGLAS: Is that because the right is personal?

MR. YOUNG: Because the right is personal, and depending upon the cases of Sweatt and the Gaines case and, of course, we differentiate between those cases, cases where there was no facility, there was no expectancy of any facility within a reasonable time, as compared with a case where there is the ability and the willingness to equalize.

JUSTICE REED: It is difficult for me to grasp what the state court of Delaware was saying when it said it was not acting within its discretion.

MR. YOUNG: Well, the Supreme Court pointed out in its opinion and stated that they were relying solely—

JUSTICE REED: It is on page 44.

MR. YOUNG: On page 57 the court cast aside—the Delaware Supreme Court—two preliminary matters upon which, perhaps, the injunction could have been or the decree could have been, handed down, but said:

> But we prefer to rest our decision upon another ground. With deference to the decisions in the Briggs and Davis cases, which we have carefully examined and considered, we cannot reconcile the denial of prompt relief with the pronouncements of the Supreme Court of the United States. If, as we have seen, the right to equal protection of the laws is a 'personal and present' one, how can these plaintiffs be denied such relief as is now available? The commendable effort of the state to remedy the situation serves to emphasize the importance of the present inequalities.

THE CHIEF JUSTICE: I think you will find some language in the Sipuel case, if I remember rightly, about "personal and present."

MR. YOUNG: Yes.

THE CHIEF JUSTICE: That was the admission into the school in Oklahoma. I think that language is in the Sipuel case.

MR. YOUNG: That is right.

THE CHIEF JUSTICE: I mean "personal and present."

MR. YOUNG: Well, there it was proper, I state, because there is quite a distinction between higher education and facilities that can or cannot be offered on a higher educational level as compared with the common school level; and the court—our contention is that the lower court, the inferior court, the Court of Chancery—was in error when it thought that it was compelled to issue the kind of decree it did without giving any regard to the public interest and to the parties involved.

JUSTICE REED: Your court says in the opinion:

To require the plaintiffs to wait another year—

I am reading at page 58—

MR. YOUNG: Yes.

JUSTICE REED: (Continuing)

—under present conditions would be in effect partially to deny them that to which we have held they are entitled. It is possible that a case might occur in which completion of equalization of facilities might be so imminent as to justify a different result, but we do not pass on that question because it is not presented.

Whether that is discretion—your position is that they are bound under the Sipuel case to give immediate relief; they thought they were bound to give immediate—

MR. YOUNG: Yes, they thought they were bound.

JUSTICE REED: To give immediate relief.

MR. YOUNG: Yes, that is correct.

In the light of what I have read from the amicus curiae brief, when it was urged that the Court should be slow in desegregating even where segregation per se was held to be invalid, our contention is that the fact that it is even more serious where the "separate but equal" doctrine is held to be valid, and where it is recognized that the state, upon a showing that any existing inequality relating to facilities and educational opportunities are capable of being corrected within a reasonable time, for a court to compel the immediate amalgamation of Negroes and whites in the same school, and then later upon a showing of equalization again separate the Negro children from the white school.

A decree requiring the defendants to equalize the facilities within a reasonable time would give the plaintiffs relief as quickly as practicable, consistent with an orderly administration of the school system and a specific adjustment of inequalities where such inequalities have been found to exist in the past.

The same situation occurred in the Virginia case and also in the South Carolina case, perhaps not with the finding that Your Honors find to exist in the opinion of the Chancellor in the lower court, but I believe that the language of—

THE CHIEF JUSTICE: The language can be found in the Virginia case, can it not?

MR. YOUNG: Not that particular finding that segregation of and by itself under the evidence is harmful. I think that they did—

THE CHIEF JUSTICE: They had findings there that it was not equal.

MR. YOUNG: That it was not equal, that is correct; and I believe there was some comment, as I recall, that whether it does harm or does not do harm is not for the Court to determine. But this is what Judge Parker had to say in disposing of the case, the South Carolina case:

> It is argued that, because the school facilities furnished Negroes in District No. 22 are inferior to those furnished white persons, we should enjoin segregation rather than direct the equalizing of conditions. Inasmuch as we think that the law requiring segregation is valid, however, and that the inequality suffered by plaintiffs results, not from the law, but from the way it has been administered, we think that our injunction should be directed to removing the inequalities resulting from administration within the framework of the law rather than to nullifying the law itself. As a court of equity, we should exercise our power to assure to plaintiffs the equality of treatment to which they are entitled with due regard to the legislative policy of the state. In directing that the school facilities afforded Negroes within the district be equalized promptly with those afforded white persons, we are giving plaintiffs all the relief that they can reasonably ask and the relief that is ordinarily granted in cases of this sort.

The Court, as it was said in the Briggs case, should not use its power to abolish segregation in a state where it is required by the constitution and laws of the state if the equality demanded by the Constitution can be attained otherwise.

This much, the court went on to say, is demanded by the spirit of comity which must prevail in the relationship between the agencies of the federal government and the state if our constitutional system is to endure.

What we ask in this case is that the Delaware Supreme Court's judgment be reversed and that the Delaware Supreme Court be instructed that affording reasonable time for the board of education to correct inequalities capable of being corrected, as we have shown, is not in violation of the Fourteenth Amendment.

JUSTICE FRANKFURTER: Mr. Attorney General, may I trouble you again? Has the Supreme Court, your Supreme Court, in terms, not as a necessary consequence of what it has decided, but has your Supreme Court in terms, taken the position that if the Chancellor finds inequality then the immediate opening of the doors of schools of whites who have no segregation in schools is a legal compulsion?

MR. YOUNG: That is, we contend, the position the Supreme Court took.

JUSTICE FRANKFURTER: Has it taken that in terms? Here is what troubles me. It is asking a great deal of this Court, for one-ninth of this Court, to overrule the judgment of the Chancellor, affirmed by the Supreme Court of the state, that the equity of the situation requires the decree that they entered.

If they base that on their interpretation of what the decisions of this Court require, then it was not the Chancellor's exercise of discretion, but it was a result caused by the requirement that they must follow the decisions of the Court.

As I read their opinions, they did not say that in terms, did they?

MR. YOUNG: No, but the general mandate, it would seem to me, the blanket mandate, in affirming the judgment of the Court of Chancery or the Chancellor—

JUSTICE FRANKFURTER: Did the Chancellor think that was the thing to do?

MR. YOUNG: He thought so, yes.

JUSTICE FRANKFURTER: That as soon as inequality is shown, then at once there must be—

MR. YOUNG: That is right.

JUSTICE FRANKFURTER: How could he? We did not do that in one of the cases.

MR. YOUNG: We tried to point out to the Chancellor that he was wrong, and we tried to point out to the Chancellor that that was not so.

JUSTICE FRANKFURTER: The question is whether he was wrong or what rule of law did he apply. If he said that in this situation, considering the circumstances in Delaware, your county or school district, or he may not have been explicit about it—that is one thing. If he says that the Supreme Court demands, "and I am an obedient judge," that is another thing.

MR. YOUNG: He said where there is an injury, as he found such to be here, then the injury should be redressed immediately.

JUSTICE FRANKFURTER: Well, that may be his view as an equity judge.

MR. YOUNG: But he based it on the equal protection clause of the Fourteenth Amendment.

JUSTICE FRANKFURTER: If I may say so, a chancellor who shows as much competence as this opinion shows, probably can read the opinions of this Court with understanding.

MR. YOUNG: There is no question about the Chancellor's competency, Your Honor.

JUSTICE FRANKFURTER: If I may say so, it was an unusual opinion, as opinions go.

MR. YOUNG: May I read from just the opinion of the Chancellor on page 203, at the bottom of the page:

Just what is the effect of such a finding of a violation of the Constitution, as has here been made. It is true that in such a situation some courts have merely directed the appropriate State officials to equalize facilities. I do not believe that such is the relief warranted by a finding that the United States Constitution has been violated. It seems to me that when a plaintiff shows to the satisfaction of a court that there is an existing and continuing violation of the 'separate but equal' doctrine, he is entitled to have made available to him the State facilities which have been shown to be superior. To do otherwise is to say to such a plaintiff: 'Yes, your Constitutional rights are being invaded, but be patient, we will see whether in time they are still being violated.'

Now, Judge Parker had that problem before him in the South Carolina case, and the same problem was there in the Virginia case. But is it a violation that is going to continue upon a showing that we, the state, are able and willing to correct the existing inequalities between the two races?

JUSTICE FRANKFURTER: Suppose your Supreme Court had said that "it is our view that when a violation of the Constitution is shown, that is such an overriding equity that we regard the inconvenience or the difficulties to the state as subordinate to that overriding equity." That would be a view of equity, the balancing of considerations by the local court, and not at all derived from the necessities of the Fourteenth Amendment?

MR. YOUNG: I agree with Your Honor.

JUSTICE FRANKFURTER: I was wondering whether that is not really implicit in these decisions?

MR. YOUNG: I do not believe so. I think that they were fully cognizant of the equal protection clause of the Fourteenth Amendment, and that they were aware of the South Carolina case at the time, the Virginia case, and that the leading cases, the Sweatt case and, of course, the Gaines case, and it was on that basis that they felt that they were compelled to make the kind of order—

JUSTICE FRANKFURTER: Automatically because there was a violation of the Fourteenth Amendment, and the Fourteenth Amendment requires automatic redress, that is your view of it?

MR. YOUNG: That is right, precisely. That is our view, and I think it is borne out by a reading of the two opinions in the Court of Chancery and in the Delaware Supreme Court.

JUSTICE REED: Mr. Attorney General, I call your attention to page 204 (a), as I understand it, of the Chancellor's opinion, and towards the bottom he says, "If it be a matter of discretion, I reach the same conclusion."

MR. YOUNG: Well, I think that is the language in the opinion, but it is clear that the decision rested—

JUSTICE REED: He thought to the contrary, too. He also said that if it is a matter of discretion "I reach the same conclusion."

MR. YOUNG: But he did reach the conclusion upon the basis and the interpretation of the equal protection clause of the Fourteenth Amendment, and that is the way the Delaware Supreme Court found that he ruled, and thought that it was proper because it was a matter of compulsion where there is such a finding.

I want to say, of course, there was much more that I would like to have brought to the Court's attention. I know it would be impossible for me to review the cases on the question of segregation per se that were so ably presented by my distinguished colleagues.

THE CHIEF JUSTICE: In addition to that, your time has expired.

MR. YOUNG: That is true. Is it at an end now?

THE CHIEF JUSTICE: Yes.

MR. YOUNG: Thank you.

ARGUMENT ON BEHALF OF RESPONDENTS

by MR. REDDING

MR. REDDING: May it please the Court, in this fifth and last case before the Court on this subject, the fundamental question is still the same as in the four preceding cases, namely, what rights has the individual to protection against arbitrary action by government?

In four cases, including the Delaware case, the government involved is the state government; in the fifth case, the government involved is the federal government.

This case differs from the other cases in that the persons who were originally plaintiffs appear here not as appellants but as respondents.

Judgment in the trial court was rendered for the persons who were originally plaintiffs, and that judgment, as well as a finding of fact that there was substantial inequality in facilities, was affirmed by the state Supreme Court.

Now, that affirmance was not merely a formal affirmance. The state Supreme Court concluded that because a constitutional question was involved, that is, a question involving the constitution of the State of Delaware was involved, it had a right to completely disregard the findings of fact of the Chancellor and make its own independent findings of fact, and it did so, and it sustained the Chancellor's findings of fact that there was substantial inequality in physical facilities.

The Chancellor made a second finding of fact. He made a finding of fact which, in language, is something like this—and I think, perhaps, I had better refer to the exact language:

> I conclude from the testimony that in our Delaware society, State-imposed segregation in education itself results in the Negro children, as a class, receiving educational opportunities which are substantially inferior to those available to white children otherwise similarly situated.

Now, the respondents here say, first of all, just as has been said in the four preceding cases, that classification on the basis of race to determine what educational facilities may be enjoyed, is arbitrary and unreasonable, and because it is arbitrary and unreasonable, it is unconstitutional.

We say that such a classification has no relationship to the education of a state's citizens.

Now, there has been some discussion arising, I think in part, from questions from Your Honors as to the basis for the type of legislation that is here under attack.

I cannot answer what the basis for this type of legislation in other states was, but I should like to indicate what I think the basis was in Delaware.

Delaware has never, by the normal process of ratification, ratified the Fourteenth Amendment. The only ratification of the Fourteenth Amendment which has occurred in Delaware, is a ratification by implication from judicial action.

When the Fourteenth Amendment was being circulated among the states for ratification, the Delaware Legislature, in joint session, concurred in a joint resolution, the words of which I shall read:

> Whereas, this General Assembly believes the adoption of the said proposed amendment to the Constitution would have a tendency to destroy the rights of the states in their sovereign capacity as states, would be an attempt to establish an equality not sanctioned by the laws of nature or of God,

therefore they refused to ratify.

Now, this is not an isolated action. That action was taken in March of 1869, and it is found recorded in 13, Laws of Delaware 256.

This is not an isolated action.

The legislature took the same action with respect to the Fifteenth Amendment. In language which is as follows, it stated:

> It is resolved that the members of this General Assembly do hereby declare their unqualified disapproval of said amendment to the Constitution of the United States, and hereby refuse to adopt and ratify the same.

I say it is not isolated, and I refer to still another resolution, if Your Honors will indulge me. This resolution was unanimously adopted by a joint session of the Delaware Legislature, and I think its language will be self-explanatory:

> Resolved that the members of this General Assembly do hereby declare uncompromising opposition to a proposed act of Congress introduced by the Honorable Charles Sumner at the last session and now on file in the Senate of the United States known as the Supplemental Civil Rights bill, and all other measures intended or calculated to equalize the Negro race with the white race, politically or socially, and especially do they proclaim unceasing opposition to making Negroes eligible to public offices, to sit on juries and to their admission into public schools where white children attend, to their admission on terms of equality with white people in churches, public conveyances, places of amusement or hotels, and to any and every measure designed or having the effect to promote the equality of the Negro with the white man in any of the relationships of life.

We say, sirs, that that is the background of this legislation.

However, Delaware did not include in its State Constitution a requirement that there be separation of Negroes and whites in public schools until 1897, the year after this Court decided *Plessy* v. *Ferguson*.

Apparently, the Delaware Legislature, which passed the amendment of the Delaware Constitution—it was amended by two successive legislatures—apparently the Delaware Legislature felt that there was warrant in *Plessy* v. *Ferguson* for a so-called "separate but equal" doctrine.

Now, we think that these resolutions indicate that this separation of the Negro and white in public schools was not based on any rational consideration.

At the trial of the case evidence was introduced further to show that such legislation was not based on any rational or reasonable grounds.

I should like the indulgence of the Court to call attention to this testimony at page 122 of the appendix of the appellees, plaintiffs below.

Dr. Otto Klineberg, a professor of psychology at Columbia University was testifying. He was asked this question—

JUSTICE REED: What was the page, please?

MR. REDDING: I am sorry, sir, page 122 of the thick blue book.

Dr. Klineberg, are there differences in inborn intellectual capacity among individuals which are determined by whether an individual is Negro or white?
A. No. There are, of course, differences in intellectual capacity, but we have no scientific evidence that those differences are determined in any way by the racial origin of the individual.

We think that completely removes any possibility of a contention that this legislation today, with the advances in scientific knowledge about the measurement of mental capacities of human beings today, could have any rational basis.

Now, the Delaware statute provides for separate but equal education for Negroes and whites. The form of the statute itself predetermined the nature of the action, that is, these plaintiffs felt that they were required to show that there was not equality although there was separation, and they attempted to do it on two bases: They showed inequality of physical facilities, and they got a finding of fact from the Chancellor which was sustained by the Supreme Court on that, and then they attempted to show inequality flowing from the harm done by segregation on the individual student.

I might say that twelve expert witnesses testified with respect to this second aspect of inequality.

I should like to call the attention of the Court to just a small portion of that testimony. I should like to call the Court's attention to the testimony of a witness whom the Chancellor characterized in his opinion as one of America's foremost psychiatrists. This witness was not testifying merely from abstractions of scientific knowledge. This witness had examined, among other Delawareans, some of the respondents in this case and, as a result of his learning and as a result of this examination, this witness testified as follows, at page 76 of this same book, which is the transcript of the testimony. Dr. Fredric Wertham[64] testified:

Now, the fact of segregation in public and high school creates in the mind of the child an unsolvable conflict, an unsolvable emotional conflict, and I would say an inevitable conflict—it is inevitable that it cause such a conflict. This conflict is, in the child's mind, what a foreign body is in the child's body.

[64]Dr. Fredric Wertham is a noted psychiatrist and author. Among his works are *The Sign of Cain* (1967), *The Show of Violence* (1949), *Dark Legend* (1941), and *Seduction of the Innocent* (1954).

Further, Dr. Wertham testified that segregation, state-imposed segregation, created an important inequality in educational opportunities for the various reasons. He said:

> Now, of course, these facts that I have mentioned are not caused only by the school segregation, but the school segregation is important, of paramount importance, for a number of reasons.

JUSTICE BURTON: Where is that?

MR. REDDING: This, I am sorry, Your Honor, is at page 86 of this same transcript of testimony. He says:

> It is of paramount importance for a number of reasons.
> In the first place, it is absolutely clear cut.

Secondly, he says, the state does it; thirdly, it is not just the discrimination, it is discrimination of very long duration; it is continuous; and fourth, it is bound up with the whole educational process.

Now, sirs, I say that the Chancellor's finding of fact with respect to the harm done in Delaware society by state-imposed segregation on the minds of these children is based on that testimony.

Some discussion has been had as to what the Supreme Court of Delaware did with that finding of the Chancellor. It is our view that the Supreme Court did not reject that finding. It is our view that that finding survives, and because we have that view, and because the Supreme Court, in our view, did not give legal effectuation to a finding of fact made by the trial court, we ask that this Court give legal effectuation to such a finding.

JUSTICE FRANKFURTER: Aren't you really asking that the decree below be affirmed?

MR. REDDING: We ask, of course, that the decree below be affirmed, but we ask that it be affirmed not merely for the reason given by the Supreme Court of Delaware, but for other considerations which this Court has taken into account in, for example, the Sipuel case and the McLaurin case.

In those cases this Court did take into account factors like the isolation of the student from other students. The Delaware Supreme Court did not take that into account, and in affirming the opinion of the Delaware Supreme Court, we respectfully ask that this Court take those factors into account and grant a judgment of affirmance which will indicate that segregation in and of itself inflicts inequalities of educational opportunities on the respondents here. So that no matter what attempt to equalize facilities may be made by the Attorney General of the State of Delaware, there will still be inequality of educational opportunity which the state is not correcting.

We think that in the Sweatt case—

JUSTICE FRANKFURTER: If we just affirmed this decree below without an opinion, that would be an end of the matter, and the plaintiffs in this case would get all they asked, would they not?

MR. REDDING: No, sir.

JUSTICE FRANKFURTER: They would be admitted into the school into which they wanted to be admitted.

MR. REDDING: They ask for the equality of educational opportunity.

JUSTICE FRANKFURTER: That is what they would get if the decree was affirmed.

MR. REDDING: They would get it, sir, but they would get it under the shadow of the threat of the Attorney General that the moment he has shown to the court that facilities are equalized they would then be ejected from the schools.

THE CHIEF JUSTICE: Was it the threat of the Attorney General or was that the condition stated by the Court?

MR. REDDING: Well, the Attorney General now threatens that, sir.

THE CHIEF JUSTICE: I say though—

MR. REDDING: I say that is the explanation of his appearance here.

THE CHIEF JUSTICE: (Continuing)—isn't that what the court said?

MR. REDDING: Yes, the court said that.

THE CHIEF JUSTICE: And he held that it would be contingent, and motions might be made if conditions were changed.

MR. REDDING: We think that—

THE CHIEF JUSTICE: Isn't that what the court said?

MR. REDDING: That is correct, sir.

JUSTICE FRANKFURTER: Did the court say that they would exclude those children if new arrangements were made? Did the court say what they would do if in the future an application were made to deal with this decree? They simply let the decree open. Almost every decree in equity is left open.

MR. REDDING: That is correct, sir. But we have no reason to believe that the court at that time will not take the same position with respect to its limitation that it took originally.

JUSTICE FRANKFURTER: Mr. Redding, we have had cases where we had to dismiss a case as moot because the child had gone through the education, a case from New Jersey, and it was a case in a totally different field[64a]—so that by the time there may be a new threat, these boys and girls might be in various universities of the country.

MR. REDDING: We feel, sir, that the decree should be affirmed.

[64a]Doremus v. Board of Education, 342 U.S. 429 (1952). The Court held that a parent could not challenge public school bible-reading after his child had graduated from high school.

166

ARGUMENT IN BEHALF OF RESPONDENTS

by MR. GREENBERG

MR. GREENBERG: If it please the Court, we are seeking affirmance of the judgment below. In addition to the reasons submitted by Mr. Redding, which, we submit, will permanently settle respondents' right to the relief which they sought, and settle on the basis of the really important factors present in this case, we submit that the judgment rendered below should at least be affirmed for the reasons given by the court below.

The court below found that the state was offering education to respondents inferior to education offered white children similarly situated.

The petitioners, on page 4 of their petition for certiorari, expressly disclaim any challenge to this finding of inequality.

To give the Court an idea of the degree of the more measurable inequalities present in this case, I had merely intended to mention a few of them, but since the Attorney General had taken them up in detail, I should like to, for a moment, go through our brief where they are listed on pages 27 through 41, and outline them rapidly so that the Court will have an idea of the severe degree of the inequality.

There is travel, and the significance of travel, as testified to by a psychologist, who indicated that travel has important consequences for the learning process, that it induces fatigue and irritability and takes up valuable portions of the child's time when he could be engaged in self-initiated activity, that is very important to the learning process.

There were inequalities in sites and buildings and inequalities in teacher preparation and there was inequality in teacher load, which the Attorney General did not bring out.

We contended there were inequalities in curricula and extracurricular activities; there was no finding that these were equal, but we submit, and the Supreme Court of Delaware found that, perhaps, they were de minimus, and nothing to be taken into account in a case of this sort, and it is our contention, concerning inequalities of, perhaps, this small nature, that a child should not be submitted to them merely because of his race.

There were inequalities in the elementary school case in sites and buildings, which the Attorney General brought out, in instructional materials and accessories, which the Attorney General brought out; there were inequalities in relative expenditures for schools 29 and 107, which I do not believe were brought out; and, very important, there were inequalities in teaching in the cases.

The teachers in the Negro elementary school were not as well trained and were not as highly rated by the County Supervisor, who had rated them as B teachers, whereas he had rated the teachers in the white schools as A teachers.

So, we submit, that the palpable, perhaps the more measurable, inequalities in this case are of a very severe and extensive nature.

The Attorney General expressed willingness in both courts below, and he expresses it in this Court to accept the decree ordering the state to equalize the schools in questions.

But, as was pointed out in a portion of the Chancellor's opinion which was read here before, the Chancellor wrote:

This would be to say, 'Yes, your constitutional rights are being invaded, but be patient, we will see whether in time they are still being invaded.'

The Chancellor cited *Sweatt* against *Painter* for this proposition, and he ruled that respondents were entitled to relief immediately in the only way that relief was available, namely, by admission to the schools with the superior facilities, and he wrote:

To postpone relief would be to deny relief,

and the Supreme Court of Delaware affirmed on this express ground.

JUSTICE JACKSON: Is it your position that the court, finding a right being denied, has no power to take into consideration the time that it will take to correct it?

MR. GREENBERG: It is our position, Your Honor, that if constitutional rights are being denied our respondents, they are entitled to those rights as quickly as those rights can be made available; and in this case they could be made available most quickly by admission to the superior facilities—that is, without regard to the other factors that have been discussed in the other cases.

JUSTICE JACKSON: You do not agree with the Attorney General's suggestion, then?

MR. GREENBERG: No. It is our position, for example, that if the state guarantees a child ten years of education, and the child has spent approximately five of those years in inferior schools, and it is possible to give him the remaining five years on a parity with white students, that to deny him the sixth, seventh, and eighth year of equality is to inflict an irreparable injury on him.

Those three years cannot be completely recaptured, and we feel there is no reason in justice or under the Fourteenth Amendment why we should not demand it.

JUSTICE FRANKFURTER: When you say there is no reason in justice, of course—

MR. GREENBERG: And under the Fourteenth Amendment.

JUSTICE JACKSON: When you say that the Attorney General's plan for a gradual correction of this situation is impossible, it has to be done all at once?

MR. GREENBERG: That is our view.

First of all, it does not afford the right and, second of all, as I intend to come to in a moment, there is no showing on this record, no showing whatsoever, and both courts so found there is no evidence that equality would occur at any time in the future.

JUSTICE FRANKFURTER: What is there in the Constitution which prevents a chancellor from taking into consideration the consequences of a decree in cases involving constitutional rights or any other rights?

MR. GREENBERG: There is nothing in the Constitution one way or another on the question.

JUSTICE FRANKFURTER: He behaved the way a chancellor should behave, in the way of balancing the public interest on one side as against an immediate relief on the other?

MR. GREENBERG: But there is no showing of any public interest—

JUSTICE FRANKFURTER: That is a different story. A chancellor has no business not to enforce a right which he decrees in the ordinary property case—

MR. GREENBERG: I think that if a showing had been made on that point, something of that sort might be taken into consideration.

JUSTICE FRANKFURTER: I was referring to the broader question that Justice Jackson raised by referring to the considerations of the Attorney General's previous answers, the whole broad problem of relief in these cases on the assumption that rights are involved.

MR. GREENBERG: That is right, sir.

I would like to address myself to something close to that question, Your Honor. There have been questions apparently in this case and in other cases concerning the administrative problems that might be involved in the integration which was involved in these cases. As to this case, we can only say that the decree of the Supreme Court of Delaware came down, I believe, on August the 28, at which time both counsel for the respondents were on vacation, and before we could even return from vacation, the children who had read about the decree in the newspaper had applied to the schools and had been admitted, and there was no more administrative problem involved than admitting anybody else. I certainly heard of nothing unusual in this particular case that would indicate any serious administrative, or any administrative, difficulty.

JUSTICE FRANKFURTER: Are you suggesting that on the broader issue there is no problem at all in just eliminating segregated school systems throughout the country, no problem at all?

MR. GREENBERG: Of course, there may be a problem, but in this case, there was no problem, and in fact no problem whatsoever.

JUSTICE FRANKFURTER: Then there is no occasion for not doing what the Delaware court did?

MR. GREENBERG: As far as administrative problems are concerned, I see no problem.

The Attorney General's contention that the schools can be equalized within one year does not take several factors into account. The first one is, how the Wilmington School Board, which is not a party to this case, and which would have to equalize the Howard School in question, can be compelled to equalize the Howard School, since it is not a party to the case. The Court of Chancery and the Supreme Court of Delaware both know that they could not order the Wilmington

Board to do anything to which it was not a party. And the Attorney General in his petition for certiorari and also in his argument nowhere indicated how Delaware courts of equity could administer the type of decree which he said that they should have handed down, as both the Court of Chancery, which would have to administer such a decree, and the Supreme Court of Delaware have ruled that they cannot engage in the sort of business which he wants them to become involved in.

I read from page 57 of the thin blue book, at the end:

... It is difficult to see how a court of equity could effectively supervise and direct the expenditure of state funds in a matter committed to the sound administrative discretion of the school authorities.

The Chancellor wrote similarly that he did not see how he could order the state to put into effect the equalization which the Attorney General suggests this Court should order the state to do.

A reference to the pages of the record to which the Attorney General referred for his assertion that equality will occur sometime in the future does not reveal that there is any likelihood of equality at all in the future. Both courts below found no likelihood of future equality.

The Court of Chancery wrote on page 352 of this thick white book:

I do not see how the plans mentioned will remove all the objections to the present arrangement.

And on page 353:

I conclude that the State's future plans do not operate to prevent the granting of relief to these plaintiffs . . .

And on page 356, he indicated that the same considerations applied to the elementary school cases. I was talking about the high school cases in the other two.

The Supreme Court of Delaware likewise noted that the Attorney General had proffered no evidence whatsoever of future equalization, and he noted that claims of equality would have to be judged when made in the future. That is on page 58 of the thin blue book.

So the Attorney General's request for a decree ordering equalization is based upon a factual premise that such equalization will occur at some ascertainable time in the future, and it is nowhere supported in the record in either of the opinions of the courts below.

THE CHIEF JUSTICE: You mean to say that the record does not show about the construction of the new high school, costing a million and a quarter dollars, that the Attorney General referred to?

MR. GREENBERG: Yes, Your Honor. It showed that a new high school is being constructed. That high school is thirty miles south of where respondents live, in the high school case, and it nowhere indicates what effect that high school will have upon the future education of respondents.

THE CHIEF JUSTICE: Does it consider the additions at Howard, and how they would be ready for use next September? Is that in the record, or is the Attorney General speaking out of the record?

MR. GREENBERG: There is a stipulation, Your Honor, which I will quote in full, and I think it will thoroughly answer your question. The stipulation is on page 36 of the clipped-in portion of the thin blue book, and Item 3 of that stipulation states:

> The present schedule of the Wilmington Board of Education calls for a transfer of grades seven, eight and nine of the Howard High School to the Bancroft School and the closing down of the Carver School at the beginning of the school year in September, 1953.

THE CHIEF JUSTICE: Is there anything about the additional facilities at Howard? We were told that there is quite a bit of it, and that that would be ready in September.

MR. GREENBERG: I think, in justice to the Attorney General, I can take the petition for certiorari and refer to every record reference that he gives. On page 5 of his petition for certiorari, speaking of future equalization, he refers first to pages R-36 and 57, which are in the clipped-in portion of this thin blue book. On page R-36 is Item 3, which we just read. On page 57, there is the statement that the court held:

> As to the Howard-Carver buildings, plans have been approved for the transfer of the junior high school pupils at Howard to another junior high school, for the enlargement of the Howard building, with additional equipment, and for the closing of Carver and the transfer of its pupils to Howard. It is said that all these changes are expected to be completed by September 1953, and that they will completely equalize the Howard facilities. It is also shown that plans are under way to build a modern high school for Negroes at Middletown, New Castle County.

That is our item. I might say that this nowhere takes into account contemplated future changes at the Claymont School, and the record indicates a very vast expansion program is under way there.

He then refers in that same paragraph to page 57, which I read, and then he refers to page A-312, which is page 312 of the thick white book. George Miller, who was State Superintendent of Education, stated:

> The construction program in New Castle County provides for a four-year high school in Middletown which is under way now, and we are just waiting for materials until that is completed.

But it nowhere indicates what effect that will have. This is thirty miles south of where respondents live. It in no way indicates what effect that will have on respondents' education.

He then in the elementary school case refers to pages R-59 to 62, where it is stated that until recently the white elementary school was favored in the receipt of public funds, and that that inequality has been eliminated, and on page 62, there is the statement that, speaking of the fact that the inequality of funds had been eliminated:

> the burden was clearly upon the defendants to show the extent to which the remedial legislation had improved conditions or would improve them in the near future. This the defendants failed to do. It is natural to suppose that with the equality of funds any

substantial disparities will shortly be eliminated, but we must take the record as it was made below.

And that only refers to the equalization of teachers in the two schools. It does not refer to any other disparities.

As Mr. Redding indicated, Your Honor, it is our contention in this case that from the Attorney General's position in this case and from the express provision in the opinion of the Supreme Court of Delaware, this litigation is open to re-segregate those plaintiffs at any time that the physical facilities, they believe, may become equalized.

Now, if the physical facilities were all that were involved in this case, it would be our contention that this merely might be another unfortunate burden that these respondents have to bear solely because of their race. But where the record proves that the injury from which the right flows will exist in segregated schools so long as segregated schools exist, we submit that this court should recognize these facts and assure the respondents' admission permanently.

JUSTICE BLACK: Do you say that the record shows that? What are you depending upon? The findings?

MR. GREENBERG: We are depending upon the findings and the evidence upon which the findings were made.

JUSTICE BLACK: Do you take the position that the findings affect the matter generally, or only in Delaware?

MR. GREENBERG: The findings expressly referred to Delaware, Your Honor, in our Delaware society. As to the other states, I have read the record in some of these other states, and there is similar evidence. But speaking of the Delaware case, the findings refer to Delaware specifically, and indeed, by our witnesses there was a very heavy emphasis upon the fact that these Delaware children were examined by one of America's most eminent psychiatrists, and by psychologists. An ex-head of the Delaware Psychological Association testified for us. The head of the Sociology Department of the University of Delaware testified for us. A professor of education at the University of Delaware testified for us. It was all to the effect that in Delaware society, this is the effect.

JUSTICE BLACK: Is that what you are limiting this part of your argument to, that on the basis of cases of this kind and the findings of fact based on oral testimony it may be expected, under the "separate but equal" doctrine to show that there is an inferiority in educational opportunity in one community where there might not be in another?

MR. GREENBERG: Yes, Your Honor, that is part of what you might call a three-prong attack. But that is only one part of it. We also contend, of course, that the classification is entirely unreasonable, but we are urging all the reasons we can for affirmance of the judgment below. And that is one of the reasons.

So as I said, in the doctrine announced in the case of *Helvering* v. *Lerner Stores*,[65] which is in our brief at page 11, we urge these additional reasons for affirmance of the judgment below.

[65]314 U.S. 463 (1941). The Court held that claims of unreasonable classification raise no question under the Fifth Amendment which contains no equal protection clause.

We urge again that this Court recognize the unreasonableness of the classification involved in this case, and also that this Court adopt as its own the factual finding of the Chancellor that state-imposed segregation in Delaware society injures the Negro child.

JUSTICE FRANKFURTER: How can we do that? The Supreme Court says that we are not going to review that. That means that we must take the testimony of Dr. Fredric Wertham, for whom I have a great respect, and say that his testimony, his appraisal and his judgment are like mathematical pronouncements, and there they are.

MR. GREENBERG: Well, Your Honor, there are several things involved. It is a very full and completely uncontradicted record. Secondly, there was a thorough review by the Chancellor.

JUSTICE FRANKFURTER: But the testimony of a witness is subject to intrinsic limitations and qualifications and illuminations. The mere fact that a man is not contradicted does not mean that what he says is so.

MR. GREENBERG: As far as that is concerned, the Chancellor—

JUSTICE FRANKFURTER: If a man says three yards, and I have measured it, and it is three yards, there it is. But if a man tells you the inside of your brain and mine, and how we function, that is not a measurement, and there you are.

MR. GREENBERG: That is true, Your Honor. But it is our contention that as far as the value to be placed upon the facts, the trial judge was able to see and hear the witness, and that is certainly in the record. The Chancellor saw him. Now, as far as the record is concerned, Your Honors are as free to review that record as the Supreme Court of Delaware. They cannot recapture the mood and the word of the witness, either, and this bears on a constitutional right.

JUSTICE FRANKFURTER: I do not know about that. They are dealing with Delaware conditions. They are dealing with situations that they know about. It makes a lot of difference, whether you have two so-called minority children in a group of twenty or two out of fifty or ten out of forty. Those are all local conditions, as to which the Supreme Court of Delaware has some knowledge, having lived there and thought about these things.

MR. GREENBERG: All we can say is that whatever consideration was given to the matter by the Delaware court, all added up to the fact that segregation injured these children. And as far as what I assume Your Honor is referring to, I assume Your Honor is referring to what other counsel has referred to, the untoward effects of the abolition of segregation.

JUSTICE FRANKFURTER: I am not referring to anything, except that we are here in a domain which I do not yet regard as science in the sense of mathematical certainty. This is all opinion evidence.

MR. GREENBERG: That is true, Your Honor.

JUSTICE FRANKFURTER: I do not mean that I disrespect it. I simply know its character. It can be a very different thing from, as I say, things that are weighed and measured and are fungible. We are dealing here with very subtle things, very subtle testimony.

MR. GREENBERG: Our only answer to that is that to the extent that it did receive a review below, and to the extent that the Chancellor was able to view these witnesses, and to the extent that the cross-examination affected their testimony, and to the extent that the Supreme Court of Delaware felt that the abolition of segregation would have any untoward effect, none of that weakens this testimony at all, because in fact segregation was abolished as far as these particular children were concerned, and they are now attending the schools.

JUSTICE FRANKFURTER: I do not mean to raise the question of testimony. All I am saying is that I do not have a record such as I would have if I merely had the Chancellor's findings or if the Supreme Court had said, "We agree with the Chancellor."

MR. GREENBERG: I agree that if more people had reviewed this—

JUSTICE FRANKFURTER: Not more; the very simple fact, the fact that the Supreme Court said, inasmuch as we deem this immaterial, we do not review it, and therefore we have merely a finding of an intermediate court, as to which I know not what the highest court of Delaware would have said if they had reviewed it.

JUSTICE BLACK: Did you say that the children are now attending these schools?

MR. GREENBERG: That is right, sir. They registered from the beginning of the semester. I thought I mentioned that the decree—

JUSTICE BLACK: I thought the argument was that they could not get in, that it would disrupt the schools.

MR. GREENBERG: The Attorney General of Delaware applied for a stay of execution, but it was not granted to him. One of the reasons was that he applied too late, and another reason was that to grant the stay would be inconsistent with the mandate.

And so for the reasons that Mr. Redding has submitted, and particularly for those reasons, because we feel that our respondents' rights can be more fully protected and more permanently protected in that way, we urge that this Court affirm the judgment below, and assure that the respondents' stay in the schools to which they have been admitted and which they are now attending will be one unharassed by future litigation, and attempts to segregate them once more.

(Whereupon, at 3:50 p.m., the argument was concluded.)

1953 ARGUMENT

Miscellaneous Orders

345 U.S. 972

June 8, 1953

No. 8. BROWN ET AL. v. BOARD OF EDUCATION OF TOPEKA ET AL.;
No. 101. BRIGGS ET AL. v. ELLIOTT ET AL., MEMBERS OF BOARD OF TRUSTEES OF SCHOOL DISTRICT #22, ET AL.;
No. 191. DAVIS ET AL. v. COUNTY SCHOOL BOARD OF PRINCE EDWARD COUNTY ET AL.;
No. 413. BOLLING ET AL. v. SHARPE ET AL.; and
No. 448. GEBHART ET AL. v. BELTON ET AL.

Each of these cases is ordered restored to the docket and is assigned for reargument on Monday, October 12, next. In their briefs and on oral argument counsel are requested to discuss particularly the following questions insofar as they are relevant to the respective cases:

1. What evidence is there that the Congress which submitted and the State legislatures and conventions which ratified the Fourteenth Amendment contemplated or did not contemplate, understood or did not understand, that it would abolish segregation in public schools?

2. If neither the Congress in submitting nor the States in ratifying the Fourteenth Amendment understood that compliance with it would require the immediate abolition of segregation in public schools, was it nevertheless the understanding of the framers of the Amendment

(a) that future Congresses might, in the exercise of their power under section 5 of the Amendment, abolish such segregation, or

(b) that it would be within the judicial power, in light of future conditions, to construe the Amendment as abolishing such segregation of its own force?

3. On the assumption that the answers to questions 2 (a) and (b) do not dispose of the issue, is it within the judicial power, in construing the Amendment, to abolish segregation in public schools?

4. Assuming it is decided that segregation in public schools violates the Fourteenth Amendment

(a) would a decree necessarily follow providing that, within the limits set by normal geographic school districting, Negro children should forthwith be admitted to schools of their choice, or

(b) may this Court, in the exercise of its equity powers, permit an effective gradual adjustment to be brought about from existing segregated systems to a system not based on color distinctions?

178

5. On the assumption on which questions 4 *(a)* and *(b)* are based, and assuming further that this Court will exercise its equity powers to the end described in question 4 *(b)*,

(a) should this Court formulate detailed decrees in these cases;

(b) if so, what specific issues should the decrees reach;

(c) should this Court appoint a special master to hear evidence with a view to recommending specific terms for such decrees;

(d) should this Court remand to the courts of first instance with directions to frame decrees in these cases, and if so what general directions should the decrees of this Court include and what procedures should the courts of first instance follow in arriving at the specific terms of more detailed decrees?

The Attorney General of the United States is invited to take part in the oral argument and to file an additional brief if he so desires.

IN THE SUPREME COURT OF THE UNITED STATES

October Term, 1953

HARRY BRIGGS, JR., et al.,
Appellants,

vs.

R. W. ELLIOTT, CHAIRMAN, J. D. CARSON, et al.,
MEMBERS OF BOARD OF TRUSTEES OF SCHOOL DISTRICT NO. 22,
CLARENDON COUNTY, S.C., et al
Appellees.

DOROTHY E. DAVIS, BERTHA M. DAVIS AND INEZ E. DAVIS, ETC., et al.,
Appellants,

vs.

COUNTY SCHOOL BOARD OF PRINCE EDWARD COUNTY, VIRGINIA, et al.,
Appellees

Case No. 4

Washington, D.C.
Monday, December 7, 1953.

The above-entitled causes came on for oral argument at 1:05 p.m.

PRESENT:

The Chief Justice, Honorable Earl Warren, and Associate Justices Black, Reed, Frankfurter, Douglas,
Jackson, Burton, Clark, and Minton.

APPEARANCES:

On behalf of the Appellants, Dorothy E. Davis, et al.:
SPOTTSWOOD W. ROBINSON, III, ESQ.

On behalf of the Appellants, Harry Briggs, Jr. et al.:
THURGOOD MARSHALL, ESQ.

On behalf of the Appellees, R. W. Elliott, Chairman, J. R. Carson, et al.,
Members of Board of Trustees of School District No. 22, Clarendon County, S.C., et al.:
JOHN W. DAVIS, ESQ.

On behalf of the Appellees, County School Board of Prince Edward County, Virginia, et al.:
T. JUSTIN MOORE, ESQ., and J. LINDSAY ALMOND, ESQ.

On behalf of the United States:
J. LEE RANKIN, ESQ., Assistant Attorney General

THE CHIEF JUSTICE: No. 2, Harry Briggs, Jr., et al versus R. W. Elliott, et al.

THE CLERK: Counsel are present.

ARGUMENT ON BEHALF OF THE APPELLANTS
by MR. ROBINSON

MR. ROBINSON: May it please the Court. At the outset I should like to point out that the argument in No. 2 and the argument in No. 4 are being combined. Mr. Marshall and I are offering two separate appeals, as I have already outlined, the appeal in No. 2 and the appeal in No. 4, and for this reason at the outset I would like the indulgence of the Court, before stating the facts, to outline the argument and the part that he will present and the part that I will undertake to present.

After stating the facts and the procedural matters, I propose to address myself to questions one and two of the Court, and to discuss the historical evidence which we submit demonstrates that the Congress that submitted it and the legislatures and conventions that ratified the Fourteenth Amendment, contemplated and understood that it would abolish segregation in public schools; that future congresses might in the exercise of their power under section 5 of the Amendment abolish segregation, and also, that it would be within the jurisdictional power in the light of future conditions to construe the Amendment as abolishing segregation of its own force.

Mr. Marshall will then address himself to questions three, four, and five and will present our arguments demonstrating that it is within the jurisdictional power in construing the Amendment to abolish segregation in public schools and our position with respect to the disposition that this Court should make of these cases in the event that it is decided that segregation in public schools violates the Fourteenth Amendment.

Both of these cases are rearguments of appeals from final decrees of three-judge District Courts, in the instance of No. 2 from the Eastern District of South Carolina, in the instance of No. 4, from the Eastern District of Virginia.

In each of these cases Negro children and their respective parents and guardians sued competent county school authorities alleging that by requiring these and other Negro children to attend separate Negro schools as commanded by the Constitutions and the laws of South Carolina and Virginia respectively, they denied them rights secured by the Fourteenth Amendment.

In each of these cases the appellants sought decrees declaring the invalidity of the state school segregation provisions and injunctions restraining the appellees from enforcing these provisions and from restricting Negro children on a racial basis in their requiring attendance in the public schools.

In case No. 2, the majority of the District Court, with Judge Waring[1] dissent-

[1]Judge J. Waties Waring (1880–1968). United States District Judge for South Carolina, 1942–1952. He ruled in 1947 that the South Carolina Democratic primary must be open to Negroes, Elmore v. Rice, 72 F. Supp. 516 (E.D.S.C. 1947). Thereafter, Waring's life was threatened and his home was stoned. An unsuccessful effort was made to impeach him in the House of Representatives. After dissenting in the lower court decision in Briggs v. Elliott, he received more personal abuse for his pro-Negro ruling and soon afterward resigned from the bench. He moved to New York and became active in various civil rights organizations.

ing following the original hearing of that case in that court, filed an opinion and entered a final decree requiring the appellees to afford the appellants involved in that case equal facilities, but declaring that the contested constitutional and statutory provisions were valid, and refusing to grant the requested injunctive relief.

On appeal from this decree this Court, Mr. Justice Douglas and Mr. Justice Black dissenting, vacated the judgment, that is, the first decree of the District Court, and remanded the case for the purpose of obtaining the view of the District Court upon additional facts in the record presented by a report which was subsequently filed in the District Court by the appellees, and to give the District Court the opportunity to take such action as it might deem appropriate in the light of the facts disclosed by that report.

The District Court then proceeded to have a second hearing. Judge Waring, in the meanwhile, had retired from the bench.

Upon this occasion after the hearing the District Court filed another opinion and entered another final decree, this time unanimously, again declaring the school segregation provision valid, and refusing to grant injunctive relief.

In case No. 4, the District Court for the Eastern District of Virginia likewise found inequalities in physical facilities and curricula, and likewise, it ordered that these inequalities be eliminated. But as to the District Court, in No. 2, it refused to invalidate or to enjoin the enforcement of the school segregation provisions.

These cases were argued before this Court at the last term. On last June 8 the Court entered an order directing reargument in the case and requesting counsel to address themselves to five questions set forth in the order so far as those questions would be relevant to the issues involved in the respective cases. It is pursuant, of course, to that order that we are here today.

I think that it is highly significant at the outset to note that each of these cases was brought pursuant to the authority conferred by the Act of April 20, 1871, section 1 of that Act, which is now codified in large measure in Title 8 of the United States Code, section 43 [now 42 U.S.C. section 1983]. That Act was entitled:

An Act to enforce the provisions of the Fourteenth Amendment to the Constitution of the United States and for other purposes.

As the Court is well aware, the Act provided, as does the present section, although the present section does not exactly conform to the original Act, though essentially the same provisions are there, that:

Any person who, under color of any law of any State, subjects or causes to be subjected any person within the jurisdiction of the United States to the deprivation of any rights secured by the Constitution of the United States shall be liable to the party injured in any action at law, a suit in equity or other proper proceeding for redress.

Involved in these cases is a statute which in the viewpoint of the appellants is in violation of the provisions of section 1 of the Fourteenth Amendment. In section 43 of Title 8 we have a statute which, in the enforcement of the provisions of the Fourteenth Amendment, creates a cause of action and confers both the power and the duty upon the federal courts to enforce that cause of action.

We submit that the statute imposes a positive duty upon the courts to determine whether, under the Fourteenth Amendment, the action of a state in imposing racial segregation in public education is valid.

I would like now to proceed to an examination of the history of the formulation, the proposal and the ratification of the Fourteenth Amendment as an aid to the Court's determination of whether the laws involved in these cases can stand consistently with the prohibitions of the Fourteenth Amendment.

Our position is this: considering the overall evidence derived from the debates and proceedings on the Fourteenth Amendment, these conclusions are supported.

First: that the Amendment had as its purpose and effect the complete legal equality of all persons, irrespective of race, and the prohibition of all state imposed caste and class systems based upon race.

And secondly, that segregation in public schools, constituting as it does legislation of this type, is necessarily embraced within the prohibitions of the Amendment.

Going first to the debates on the Fourteenth Amendment itself, there is considerable evidence of the intention of the framers to broadly provide for the complete legal equality of all men, irrespective of race, and to broadly proscribe all caste and class legislation based upon race or color.

There is also some reference specifically to the impact which the proposed Amendment would have upon State imposed segregation in public schools. I propose to address myself to both categories of evidence.

When the 39th Congress, which formulated the Fourteenth Amendment, convened in December of 1865, it was cognizant of, and it was confronted with, the so-called Black Codes which had been enacted throughout the southern states.

In brief summary, these laws imposed and were designed to maintain essentially the same inferior position which Negroes had occupied prior to the abolition of slavery. As a matter of fact, they followed pretty much the legal pattern of the antebellum slave codes.

For example, they compelled Negroes to work for limited pay, they restricted their mobility, they prohibited their testimony in court against a white person, and contained innumerable provisions for segregation on carriers and in public places. In some of these codes there were expressed prohibitions upon the attendance by Negroes of the public schools provided for white children.

I would like to emphasize, as this Court has in its previous decisions recognized, that the existence of these laws was largely responsible for the Fourteenth Amendment and the contemporaneous civil rights legislation.

We find in the debates and proceedings on the Fourteenth Amendment abundant evidence demonstrating that the radical Republicans in the 39th Congress desired and intended that the Fourteenth Amendment would effect both the invalidation of the existing Black Codes and any and all future attempts to impose governmentally caste distinctions predicated upon race.

Among the items of evidence which demonstrate this broad overall purpose in effect of the Amendment, I would like to make reference to the following: When the resolution was introduced into the Senate which embraced the provision which is now section 1 of the Fourteenth Amendment, with simply the addition of the citizenship clause, in other words, House Resolution 127, Senate Howard[2] opened

[2]Senator Jacob M. Howard (1805-1871) of Michigan. Whig representative, 1841-1843; one of the founders of the Republican party in 1854; Republican senator, 1867-1871.

the debate in the Senate—as a matter of fact, he was speaking for the Joint Committee on Reconstruction, which had formulated the provision, mindful, as I said before, that it did not yet contain the citizenship clause, but did contain the privileges or immunities, the equal protection and due process clauses—speaking for the Joint Committee, because Senator Fessenden,[3] one of its co-chairmen, was ill, he made these significant statements.

He referred to the last two clauses of the first section. He said that these two clauses disabled a state from depriving not merely a citizen of the United States, but of any person, whoever he may be, of life, liberty or property without due process of law, and from denying him the equal protection of the laws.

This, Senator Howard says abolishes all class legislation in the states and does away with the injustice of subjecting one caste of persons to a code not applicable to another.

It prohibits the hanging of a black man for crime for which the white man is not hanged. It protects the black man in his fundamental rights as a citizen with the same shield which it throws around the white man.

Here we have an explicit declaration by one of the co-chairmen of the committee of Congress which formulated what is now essentially section 1 of the Fourteenth Amendment, and that is the scope that he ascribed to it.

As a matter of fact, during the course of the same speech introducing the bill into Congress, Senator Howard had this to say:

> I look upon the first section taken in connection with the fifth section as very important. It will, if adopted by the States, forever disable every one of them from passing laws infringing upon those fundamental rights and privileges which pertain to citizens of the United States and to all persons who may happen to be within their jurisdiction.
>
> It establishes equality before the law, it gives to the humblest, the poorest, the most despised of the race the same rights and the same protection before the law that it gives to the most powerful, the most wealthy and the most haughty.

Consequently, certainly in the opinion of Senator Howard, the due process and equal protection clauses would sweep away, in his language, all class legislation.

Similarly, during the Senate debates, Senator Poland[4] addressed himself to section 1, and he made a somewhat similar declaration. As a matter of fact, he pointed out the existence of the Black Codes. He made reference to them specifically:

> We know that State laws exist and some of them of very recent enactment, in direct violation of these principles.

Then he went on to give the Amendment the scope which he thought it was entitled to.

[3]Senator William P. Fessenden (1806–1869) of Maine. Whig representative, 1841–1843; Whig and Republican senator 1854–1864; Secretary of the Treasury, 1864–1865; Republican senator, 1865–1869. He was one of the seven Republican senators who voted to acquit President Andrew Johnson in his impeachment trial in May, 1868.

[4]Senator Luke P. Poland (1815–1887) of Vermont. Republican senator, 1865–1867; representative, 1867–1875 and 1883–1885.

The statements in this regard were by no means confined to the proponents of the Amendment. As a matter of fact, after the citizenship clause had been added to the Amendment, Senator Davis[5] of Kentucky had this to say:

> The real and only object of the first provision of this section [speaking of the citizenship clause which the Senate has added to it] is to make Negroes citizens, to prop the Civil Rights Bill and to give them a more plausible if not a valid claim to its provisions, to press forward to a full community of civil and political rights with the white race, for which its authors are struggling and mean to continue to struggle.

Over in the House when Representative Stevens[6] introduced Resolution 127, he made a similar declaration with respect to scope.

> I can hardly believe that any person can be found who will not admit that every one of these provisions [in the first section] is just.

As a matter of fact, Congressman Stevens says they are all asserted in some form or another in our Declaration or organic law. He pointed out, however, that the Constitution limits the action of Congress; that in this area it was not a limitation upon the States and said that the Amendment supplied that defect and allowed Congress to correct the unjust legislation of the states, and here again referring to the Black Codes, in so far as that law which operates upon one man shall operate equally upon all.

He later on made further reference to the fact that the Amendment was necessary by what he termed the oppressive codes which had become law in the southern states, pointing out that unless the Constitution should restrain these states, "those States will, I fear"—to use his language—"will all keep up this discrimination, and crush to death the hated Freedmen."

And just as in the Senate, we had others who took the floor in the discussion. I might make reference to the statement which was made by Congressman Randall[7] of Pennsylvania, the statement that was made by Congressman Rogers of New Jersey.[8] Now, they were men who opposed the Amendment.

Yet, their statements which we have set forth in our brief show that they also recognized as one of the clauses, as the great occasion for the Fourteenth Amendment, the existence of these racial laws in southern states, and recognized that if the Amendment were in fact adopted, it would have an impact upon such laws of the character which we describe.

I should also like to direct the Court's attention specifically to the statement of Mr. Bingham,[9] who has very appropriately been described as the Madison of

[5]Senator Garrett Davis (1801–1872) of Kentucky. Whig representative, 1839–1847; Whig and Democratic senator, 1861–1872.

[6]Representative Thaddeus Stevens (1792–1868) of Pennsylvania. Whig and Republican representative, 1849–1853 and 1859–1868; Leader of the radical Republicans after the Civil War and Chairman of the managers of the House conducting the impeachment proceedings against President Andrew Johnson.

[7]Representative Samuel J. Randall (1828–1890) of Pennsylvania. Democratic representative, 1863–1890.

[8]Representative Andrew J. Rogers (1828–1900) of New Jersey. Democratic representative, 1863–1867.

[9]Representative John A. Bingham (1815–1900) of Ohio. Republican representative, 1855–1863 and 1865–1873; one of the House managers in the impeachment proceedings against President Andrew Johnson.

the first section of the Fourteenth Amendment. Mr. Bingham made a very notable speech in the House during the debates on the Amendment.

He said that the need for the first section was, to use his language, "one of the lessons that had been taught by the history of the past four years of terrific conflict."

He pointed out that the Amendment did not take away rights which were properly reserved to the states, for in his opinion, and in his language, no state ever had the right under the forms of law, or otherwise, to deny to any Freedmen the equal protection of the law or to abridge the privileges or immunities of any citizen of the Republic, although many of them have assumed and exercised that power and that without remedy.

Going specifically to the evidence which was directed to the issue of public school segregation, I should like first to point out that on the Fourteenth Amendment debates proper, we find only one specific reference to school segregation, and that was the reference that was made in the House by Representative Rogers at the time that Resolution No. 63 was up for consideration. Resolution 63 was the predecessor of 127, and the relationship between the two of them I shall undertake to establish in just a moment.

But during this speech, Representative Rogers made a direct attack upon the proposed Amendment which at that time simply provided that Congress should have the power to make all laws which shall be necessary and proper to secure to the citizens of each state all privileges and immunities of citizens of the several states, and to all persons in the several states equal protection in the rights of life, liberty and property.

Perhaps I should undertake at this moment to demonstrate that connection which I mentioned. H.R. 63 was the bill which had been reported by the Joint Committee on Reconstruction, and it was a bill drafted by Mr. Bingham. H.R. 127, which eventually became, with two significant changes, the Fourteenth Amendment, was also drafted so far as the provisions of section 1 of the Amendment were concerned by Mr. Bingham.

Mr. Bingham introduced Resolution 63 in the House first, and it is notable at this point to say two things which I think are very significant.

In the first place, H.R. 63 was proposed simply to grant to Congress the power to enact laws of a certain character. Pursuant to this authority, assuming as I do that this would have been the construction given to H.R. 63 had it become a constitutional amendment, pursuant to this authority Congress might undertake to pass laws which would outlaw this or that embraced within the scope of the prohibition.

Later on—and the proceedings of the Joint Committee on Reconstruction indicate the various drafts, the various attempts, the various procedures which were gone through and finally deriving the present language of the trilogy of the first section—the form was changed, and it was changed and rewritten by Mr. Bingham to state as a direct prohibition upon the states the disabilities with respect to the things which were embraced within that section.

Now it was, as I said before, at the time that H.R. 63 came up for consideration in the House that Representative Rogers made reference to school segregation. As a matter of fact, he attacked this proposal. He termed it "more dangerous to the liberties of the people and the foundations of the Government than any proposal for amending the Constitution heretofore advanced". He said this amendment would destroy all state legislation distinguishing Negroes on the basis of race.

With respect to schools specifically he had this to say:

> In the State of Pennsylvania there are laws which make a distinction with regard to the schooling of white children and the schooling of black children. It is provided that certain schools shall be designated and set apart for white children, and certain other schools designated and set apart for black children.
>
> Under this amendment Congress would have the power to compel the state to provide for white children and black children to attend the same school upon the principle that all the people shall have equal protection and all the rights of life, liberty and property and all the privileges and immunities of citizens of the several States.

I think that it is also highly significant that during these debates no one denied that H.R. 63 had the scope that Mr. Rogers said that it did.

Throughout the debates there is practically no dispute as to the scope of H.R. 127, which eventually became the trilogy of the Fourteenth Amendment. As a matter of fact, Representative Bingham, who was contemporaneously amending the 1866 Civil Rights Act, to which I will make reference shortly, because of its broad anti-discrimination provisions, and claiming that it lacked constitutional foundation, naturally did not make any dispute of Representative Rogers' appraisal of the wide scope of H.R. 63.

On the contrary, Mr. Bingham in a colloquy with Mr. Hale,[10] two days later indicated his appraisal in just about the same terms. He was asked at that time a question in that regard, and at that time Mr. Bingham pointed to the equal protection clause of his constitutional proposal as justifying the scope which he attributed to the amendment.

In addition to the debates and proceedings on the Fourteenth Amendment proper, there is other evidence which in our opinion is helpful in promoting an understanding of the purposes and effects of the Fourteenth Amendment and of the correctness of our conclusions in this regard.

One of the most important of these items of evidence in my opinion is the Civil Rights Act of 1866. The 39th Congress had an occasion to contemporaneously consider, in addition to the Fourteenth Amendment, this piece of civil rights legislation.

I think that it is very important that at the outset I should point out that these two measures are related, this measure, rather, is related to the Fourteenth Amendment by something more than a mere coincidence in terms of time or subject matter.

The Fourteenth Amendment was actually proposed after members of the 39th Congress stated that the civil rights guaranteed by statute, particularly the Civil Rights Act of 1866, were vulnerable to future political attack or might be struck down as unconstitutional.

Consequently the legislative history of the Act of 1866 is a relevant and important part of the background of the Fourteenth Amendment. This is particu-

[10]Representative Robert S. Hale (1822–1881) of New York. Republican representative, 1866–1867 and 1873–1875.

larly true in our opinion since, as I will later undertake to show, the scope of the Fourteenth Amendment was broader than the scope of this Act.

Going through this as deeply as time will permit, the Civil Rights Act came about in the form of a bill introduced by Senator Trumbull[11] which intended to prohibit in the terms of the bill "any discrimination in civil rights or immunities among the people of the United States on account of race, color or previous condition of servitude," and also containing other provisions to the effect that all persons should have full and equal benefit of all laws for the security of their persons and property, and enumerating certain rights, the right to sue, the right to make contracts, to own and inherit property and that type of thing, which the latter provision would provide.

Senator Trumbull introduced the bill and, upon its introduction, he gave it a very broad scope. He said that in his opinion any statute which was based on race, which was not equal to all persons and which deprived any citizen of civil rights which are secured to other citizens, is in fact a badge of servitude which in his opinion was prohibited by the Constitution.

When the bill was introduced, there were two things that were considered by the houses of Congress with regard to this act. First was its constitutionality, and I don't think I need to needlessly consume the time of the Court on that issue, but simply point out that opponents of the bill took the position there was nothing in the Constitution at that time to justify the enactment of such a law.

There were others on the other side who asserted that the bill was constitutional.

And the second big issue that was involved in the proceedings in this regard was the scope of the bill. Time and again the Democrats and the more conservative Republicans in the Senate and in the other House of Congress had occasion to state that this bill, if Congress passed it, would have a very, very broad effect.

It would have an effect which would deprive the states of all power to make or impose racial distinctions or classifications, and some of these people made specific reference to the impact of the provisions of the first section of this bill, the "no discrimination" of this bill upon public school segregation.

JUSTICE FRANKFURTER: Mr. Robinson, what attitude do you think the Court is called upon to manage, what weight is to be given, or how is it to ever deal with individual utterances of this, that or other congressmen or senators?

MR. ROBINSON: I do not, Mr. Justice Frankfurter, take the position as this Court has on previous occasions stated that it would insist that the meaning of a constitutional provision or of a statute is to be determined by any isolated statement of any individual proponent or opponent of the legislation.

At the outset, however, I tried to point out what was the great occasion, in other words, what there was in the history of the times which presented the occasion for the constitutional amendment. Perhaps I should have earlier pointed out that the same thing, the racial laws in the southern states, constituted the basis,

[11]Senator Lyman Trumbull (1813–1896) of Illinois. Republican senator, 1855–1873; one of seven Republican senators to vote against the impeachment of President Andrew Johnson.

the occasion for the enactment, for the promulgation and eventual enactment in limited form, of the Civil Rights Act of 1866.

JUSTICE FRANKFURTER: Do you think we can get out of the debates anything more than Mr. Justice Miller[12] got out of them at the time of the *Slaughter-House Cases?*

MR. ROBINSON: Yes, I think so, Mr. Justice Frankfurter. As I recall Mr. Justice Miller's opinion in the *Slaughter-House Cases,* he recognized also that the great purpose of the Fourteenth Amendment, the occasion for the enactment of it, for the adoption of the Fourteenth Amendment—and I think that what additionally we got out of the debate is not simply a statement here or a statement there with respect to the broad overall purpose and effect, the fundamental thing that a constitutional amendment is supposed to accomplish, but what we get is a general understanding by people who are in the body promulgating that provision as to what scope it was intended to have.

JUSTICE FRANKFURTER: And the understanding you get or you think we ought to get goes beyond the terms which Justice Miller put it in the *Slaughter-House Cases.*

MR. ROBINSON: Well, I do not in any wise, of course, intend in any way to cut down on anything that Mr. Justice Miller stated in that connection. We offer the evidence in the congressional debates on the Amendment and other debates—

JUSTICE FRANKFURTER: I grant you we solicited and elicited that. But I just wondered now that we have got it, what are we to get out of it? The fact that a man in your position says, "This is a terrible measure and if you pass it we will do this and that," does that tell me that this measure does do this and that?

MR. ROBINSON: To this extent, sir. So far as the statement standing alone is concerned, I would attribute no value to it. But when a man makes that statement and he is joined in it by others, he is not disputed by anyone, we have a condition of general understanding that is demonstrated by the overall statements pro and con in that particular connection. I think we get assistance.

JUSTICE FRANKFURTER: You think if an opponent gives an extreme interpretation of a proposed statute or constitutional amendment in order to frighten people on the other side, and the proponents do not get up and say "Yes, that is the thing we want to accomplish," that means they believe it, do you?

MR. ROBINSON: Well, I will have to put it in these terms. I would not, of course, sir, know the motive of the person making that statement.

---

[12]Justice Samuel Miller (1816–1896) of Iowa. A doctor until he was thirty, he then studied law and became a leading lawyer in his state before being appointed to the Supreme Court by President Lincoln in 1862. One of the outstanding Justices of his time, he sat on the Court until 1890. He wrote the Court's opinion in the Slaughter-House Cases, 16 Wall. 36 (1873).

JUSTICE FRANKFURTER: I know, but what does silence mean?

MR. ROBINSON: I think when you have statement after statement with respect to broad overall purpose—

JUSTICE FRANKFURTER: By individual members?

MR. ROBINSON: By individual members.

JUSTICE FRANKFURTER: That the proposal has—

MR. ROBINSON: On other sides, if you please, on both sides, coupled with the fact of almost an entire absence of evidence to the contrary showing that anyone there had a different understanding or a different opinion as to what scope it would have.

JUSTICE FRANKFURTER: Namely, they wanted this proposal to put an end to treating white and colored differently before the law in all its manifestations?

MR. ROBINSON: That is correct, sir.

JUSTICE FRANKFURTER: That is all you get out of it?

MR. ROBINSON: In all of its manifestations.

JUSTICE FRANKFURTER: Then the question is whether this is one of its manifestations.

MR. ROBINSON: I beg your pardon, sir.

JUSTICE FRANKFURTER: Then the question is whether this is one of its manifestations.

MR. ROBINSON: Our position in this regard, Mr. Justice Frankfurter, is that when you consider overall what these people said, what from the facts of history it appears, what Mr. Justice Miller, if you please, said was the purpose and the intended scope of the Amendment, we come up with a broad, general purpose that necessarily embraces a prohibition against the type of state activity which we have presented to the Court in these cases.

I do not mean in any respect to divorce from the other factors which this Court normally utilizes to determine the scope of a constitutional amendment, the debates and proceedings, but simply to relate them in the fashion in which I have undertaken to do.

I will simply make brief reference to the remaining congressional legislation, out of the consideration of time. As I have pointed out, Senator Cowan,[13] of Pennsylvania, in the Senate made a specific reference to the scope of the Civil Rights Act in its original form, stating that it would outlaw school segregation.

[13]Senator Edgar Cowan (1815–1885) of Pennyslvania. Republican senator 1861–1867; opposed Reconstruction policy of radical Republicans and was not reelected.

Senator Howard made a statement with respect to its outlawing all state laws discriminating on the basis of civil rights. As a matter of fact, as we have set forth in our brief, there was speech after speech in each House devoted not only to the broad general intention of the Act, but also with respect to segregation in public schools.

Over in the House the same Representative Rogers, who said that the Fourteenth Amendment would abolish school segregation, said that the original form of the Civil Rights Act would also have that effect.

Now the importance of all that comes to this. After all of this discussion, particularly the raising of objections as to the constitutionality of the Act, Representative Bingham took the floor, stated that he was thoroughly in favor of the provisions of the things which the proponents of the Act were attempting to accomplish. He had an objection not to the scope of the bill, but he did have one to its constitutionality.

He then stated that in his opinion while the objectives that were objectives properly to be attained, they were to be attained by a constitutional amendment, and not by a statute which, in his opinion, was not justified by the provisions of the Constitution as it then existed. He made it very plain, however, that his objection in this particular regard was not the scope. His objection was to constitutionality.

Now, as a matter of history, Mr. Bingham had just introduced in the House a few days before H.R. 63 which was, as I have said, the forerunner of the Fourteenth Amendment, so consequently, he already had before the Congress a proposal which, if adopted, would, in his opinion, constitute or provide a constitutional basis for the type of legislation which was involved in the Civil Rights Act.

Now, at this point the discussions and the debates make it perfectly plain that the action of the Congress in eliminating the broad no-discrimination clause in the first part of the Civil Rights Act of 1866, and enacting the rest, the balance of the Act in a more limited form, did so for the reasons that were suggested by Mr. Bingham.

As a matter of fact, in this regard we haven't been able to find anything in history that discloses, as our opponents contend, that the rights which are embraced in, and the prohibitions imposed by, the Fourteenth Amendment are no larger than those which are embraced in or imposed by the Civil Rights Act of 1866.

I think this contention ignores the evolution of the Fourteenth Amendment in so far as its relation to the Civil Rights Act of 1866 is concerned. It will be recalled, as I have previously said, that some members of Congress stated that the bill in its original form would outlaw school segregation.

It is another fact that Mr. Wilson[14] in the House claimed that the Act as originally proposed would not effect school segregation, and it was at that point that Mr. Bingham disputed his construction of the Act and asserted that the bill was as broad as the conservatives charged and that while he favored such sweeping objections, he felt that they could not be legally justified except by a new constitutional amendment.

[14]Representative James J. Wilson (1828–1895) of Iowa. Republican representative, 1861–1869; Republican senator, 1883–1895; one of the House managers in the impeachment trial of President Andrew Johnson.

Consequently, when the 39th Congress eliminated the no-discrimination clause and restricted the scope of the Act, they did so both on the basis of Mr. Bingham's construction of the breadth of the Act and his assertion that there would be forthcoming a constitutional amendment of broad scope.

It is very evident that House Resolution 127, which finally became section 1 of the Fourteenth Amendment, with the addition of the citizenship clause, was even broader than H.R. 63 which was before Congress at that time.

Now, I should like to point out that during the debates on the proposed Amendment, it was charged that the radical Republicans were simply undertaking to provide a constitutional basis for the Civil Rights Act which had already been enacted. At this point the proponents of the Amendment made their purpose clear.

They pointed out that they intended not to adopt a constitutional amendment of restrictive scope, but first they wanted to place the rights to be secured by the constitutional amendment beyond the power of repeal by future congresses. A congressional act would not do this, but a constitutional amendment would.

They also made it plain that what they wanted to assure was the constitutionality in the future of any subsequent legislation which would have as broad a scope as did the '66 Act at the time it was originally introduced. And they also made it plain that they intended to enable the judiciary to give full and complete protection to the rights secured.

We don't find in the debates, nor do we find elsewhere, any such limiting scope attributable to the Fourteenth Amendment as is claimed. As I have had occasion to say, Senator Howard in the Senate, and Mr. Stevens in the House, introducing the bill for the Joint Committee on Reconstruction—I am speaking about 127 now, the Fourteenth Amendment—gave it a scope which far exceeded the Civil Rights Act of 1866.

I should also like to make this final point. That in adopting the Civil Rights Act of 1866, Congress enumerated in its final form as it was enacted, enumerated the rights protected.

I have already explained the reasons why that was done. But unrestricted by this consideration in drafting a constitutional provision, Congress used broad, comprehensive language to describe the standards necessary to guarantee complete Federal protection.

In one of the very early cases, construing the Fourteenth Amendment, *Strauder* v. *West Virginia,* this Court had occasion to point that out. It said:

> The Fourteenth Amendment makes no effort to enumerate the rights it designs to protect. It speaks in general terms, and those are as comprehensive as possible.

I will make brief reference to the legislation following the proposal of the Fourteenth Amendment by Congress and indeed, following its ratification by the states. We have set forth in our brief in considerable detail the proceedings in Congress relating specifically to school segregation. By reason of the division of time which we desire in undertaking to present the argument in these two cases, time simply will not permit me to get into it.

I would like to point out, however, that from beginning to end, all the way through, considering the evidence over all, there was an overwhelming mass of opinion that under the Fourteenth Amendment Congress could constitutionally legislate with respect to the elimination of segregation in public education.

JUSTICE REED: Do you think that legislation by Congress would add anything to the strength of your position?

MR. ROBINSON: In so far as this—

JUSTICE REED: In so far as segregation is concerned in the schools.

MR. ROBINSON: Oh, yes, I think if we had a congressional act, sir, that we probably would not have to be here now. However, I do not think that legislation by Congress in anywise detracts from the power of the judiciary to enforce the prohibitions of the Fourteenth Amendment.

JUSTICE REED: [The] provision granting new legislative power to Congress is useless?

MR. ROBINSON: Well, I would put it this way. As I understand section 5, section 5 was designed to give Congress the authority to legislate in this area if it so desired, within the scope of its legitimate sphere. I am speaking, of course, about the limitations of section 1. However, the separation of the provisions of section 1 and 5 we think is very, very significant.

JUSTICE REED: Was 5 intended only for punishment of violations?

MR. ROBINSON: For remedies, for remedies in so far as congressional action could afford them with respect to the prohibitions of section 1. But actually, as a matter of history, Mr. Justice Reed, the change was made from the original form of the Fourteenth Amendment as it was set up in H.R. 63 and H.R. 127 to make this a direct prohibition on the states not necessitating any congressional action, and as a matter of fact, of course, thereby empowering the courts to determine as a judicial matter acts of a state which were claimed to be in contravention thereof.

I should like to make brief reference to the evidence with respect to state ratification. We have again in our briefs set this forth in considerable detail.

I think the states will pretty largely fall in these general classifications. First we have the states which had seceded from the Union and which were seeking readmission. We have ten in this class who were not in the Union at the time the Fourteenth—well, the ten southern states which had seceded, except Tennessee. I think for all practical purposes Tennessee can be classified in about the same fashion.

Our position in that regard simply is that in view of the fact that these states were specifically required to adopt new constitutions in all respects in conformity with the provisions of the federal Constitution, in view of the highly significant fact that at the time these states came back into the Union they contained in their constitutions no reference to race, no reference to school legislation, I mean to racial segregation in schools, in view of the fact that these restrictions appear in the laws of those states only at a later time, that under those circumstances that fact is of great significance in so far as a determination as to what their understanding of the Fourteenth Amendment was to serve.

Additionally, the point which I urge in that connection was the fact that they were required to ratify the Fourteenth Amendment as a condition of readmission. Also, the newly admitted state, Nebraska, which came in at this time, the history which we set forth in our brief I think is sufficient to demonstrate that Nebraska's understanding with respect to the meaning of the Fourteenth Amendment was that it was not of a character which would permit of public school segregation.

Now, the rest of the cases fall in different categories. We have cases in which there were segregation laws at the time the Amendment was adopted. When the Amendment was adopted, those laws were eliminated, more or less at longer or shorter intervals after the adoption of this Amendment.

We think that the action of the states in this connection is of great significance. There were also states in which segregation in public schools was practiced administratively, some instances in which it was practiced without any statutory authority at all, and we have pointed out in our effort to respond to the Court's question in this particular regard the fact that in a good many instances those states changed their laws as well. Time will simply not permit me to go down the list with respect to the others, but I want to emphasize this point.

We do not claim that every state in the Union understood the Fourteenth Amendment as abolishing school segregation. But we do submit that considering the evidence overall, there was substantial understanding which is to be derived principally not from what the states said, because you can't get that, but from what the states did, that the Fourteenth Amendment would have the scope that we attribute to it, and that consequently, school segregation laws would be invalidated.

In conclusion, with respect to this historical evidence, I would like to say this. I think it is very clear that the framers intended to destroy the Black Codes. I think it is clear that they intended to deprive the states of all power to enact similar laws in the future.

I think the evidence overall is clear that it was contemplated and understood that the state would not be permitted to use its power to maintain a class or caste system based upon race or color, and that the Fourteenth Amendment would operate as a prohibition against the imposition of any racial classification in respect of civil rights.

I think secondly, it is very clear that the breadth of the Amendment is such that it necessarily encompasses school segregation, consequently is one of the activities which the Amendment was designed to protect. Necessarily, it would be invalidated by its provisions.

I further submit that the overall evidence establishes substantial understanding by the states ratifying the Fourteenth Amendment that it would prohibit such segregation. The historical evidence in our opinion, also demonstrates—well, there isn't any question about this—that under section 5 Congress could abolish such segregation and that the judiciary in the enforcement of the provisions of section 1, in the light of future conditions, could construe the Amendment as abolishing segregation of its own force.

(Short recess)

THE CHIEF JUSTICE: Mr. Marshall.

ARGUMENT ON BEHALF OF APPELLANTS

by MR. MARSHALL

MR. MARSHALL: May it please the Court, Mr. Robinson has addressed himself particularly to the congressional history and specifically to the first two questions asked by the Court. I would like for a moment to review particularly questions two and three.

As I understand it, the second question raised the question about Congress in submitting the Amendment as to whether future Congresses would have the power; and (b) was as to whether or not it was within the judicial power in the light of future conditions to construe the Amendment as abolishing such segregation of its own force; and then we get to question three, which is the one I would like to address myself to for the first part of this argument, namely, that, as I understand it, the Court is first requesting us to make the assumption that the answers to questions two (a) and two (b) do not dispose of the case, and on this assumption we are requested to direct our attention [to] the specific question as to whether or not the Court—this Court—has judicial power in construing the Fourteenth Amendment to abolish segregation in the public schools. And our answer to that question is a flat "yes."

But in answering the question, we want to develop from the legal precedents in this case the necessary answer, and to us these legal precedents divide themselves into three groups; and it would be normal and, perhaps, would be more logical to cover these groups of cases in chronological order.

But, however, with the permission of the Court and for the purpose of this argument, we would like to divide them as follows: in the first group to discuss the cases this Court has handed down in the recent years construing the Fourteenth Amendment and the Fifth Amendment, in both instances in regard to the power of the Government, federal or state, to use race, class or national origin for classification purposes.

Then, we would like to go to the second group, being the decisions of the Court construing the Fourteenth Amendment during the period immediately subsequent to the ratification of the Fourteenth Amendment.

We believe that a review of these two groups of cases will show that during these two periods, this Court uniformly gave to the Amendment the broad scope which the framers intended, as set forth by Mr. Robinson.

If there were no other cases on the point, the answer to question three would be simple. However, there is a third group of cases, including at least two decisions, and some others inferentially in that group, which are heavily relied upon by the appellees as compelling a contrary decision of this Court. These cases, obviously, are the ones alleged to support the "separate but equal" doctrine.

With that preliminary statement, I would like to get to this first group of cases.

JUSTICE JACKSON: May I suggest, I do not believe—

MR.MARSHALL: Yes, sir.

JUSTICE JACKSON: I do not believe the Court was troubled about its own cases. It has done a good deal of reading of those cases.

MR. MARSHALL: And the first group are all from this very Court; I was just trying to relate them.

JUSTICE JACKSON: Good.
Maybe the question was more nearly, instead of power—in the strong sense—I only speak for myself not for others—it is the question of the propriety of exercising judicial power to reach this result, if the result would be reached, in the absence of any legislation. I do not think it was a question of power in the sense that our cases have dealt with it. It is a question—

MR. MARSHALL: Well, so far—if I understand you correctly, Mr. Justice Jackson, you mean power that would come from the legislative history of the Fourteenth Amendment?

JUSTICE JACKSON: Whether the Amendment, with what light you can throw on it, makes it appropriate for judicial power, after all that has intervened, to exercise this power instead of—

MR. MARSHALL: Leaving it to the Congress.

JUSTICE JACKSON: That is right.
I do not like to see you waste your time on a misunderstanding, because I do not think we had any doubt about our cases. Things are so often read—

JUSTICE FRANKFURTER: And the books.

MR. MARSHALL: Believe it or not, I have read about it.
I think then that I should change and leave out the first group, for the time being, and go to the other group beginning with *Slaughter-House,* because the reason I would like to discuss those—because, for example, Mr. Justice Frankfurter raised the question about Mr. Justice Miller in the *Slaughter-House Cases,* and I wanted to add to that the fact that we cannot ignore the opinion of Justice Strong₁₅ in the *Strauder* v. *West Virginia* case, and at that stage of the argument I wanted to say that in these decisions at that period of time they recognized the exact same legislative historical argument that we have just completed; and the *Slaughter-House Cases,* as I read it, stands for the proposition, and at least it has been cited by this Court all the way up at least to the covenant cases of *Shelley,* that the Fourteenth Amendment and the intent that you get from the framers of it, is definitely on the broad purpose that we allege here.

¹⁵Justice William Strong (1808–1895) of Pennsylvania. Although originally a Democrat, he switched to the Republicans and strongly supported the Union cause, voting to uphold federal conscription and the Legal Tender Act while on the Pennsylvania Supreme Court (1857–1868). He was appointed to the Supreme Court by President Ulysses Grant in 1870 and wrote a number of opinions interpreting the Civil War amendments and the new civil rights statutes enacted under them.

As to whether or not Congress intended to leave this matter to Congress, I submit that one of the short answers is that Title 8, section 43, [now 42 U.S.C. section 1983] which is the statute that we base all of these cases on, says specifically in its enacting clause adopted in 1871, which we have in our brief, that "this bill is enacted for the purpose of enforcing the Fourteenth Amendment."

Congress has already acted and, in that act I am sure it will be remembered that it says that anyone acting under color of state statute, who denies anyone rights guaranteed by the Constitution or laws of the United States shall have a right of action in law or in equity. The original statute said "in the District Court or Circuit Courts," and in codifying it they, of course, have left out the Circuit Court point.

But if there is a need for congressional action, it is there, and in *Strauder* against *West Virginia* Mr. Justice Strong, in his opinion and we quote it in our brief on page 22 and 23 the language which we believe—either I have the wrong brief or—it is there, 33.

THE CHIEF JUSTICE: I would like to have you discuss the question of power because I believe that is the question the Court asked you to discuss.

MR. MARSHALL: The power.

THE CHIEF JUSTICE: Yes, the power.

MR. MARSHALL: Yes, sir. On the power, Mr. Chief Justice Warren, we take the position, and we have covered it in the brief—

THE CHIEF JUSTICE: Yes.

MR. MARSHALL: —and that was the part that Mr. Robinson was to deal with this morning, and it is our understanding that the Fourteenth Amendment, following the Civil Rights Law, but not limited to the Civil Rights Act of 1866, in the debates, it is obvious, especially in the later debates, that left with the courts of the land was this problem of deciding as to the interpretation, so that as to power, it is our position that the Court gets specific power in addition to the regular judiciary act, in this Act of 1871, Title 8, which is not Title 8, section 43 which, I submit, not only gives the federal courts power, but imposes upon the federal courts a specific duty which is different, and this is where we get our power point, and we thought that was sufficient.

THE CHIEF JUSTICE: Yes.

JUSTICE FRANKFURTER: Mr. Marshall—

MR. MARSHALL: Yes, Mr. Justice Frankfurter.

JUSTICE FRANKFURTER: —you trouble me about saying there has been legislation.

You are not resting your claim here on the Act of 1871 and are then discussing whether that Act is constitutional?

MR. MARSHALL: No, sir.

JUSTICE FRANKFURTER: You have to—you are resting, as I understand it, on the compulsions, the implications, derived from the Fourteenth Amendment, as such, in your cases?

MR. MARSHALL: Yes, sir.

JUSTICE FRANKFURTER: So I do not know why you constantly revert to the fact that Congress has already exercised the power. I do not understand what you mean by that.

MR. MARSHALL: Well, as I understand, running through the questions, especially those in number two, the second question—and, fortunately, in so far as this case is concerned, the appellees here claim that Congress has no power to legislate in this field at all and, as I understand their position, the courts and Congress and nobody else can touch it, it is a matter solely for the states.

JUSTICE FRANKFURTER: That we have not got here.

MR. MARSHALL: No, sir; but it is our position that the Fourteenth Amendment was intended to leave to the courts the normal construction of the statute—I mean of the Constitution—and this Act of 1871 is merely recognizing that.

JUSTICE FRANKFURTER: I do not know what that Act has to do with this, our problem. If your claim prevails, it must prevail by virtue of what flows out of the Fourteenth Amendment, as such?

MR. MARSHALL: And would be—

JUSTICE FRANKFURTER: And so far as I am concerned, 1871 need not be on the statute books.

MR. MARSHALL: And we would still have a valid—

JUSTICE FRANKFURTER: And does not help me any.

MR. MARSHALL: Yes, sir.

JUSTICE FRANKFURTER: All right, I understand.

MR. MARSHALL: As I understand it, Mr. Justice Frankfurter, if I may for a minute leave the congressional debates, because I think on the matter of time—and go to the *Strauder* and the *Slaughter-House Cases* which, I think, are the key to this situation, because they were decided at the time nearest to the Fourteenth Amendment—and the *Slaughter-House Cases,* Justice Miller's opinion has been, as I said, cited over and over again, and there is no question that that opinion makes it clear that the Fourteenth Amendment was adopted for the express purpose, and the purpose was, to correct the situation theretofore existing in regard to the treatment of Negroes, slave or free, in a different category from the way you treated the others.

Then, in that particular instance on page 81, which is cited on page 33 of our brief, it is stated that, "The existence of laws in the States where the newly emancipated Negroes resided, which discriminated with gross injustice and hardship against them as a class, was the evil to be remedied by this clause, and by it such laws are forbidden." That is the expression that is nearest to the time of the Amendment.

JUSTICE FRANKFURTER: Wouldn't you say, sir, we do not have to elaborate that because the whole point—not the whole point, but one of the difficulties or one of the assumptions that has to be remedied by later cases—was the intimation of Justice Miller that it was related exclusively to equalizing things?

MR. MARSHALL: Yes, sir.

JUSTICE FRANKFURTER: So one does not have to argue that the Fourteenth Amendment, the target of the Fourteenth Amendment, was to give Negroes certain rights.

MR. MARSHALL: I think so, sir.

JUSTICE FRANKFURTER: I do not see that that needs any argument.

MR. MARSHALL: The only thing that was preliminary to this, Mr. Justice Frankfurter, was that in the Strauder case—and I think that is the one that is really on the point for this particular issue, in *Strauder* v. *West Virginia*—it was made clear, one thing which I would have considered obvious all along—and that is the constitutional amendments are setting down rules—I mean broad principles and not rules—of conduct, as such, and they are put in broad language.

Well, *Strauder* mentions that.

But the important point is that in the Strauder case the decision in that Court makes it clear that they did not intend to enumerate these rights; and that, to my mind, is the crux of whether or not the Court has power to deal with segregation.

Certainly it did not mention it in the Amendment itself, and a lot of items it did not mention. But when you read the debates, as Mr. Robinson explained, you cannot escape this point: that the Amendment was adopted for the express purpose of depriving the states of authority to exercise and enforce the existing Black Codes; that by putting it in the Constitution it was obviously intended that the states would not have power in the future to set up additional Black Codes; and to use the language of this Court in one case, *Lane* v. *Wilson*,[16] whether it is sophisticated or simple-minded; and the part that is to my mind crucial in this case, is that until this time the appellees have shown nothing that can in any form or fashion say that the statutes involved in these cases are not the same type of statutes discussed in the debates and in the decision of the Court nearest to that, namely, the Black Codes, and I do not see how the inevitable result can be challenged, because they are of the exact same cloth, when you go to these Black Codes.

They do, however, on the question of power argue that the State of South Carolina and the State of Virginia have themselves worked out this problem, and for that reason they have found they have to have segregation.

---

[16]Lane v. Wilson, 307 U.S. 268 (1939). The Supreme Court upheld a suit for damages by a Negro against Arkansas officials who had unlawfully prevented him from voting.

The only way they can keep schools would be to keep segregation and for that reason, as I understand their argument, that reason takes them out of the general flow of invidious legislation under the Fourteenth Amendment; and then they say that there is no definite material in the debates that shows the intent of Congress to include segregation in public education. We submit that that is not the way to approach this problem.

Once we admit, either by reading the legislative debates or reading cases such as *Strauder,* the *Slaughter-House Cases* and the other cases, once we arrive at the conclusion that the Fourteenth Amendment was intended to strike down all types of class and caste legislation [that] on its face involves class, then it seems to me that the only way the appellees can destroy that very clear and logical approach is to show that it was intended not to include schools, not include segregation, and then we have the very interesting position—they immediately recognize that in their briefs, especially in the South Carolina brief, because they say that the McLaurin case involves "separate but equal" doctrine, and certainly if ever there was a case that did not involve "separate but equal," it was *McLaurin,* because as soon as the McLaurin case recognizes the broad intent of the Fourteenth Amendment to cover in progressive stages education, graduate education, I mean, excuse me, legal education, then graduate education; and, as I understand the task the appellees have by force addressed themselves to, it is that even admitting that education is within the purview of the Fourteenth Amendment, when you get to elementary and high schools this Court loses its power to decide as to whether or not segregation in elementary and high schools is illegal.

Now, as to the power argument, it seems to me that that is it in the simplest fashion, and despite the fact that we thought we were obliged to develop it, I think that is a shorthand statement of our position on it, and I think it has not been met, at least up to this point, in any of the briefs and cases.

JUSTICE FRANKFURTER: I should suggest that the question is not whether this Court loses its power, but whether the states lose their powers. I understand the answer you make to it—

MR. MARSHALL: It is my understanding, yes, sir, I think definitely, Mr. Justice Frankfurter, that a reading of the two briefs in this case demonstrates clearly that as of this time we have a test to see whether or not the public policy, customs and mores of the states of South Carolina and Virginia or the avowed intent of our Constitution—as to which one—will prevail.

For example, in their briefs they rely on the fact that, they mention the fact that there is such a thing as racial prejudice, and this is this and that is that, and I would like to, if I could, quote to you one case in our reply brief which, at least is I know, not news to the Court, but it was news to us. I am sure the Court is familiar with the case of *Tanner* v. *Little.*[17] I am not advocating the actual final decision in that case as of this time, but in the language in that case, which involved as you may remember, the green stamps by trading stores—the language is cited on

[17]Tanner v. Little, 240 U.S. 369, 382 (1916). The Court upheld a Washington state law requiring a tax of $6,000 on businesses that gave away trading stamps.

pages 8 and 9 of our brief, and I submit that it is in the middle of a paragraph, is that:

> Red things may be associated by reason of their redness, with disregard of all other resemblances or of distinctions. Such classification would be logically appropriate. Apply it further: make a rule of conduct depend upon it, and distinguish in legislation between red-haired men and black-haired men, and the classification would immediately be seen to be wrong; it would have only arbitrary relation to the purpose and province of legislation.

In these cases the only way—and if I will stay with the power point a short while longer, there would have to be a showing in order to sustain this legislation under the broad power of this Court to construe statutes under the reasonable classification doctrine.

They would have to show, and we have shown to the contrary—they would have to show, one, that there are differences in race; and, two, that differences in race have a recognizable relationship to the subject matter being legislated, namely, public education. That is a rule that has been uniformly applied by this Court in all other challenges that a classification is unreasonable. Those cases, of course, are also set out in our brief.

The other side in the South Carolina case says that the rule is a general rule, and the state has these powers; and they cite, of all cases to support that, *Yick Wo* v. *Hopkins*,[18] which this Court is thoroughly familiar with, the principle established in that case, which is directly to the contrary.

So, on the power point, it seems to me that there are only two relative groups of arguments: one, the congressional side, and the other, in addition to the recognized cases, the regular reasonable classification cases.

Now, with that, it seems to me that if I am correct in interpreting Mr. Justice Jackson's position, that that is what that point involves, it seems to me that is a sufficient answer to it, and if it is, I would conclude it by going back to the difference between the cases and the cases on the other side, because I feel obliged to touch the cases that the other side, of course, relies on and the lower courts relied on, beginning with the *Plessy* v. *Ferguson* case, and its doctrine.

In our brief we have pointed out the obvious ways that those cases could be distinguished. For the purpose of this argument and for the purpose of answering the specific question of this Court, we believe that it is proper for us to say here and now that the distinction, for example, in the *Plessy* v. *Ferguson* case, that it involved railroads instead of education, transportation against education, is a point of distinction, but for this point there is none, in fact, because it has been recognized as the originator of the "separate but equal" doctrine.

The next case that is near to the point is the *Gong Lum* v. *Rice* case, which was different; they did not raise the issue of the validity of the classification. All they were objecting to, and possibly it is understandable that the Chinese child was

---

[18]Yick Wo v. Hopkins, 118 U.S. 356 (1886). A San Francisco ordinance required all laundries to be made of brick or stone but permitted the board of supervisors at its discretion to give licences to wooden structures. The Supreme Court held that the law, although seemingly impartial and fair, was directed against Chinese laundries, generally built of wood, and thus violated the equal protection clause.

objecting to being classified as a Negro and put in an inferior school. Maybe that is—but so far as the law in the country today is concerned, that decision stands for the proposition that a state has a right to classify on the basis of class, race or ancestry, and our position on that is merely that the Gong Lum case, and the "separate but equal" doctrine of *Plessy* v. *Ferguson,* is just out of step with the earlier decisions in *Slaughter-House* and *Strauder* v. *West Virginia,* and the recent cases in this Court.

The other point which is made—

JUSTICE REED: But to reach that you have to take the Sweatt case based on the "separate but equal" doctrine.

MR. MARSHALL: No, sir; I only say the McLaurin case does not embrace the "separate but equal" doctrine.

I think in *Sweatt* v. *Painter,* the truth of the matter is that the decision was able to find that these intangibles produced inequality, and to that extent—

JUSTICE REED: But didn't the McLaurin case—

MR. MARSHALL: There was none of that.

JUSTICE REED: Granting the facts in the statement showed that they were equal—

MR. MARSHALL: Yes.

JUSTICE REED: But didn't the fact that they did not have the opportunity for association or discussion have any effect on it?

MR. MARSHALL: Yes, sir.

JUSTICE REED: And that, therefore, since they were graduate students, they did not have equal opportunities.

MR. MARSHALL: As I read it, sir—the best I could do is read it—as I understand it, the conclusion in there in two particular places, he says that in a situation of this type the state is deprived of the power to make distinctions, and the other point it says, to make any difference in treatment, but it was my idea that the thrust of the *McLaurin* opinion is that segregation in and of itself, at least as far as graduate training is concerned, is invalid, and that it was that conclusion was reached by first finding out—

JUSTICE REED: But they gave the reasons why, for undergraduate students, because they did not give equal opportunity.

MR. MARSHALL: But the only reason, I submit, Mr. Justice Reed, on the McLaurin case and these cases is age, age of students, and the fact that obviously graduate training is different from elementary training and high school training. But it has a difference, to use the language about another point in the McLaurin case, there is constitutional difference or rather it is insignificant as to the minor points, because if I understand, if we follow that to the logical conclusion, I do not have the slightest idea of where the line would be; whether the line would be at the college level, the junior college level, or the high school level, as to where this discussion with other pupils is of benefit.

JUSTICE FRANKFURTER: Am I wrong in thinking that you must reject the basis of the decision in McLaurin for purposes of this case?

MR. MARSHALL: You mean reject the basis of the fact that they were not allowed to associate?

JUSTICE FRANKFURTER: No. The basis was the criterion of those cases was whether each got the same thing. Your position in these cases is that that is not arguable, that you cannot differentiate, you cannot enter the domain of whether a black child or a white child gets the same educational advantages or facilities or opportunity. You must reject that, do you not?

MR. MARSHALL: We reach—

JUSTICE FRANKFURTER: Therefore, that is what I mean by saying you must reject the basis on which those cases went.

MR. MARSHALL: We reject it to this extent: I think I am—

JUSTICE FRANKFURTER: You reject the Delaware ground of decision, don't you?

MR. MARSHALL: Absolutely.

JUSTICE FRANKFURTER: Well, therefore, you reject the basis of the McLaurin case.

MR. MARSHALL: I think so far as our argument on the constitutional debates is concerned, and these two cases, that the state is deprived of any power to make any racial classification in any governmental field.

JUSTICE FRANKFURTER: So I understand.

MR. MARSHALL: But I do have to qualify it to this extent: I can conceive of some governmental action—to be perfectly frank, sir, we have discussed the point of census-taking—so they could take the census and name in the census, but so long as it affects not either group—but in any area where it touches the individuals concerned in any form or fashion, it is clear to me, to my mind, under the Fourteenth Amendment that you cannot separate people or denote that one shall go here and one shall go there if the facilities are absolutely equal; that is the issue in this case, because in the South Carolina case especially it is admitted on record that every other thing about the schools is equal, schools, curricula, everything else. It is only the question as to the power of the state to—

JUSTICE FRANKFURTER: Well, the Delaware case tests that. You are opposed to—you are in favor of the requested equality there, because I do not know whether you are—

MR. MARSHALL: Yes, sir.

JUSTICE FRANKFURTER: That is generally under your wing?

MR. MARSHALL: It is not only under our wing, sir; we are very proud of the fact that the children are going to school there, and they are demonstrating that it can be done.

JUSTICE FRANKFURTER: All I am saying is that with reference to the basis on which the Delaware decision went, you reject—

MR. MARSHALL: Yes sir.

JUSTICE FRANKFURTER: I follow that.

MR. MARSHALL: Well, it seems to me, sir, that there is considerable— there is an opening for argument that, after all, the Court is interpreting the phrase "equal protection" underlining the word "equal," and for that reason, that is the reason in our record in the case we felt obliged to show that these, what we considered as intangibles in the Sweatt case, were there in this case and, if necessary, the doctrine of *Sweatt* and *McLaurin* could automatically on all fours come there except for the question of difference of schools.

JUSTICE FRANKFURTER: But the point is important whether we are to decide that the facilities are equal or whether one says that is an irrelevant question, because you cannot apply that test between white and black.

MR. MARSHALL: In this case it is irrelevant—

JUSTICE FRANKFURTER: All right.

MR. MARSHALL: (continuing) —for two reasons: one, it is not in the case because we have agreed that equality is outside the case, and our argument is deliberately broad enough to encompass a situation regardless of facilities, and we make no issue about it.

JUSTICE FRANKFURTER: I understand that, but that will be a ground on which the series of cases in the McLaurin case—the point of my question is that I think we are dealing with two different legal propositions; *McLaurin* is one and what you are tendering to the Court is another.

MR. MARSHALL: The questions raised by this Court in June, as we understand it, requested us to find out as to whether or not class legislation and, specifically segregation, whether or not it, in and of itself, with nothing else, violated the Fourteenth Amendment.

We have addressed ourselves to that in this brief, and we are convinced that the answer is that any segregation, which is for the purpose of setting up either class or caste legislation, is in and of itself a violation of the Fourteenth Amendment, with the only proviso that normally, in normal judicial proceedings, there must be a showing of injury or what have you. That is our position and that is up—

JUSTICE REED: That is solely on the equal protection clause?

MR. MARSHALL: Solely on the equal protection clause except, sir, that is true in South Carolina, but we are arguing two cases together.

In Virginia we rely on equal protection and due process both, but the argument in our brief is limited to equal protection; not that we have discarded due process, but we did not have to get to it because of the wording of the questions of the Court.

But we think it is a denial of both. I urge particularly the equal protection clause because it seems to me, at least from the restrictive convenant case, the Shelley case on that. These rights are beginning to fall into the equal protection clause rather than the due process clause, but we do not abandon the due process clause at all.

JUSTICE FRANKFURTER: In the District of Columbia case—

MR. MARSHALL: Automatically—

JUSTICE FRANKFURTER: (continuing) —the opposite would happen.

MR. MARSHALL: In the District of Columbia—we are not the lawyers in that case—we are all working together on it—they, of course, are relying on the due process clause and they have the cases that support that; so I would say that in so far as there is a due process argument to be in the District of Columbia and Virginia, they would be related except for the difference that in the District of Columbia this Court has broad power—

JUSTICE FRANKFURTER: Your argument comes down to this: If in one of the states in which there is a large percentage of Negro voters, a preponderance, where we get a situation where X state has a preponderance of Negro voters who are actually going to the polls, and actually assert their preponderance and install a Negro governor to the extent that more money is spent for Negro education, better housing, better schools, more highly paid teachers, where teachers are more attracted, better maps, better schoolbooks, better everything than the white children enjoy—and I know I am making a fantastic, if you will, assumption—

MR. MARSHALL: Yes.

JUSTICE FRANKFURTER: (continuing) —and yet there is segregation, you would come here and say that they cannot do that?

MR. MARSHALL: If it is done by the state, the state has been deprived of—

JUSTICE FRANKFURTER: That is your position; that is the legal—

MR. MARSHALL: I think, sir, that is our flat legal position, that if it involves class or caste legislation—

JUSTICE FRANKFURTER: That is the antitheses of the McLaurin and the Gaines doctrine.

MR. MARSHALL: Well, of the Gaines case, certainly so, sir, because I, for one, do not believe that the language used by Chief Justice Hughes was—I mean, I just do not consider it as dictum when he said that they operated under a doctrine, the validity of which had been supported.

I think that *Gaines* was interpreted within the "separate but equal" doctrine.

I think *Sipuel* was, with the addition of "you have to do it now."

I think that *Sweatt* and *McLaurin,* if I could disagree for a moment, are moving between the two; that is the way I look at it.

JUSTICE FRANKFURTER: My only purpose is to try to see these things clearly without a simplifying darkness, and to try to see it clearly.

MR. MARSHALL: Yes, sir. But I do not believe—the point I wanted to make clear is that we do not have to—this Court does not have to—take my position to decide this case. Because of what I told you a minute ago, they could take up that material in those other records and find that the children were not getting an equal education, but it would not help in the situation.

JUSTICE FRANKFURTER: No, but if that line is taken, then the whole problem that you bring your weight to bear on is opened, and in each case we have to decide that.

MR. MARSHALL: I think so, sir.

JUSTICE FRANKFURTER: I did not suppose that you would say that we had to open this case, that they were not equal, whether psychologically, whether buildings, whether they spent X million dollars for white, or X minus Y for the black, that does not open any doctrine?

MR. MARSHALL: No, sir; and the Delaware case, if I can go to that without going outside of the record, demonstrates a situation more so than it does in South Carolina, because in Delaware so long as the schools are unequal, okay. And then the schools are made equal, and if I understand the procedure, you move the Negroes back to the colored school, and then next year you put ten more books in the white school, and the colored school is unequal, and I do not see how that point would ever be adequately decided, and in truth and in fact, there are no two equal schools, because there are no two equal faculties in the world in any schools.

They are good as individuals, and one is better than the other, but to just—that is the trouble with the doctrine of "separate but equal"; the doctrine of "separate but equal" assumes that two things can be equal.

JUSTICE REED: There is not absolute equality, but substantially equal, in accordance with the terms of our cases.

MR. MARSHALL: Yes, sir; starting with *Plessy* the word "substantial" and we say in our brief—I mean we are absolutely serious about it—that the use of the word "substantial" emphasizes that those cases in truth and in fact amend the Fourteenth Amendment by saying that equal protection can be obtained in a substantially equal fashion, and there is nothing in the debates that will hint in the slightest that they did not mean complete equality—they said so—to raise the

Negro up into the status of complete equality with the other people. That is the language they used.

"Substantial" is a word that was put into the Fourteenth Amendment by *Plessy* v. *Ferguson,* and I cannot find it, and it cannot be found in any place in the debates.

If it please the Court, we would like to, if possible, conserve the balance of the time for rebuttal. Mr. Robinson was a little over his time, and I cut mine down. Unless there are any questions on this particular point, because we still have some time left, I would like to leave that for rebuttal.

THE CHIEF JUSTICE: Thank you.
Mr. Davis?

ARGUMENT ON BEHALF OF APPELLEES R. W. ELLIOTT, ET AL

by MR. DAVIS

MR. DAVIS: May it please the Court, I suppose there are few invitations less welcome in an advocate's life than to be asked to reargue a case on which he has once spent himself, and that is particularly unwelcome when the order for reargument gives him no indication whatever of the subjects in which the Court may be interested, and, therefore, I want to at the outset tender the Court my thanks and, I think, the thanks of my colleagues on both sides of the desk for the guidance they have given us by the series of questions which they asked us to devote our attention to, and in what I shall have to say, I hope to indicate the answers which, for our part, we give to each one of them.

At the previous hearing of this case I think all counsel on both sides of the controversy, and in every case, realizing that it was an act of mercy and, perhaps, even of piety, not to increase the reading matter that comes to this Court, briefed the case in rather concise fashion. An effort was apparent, and I am sure I shared it, to condense the controversy to the smallest compass it would bear.

Now, for a rough guess I should think the motion for reargument has contributed somewhere between 1500 and 2000 pages to the possible entertainment, if not the illumination, of the Court. But I trust the Court will not hold counsel responsible for that proliferation.

Most of us have supported our answers to the Court's questions by appendices addressed to the action of Congress, to the action of the ratifying states, and in our particular case, to the history of the controversy within the State of South Carolina.

In view of the fact that His Honor, the Chief Justice, was not on the bench at the time of the other argument, perhaps I should outline the present posture of the South Carolina case of Briggs and Elliott.

It was brought, as Mr. Robinson correctly stated, upon two grounds: A suit by infant Negro children in Clarendon County School District No. 22 which, by a subsequent reorganization, became a part of District No. 1, by their parents and next friends, asserting that they were denied the equal protection of the laws on two grounds: first, that section 7 of Article 11 of the Constitution of South Carolina forbade integrated schools; commanded that the white and colored races should be taught in separate schools, and that the statute, in pursuance of that

Constitution, section 5277 of their code, made a similar provision, and that both were in violation of the Fourteenth Amendment to the Constitution of the United States per se.

Second, that be that as it may, inequalities existed between the educational facilities furnished to the white and black children, to the detriment of the black.

The State of South Carolina came in and admitted that those inequalities existed, and declared its intention to remove them as promptly as possible.

Evidence was taken, the District Court decreed that the Constitution and statute of South Carolina did not violate the Amendment; found the existence of the admitted inequality, and enjoined its immediate removal, gave to the State of South Carolina the period of six months to report what steps had been taken to implement that decree.

At the end of that time a report came in which came to this Court, and was returned to the District Court, and upon a second hearing, a further report came in.

It was made to appear that the promise of the State of South Carolina to remove this inequality was no empty promise; that it had authorized, its legislature had authorized, a bond issue of $75 million to equalize the physical facilities of the schools, supported by a 3 per cent sales tax; that the curricula had been equalized, the pay of teachers had been equalized, transportation had been provided for children, white and black; and the accuracy of those reports being admitted—and I am merely summarizing it—the court below held that it was clear that by the first of September, 1952, that the inequalities had disappeared.

It then entered an order enjoining the further removal of such inequalities as might have existed, and declared the Constitution and the statute to be valid and non-violative of the Fourteenth Amendment.

We have then in South Carolina a case, as Mr. Marshall has so positively admitted, with no remaining question of inequality at all, and the naked question is whether a separation of the races in the primary and secondary schools, which are the subject of this particular case, is of itself per se a violation of the Fourteenth Amendment.

Now, turning to our answers, let me state what we say to each one of them. The first question was what evidence is there that the Congress which submitted to the state legislatures and conventions which ratified the Fourteenth Amendment contemplated or did not contemplate, understood or did not understand that would abolish segregation in public schools?

We answer, the overwhelming preponderance of the evidence demonstrates that the Congress which submitted, and the state legislatures which ratified, the Fourteenth Amendment did not contemplate and did not understand that it would abolish segregation in public schools, and in the time that is afforded, I hope to vindicate that categorical reply.

Our friends, the appellants, take an entirely contrary view, and they take it, in part, on the same historical testimony; certain fallacies underlie, I think, their course in reaching that conclusion. Some of them are apparent in their brief, and I have not found that they touched upon them in oral argument.

The first fallacy which appears in their brief, in their recounting of history, is the assumption, wholly unwarranted, as I think, that the antislavery pre-Civil

War crusade, the abolitionist crusade, was directed not only against slavery but against segregation in schools.

I do not think that thesis can be sustained, for the thrust and movement of the abolitionist crusade was directed toward one thing, and one thing only: the abolition of the institution of slavery, and from that nothing can be deduced which is helpful to the Court in its study of this section of history.

I think the next unjustified assumption which, again I am referring to my adversaries' brief and not to their oral presentation, was that the radical Republicans controlled the action of the 39th Congress. That again is an unwarranted assumption.

The 39th Congress never went as far as some of the radical Republicans wished it to go and, perhaps, there has never been a Congress in which the debates furnished less real pablum on which history might feed. It was what Claude Bowers calls in his book *The Tragic Era*, well-named—flames of partisan passion were still burning over the ashes of the Civil War.

In the Senate there were such men as Sumner, who made a lifelong crusade in favor of mixed racial schools from the time that he was counsel for the plaintiff in *Roberts* v. *Boston* in '49—he never missed an opportunity to bring the question forward, and never succeeded in having it enacted into law, except by the legislature of Massachusetts in 1855.

There were men who stood with Sumner, his colleague, Henry Wilson of Massachusetts,[19] and on the other side, equally critical, men like Cowan of Pennsylvania, and Garrett Davis of Kentucky,[20] and others, resented all of the Civil War Reconstruction legislation, and whenever they had an opportunity to attack it, painted it in the blackest colors that they could devise.

In the House, Thaddeus Stevens, called by historians perhaps the most unlovely character in American history, more concerned to humiliate the aristocrats of the South, as he called them, even than to preserve the rights of the Negro. His policy was confiscation of all estate over $10,000 and two hundred acres, of which $40 an acre should be given to every adult Negro, and remainder should be sold to pay the expenses of the war. He wanted the South to come to Washington as suppliants in sackcloth and ashes. He had his echoes.

On the other side there were resistors like Rogers of New Jersey, a Democrat from New Jersey, who never missed an opportunity to criticize every one of the bills that were presented on the ground that they would forbid segregated schools. That echo came from Rogers almost as regularly as the contrary view came from Sumner.

Now, if I gather my friends' position both in brief and argument, they hope from the debates of such a Congress to distill clear, specific evidence of congressional intent.

I do not think that is possible, but there is a source from which congressional intent can be gathered, far more reliable, far less hope for challenge by anyone.

What did the Congress do? And when we study the legislation enacted by

[19]Senator Henry Wilson (1812–1875) of Massachusetts. Free Soil and Republican senator, 1855–1873; Vice President of the United States under President Ulysses S. Grant, 1873–1875.

[20]See no. 5, *supra*.

Congress immediately before, immediately after, and during the period of the discussion of the Fourteenth Amendment, there can be no question left that Congress did not intend by the Fourteenth Amendment to deal with the question of mixed or segregated schools.

There is another fallacy in the presentation of the case by the appellants. They take for granted they can quote any senator, congressman, or other character in favor of racial equality, they can count him down in the column of those who were opposed to segregated schools, which is a clear non sequitur and a begging of the question.

We are not concerned here with the mandate of the Constitution that the Negro, as well as the white, shall enjoy the equal protection of the laws.

The question with which Your Honors are confronted is, is segregation in schools a denial of equality where the segregation runs against one race as well as against the other, and where, in the eye of law no difference between the educational facilities of the two classes can be discerned.

Now, I think those remarks sum up most of what I care to say by way of direct reply to the argument of the appellants.

There is a third point of view presented to Your Honors. We say the intent of Congress was clear not to enter this field. We say the intent of the ratifying states was equally clear, the majority of them, not to enter this field.

The Attorney General is present, acceding to the invitation of the Court, with a brief, and a very large appendix reciting the history of the legislation. He reaches the conclusion, or those who speak for him—I am not speaking in the personal sense but only of the office—he reaches the conclusion, as stated in his brief, historical facts, after some four hundred pages of recital, are too equivocal and inconclusive—I am having some trouble with my own chirography here—the historical facts are too equivocal and inconclusive to formulate a solid basis on which this Court can determine the application of the Amendment to the question of school segregation as it exists today.

After so prolonged a study, as has evidently been made, it does seem rather a lame and impotent conclusion, not calculated to be of a great deal of help to the Court, and I think the cause of that despair on the part of the learned Attorney General and his aides, is that they have fallen into the same fallacy into which the appellants have fallen. They endeavor by collating all that was said on either side whenever the question raged, and it was not a single instance—they hope out of that to distill some attar that will exhibit what can fairly be called the congressional intent.

It is no wonder, that having plunged into that Serbonian bog, they are in a state of more or less despair when they are able to emerge.

Now, Your Honors then are presented with this: We say there is no warrant for the assertion that the Fourteenth Amendment dealt with the school question. The appellants say that from the debates in Congress it is perfectly evident that the Congress wanted to deal with the school question, and the Attorney General, as a friend of the Court, says he does not know which is correct. So Your Honors are afforded the reasonable field for selection. (Laughter.)

Now, we say that whatever may have been said in debate, and there is not an angle of this case that would not find, if that were the decisive question, support in what some person might have said at some time, but Congress by its action demonstrated beyond a peradventure what scope it intended to employ.

I hoped at one time that it would be possible to take up each action of Congress upon which we rely and vindicate our interpretation of it. I see now that I underestimated the time that would be at my disposal, or overestimated my power of delivery.

I shall have to speak now more or less in word of catalog and leave to our brief and to our appendices confirmation of the relevancy of these incidents.

In the 39th Congress the first supplemental Freedmen's Bureau bill passed, giving the Freedmen's Bureau power to buy sites and buildings and schools for freedmen, refugees, and their children; and, of course, the freedmen and the refugees were of the colored race.

There was provision that if certain cataloged rights were denied, military protection should be given. What was that catalog? To make and enforce contracts, sue, be sued, be a party and give evidence, inherit, purchase or dispose of real or personal property; have full and equal benefit of all laws and proceedings for the security of person and estate, and be subject to like punishments, pains and penalties as with others, and none beside.

What did the Freedmen's Bureau do? It was the pet and child of Congress and, acting under its constant supervision, they installed separate schools throughout the South, so separate indeed that history records one complaint by the City of Charleston that they had seized, occupied, and taken over all the school buildings in the city, filled them with their Negro wards, and the white children no longer had any buildings to which to resort; the Civil Rights Act of 1866, where the rights to be protected by it were cataloged almost in the identical language of the Freedmen's Bureau Bill, the difference being that the Freedmen's Bureau Bill ran only in those states in which the process of the courts had been interrupted, which was a euphemism, being those states that had been occupied by the Confederate and Federal army, and the Civil Rights Act of 1866 was designed to be nation-wide.

It is not surprising that its language conformed to the language of the Freedmen's Bureau. They were both introduced at the same time by Senator Trumbull, the chairman of the Judiciary Committee of the Senate, and they made their way through Congress in much the same fashion.

After the Civil Rights Act of 1866 had passed the Senate, it went to the House for consideration. There it was introduced, sponsored, discussed by Congressman James Wilson[21] of Iowa, who was chairman of the Judiciary Committee, and when Brother Rogers, with his usual complaint that it would do away with the separate schools, and others joined him in taking that point of view, at that time Wilson said on the floor that the Act did not mean that their children should attend the same school, and, in effect, that it was absurd so to interpret it.

Now, the pertinency of that is due to the connection which counsel has stated between the Civil Rights Act and the Fourteenth Amendment. It was the constant claim of those who favored the Fourteenth Amendment, Stevens and Sumner, both speaking to it, that it was intended to make the Civil Rights Act not only constitutional and quiet Bingham's doubt and conscience, but to make it irrepeal-

[21]See no. 14, *supra*.

able so that, as Stevens said, whenever the Democrats and their Copperhead allies came back to Congress, they would not be able to repeal it.

I will pass over, for the moment, some other legislation, which I will come back to, that occurred in the 39th Congress.

We came to the reinstatement of the seceded states. Congress passed an Act, by virtue of which they might, in compliance, send their senators and congressmen back.

Now, in the 39th Congress, Sumner had put forward his prescription for their readmission. He had five headings for it, of which the fourth was this: that the seceding states, if they wished to return, should adopt constitutions, which among other things, would provide for the organization of an educational system for the equal benefit of all, without distinction of color or race.

The Reconstruction Act was adopted in the succeeding Congress and it called for a catalog of performances to be carried out by the states desiring readmission. Did they say anything about Sumner's educational plank? Not a word. Was any requirement made of the state as to educational provision? None whatever.

When they came to admit the State of Arkansas, Senator Drake[22] of Missouri offered an amendment in which he provided that the constitution of the petitioning state should provide no denial of the elective franchise or any other right. He offered that as an amendment to the bill admitting the State of Arkansas.

Controversy arose as to the meaning of "any other right." Then it was asserted that there would enter the question of schools. It was stricken out, and the Drake Amendment adopted without—and Senator Frelinghuysen,[23] who had been chairman of the Joint Committee on Reconstruction, said that neither the Drake Amendment or the Fourteenth Amendment touched the question of separate schools. That is once I think it is proper to quote from a debate.

There came then the amnesty bill amendments. Congress passed an amnesty bill. When it was before the Senate, Sumner offered his supplemental Civil Rights Act, which provided expressly for mixed schools.

The Judiciary Committee twice reported it adversely, and Sumner flanked them by offering it then as an amendment to the amnesty bill. In that form it was debated and, finally, a vote was taken which was 28 to 28, and the Vice President broke the tie in Sumner's factor. It was the high-water mark of his achievement.

The amnesty bill, so amended, went to the House.

It failed of passage in the Senate, where it needed a two-thirds vote under the terms of the Fourteenth Amendment. It failed of passage in the Senate and the Senate did nothing more with it.

Then it went to the House, and the House failed to pass it. The weight of the Sumner Amendment was too much for the bill to carry.

Bills to require mixed schools in the District of Columbia were defeated in the 41st and the 42nd Congress.

[22]Senator Charles D. Drake (1811–1892) of Missouri. Republican senator, 1867–1870; Chief Justice of Court of Claims, 1870–1885.

[23]Senator Frederick T. Frelinghuysen (1817–1885) of New Jersey. Republican senator, 1866–1869 and 1871–1877: Member of Hayes-Tilden Electoral Commission (1877); Secretary of State under President Chester A. Arthur, 1881–1885.

Then came the Civil Rights Act of 1875, which was passed only after the Kellogg Amendment[24] striking out the reference to schools, churches, cemeteries, and juries, and passed in that form.

Then, in 1862 Congress set up its first school for Negroes in the District on a segregated basis. In 1864 it dealt with that question again on a segregated basis.

In 1866, the 39th Congress, it passed a donation of certain lots to be given to schools for Negroes only. It passed a second Act in the same Congress dealing with the distribution of funds between the Negro and the white schools.

In 1868 it dealt with the question again on the segregated basis, and has so continued to this day.

I know that Your Honors are shortly going to hear a case which challenges the validity of those statutes; and be they valid or invalid, for the purposes of my present argument it is immaterial. They are enough to show what the sentiment of Congress was, what its determination was on this specific question, and it is no answer to say that Congress is not controlled by the Fourteenth Amendment. Of course, it is not; but is it conceivable to any man that Congress should submit to the states an amendment destroying their right to segregated schools and should contemporaneously and continuously institute a regime of segregated schools in the District of Columbia?

I should think that if a congressman, who was responsible for submitting to the state an amendment shearing them of power—he would have quite an explanation to make if he got home, if he said he had not done exactly the reverse in the District of Columbia.

Then it is suggested in the brief for the learned Attorney General—and I think similar comment, perhaps, by the appellants—that these two instances in the 39th Congress, these two legislative recognitions of separate schools in the District, which was taking place when the Fourteenth Amendment was taking form and substance—they say that those were mere routine performances, that they came very late in the congressional session, that they were not even honored by having any debate.

Apparently, to have a law which is really to be recognized as a congressional deliverance, it must come early in the session, it must be debated, and the mere fact that it is passed by unanimous consent and without objection more or less disparages its importance as an historical incident. I have never, that I can recall, heard a similar yardstick applied to congressional action.

There isn't time to go over the states. They are covered by our appendix and these other appendices. We classified them, too.

We say that there are nine states that never had segregated schools. There were those states in the northern territory, and there weren't enough Negroes to make it worthwhile. There were five states—I am speaking now of the ratifying states, not of the ratifying—of the thirty-seven states that were then in existence, there were about five states where there had been segregation, and they contem-

[24]The original version of the bill which became the Civil Rights Act of 1875 contained a clause requiring integrated schools. The House Judiciary Committee added a provision permitting separate but equal school facilities to be maintained. Representative Stephen W. Kellogg of Connecticut introduced a successful amendment striking all references to schools in the bill whether for or against separate schools.

poraneously discontinued. Those were Connecticut, Louisiana, Michigan, Florida and South Carolina. Three of those states returned to segregation as soon as the Reconstruction period was over. There were four states that had segregation. I am speaking of the period now from '66 when the Amendment was submitted to '68 when it was proclaimed.

There were four states with segregation who refused to ratify and continued segregation. They were California, Kentucky, Maryland and Delaware. Delaware didn't ratify it until 1901.

There were two border states that had segregation both before and after ratification, and have continued it to this day. They are Missouri and West Virginia.

There were nine northern states that either continued segregation they already had or established it immediately after the ratification of the Fourteenth Amendment: Illinois, Indiana, Kansas, Nevada, New Jersey, New York, Ohio, Oregon and Pennsylvania.

And then—and I can find no evidence that my friends appreciate the significance of this fact—of the reconstructed states who ratified in order to get their delegate, their congressmen and senators back to Washington, eight Reconstruction states in the same Reconstruction legislature, Republican controlled, the same legislature which ratified the Fourteenth Amendment passed statutes continuing or immediately establishing segregated schools. I regard that as a fact of great significance.

If there was any place where the Fourteenth Amendment and its sponsors would have blown the bugle for mixed schools and asserted that the Fourteenth Amendment had settled the question, surely it would have been those eight states under Reconstruction legislation, sympathetic to the party which was responsible for the submission of the Fourteenth Amendment.

Now the appellants say in their brief that three-fourths of the ratifying states gave evidence that they thought the Fourteenth Amendment had abolished segregated schools. I can find in the history as detailed by all of these appendices no warrant whatever for any such assertion, for any such proportion of nonconcurring states. That is before Your Honors in the appendices, and you must, between the three points of view that I have indicated, make your selection.

The second question: Neither the Congress, in submitting, or the states, in ratifying, the Fourteenth Amendment understood that compliance with it would require the immediate abolition of segregation in public schools.

It was nevertheless the understanding of the framers of the Amendment that future Congresses might, in the exercise of their power under section 5 of the Amendment, abolish segregation or, (b), that would be within the judicial power in light of future conditions to construe the Amendment as abolishing such segregation of its own force, and to that we answer it was not the understanding of the framers of the Amendment that future Congresses might, in the exercise of their power under section 5 of the Amendment, abolish segregation in public schools.

And, (c), it was not the understanding of the framers of the Amendment that it would be within the judicial power, in light of future conditions, to construe the Amendment as abolishing segregation in public schools of its own force.

It was not the understanding of the framers that Congress might, in the exercise of the power under section 5 of the Amendment, abolish segregation, and if we are right in the initial proposition that neither Congress nor the states thought the Amendment was dealing with the question of segregated schools, obviously section 5 of the Amendment could not give Congress more power than the Amendment itself had originally embraced.

But the power given to Congress we had noted in section 5 is the power that—I thought I had the exact language—to enforce the provision of this article. And section 5 is not a Trojan horse which opened to Congress a wide field in which Congress might expand the boundaries of the article itself.

JUSTICE JACKSON: Mr. Davis, would not the necessary and proper clause apply to the Amendment as well as to the enumerated powers of the instrument itself? In other words, if Congress should say that in order to accomplish the purposes of equality in the other fields, the abolition of segregation was necessary, as a necessary and proper measure, would that not come under it, or might it not come under the necessary and proper clause?

In other words, I mean is it limited to just what is given in the Amendment or does the necessary and proper clause follow into the amendments?

MR. DAVIS: Well, if you can imagine a necessary and proper clause which would enforce the provisions of this article by dealing with matter which is not within the scope of the article itself, which I think is a contradiction in terms, that is a paradox. Congress could do what the Amendment did not warrant under the guise of enforcing the Amendment.

JUSTICE FRANKFURTER: But you can look for the necessary and proper clause to determine whether it is something appropriate within the Amendment.

MR. DAVIS: Quite so. That is if you use, choose, a monetary clause, related to congressional wisdom and policy, and to the judicial power, in answer to that question, we say that you interpret the Amendment as including something that it does not include is not to interpret the Amendment but is to amend the Amendment, which is beyond the power of the Court.

The third question: On the assumption the answers to questions 2 (a) and (b) does not dispose of the issue, is it within the judicial power in construing the Amendment to abolish segregation in the public schools, and we answer it is not within the judicial power to construe the Fourteenth Amendment adversely to the understanding of its framers as abolishing segregation in the public schools.

Before we answer, we preface that with an expression of the extreme difficulty we have in making the initial assumption on which that question is based, where in our humble judgment the answers to questions 1 and 2 (a) and (b) do dispose of the issue in this case and dispose of it in the clearest and most emphatic manner.

We go on in our answer: Moreover, if in construing the Amendment the principle of *stare decisis* is applied, controlling precedents preclude a construction which would abolish segregation in the public schools.

Now we are cognizant of what this Court has said not once but several times, and what some of us have heard outside the Court as to the scope of *stare decisis* in constitutional matters, and it has been accepted that where there is a pronounced dissent from previous opinions in constitutional matters, mere difficulty in amendment leaves the Court to bow to that change of opinion more than it would of matters of purely private rights.

But be that doctrine what it may, somewhere, sometime to every principle comes a moment of repose when it has been so often announced, so confidently relied upon, so long continued, that it passes the limits of judicial discretion and disturbance.

That is the opinion which we held when we filed our former brief in this case. We relied on the fact that this Court had not once but seven times, I think it is, pronounced in favor of the "separate but equal" doctrine.

We relied on the fact that the courts of last appeal of some sixteen or eighteen states have passed upon the validity of the "separate but equal" doctrine vis-a-vis the Fourteenth Amendment.

We relied on the fact that Congress has continuously since 1862 segregated its schools in the District of Columbia.

We relied on the fact that twenty-three of the ratifying states—I think my figures are right, I am not sure—had by legislative action evinced their conviction that the Fourteenth Amendment was not offended by segregation, and we said in effect that that argument—and I am bold enough to repeat it here now—that in the language of Judge Parker in his opinion below, after that had been the consistent history for over three-quarters of a century, it was late indeed in the day to disturb it on any theoretical or sociological basis. We stand on that proposition.

Then we go on that even if the principle of *stare decisis* in controlling precedents be denied, the effect of the Amendment upon public school segregation examined de novo, that the doctrine of reasonable classification would protect this from the charge of any policy that is brought against us.

In Clarendon School District No. 1 in South Carolina, in which this case alone is concerned, there were in the last report that got into this record something over a year or year and a half ago, 2,799 Negroes, registered Negro children of school age. There were 295 whites, and the state has now provided those 2,800 Negro children with schools as good in every particular.

In fact, because of their being newer, they may even be better. There are good teachers, the same curriculum as in the schools for the 295 whites.

Who is going to disturb that situation? If they were to be reassorted or comingled, who knows how that could best be done?

If it is done on the mathematical basis, with 30 children as a maximum, which I believe is the accepted standard in pedagogy, you would have 27 Negro children and 3 whites in one school room. Would that make the children any happier? Would they learn any more quickly. Would their lives be more serene?

Children of that age are not the most considerate animals in the world, as we all know. Would the terrible psychological disaster being wrought, according to some of these witnesses, to the colored child be removed if he had three white children sitting somewhere in the same school room?

Would white children be prevented from getting a distorted idea of racial relations if they sat with 27 Negro children? I have posed that question because it is the very one that cannot be denied.

You say that is racism. Well, it is not racism. Recognize that for sixty centuries and more humanity has been discussing questions of race and race tension, not racism.

Say that we make special provisions for the aborginal Indian population of this country, it is not racism.

Say that the twenty-nine states have miscegenation statutes now in force which they believe are of beneficial protection to both races. Disraeli said, "No man," said he, "will treat with indifference the principle of race. It is the key of history."

And it is not necessary to enter into any comparison of faculties or possibilities. You recognize differences which racism plants in the human animal.

Now, I want to spend some time on the fourth and fifth questions. They give us a little disturbance, and I don't feel they will greatly disturb the Court.

As to the question of the right of the Court to postpone the remedy, we think that adheres in every court of equity, and there has been no questions about it as to power.

The fifth question, whether the Court should formulate a decree, we find nothing here on which this Court could formulate a decree, nor do we think the Court below has any power to formulate a decree, reciting in what manner these schools are to be alternative at all, and what course the State of South Carolina shall take concerning it.

Your Honors do not sit, and cannot sit as a glorified Board of Education for the State of South Carolina or any other state. Neither can the District Court.

Assuming, in the language of the old treaties about war, it is not to be expected and that God forbid, that the Court should find that the statutes of the State of South Carolina violated the Constitution, it can so declare.

If it should find that inequality is being practiced in the schools, it can enjoin its continuance. Neither this Court nor any other court, I respectfully submit, can sit in the chairs of the legislature of South Carolina and mold its educational system, and if it is found to be in its present for unacceptable, the State of South Carolina must devise the alternative. It establishes the schools, it pays the funds, and it has the sole power to educate its citizens.

What they would do under these circumstances, I don't know. I do know, if the testimony is to be believed, that the result would not be pleasing.

Let me say this for the State of South Carolina. It does not come here as Thad Stevens would have wished in sack cloth and ashes. It believes that its legislation is not offensive to the Constitution of the United States.

It is confident of its good faith and intention to produce equality for all of its children of whatever race or color. It is convinced that the happiness, the progress and the welfare of these children is best promoted in segregated schools, and it thinks it a thousand pities that by this controversy there should be urged the return to an experiment which gives no more promise of success today than when it was written into their Constitution during what I call the tragic era.

I am reminded—and I hope it won't be treated as a reflection on anybody—of Aesop's fable of the dog and the meat: The dog, with a fine piece of meat in his mouth, crossed a bridge and saw the shadow in the stream and plunged for it and lost both substance and shadow.

Here is equal education, not promised, not prophesied, but present. Shall it be thrown away on some fancied question of racial prestige?

It is not my part to offer advice to the appellants and their supporters or sympathisers, and certainly not to the learned counsel. No doubt they think what they propose is best, and I do not challenge their sincerity in any particular period but I entreat them to remember the age-old motto that the best is often the enemy of the good.

ARGUMENT ON BEHALF OF APPELLEES, COUNTY SCHOOL BOARD OF PRINCE EDWARD COUNTY, VA., ET AL.

by MR. MOORE

MR. MOORE: May it please the Court, in undertaking to present the Virginia case, and in view of the fact that the facts are now so similar to those in the South Carolina case, I am aware that there will necessarily be covering of much of the same ground that my distinguished friend and associate, Mr. Davis, has covered. But we feel that we should present our own point of view.

Starting first with a very interesting table, if Your Honors will look at page 211 and 212 of our brief, you will get a very quick and vivid conception of the impact that a decree such as is asked for against South Carolina and Virginia in these cases would produce.

As you will see from page 212, we have there shown you the population by race in every state in this Union, and according to the 1950 census, and as you will see from that table, the proportions vary from practically zero up to 45.3 per cent in Mississippi, with, near the bottom there, 22.1 per cent in Virginia.

Now, if you look at page 211, you will see another very striking set of figures which shows that in these seventeen states in which segregation is now required, plus the District of Columbia, there is, according to this census, ten and a half million Negroes, 40,400,000 white, and that approximately 70 per cent of the entire Negro population of the Nation is in these seventeen states and in the District of Columbia.

It is very striking that the total percentage of the Negroes to total population is approximately 10 per cent, as you will notice there, 10 per cent of the total.

In other words, there are 15,000,000 Negroes, according to the last census in the Nation as a whole, with ten and a half million of those Negroes, or approximately 70 per cent, in these seventeen states plus the District, so that when our opponents talk about the effect of segregation in some of these Northern and Western States, they are not talking about the practical condition with which we are here faced.

In other words, there is actually today one-third of the nation in these seventeen states which, by law, has required segregation, approximately one-third of the population which lives in that situation.

Now, that focuses attention, we believe, at the outset, upon the facts of each situation, so that you cannot talk about this problem just in a vacuum in the manner of a law school discussion.

Now, this particular case, I believe, should be very briefly referred to as to the facts just as was done in the South Carolina case, particularly in view of the fact that the present Chief Justice was not sitting at that a year ago.

This case comes from one of the smaller and poorer counties in Virginia, Prince Edward County. It is about 130 miles from this very spot.

There were three high schools in Prince Edward County at the time this litigation arose. The best of those was the Farmville High School for whites, the poorest was the Worsham High School for whites, and in the middle was the Moton School for Negroes.

Now the record shows that the school authorities during the ten-year period just before this suit was filed had had a very unexpected and difficult problem. In 1941 there were 540 white high school students in the county and only 208 Negro students. In ten years, by 1951, those relationships had changed tremendously.

The white school students numbered 405 while the Negroes had increased to 463. In other words, there had been a decline of 25 per cent in the white, but an increase of 120 odd per cent in the colored.

Now, of course, during that period, during much of the time, it was not practical to obtain the necessary materials for construction of facilities that would be absolutely equal. But we are glad to say that in quality that does not any longer exist. The new Moton Negro High School has now been completed, which was in process of construction when we were here a year ago. It has been completed at a cost of something more than $800,000.

The details of that are shown in Appendix at the end of our brief where there are certificates furnished there by the architects and Superintendent of Schools, showing that money being furnished either through loans or grants from the State of Virginia.

And it is a striking fact that this is just not an isolated case. This brand new high school which has now been completed and was occupied beginning the first of September, is only one of a large number of similar projects. The state has in effect a program over the next four years of more than 250 millions of dollars, with a view to equalizing the facilities. They are able to do it, they intend to do it, and according to the records in this case, about half of the job has been done.

Now, just as in the South Carolina case, this suit was brought with two purposes. The first was the charge that segregation per se was a violation of the Fourteenth Amendment, and to support that charge, the appellants here introduced expert testimony. I, of course, cannot go into that in detail here. We reviewed that a year ago. But it is sufficient to say that if expert testimony ever was discredited, the testimony in this case was.

Now, on the other hand, on our side of the case—and this is the most distinctive feature of this case—we called seven distinguished experts ourselves and attacked the theories, the factual theories that were relied on by the other side, four distinguished educators, a psychiatrist, a psychologist and a distinguished professor of Columbia University, the head of the Department of Psychology.

And through our testimony we show perfectly clearly that the factual contentions that were made by the other side as to detriment to the Negro child were not borne out, as a matter of fact. And the court found on the crucial point in its opinion to this effect. The court said:

> In this milieu we cannot say that vast separation of white and colored children in the public schools is without substance in fact or reason. We have found no hurt or harm to either race.

Now, it is striking that in three of these five cases there was no evidence presented countervailing the Negro's evidence. In the Kansas case, the District case and the Delaware case, expert evidence was presented which was not contradicted by opposing evidence.

In the South Carolina case there was some opposing evidence, not to any great degree such as was in the Virginia case, so that the Virginia case really stands out in opposition, for example, to the Kansas finding where the Virginia court has found on the evidence, after five days of hearings, that the Negroes have failed to prove their case as a matter of fact.

Now, there was an inequality of facilities which we admitted. We were required by the lower court to equalize. We have now done that, and so far as we know, we are precisely in the same situation as the South Carolina case. I don't think there is any dispute about that now from our friends on the other side.

Now, may I just, for a moment, touch questions four and five. Question four in substance is an inquiry as to our position on the question of gradual adjustment if the Court finds against us. We think it is perfectly clear, as Mr. Davis has pointed out, that in the event we are faced with the distressing situation of an adverse decree, that the Court as a court of equity plainly has the power and the duty, in situations like this, to permit a gradual adjustment, as a court of equity considering a balancing of equities. That is all briefed and I don't want to take up time in that discussion.

On the fifth question, the question is whether or not if there is an adverse decree, whether the case should be remanded to the lower court or should a master be appointed, or some other way that the matter should be handled.

We think it is perfectly clear that if there should be this unhappy, unfortunate decree, that the case should be remanded to the lower court where local conditions could be considered, where new evidence would be received. Considering what might be appropriate in Kansas, wouldn't necessarily be appropriate in South Carolina or Virginia.

JUSTICE FRANKFURTER: What kind of guidance, if any, should be given to the district court on this unhappy hypothesis of your argument?

MR. MOORE: It really distresses me to face that question. About all I can say, Your Honor, is we feel the courts should be given the broadest possible discretion to act along reasonable lines. It is a matter of a reasonable exercise of discretion. That is the best answer, I believe, I can give.

JUSTICE FRANKFURTER: I suppose, and Mr. Davis touched on it before when it was asked, it is one thing to ask a district court to lay out districts, school districts.

MR. MOORE: Yes.

JUSTICE FRANKFURTER: I suppose that is one thing. But to have the parties or the state which would be involved, whatever the political unit, say "This is what we are going to do" and have the district court pass on whether that conforms to this hypothetical decree, is another thing, isn't it?

MR. MOORE: Well, Your Honor, we think, to further answer the question—I did not intend to just drop it summarily.

JUSTICE FRANKFURTER: I beg your pardon, I am sorry. Please go your own way, Mr. Moore.

MR. MOORE: No, no, I want to answer Your Honor. We think that following the theory of, say, the antitrust cases, that the party certainly should be allowed to present a plan, rather than for the Court just to hand down a plan. Perhaps that is a more accurate and a better answer. I did not give quite as fluent an answer as I should have originally.

JUSTICE FRANKFURTER: In the Paramount Case in New York,[25] as you know—

MR. MOORE: Yes.

JUSTICE FRANKFURTER: —there was I don't know how long a proceeding before Judge Hand and his associates in which there was conformity by the parties going on as proposed by what this Court decided, which was made a matter of independent extensive litigation and consideration.

MR. MOORE: That's right.

JUSTICE FRANKFURTER: Is your suggestion that kind of solution?

MR. MOORE: That's right. I think undoubtedly that the decree should be a decree that would give broad discretion and permit the parties involved to present an appropriate plan that would be in conformity with the decision of this Court, but leaving a great deal of latitude for the parties to present their own kind of plan.

Now in view of the discussion of Mr. Davis, I am going to pass rather rapidly on the first question.

The remaining questions which Your Honors posed for us to investigate and discuss might be summarized very briefly in this way. The Court said to us to investigate what was the Congressional understanding and intent of the framers of the Fourteenth Amendment with respect to this matter of its impact on schools, both from the standpoint of that time and from the standpoint of what they contemplated future Congresses might do or what this Court might do.

Secondly, what was the understanding and intent of the 33 out of the 37 States that ratified, and the third question was what is the judicial power of this Court? To what extent is it properly within the judicial power of this Court to outlaw segregation just by force of the Amendment and the decision of this Court.

Now there are six major pieces of legislation that were involved in that first question. I will just enumerate them for convenience, and then touch only the more important ones.

The first one was the Freedmen's, the first supplemental Freedmen's Bureau Bill in this 39th Congress of 1866 which, as Mr. Davis pointed out, provided for certain relief, authorized certain relief for these freedmen, but nowhere is the effect on mixed schools really involved in that at all.

[25]United States v. Paramount Pictures, 334 U.S. 131 (1948). The practice of motion picture companies charging uniform license fees to exhibitors and requiring uniform booking arrangements was found to violate the Sherman Act. Extensive litigation on appropriate relief followed the original Supreme Court decision.

The second is the Civil Rights Act of 1866. The third is the Fourteenth Amendment Resolution. The fourth is the legislation with regard to district schools. The fifth are the amnesty bills and sixth is the Civil Rights of 1875.

Now it is a striking thing that that first supplemental Freedmen's Bill undertook to cover almost precisely the same rights, the same subject matter as the Civil Rights Act of 1866.

The supplemental Freedmen's Bill covered only the seceding states.

The Civil Rights Act of 1866 covered all the states. The Rights bill fell into five groups, and everywhere through the debates you will see these five groups of rights being dealt with.

The first was the right to contract. The second was the right to hold property, to inherit it, to transfer it, to lease it and what not.

The third was the right to sue and be sued and give evidence in court.

The fourth was the right to equal security, no improper seizures, no searches and so forth. Equal rights in respect of security.

And the fifth was a group of rights that assured equal punishment for the same offenses.

Now, it is very striking that when this Civil Rights Act of 1866 was submitted, it was submitted by Senator Trumbull, who, as we show repeatedly in our brief, very clearly and finally came out very definitely on the specific point—and he was the proponent—that the right to go to public school was not regarded as a civil right. That is what he said repeatedly in those days.

Now that was the five groups of rights that was covered. Notice what he said. I want to just leave in these few moments in your minds two quotations.

I agree entirely with the thought expressed this morning that you can't judge the intent of Congress by what one senator might have said here or what another congressman said there, but as this Court has repeatedly said, what the sponsors of the legislation say is entitled to particular weight.

That is the Duplex doctrine,[26] that is the doctrine in the Calvert case[27] which Mr. Justice Douglas repeatedly delivered the opinion on, and I want to leave in your minds what these two sponsors said.

Trumbull, as the sponsor of the Civil Rights Act, Wilson in the House, who was Chairman of the Judiciary Committee, and here is what Trumbull said:

> The first section of this bill defines what I understand to be civil rights, the right to make and enforce contracts, to sue, to be sued, to give evidence, to inherit, purchase,

[26]Duplex Printing Press Co. v. Deering, 254 U.S. 443 (1921). The Supreme Court upheld an action for damages under the antitrust law against a union despite a labor organization exemption granted by the Clayton Act. In commenting on the Congressional debates on the labor exemption, the Court noted: "it has come to be well established that the debates in Congress expressive of the views and motives of individual members are not a safe guide . . . in ascertaining the meaning and purpose of the law-making body." 254 U.S. at 474.

[27]Schwegmann v. Calvert Corp. 341 U.S. 384 (1950). The Supreme Court found that fair trade laws passed by Louisiana did not permit a manufacturer of liquor to stop non-signing merchants from selling below the fair trade price despite the Miller-Tydings Act generally sanctioning fair trade laws. In referring to the statutory history of the Act, Justice Douglas noted: "The fears and doubts of the opposition are no authoritative guide to the construction of legislation." 341 U.S. at 394.

sell, lease, hold, convey real and personal property. It is confined exclusively to their civil rights.

And you couple that with his own statement that the right to go to school is not a civil right. Here is what Wilson said over on the House side:

Nor do they mean that children shall attend the same schools. These are not civil rights.

Later on he said:

When he talks about setting aside the school laws of the States by the bill now under consideration, he steps beyond what he must know to be the rule of construction which must apply here.

And when you read these debates, as I hope to show you tomorrow, there were three types of rights which they all finally admitted were not civil rights.

The first one was the right to vote, which was never given until the Fifteenth Amendment. The second was the right to marry a white woman or the other way. The third was the right to go to mixed schools.

Now as I hope to show Your Honors tomorrow morning, those were certainly three vital rights in spite of all this talk about equality of men which was never intended to be given under that bill.

Now the Attorney General, as Mr. Davis points out, says that in view of this conflict, he sets one off against the other. He says he doesn't believe any interpretation is practical here.

He asserts that the proponents and opponents both express the view that the act would outlaw or would not outlaw separate but equal schools. Two of the people he refers to are Kerr and Delano,[28] I will have you bear in mind. They were speaking of cases where there were schools for whites and no schools for Negroes.

Senator Cowan, the only senator who insisted on the point of view that it might open up the schools, as we point out in our brief, later changed his mind in the light of further debate, and he said he became convinced that the rights are here, that the rights are those which I here enumerated.

And only Rogers of New Jersey, the most bitter opponent, stands out in the House in the final showdown, who was insistent that the right to go to school, the mixed schools, might be produced.

As we said in the Calvert case, may I just close this part of the discussion with this question. The Court said here: "The fears and doubts of the opposition are no authoritative guide to the construction of legislation. It is the sponsors that should be looked to when the meaning of the statutory words is in doubt." Now that brings me to the Fourteenth Amendment itself.

(Whereupon at 4:30 p.m., the Court arose.)

(Oral argument was resumed at 12:10 p.m., December 8, 1953.)

[28]Representative Michael C. Kerr (1827–1876) of Indiana. Democratic representative, 1865–1873 and 1875–1876. Representative Columbus Delano (1809–1896) of Ohio. Republican representative, 1865–1862 and 1868–1869; Secretary of the Interior under President Ulysses S. Grant, 1870–1875.

THE CHIEF JUSTICE: This is in the matter of a hearing before the United States Supreme Court in the segregation cases held on Tuesday, December 8, 1953.

ARGUMENT ON BEHALF OF THE APPELLANTS—Resumed

by MR. MOORE—Resumed

MR. MOORE: May it please the Court, at the adjournment yesterday afternoon I had referred briefly in presenting our side of the Virginia case, to the fourth and fifth questions.

Perhaps I was very brief, but we felt in comparison with these other great questions, that we dealt with those very fully in our brief, and I hope my statement was sufficient as to our position as to gradual adjustment and as to the kind of decree in the event of an adverse decision.

I started in the discussion of the first great question, one, as to congressional intent and understanding. In view of Mr. Davis' very extensive discussion on that matter and also on the question of the states' understanding, I shall try to be quite brief on those two next questions, and will simply try to pinpoint what we regard as the high points as to both those matters, and give the greater part of my time to what we believe now, in view of questions from the Court as well as from the former hearing, what is perhaps the larger question as to judicial power.

Your Honors will recall that I had pointed out that there are six classes of legislation which throw a great deal of light on the intent of Congress. I had touched on the first two, the Freedmen's Bill which is significant here only in this respect: that that was the first bill in which Congress had undertaken to provide for the Negro for public schools at public expense, and the significant thing is they were separate schools.

I had then proceeded to discuss the 1866 Civil Rights Act and had undertaken to point out to you the great change that was made in that Act.

As the Act was originally introduced, it had broad language which provided that all discrimination in civil rights and immunities as to all inhabitants on account of race is prohibited. And because of constitutional questions that had been raised and arguments on policy, that language was changed around to the specific language that you now find in the bill as it was finally passed.

Now I had pointed out that there were these five groups of rights that were listed, and the sponsors of the bill made clear that those were the rights intended, and only those.

Now there is no difficulty about *Strauder* when you look at it in that light.

The fourth group of rights was their right to equal security, and all that *Strauder* held was the right to have a Negro possibly on the jury was a part of his right of equal security.

I also tried to point out that there were three classes of rights which, by debate, was clearly eliminated in that list of rights. The first was the right of suffrage which, as we all know, in spite of this argument about equal rights was never given the Negro until two years later in 1870 when the Fifteenth Amendment was passed, although the Thirteenth had freedom from slavery.

The second was the right of intermarriage which was clearly not intended to be included, in spite of the broad language, and this right of mixed schools. Now those were three that were clearly pointed out in all the debates and were not intended to be covered.

That brings us therefore to the third important piece of legislation which was the Fourteenth Amendment itself. As Your Honors recall, that Amendment really sprung out of the debates on the Civil Rights Act, because it was argued that the Civil Rights\Act, even in spite of the Thirteenth Amendment that freed the slaves, was still not constitutional. So the Amendment sprung from that.

It came from the Joint Committee on Reconstruction. That Committee was composed of nine representatives and six senators. The majority were radicals, although Senator Sumner was considered too radical for membership, we find, from a very interesting letter from Senator Fessenden's son. It is in our opinions. His friends wouldn't put him on there.

The chairman was Senator Fessenden of Maine and he was ill much of the time, and Senator Howard of Michigan took the lead in his place. The House leader was the famous co-chairman, that is, Stevens.

Now the Amendment here again is debated in two forms very much like the Civil Rights Act. In its first form it purported to confer on Congress the affirmative power to make all laws that were necessary to secure privileges and immunities and equal protection. That version though was considered too broad, just as was the broad language in the original Civil Rights Act.

And finally in May of that year the Amendment was reported in the form that is now found, and as Your Honors probably are thoroughly familiar with it, there are two sentences really in the first section.

The first was the sentence put in by Senator Howard which defined citizenship, that everyone born and naturalized in this country, regardless of race, was a citizen, and the second sentence which Mr. Bingham wrote, was the same section we are here concerned with, which switched around the approach to the matter from a grant of affirmative power to Congress to a denial of power to the states.

Now in both the House and the Senate the debates made one thing clear. The purpose of the first section of the Amendment was simply to write the Civil Rights Act into the Constitution. Stevens, the sponsor in the House, said that, Howard of Michigan said that, and numerous others, which I will not take time to enumerate.

The reasons were very interesting. The Democrats persistently charged the Republicans with trying to constitutionalize the Civil Rights Act. They said, "That is all you are trying to do is to legalize it."

On the other hand, the Republicans replied, "Yes, that is what we want to do, but we want to nail it down so it can't be repealed."

That is what Stevens said in perfectly clear language as the leader, and as I pointed out yesterday, we look primarily to Stevens and Howard, people like that, and Wilson in the House, to find out really what they are talking about, the proponents.

Now the appellants here assert two things. They first quote these broad statements about equal privileges and immunities that certain members of Congress and the Senate wanted to assure, and next they assert that the Amendment went beyond those civil rights that we have in the Civil Rights Act.

Neither statement in our judgment is a safeguard to this Court because it is perfectly plain from the extracts in our brief and appendix and in the South Carolina brief, that these radical people never were able to go as far as they wanted. Stevens admitted that frankly. So did Howard at the end.

So the Amendment was proposed in the form with these two sentences, Howard's definition of citizenship and Bingham's statement of denial of rights to the States to deny equal protection of the laws.

Now the debates give convincing evidence that it was not intended to abolish segregated schools, but confirmation comes from two other sources which were mentioned, one of them particularly yesterday. I will just touch it very briefly.

The next step is the District school legislation which our opponents, our colored friends, saw fit in their brief to completely ignore, and which the Attorney General comes in and dusts off with just a gesture, saying it was dealt with casually.

The most significant thing in that legislation, Your Honors, aside from the fact that just a month after slavery was abolished here in the District in 1862 and separate schools were set up for Negroes, is this fact: I am not going to review it all, but keep in mind this fact, that in 1866, in July, 1866, within one month after the Fourteenth Amendment was proposed in June, 1866, this Congress, the same 39th Congress passed these two bills in which they dealt with these separate schools.

In one case they provided for property to be transferred for the use solely of those schools. In the second bill they appropriated money in proportion to the number of Negroes to whites, and yet these gentlemen are bold enough to come up and say because that legislation passed without great debate, that it was not carefully considered.

Now passing on from the District school legislation, let's take the next important piece of legislation. I will mention it. It was the amnesty bills.

Those bills were debated with greatest heat in Congress with a view to granting amnesty to Southerners who participated in the war. And on two occasions Charles Sumner undertook to draft, to tack onto those bills his Civil Rights bill, which included a requirement that the Negroes should be given equal status as to schools, churches, cemeteries, theaters and what not. And in respect to each of those he lost out, and the bills were finally passed without them.

Now one more reference and I am through with this part of the case. We should not lose sight of the 1875 Civil Rights Act. This matter was not finally ended until the 1875 Act was dealt with, the famous right, the famous act, which was held unconstitutional in the *Civil Rights Cases*.

And therein in respect of that Act which was introduced by General Butler of Massachusetts,[29] the effort was being made as the last effort on this matter to write into the civil rights bill the fact that the Negroes should be given equal status in schools, churches, cemeteries, theaters and what not.

Finally, in order to get something passed because the Republicans lost out, there were a hundred people who lost their seats in Congress just about that time

[29]Representative Benjamin F. Butler (1818–1893) of Massachusetts. Major General of the Union Army, Republican representative, 1867–1875 and 1877–1879. He was one of the radical Republican leaders in Congress and one of the House managers in the impeachment proceedings against President Andrew Johnson. He also served as Governor of Massachusetts, 1882–1884.

on the Republican side, and to try to get something through, they struck out all reference to schools and the cemeteries and things of that sort and the Act was passed without it, and that was the last effort made to write into this legislation all of this business about equal rights as to schools.

So how our friends on the other side can get comfort out of that story when they can point only to Rogers of New Jersey and occasionally to a remark made by Senator Cowan is beyond us to understand.

Now let me turn just very briefly to the state end of this. There is a very interesting chart in our brief. I have called Your Honors' attention to one yesterday, which was the chart of the 1950 Census.

If you look at page 150, you will see the Census of 1870 where for the first time after the Amendment was adopted, we get a Census including the Negro, and that chart is very illuminating as to what was done with these states.

Mr. Davis discussed it yesterday, and I will not take much time on it. I will just comment on two or three points.

As you see from that chart, there are five states, including Maine, New Hampshire, and so forth, where the question of segregation never was even pertinent at all, never even came up, and in those states the Negro was not quite two-tenths of one per cent of the population.

There is another group of states, such as Massachusetts, Michigan, and so forth, where slavery had been abolished before the Amendment, or where it was abolished about that time, and it is less than one per cent of the Negroes in those States, so it was of no moment.

You then turn to the twenty-three states, the principal ones that are left. My friend, Judge Almond, who will follow me in a brief talk about the seceding states as to which there is an abominable conspiracy charged here by our opponents, is going to talk about the seceding states. But there what happened was that the same legislature that adopted the Fourteenth Amendment passed these laws that required segregation.

Well, how could that be clear evidence that they didn't understand that the Amendment prevented that? But I submit to you that the significant thing in this whole state story is the fact that there were seven of the great states—and I will name them, New York, New Jersey, California, Illinois, Missouri, Ohio and Pennsylvania—as to which our opponents are unable to lay any finger of scorn, and every one of those states had segregation before the Amendment was adopted, and they continued segregation for years thereafter; in California until 1880, in Illinois until 1874, in New Jersey until 1881, in Ohio until 1887, in Pennsylvania until 1881, and in New York until 1930.

And in addition to that, we have the Supreme Courts of those states—Ohio was the first in 1871—which passed directly on the matter and held that the equal facilities, equal doctrine, was not in violation of the Constitution. California filed suit with the decision of its Supreme Court, then Pennsylvania and New York. I will not take further time on it. The record is perfectly clear. And how these gentlemen try to explain away that record with respect to those states is beyond our understanding.

Now turning finally to the third question as to judicial power, as we understood that question, we understood that the Court had in mind in asking us whether the Court had judicial power of itself to abolish segregation, we understood that the Court had in mind perhaps three approaches to it, which I will deal with very briefly.

The first is whether or not this is a case where there should be a restraint of judicial power and the matter left to the legislative bodies.

The second is whether or not in the light of precedents this is a case lasting over these hundred years where it would be an abuse of power in the light of that history. It is what Mr. Davis called yesterday the time when there should be some time a period of repose when a matter is really settled. That is the second question.

And the third branch is whether or not there is some idea here of a living constitution and changing conditions that should make a difference. I am going to talk just very briefly about those three.

As we pointed out, segregation in education does exist in these seventeen states and the District where 55 million people live. In many of these states it is written into the constitution.

And we submit that the first point to bear in mind on this phase of the case is the principle that was mentioned in Justice Jackson's opinion here yesterday, and so well put by Justice Brandeis many years ago: that in a situation like this the statute of a particular constitution comes before Your Honor with a presumption of constitutionality.[30]

In the second place, we point out that this is not a case of some novel or modern experiment such as has been involved in so many cases before Your Honors where these old doctrines have been attempted to be applied to some modern situation. Here the statute is as old as the Constitution itself, and the novel principles are those that are brought in issue here by our opponents.

Finally, we must refer to the field of legislative action. Mr. Justice Holmes has very well expressed the thought when he said:

> Legislatures are ultimate guardians of the liberties and the welfare of the people in quite as great a degree as the courts.[31]

We submit that the Court must coordinate the field for its operations with that of the legislative branch in a case particularly of this kind. What we urge is that the size, the history of this problem before the Court here, makes it clear that the solution should be left with the legislatures.

This case presents a matter, we submit, for judicial restraint if there ever was a case presented. We don't mean judicial restraint here in the sense of these political cases such as have been referred to by the other side. What we do urge is that this question should be left to the duly elected representatives of the people.

Now in touching just the second question as to what is the true situation here in the light of history of the decisions of this Court and the many state courts, in view of questions between Mr. Justice Frankfurter and Mr. Marshall yesterday, I can touch that very briefly.

---

[30]United States v. Gambling Devices, 346 U.S. 441 (1953). On December 7, 1953, the Court in an opinion by Justice Jackson upheld the constitutionality of a federal law prohibiting the shipment of gambling machines in interstate commerce.

[31]Missouri, Kansas and Texas Ry. Co. v. May, 194 U.S. 267, 270 (1904).

I need only point out that his "separate but equal" doctrine is not a new doctrine. It is more than one hundred years old.

It was first presented to the nation in *Roberts* against *Boston* in 1849, and there was upheld under the Massachusetts Constitution in fundamentals like we have here.

From that time on it got written in the various state statutes, as I have just pointed out. It was continued, it was debated back and forth in the halls of Congress here between 1862 and 1875. In states like Virginia and Georgia it was written into fundamental law in 1870.

These state court cases came along in 1871, 1873 and 1874. In *Hall* v. *DeCuir* in 1877 Mr. Justice Clifford there in the Steamboat case, where the State of Louisiana in a legislature dominated by Negroes and carpetbaggers had passed a law requiring the mixing of people on these boats, that was held unconstitutional under the commerce clause, and he had recognized the doctrine in his concurring opinion there.[32]

So the Court came in 1896 to *Plessy* v. *Ferguson.* There was nothing new to present, and I am glad to find that our gentlemen on the other side here differ from their position here a year ago. They do not come here trying to distinguish *Plessy* v. *Ferguson* and *Gong Lum* from this case. They were here a year ago saying *Plessy* v. *Ferguson* was a railroad case, and the Gong Lum case was a Chinese case, and they could be distinguished, but I am very glad Mr. Marshall marched right up to the point.

He said, "Now, we are asking that this Court go further than it has ever gone before and overrule *Plessy* v. *Ferguson* and *Gong Lum*" because that is what has got to be done for the decree that he asks to be entered.

I am not going to review these more recent cases. As was pointed out, it was admitted here yesterday these gentlemen are not happy with these recent cases of *Sweatt* v. *Painter* nor *McLaurin,* for that matter. McLaurin there in the Department of Education in Oklahoma was set apart, true enough, but he was set apart in a way so it was just as if he had the sign, "Here is a leper, here is a leper, don't touch him." In very proper words said, "Well, you can't do that. That is not any proper application of the doctrine."

So we find the Court under the Chief Justice saying in *Sweatt* v. *Painter,* which they don't like on the other side, "Nor do we need to reach the petitioners' contention that *Plessy* v. *Ferguson* should be reexamined."

Now coming finally to the last phase of this matter that I just spoke of, and that is whether or not there are changed conditions that may warrant some different application of the doctrine.

The appellants urge that these precedents should be overruled. They don't urge merely changed conditions. Practically every argument these gentlemen present, Your Honors will find that Charles Sumner presented just as effectively and just as oratorically in 1870 and in that period as they presented it.

The real crux of their argument is the fact they contend that the mere act of

[32]Hall v. DeCuir, 95 U.S. 485 (1878). A Louisiana state law passed in 1869 by a Reconstruction legislature required integration of common carriers within the state. It was held unconstitutional as a burden on interstate commerce.

separation is a badge of inferiority, and that was his theme, that is what he dedicated his life to long before the Amendment and until his death in 1874.

Now if we are going to look at this matter from the standpoint of precedent, the rule is pretty simple. The rule is that the state may classify and the test of its classification is merely within the bounds of reason. Mr. Justice Hughes well said, quoting him:

The inquiry must be whether considering the end in view, the statute passes the bounds of reason and assumes the character of a mere arbitrary fiat.[33]

Now how is "reasonable" to be decided here? It can't be decided in a vacuum. It has got to be decided in the light of all the surrounding facts.

Now what are the local conditions in Virginia where we are concerned? In our case the superintendent, State Superintendent of Public Construction testified that the people, Negroes and whites alike, believed that the best interests of both the whites and the Negroes are that the separate schools are best. A former Superintendent of Public Education testified that segregation caused no warped personalities, and that the general welfare would be definitely harmed by mixed schools in Virginia.

A distinguished child psychiatrist testified in this case that the amalgamation would result in increased anxieties which would be detrimental to both races.

The Chairman of Psychology in the Department of Columbia testified—and he is a Virginia boy educated in Virginia, went up to the big city where he has been a great teacher for these many years—he testified with full knowledge of Virginia conditions that the result of segregation in Virginia produced better education for both races.

Now what are we going to do with that testimony? Are we just going to disregard it? Can this Court now say that on the basis of this record, segregation is beyond the bounds of reason, that it is an arbitrary fiat? We don't believe so.

I would like to say this in conclusion, may it please Your Honors. We are trying to be fair as we know how about this matter. It is a matter on which there is great feeling in these seventeen states.

We recognize that there are a great many people of the highest character and position who disapprove of segregation as a matter of principle or as ethics. We think that most of them really do not know the conditions, particularly in the South, that brought about that situation.

That was true of all these witnesses, these experts that appeared in our Virginia case. They did not know a thing about Virginia, they all admitted, and they are not familiar with the way in which it is gradually being worked out. But those feelings that I refer to are not relevant here.

Mr. Justice Holmes had very well put the thought when he said:

There is nothing that I deprecate more than the use of the Fourteenth Amendment beyond the absolute compulsion of its words to prevent the making of social experiments that an important part of the community desires, in the insulated chambers afforded by the several States, even though those experiments may seem futile or even noxious to me and to those whose judgment I most respect.[34]

[33]Purity Extract and Tonic Co. v. Lynch, 226 U.S. 192, 204 (1912).
[34]Truax v. Corrigan, 257 U.S. 312, 344 (1921).

Is that sound? We believe it is. And just look at the picture that faces the seventeen states as I leave this matter with you.

These states start at Maryland. They go all the way down to Texas, to the Gulf of Mexico. They go out as far west as Missouri and Oklahoma, with a third of the nation included in those states with ten and a half million Negroes in those states, 70 per cent of the Negroes in the whole nation in those states.

During this hundred-year period since *Roberts* and *Boston* has been the law, millions and millions of dollars have been spent in building up these systems. There are thousands of school houses, fine school houses, all over these seventeen states. As a matter of fact, these gentlemen here have one of the finest school buildings in the Nation just completed, which they moved into on September the first.

What are we to do with that situation? Are we to go and put in this county—there are about five and a half Negroes to every five white persons—shall we put one Negro along with every white child in high school when that is the best high school?

I say to you that there is looking down on you from every one of these high school sections, every elementary school in these seventeen states with anxiety as to what you shall do with this.

In our humble judgment there is not anything that could be more serious than an adverse decision. And I want to leave that matter just with this thought which our friend Judge Parker in the South Carolina case has expressed better than anywhere I know. Here is the way he summed it up, after referring to *Plessy* v. *Ferguson* and *Gong Lum* and the great judges that sat in those cases. He said:

> To this we may add that, when seventeen states and the Congress of the United States have for more than three-quarters of a century, required segregation of the races in the public schools, and when this has received the approval of the leading appellate courts of the country including the unanimous approval of the Supreme Court of the United States at a time when that Court included Chief Justice Taft, Justices Stone, Holmes and Brandeis, it is a late day to say that such segregation is violative of fundamental constitutional rights.

> It is hardly reasonable to suppose that the legislative bodies of so wide a territory, including the Congress of the United States, and the great judges of high courts, have knowingly defied the Constitution for so long a period or that they have acted in ignorance of the meaning of its provisions. The constitutional principle is the same now that it has been throughout this period; and if conditions have changed so that segregation is no longer wise, this is a matter for the legislatures and not for the courts. The members of the judiciary have no more right to read their ideas of sociology into the Constitution than their ideas of economics.

Thank you.

THE CHIEF JUSTICE: General Almond.

ORAL ARGUMENT ON BEHALF OF THE APPELLEES
COUNTY SCHOOL BOARD OF PRINCE EDWARD COUNTY, VIRGINIA, ET AL

by MR. ALMOND.

MR. ALMOND: May it please the Court, Mr. Moore assigned to me a rather Herculean task, and I have no time in which to address myself to that phase of the case which I would like to discuss.

As the only official of one of the seceding states privileged to actively participate in this case, I just want to, if Your Honors please, take a few moments, the
few moments which remain, to bring to your attention this phase: what are they
here asking for?

They are asking this Court, contrary to the intention of the Congress which
proposed the Fourteenth Amendment, as evidenced irrevocably by the records of
that historic session and during those years, they are asking you to make a decision contrary to the spirit, the intent and purpose of the Fourteenth Amendment.

They are asking you to amend the Constitution of the United States and to
go further than the Congress ever intended that this Court should go.

They are asking you to disturb and tear down the principle of *stare decisis*
enunciated so clearly in 1896 in *Plessy* v. *Ferguson,* reimplemented again in
1899 in *Cumming* v. *Board,* clearly enunciated again in 1927 in *Gong Lum* v.
Rice, and even though driven to the wall yesterday, the ingenious counsel of the
opposition in a fruitless effort to confess and avoid, finally admitted that the very
basis of the latest decisions of this Court on that subject beginning with *Gaines* v.
Canada in 1938, followed by *Sipuel* in 1948, by *Sweatt* v. *Painter* and *McLaurin* in
1950, that the very basis of those latter cases was predicated upon the doctrine
enunciated in *Plessy* v. *Ferguson:* separate but equal facilities do not offend any
provision of the Constitution of the United States.

They are asking you to overturn the principle of *stare decisis* laid down by
this Court and the courts of last resort of every state in this Union that a solemn
constitutional provision or legislative enactment carries with it the highest presumption known to law, that it is a valid exercise of the powers of the body which
enacted it.

They are asking you to disturb the unfolding evolutionary process of education where from the dark days of the depraved institution of slavery, with the help
and the sympathy and the love and respect of the white people of the South, the
colored man has risen under that educational process to a place of eminence and
respect throughout this nation. It has served him well.

In those days as now, the states were dealing with the question of policy.
Questions have been asked here or submitted by this Court as to what directions
there should be in any adverse decree handed down, adverse to the appellees in this
case. I like the language of Mr. Justice Holmes when he said—I believe it was Mr.
Justice Holmes—no, probably not, but in the case of International Salt in 332
U.S.:[35]

> It is not the province of the appellate court to write decrees. That is within the
> province and the equipment of the District Court.

I would say to this Court on that question, in the event of an adverse decision
to our side, that the case be remanded with direction to the lower court to conduct
a hearing taking into consideration the vast administrative difficulties which
would be occasioned as a result of such a decision.

[35]International Salt Co. v. United States, 332 U.S. 392 (1947). The International Salt
Co. leased its patented machines with a requirement that the lessee could purchase only
International Salt products for the machine. This was held to violate the Sherman Act. The
District Court was directed to frame an appropriate decree for relief.

We must determine from Virginia what we are going to do with our compulsory attendance law in the event of an adverse decision. We must determine whether we will have one system or three systems, if the dual system is destroyed.

It is a matter, sir, of great import to these states affected. What crime has Virginia committed? She has within the last fifteen years gone further in the promotion of education on an equal facilities basis than almost, I can say, any state in the South.

Within the last four years she has appropriated 75 millions of dollars which has been more than matched by the political subdivisions, to increase the facilities of our public school system, and most of that has been spent to equalize facilities which needed to be equalized.

JUSTICE FRANKFURTER: General Almond, let me ask you a question to see whether I understand your suggestion.

MR. ALMOND: Yes.

JUSTICE FRANKFURTER: Of these systems, the choice is of going to what is called an integrated school but in default of that, deciding of the choice than, it will be shepherded into one or the other, is that what you mean by the decree?

MR. ALMOND: I didn't mean, Mr. Justice Frankfurter, shepherding in that sense.

JUSTICE FRANKFURTER: That is a bad word. If they do not choose to go to unmixed schools, then they would have to go to a separate school, is that right, if they do not choose to go to a mixed school which is open to them, then they would have to go to one or the other, is that what you mean, General Almond?

MR. ALMOND: I said, sir, that that is the matter of policy which the states—

JUSTICE FRANKFURTER: Yes, I understand, but is that what you meant?

MR. ALMOND: Yes.

JUSTICE FRANKFURTER: Those are the three which you have in mind?

MR. ALMOND: That is right, sir, which the state would have to determine.

JUSTICE FRANKFURTER: Yes, I understand that. It is a very hypothetical answer on that, but I just wanted to understand you.

MR. ALMOND: That is a matter of legislative policy.

Now, if Your Honors please, I guess my time has just about expired. I would like to say one thing in behalf of the seceding states, if there was ever such a thing, why they have been indicted by the opposition of treachery, of fraud, of conniving to subvert the Fourteenth Amendment.

I ask our friends of the opposition to consider this: That when the constitutional conventions were created in the South, think of their composition. There were 101 delegates to the constitutional convention which framed the new constitution of the great State of Alabama. Of these there were 18 Negroes, 38 carpetbaggers and 45 scalawags.

Now I do not use those two latter terms in any sense of approbium. Mr. Webster defines a carpetbagger as a roving venturer meddling in the politics of a locality in which he has no interest. History defines a scalawag as a white southerner who associated with the machinations of the carpetbaggers.

Now Georgia's constitutional convention of 1867 and '68 consisted of 131 scalawags, 37 Negroes, 9 carpetbaggers and 12 conservative whites. The convention that prepared the new constitution for Virginia was composed of 24 Negroes, 26 carpetbaggers, 14 scalawags and 35 conservative whites.

I ask them when they indict these states for perpetrating a fraud by not placing certain provisions in their constitutions until after readmissions has been accomplished, and then turning around as they said and enacting mixed school law, if a fraud was perpetrated, who was the perpetrator.

We should remember also in this indictment against the southern states that governors were sent in as importations from as far away as Maine, Kansas and Pennsylvania, and those governors recommended to the very legislatures which ratified the Fourteenth Amendment that a school system should be established on a segregated basis. They did that because they understood the facts of life and knew that in no other way could that question then, as we maintain now, be solved to the benefit of both races.

REBUTTAL ARGUMENT ON BEHALF OF APPELLANTS, HARRY BRIGGS, JR., ET AL.

by MR. MARSHALL

MR. MARSHALL: May it please the Court, there are several points I would like to clear up preliminarily, and then I would like to make sure that our position is correctly stated, and as it relates to statements made by counsel on the other side.

JUSTICE FRANKFURTER: Mr. Marshall, I do not want to interrupt your closing argument, but I hope before you sit down you will state to the Court whether you have anything more to say on the question of remedies.

MR. MARSHALL: Yes, sir.

JUSTICE FRANKFURTER: In case you should prevail, more than is contained in your brief.

MR. MARSHALL: Yes, sir, I would be glad to get to that first, Mr. Justice Frankfurter.

In our brief we found ourselves, after having given as much research as we could, in a position where we intelligently could not put forth a plan. We find that in the briefs of the other side they recognized there would be certain administrative problems involved, and anything else that they mentioned we, of course, well, not of course, we do not recognize as being valid for this Court to consider.

On the other hand, we spent as much time as we could during the time of filing and the present time on the United States Government's suggestion as to the decree, and so far as we are concerned, it appears to us that there are administrative problems, there would be administrative problems, and that the decree of this Court could very well instruct the lower court to take into consideration that factor, and if necessary give to the state involved a sufficient time to meet the administrative problems, with the understanding so far as we are concerned that I do not agree with the last part of the Government [brief], that if it isn't done within a school year, that they could get more time for this reason, sir.

I can conceive of nothing administrative-wise that would take longer than a year. If they don't have staff enough to do these administrative things, the sovereign states can hire more people to do it.

So for that reason I don't think it should take more than a year for them to adequately handle the administrative techniques, and I submit that a longer period of time would get the lower court into the legislative field as to whether or not to do it this way or that way.

Specifically, I am a firm believer that especially in so far as the federal courts are concerned, their duty and responsibility ends with telling the state, in this field at least, what you can't do.

And I don't think anybody is recommending to this Court that this Court take over the administrative job. Obviously, that is not recommended by anyone. So with that, I think that is our position.

We said in the opening brief that if any plans were put forth, we would be obliged to do it, we wanted to do it, and that is our position on the limited point.

It gets me, if it please the Court, to one of the points that runs throughout the argument in the brief on the other side, and that is that they deny that there is any race prejudice involved in these cases. They deny that there is any intention to discriminate.

But throughout the brief and throughout the argument they not only recognize that there is a race problem involved, but they emphasize that that is the whole problem. And for the life of me, you can't read the debates, even the sections they rely on, without an understanding that the Fourteenth Amendment took away from the states the power to use race.

As I understand their position, their only justification for this being a reasonable classification is, one, that they got together and decided that it is best for the races to be separated and, two, that it has existed for over a century.

Neither argument, to my mind, is any good. The answer to the first argument is in two places, if I may for a moment address myself to it. This one that Mr. Davis and Mr. Moore both relied on, these horrible census figures, the horrible number of Negroes in the South—and I thought at some stage it would be recognized by them that it shows that in truth and in fact in this country that high percentage of Negroes they talk about can be used to demonstrate to the world that in so far as this country is concerned, two-thirds of the Negroes are compelled to submit to segregation.

They say that is the reason for it. The best answer is in the record in the Clarendon County case, where the only witness the other side put on on this point—and a reading of it will show he was put on for the express purpose—he is a school administrator—of explaining how the school system would be operated under the new bill that was going to tax people, but they dragged this other point in and made him an expert in race relations and everything else.

He emphasized—well, the best way to do it is this way on page 119 of the record in the Briggs case:

> What I was saying is that the problem of the mixed groups and racial tensions is less in communities where the minority population is small. That has been true of the testimony I have heard.
> Then the question: "Well, Mr. Crow," incidentally, that was his name, Mr. Crow, assuming that in Clarendon County especially in School District No. 22 the population was 95 per cent white and 5 per cent Negro, would that change your opinion? Answer. No.
> Question. Then that is not really the basis of your opinion, is it?
> Answer. The question that you have asked me is in my opinion, will the elimination of segregation be fraught with undesirable results, and I have said that I thought it would. That may not be stating your question exactly, but that is still my answer.
> Question. As a matter of fact, Mr. Crow, isn't your opinion based on the fact that you have all of your life believed in segregation of the races? Isn't that the reason, the real reason, the basis of your opinion?
> Answer. That wouldn't be all.
> Question. But it is a part of it?
> Answer. I suppose it is.

And that answers all of those arguments about this large number of people involved. They are all American citizens who, by accident of birth, are a different color, and it makes no difference one way or another in so far as this Court is concerned.

Then, in that same vein, Attorney General Almond gets to the name-calling stage about these state conventions. Well, let's go up to the later convention in his State of Virginia. I don't believe that the man I am now going to quote can be characterized as anything but a respected former senator of the United States, and in debating the section in the latter Constitution of Virginia, not the one in this period, but the later one, Senator Carter Glass, who was a delegate to the convention, spoke thusly in the debates:

> Discrimination, that is precisely what we propose. That exactly is what this Convention was elected for, to discriminate to the very extremity of permissible action under the limitations of the federal Constitution.

That is quoted in the statement of jurisdiction in the Virginia case on page 11. And another answer I submit is quoted in our reply brief involving the University of North Carolina Law School case which was decided adversely to the Negro applicants in the district court, and on appeal to the Fourth Circuit Court of Appeals, the very Circuit that is involved here, in an opinion by Judge Soper of Maryland met this question of what we are doing is for the benefit of the white and Negro people alike, saying:

> The defense seeks in part to avoid the charge of inequality by the paternal suggestion that it would be beneficial to the colored race in North Carolina as a whole, and to the individual plaintiffs in particular, if they would cooperate in promoting the policy adopted by the State rather than seek the best legal education which the State provides. The duty of the federal courts, however, is clear. We must give first place

to the rights of the individual citizen, and when and where he seeks only equality of treatment before the law, his suit must prevail. It is for him to decide in which direction his advantage lies.[36]

As to this time of how long segregation has been in existence in the South, the same argument has been made in every case that has come up to this Court, the argument of *stare decisis,* that you should leave this because it has been long standing, the "separate but equal" doctrine, and that there are so many states involved, was made in even more detailed fashion in the Sweatt brief filed by Attorney General Price Daniel,[37] and as an aside, it is significant that in the Virginia brief on the last page they go out of their way to pay acknowledgement to that brief filed by the Attorney General, which was obviously discarded by this Court.

There is not one new item that has been produced in all of these cases. And we come to the question as to whether or not the wishes of these states shall prevail, as to whether or not our Constitution shall prevail.

And over against the public policy of the State of Virginia and the State of South Carolina is an Amendment that was put in the Constitution after one of the worst wars that was ever fought, and around that constitutional provision we say that the public policy of the United States does not look to the state policy, but looks to our government.

And in the brief we have filed in our reply brief, we quote from a document which just came out, at least we just got ahold of it a couple of weeks ago, monograph, which we cite in our brief from the selective service of our Government, and we have some quotes in our brief.

I don't emphasize or urge the quotes as such, but a reading of that monograph will convince anyone that the discriminatory segregation policies, education and otherwise in the South, almost caused us to lose one war, and I gather from the recommendations made in there that unless it is corrected, we will lose another.

Now that is the policy that I understand them to say that it is just a little feeling on the part of Negroes, they don't like segregation. As Mr. Davis said yesterday, the only thing the Negroes are trying to get is prestige.

Exactly correct. Ever since the Emancipation Proclamation, the Negro has been trying to get what was recognized in *Strauder* v. *West Virginia,* which is the same status as anybody else regardless of race.

I can't, for the life of me—it seems to me they recommend to us what we should do. It seems to me they should show some effort on their part to conform their states to the clear intent of past decisions.

For example, the argument was made in *McLaurin* and *Sweatt* of what would happen if these decisions were granted, and indeed the brief, joint brief filed by the Attorneys General of all the states, and if I remember correctly it was signed by General Almond, said that if this Court broke down exclusion and segregation in

[36]McKissick v. Carmichael, 187 F 2d 949, 953–54 (4th Cir. 1951). One of the plaintiffs in that action was Floyd McKissick, later chairman of CORE and a militant civil rights leader.

[37]Price Daniel (1910–   ) former Governor of Texas (1956–1963), U.S. Senator (1953–1956), and State Attorney General (1946–1953). He argued Sweatt v. Painter for the State of Texas.

the graduate and professional schools, or maybe it was the law schools—I know exactly what they said—the schools would have to close up and go out of business.

And the truth of the matter—and we cite in our record the figures that show that since that decision there are now 1500 Negroes in graduate and professional schools in heretofore all white universities, 1500 at least in twelve states, one of the states significantly out of the group being South Carolina.

It is also pointed out in our brief a very long list of private schools in the South, which as a result, with no legal binding upon them at all, do so.

It is also significant that in states like Arkansas—I could name four or five—without any lawsuit, segregation was broken down. The truth of the matter is that I for one have more confidence in the people of the South, white and colored, than the lawyers on the other side. I am convinced they are just as lawful as anybody else, and once the law is laid down, that is all there is to it.

In their argument on the congressional debate, they do a job too well. They say no education was intended to be covered by the Fourteenth Amendment.

Obviously, that is not correct, because even their pet case, *Plessy* v. *Ferguson*, recognized that education was under the Fourteenth Amendment.

Then Mr. Moore goes to great detail to point out that the Fourteenth Amendment could go no further than the Civil Rights Act, and he emphasized yesterday and he emphasized today that in addition to that, there were some rights that were deliberately excluded.

His language is "clearly eliminated," and then he says, "Suffrage was clearly not intended to be included."

And how anyone can stand in this Court, having read the opinion of Mr. Justice Holmes in the first Texas Primary case,[38] and take that position is beyond me, because that decision, in the language of Mr. Justice Holmes, said specifically that they urged the Fourteenth and Fifteenth Amendments, but we don't have to get to the Fifteenth Amendment because the Fourteenth Amendment said that the states can do a lot of classifying which we, speaking as a Court, can't seem to understand, but it is clear that race cannot be used in suffrage. So I don't see the purport of any of that argument.

JUSTICE FRANKFURTER: Do you think the Fifteenth Amendment was redundant, superfluous?

MR. MARSHALL: No, sir, definitely not.

JUSTICE FRANKFURTER: So if it had not been there, it would have been included in the Fourteenth?

MR. MARSHALL: I think definitely under the reasoning of Mr. Justice Holmes, it would have been.

JUSTICE FRANKFURTER: That is superfluous, then it is an extra.

[38]Nixon v. Herndon, 273 U.S. 536 (1927). The Texas statute barring Negroes from participating in Democratic party primary elections was held unconstitutional. Later attempts by Texas to keep Negroes from voting in the primary were voided in Nixon v. Condon, 286 U.S. 73 (1932), Smith v. Allwright, 321 U.S. 649 (1944) and Terry v. Adams, 345 U.S. 461 (1953).

MR. MARSHALL: It is an extra.

JUSTICE FRANKFURTER: An extra.

MR. MARSHALL: I just—maybe it is timidity, but I just can't say a constitutional amendment is superfluous, but if you are asking me if I think Mr. Justice Holmes was absolutely correct, definitely, yes, sir.

That brings me to the other point which I want to make clear. It involves the questions yesterday about our position as to the McLaurin case, and I am a little worried in thinking of what I said yesterday as to whether the position was absolutely clear. And it is suggested today that the position we take in this case is a negation of the McLaurin case, and as to whether or not the McLaurin case is a negation of the "separate but equal" doctrine, and it is argued that McLaurin had a constitutional grievance, because he was denied equality, but in the McLaurin case the answer is that the only inequality which he suffered is that which is inherent, emphasis on "inherent," if you please, in segregation itself.

He had the same schools, same everything else, but he had this segregation, so that is inherent. And if McLaurin won because he was denied equality, it is also true and much more important that he suffered constitutional inequality in the enjoyment of these identical offerings.

And it follows that with education, this Court has made segregation and inequality equivalent concepts. They have equal rating, equal footing, and if segregation thus necessarily imports inequality, it makes no great difference whether we say that the Negro is wronged because he is segregated, or that he is wronged because he received unequal treatment.

We believe that what we really ask this Court is to make it explicit what they think was inevitably implicit in the McLaurin case, that the two are together. But most certainly I do not agree, and I want to make it clear, that the McLaurin case is under the one-way, and I think that with this understanding, the Court has no difficulty in our position at least.

And finally I would like to say that each lawyer on the other side has made it clear as to what the position of the state was on this, and it would be all right possibly but for the fact that this is so crucial. There is no way you can repay lost school years.

These children in these cases are guaranteed by the states some twelve years of education in varying degrees, and this idea, if I understand it, to leave it to the states until they work it out—and I think that is a most ingenious argument—you leave it to the states, they say; and then they say that the states haven't done anything about it in a hundred years, so for that reason this Court doesn't touch it.

The argument of judicial restraint has no application in this case. There is a relationship between Federal and State, but there is no corollary or relationship as to the Fourteenth Amendment.

The duty of enforcing, the duty of following the Fourteenth Amendment is placed upon the states. The duty of enforcing the Fourteenth Amendment is placed upon this Court, and the argument that they make over and over again to my mind is the same type of argument they charge us with making, the same argument Charles Sumner made. Possibly so.

And we hereby charge them with making the same argument that was made before the Civil War, the same argument that was made during the period between the ratification of the Fourteenth Amendment and the *Plessy* v. *Ferguson* case.

And I think it makes no progress for us to find out who made what argument. It is our position that whether or not you base this case solely on the intent of Congress or whether you base it on the logical extension of the doctrine as set forth in the McLaurin case, on either basis the same conclusion is required, which is that this Court makes it clear to all of these states that in administering their governmental functions, at least those that are vital not to the life of the state alone, not to the country alone, but vital to the world in general, that little pet feelings of race, little pet feelings of custom—I got the feeling on hearing the discussion yesterday that when you put a white child in a school with a whole lot of colored children, the child would fall apart or something. Everybody knows that is not true.

Those same kids in Virginia and South Carolina—and I have seen them do it—they play in the streets together, they play on their farms together, they go down the road together, they separate to go to school, they come out of school and play ball together. They have to be separated in school.

There is some magic to it. You can have them voting together, you can have them not restricted because of law in the houses they live in. You can have them going to the same state university and the same college, but if they go to elementary and high school, the world will fall apart. And it is the exact same argument that has been made to this Court over and over again, and we submit that when they charge us with making a legislative argument, it is in truth they who are making the legislative argument.

They can't take race out of this case. From the day this case was filed until this moment, nobody has in any form or fashion, despite the fact I made it clear in the opening argument that I was relying on it, done anything to distinguish this statute from the Black Codes, which they must admit, because nobody can dispute, say anything anybody wants to say, one way or the other, the Fourteenth Amendment was intended to deprive the states of power to enforce Black Codes or anything else like it.

We charge that they are Black Codes. They obviously are Black Codes if you read them. They haven't denied that they are Black Codes, so if the Court wants to very narrowly decide this case, they can decide it on that point.

So whichever way it is done, the only way that this Court can decide this case in opposition to our position, is that there must be some reason which gives the state the right to make a classification that they can make in regard to nothing else in regard to Negroes, and we submit the only way to arrive at this decision is to find that for some reason Negroes are inferior to all other human beings.

Nobody will stand in the Court and urge that, and in order to arrive at the decision that they want us to arrive at, there would have to be some recognition of a reason why of all of the multitudinous groups of people in this country you have to single out Negroes and give them this separate treatment.

It can't be because of slavery in the past, because there are very few groups in this country that haven't had slavery some place back in the history of their groups. It can't be color because there are Negroes as white as the drifted snow, with blue eyes, and they are just as segregated as the colored man.

The only thing can be is an inherent determination that the people who were formerly in slavery, regardless of anything else, shall be kept as near that stage as is possible, and now is the time, we submit, that this Court should make it clear that that is not what our Constitution stands for.

Thank you, sir.

THE CHIEF JUSTICE: Mr. Rankin.

ARGUMENT ON BEHALF OF THE UNITED STATES

by MR. RANKIN

MR. RANKIN: May it please the Court, as this Court well knows, the United States appears in this action as a friend of the Court, and the only excuse for us to be here is because of the assistance that we may be able to give the Court in regard to this problem before it.

When these questions were asked by the Court as a part of the request for reargument in this matter, we approached them with the idea of how much we might be able to help the Court in answering the questions, and we felt it incumbent upon us in the Department of Justice to try to arrive at the truth in the background and the history as the Court inquired for it. And we saw it as our duty to approach that history much as historians would, and try to draw from it the facts just as objectively as any party could on either side, for someone who had no personal interest in the case. That was the approach that we made to this case in trying to help the Court in the answer of these questions.

We have been chided because we did not come forth in our brief in answer to the questions with certain history. We did not conceive it as our duty to develop any history. We thought it our duty to present what the history showed, whether it hurt or helped either side.

We have no apology to Your Honors or to the country for the manner in which we have developed the history involved in this case and the Fourteenth Amendment, and on behalf of the Attorney General and myself personally, I want to express publicly my appreciation for the work that was done, as some of you well know, by others and myself on this, in order to present a factual history of the entire matter that the Court could rely on and not have to do independent work in regard to it.

But these questions were not in vain. There are great lessons that can be drawn from them, and they are important to this Court in helping them to decide this, one of the greatest cases that this Court has had before it.

Why do those questions seem important? Because they clean out some of the unimportant elements, some of the claims that cannot be sustained by history, and leave the Court with the naked problems of what this Amendment means to every American citizen who loves this country and this Constitution.

Many claims have been made in these cases about the acts of Congress, and the only way to determine the validity of those claims is to look at what Congress did, what was said about them, and we have rejected masses of material and tried to boil it down.

I apologize for the size of the work we left for the Court, but it is the best we could do, and we tried to eliminate all we could. However, in looking at what happened, we have tried to follow the standards this Court has laid down in many decisions, *Maxwell* v. *Dow*[39] is one of them, in which the Court would not pick out an isolated remark, part of debates, something of the opponents or the proponents, in connection with a certain piece of legislation, and even that rule did not apply in constitutional matters.

And we have rejected purposely those various statements, but pointed them out to the Court so the Court could consider them for what they are worth.

But we say when Congress considered the question of segregation in the schools in the debates that extended over a period of months in this matter, that you cannot rely on those statements as showing that Congress decided this particular question before the Court.

They are too sketchy under the rules laid down by this Court to rely on. There we get to the middle of the road. We are not satisfactory to either side. We turn up with conclusions that the evidence does not sustain the plaintiff's position nor the position of the states. But regardless of who it hurts, it is there and it cannot be overlooked.

Now to deal directly with a few of these problems, let us look at what happened in the District of Columbia, and on its face the fact that two enactments were passed by the same 39th Congress dealing with this question of schools and separate schools in the District might seem of grave importance as to the interpretation by Congress.

But we show you what happened. We show the consideration or lack of it that Congress gave to that particular problem.

The separate schools question was considered by Congress back in 1862. The 39th Congress considered only two things. One was whether to give three lots for the use of the colored schools in the District, and the other was to allocate certain funds. There were no committee reports, no participation by the members of the Reconstruction Committee. There was no debate, and we show you on page 71 in the supplement to our brief the detail of the material that Congress considered on the same day.

Now, gentlemen, with your experience I am sure that Your Honors know that in that particular instance the history is of great help to this Court, because it does not show that Congress determined at that time that segregation should be continued as the policy under the Fourteenth Amendment to the Constitution.

Congress just did not consider that matter, and they did not have time for it and it wasn't the way that those matters are determined by Congress as we well know, and the things that this Court considers in regard to it.

In addition to that, we must keep in mind, as the Court well knows in connection with the Thompson[40] case, that at that time Congress did not have the same

[39]176 U.S. 581 (1900). The Supreme Court held a state need not proceed in a criminal action by indictment, nor must it try a defendant before a twelve man jury under the Fourteenth Amendment. Thus, a conviction for robbery returned by an eight man Utah jury was upheld. The case has been overruled by the Supreme Court in Duncan v. Louisiana, 391 U.S. 145 (1968).

[40]District of Columbia v. John R. Thompson Co., 346 U.S. 100 (1953). A District of Columbia restaurant was prosecuted for refusing to serve Negroes under an 1873 law passed by a temporary legislative assembly of the District. The law was held to be still in force.

responsibility in the administration and conduct of the District of Columbia that it has today; that it had its own government, and it wasn't until 1871 that the change was made where Congress undertook the detailed supervision of the District.

So we are saying that that event in itself doesn't show the Congress understood that the Fourteenth Amendment was to permit segregation in the schools of this nation.

Then we turn to the action of the states.

JUSTICE FRANKFURTER: Before you do that, Mr. Attorney General, I suppose you would say that the action since 1871 is too ex post facto to be relevant.

MR. RANKIN: Very largely, Your Honor. It all is removed from the scene. Changes have occured in Congress over the years. The framers were not participants in most of that action, and the Fourteenth Amendment was not involved in those questions.

JUSTICE FRANKFURTER: But it could in any event be involved, but I think so far as any inference is to be drawn from what Congress did or did not do, the early legislation, you put to one side for the reason that you have given. That would be significant becamse Congress was then contemporaneous, it was the same Congress about the same time as those that submitted the Fourteenth Amendment.

But since 1871 Congress has continued to pass legislation year after year acknowledging or authorizing—which is it—acknowledging or authorizing segregation in the District, both. Whatever it is, there have been appropriations recognizing the fact of segregation, and such has been the policy of the District, is that correct?

MR. RANKIN: That is right.

JUSTICE FRANKFURTER: To this day.

MR. RANKIN: That is right.

JUSTICE FRANKFURTER: From 1871, when Congress had sole charge, you would say we can't attribute constitutional verification to Congress passing the appropriations act.

MR. RANKIN: That is correct. That is our position.

JUSTICE REED: I understood you to attribute it to after 1896. What about the period from 1866 until '96, where the question hadn't been raised, where they went ahead and appropriated for the District schools which had segregation. Does that give any indication to you of the attitude of the Congress or the meaning of the Fourteenth Amendment?

MR. RANKIN: We don't consider that there is anything to show that that was an interpretation with knowledge as required by the opinions of this Court in the past concerning the meaning of the Fourteenth Amendment with regard to segregation in the schools in the District or any place else.

When you go back into the—

JUSTICE REED: What about the 1875 Act?

MR. RANKIN: When you go into the history of the 1875 Act, as we have set out in detail, the consideration before Congress was whether or not the law would be passed with a provision for mixed schools or with an amendment that was offered for separate and equal. Both of them lost.

How you can possibly draw any inference from such action that one side won that contest rather than the other is what we cannot follow. We think that Congress by not enacting separate and equal, and failing to enact for mixed schools, left the question in abeyance as far as that particular action is concerned.

JUSTICE REED: Or left it to the states.

MR. RANKIN: No, I think it left it to the Fourteenth Amendment which had already been passed by the Congress and ratified by the states, and it was appreciated at that time that this Court would have the problem to protect those rights as they were declared in section 1.

JUSTICE REED: The Fourteenth Amendment, in the light of the history that had gone on from 1866 to 1875—

MR. RANKIN: Well, that history as we saw it—

JUSTICE REED: I mean the history of the states.

MR. RANKIN: Well, the history of the states, if the Court will look—

JUSTICE REED: You are coming to that next?

MR. RANKIN: Yes. We will look into that picture.

JUSTICE JACKSON: Before you go into that, isn't the one thing that is perfectly clear under the Fourteenth Amendment, that Congress is given the power and the duty to enforce the Fourteenth Amendment, by legislation. You don't disagree with that, do you? You believe that, don't you?

MR. RANKIN: No, there is no question but—

JUSTICE JACKSON: And the other thing that is clear is that they have never done, have never enacted an act that deals with this subject.

MR. RANKIN: There is no question but what Congress has the power under section 5 to enforce the Fourteenth Amendment.

JUSTICE JACKSON: And if the Amendment reaches segregation, they have the power to enforce it and set up machinery to make it effective. There is no doubt about that, is there, and it hasn't been done.

Now if our representative institutions have failed—is that the point?

MR. RANKIN: No, because this Court has in our understanding concurrent jurisdiction.

JUSTICE JACKSON: Have you taken it over?

MR. RANKIN: No. You both have a responsibility, and neither one can give that responsibility up to the other in our conception. There is a concurrent responsibility, and the Court has recognized it in numerous cases where it has interpreted and applied the Fourteenth Amendment.

It has not waited for Congress to act under section 5, but it has looked at section 1 and the other sections of the Amendment to see what they meant, and the force of that language that was used at that time in adopting the intention and purpose of the framers as expressed and tried to give a liberal interpretation to carry out the purposes that were pervading in the passing of the Amendment.

JUSTICE JACKSON: I suppose that realistically the reason this case is here was that action couldn't be obtained from Congress. Certainly it would be here much stronger from your point of view if Congress did act, wouldn't it?

MR. RANKIN: That is true, but there are many cases that the Court well recognized I know, upon any reflection, and has in its opinions, that if the Court would delegate back to Congress from time to time the question of deciding what should be done about the rights, the constitutional rights of a party appearing before this Court for relief, the parties would be deprived by that procedure from getting their constitutional rights because of the present membership or approach of Congress to that particular question.

And the whole concept of constitutional law is that those rights that are defined and set out in the Constitution are not to be subject to the political form which changes from time to time, but are to be preserved under the holdings of this Court over many, many years by the orders of this Court granting the relief prayed for.

JUSTICE FRANKFURTER: The thing to be said, or is it to be said fairly, that not only did Congress not exercise the power under section 5 with reference to the States, but in a realm which is its exclusive authority, it enacted legislation to the contrary.

Now I understand the argument that from 1871 to date you do not get that which has contemporaneous significance, but it does indicate, or does it indicate—I ask you that—any understanding on the part of successive Congresses that segregation was not ruled out by the Constitution, not the Fourteenth Amendment. I take that whatever you have to say about the District you will be saying during this hour?

MR. RANKIN: Yes.

JUSTICE FRANKFURTER: The Fourteenth Amendment apart, which does not bind the federal government of course, but whatever is to be drawn out of the Fifth Amendment through the action of Congress for what is now eighty years, has contradicted the assumption that the Fourteenth Amendment as reflected by the due process of the Fifth, bars such action.

MR. RANKIN: Well, we think that the action regarding the District back in 1862 when the Amendment was before the 39th Congress does not give any bearing upon the action in adopting the Fourteenth Amendment.

JUSTICE FRANKFURTER: I understand that. Because after all what precedes, as Justice [Bradley] said in the *Legal Tender Cases* [41] when we got that Amendment and the antecedent—but it does seem to be underlying some implicit belief on all the Congresses from 1871, that such legislation does not contravene the deepest presuppositions of our Constitution, or am I overstating what that means or are you saying that legislation does not mean anything but what it does? It just segregates, that is all.

MR. RANKIN: Well, not exactly. It seems that you have to find a conscious determination by Congress that segregation was permitted under the Fourteenth Amendment.

JUSTICE FRANKFURTER: You think legislation by Congress is like the British Empire, something that is acquired in a fit of absentmindedness? (Laughter)

MR. RANKIN: I couldn't make that charge before this Court, and I wouldn't want to be quoted in that manner. There might be times that that occurred, but I think Congress is well aware that when that does happen, the subject matter does not deserve greater consideration than it has at the moment, and that it is ordinarily pretty well taken care of under the processes.

With regard to the entire question, it seems that there should be another factor that the Court should consider in this matter.

JUSTICE REED: Are you going to discuss later the action of the states?

MR. RANKIN: Yes. I will proceed now to the question of the legislation of the states in regard to this matter.

JUSTICE REED: The issue of the states, the seceding states?

MR. RANKIN: Yes. In the ratification of the Amendment and the readmission of the seceding states, much is assumed in connection with that by the parties. We find that the evidence, the record of history, does not sustain that.

There were no references to the Fourteenth Amendment and its effect, and the history of the times shows why there were not. We must look back to that period and recognize the condition of the entire country, and particularly the South that had just been occupied, was in the process of occupation, the condition of the Negroes who were entirely illiterate but were freedmen, and the problem of what to do about their education, and the many things dealing with them in the situation where they had just been slaves.

We must remember the condition of education throughout the North. It was far different than the progress that had been made up to this day. And that in the South there were very few public schools.

[41]Legal Tender Cases, 12 Wall. 457 (1871). The Court upheld the issuance of greenbacks without specie backing during the Civil War and the requirement that they be accepted in repayment of all debts, public and private. A contrary decision in Hepburn v. Griswold, 8 Wall. 603 (1870) was overruled. Justice Joseph P. Bradley (1813–1892) in a concurring opinion examined the practice of states issuing paper bills of credit at the time the Constitution was adopted to show that such power existed in the colonial period.

The public schools were largely for the poor, and other people went to the private schools, and there was a prohibition against the Negro going to any school because it might make him rebellious.

Now when you take all of that into account and consider what happened at that time, it seems to us that it is very revealing, but you can't draw any conclusions from that legislation that there was any conscious understanding that the Fourteenth Amendment provided or permitted segregation in the public schools.

A perfect example is shown in the appendix to our brief on page 352 where we set out the history about South Carolina. There was a state where reconstructionists, scalawags, the radical Republicans, carpetbaggers, and all of the others that have been remarked about here, had control of the convention that ratified this Amendment. And you recall the circumstances. They had to do certain things, three things in order to get back into the Union.

Now arguments were made at great length about the terms of the Constitution for the State of South Carolina, and during those arguments much was said about the schools, and the facts were that the Negroes had taken over the public schools, such as they were, in the important cities at that time in South Carolina, and had them in their possession, to try to teach the Negroes something, because they had to start from scratch.

And during those debates when the question was presented about whether they should have mixed schools or separate schools, nothing was said about the effect of the Fourteenth Amendment, although it was provided in the Constitution that there could be no distinction in the schools based upon race or color.

Now that is in a convention that was under complete control of the Reconstruction forces, and we say from that you just cannot properly say that the history shows that anyone had any conscious understanding at the time those various acts were passed that the Fourteenth Amendment would permit segregation in public schools.

It just wasn't there, because in those debates, as shown in the appendix again, all they would have had to say was "look at the Fourteenth Amendment, it prohibits this very thing."

Instead of that, one of the parties who was in control of the schools actively trying to get education for the Negroes, said, "Maybe the Negroes will attend the same schools as the whites, or the whites will come into the schools of the Negroes now in our possession." Nobody saw fit to say anything about the effect of the Fourteenth Amendment.

Now if you will look back at the history of the schools in the North and also throughout the South, you will see that everybody was involved in the problem of "What are we going to do to educate the Negro? He is a free man, he is a part of our citizenry like any white man. He has no background for education. Many of them are of mature years, as well as the children."

And they were so involved in that problem that the effect of the Fourteenth Amendment and whether it permitted or would allow segregation in the public schools was just not discussed by anyone.

And I don't think you can draw from that any assumption that by those legislative acts when there was not discussion of the problem, that it was intended or understood by anyone that the Fourteenth Amendment would permit, in spite of its language, segregation of the Negro in the public schools.

JUSTICE JACKSON: Mr. Rankin, I would like to ask you this. You have studied this much more than I have had a chance to, and I almost hesitate to ask a question in a case of this kind because people jump to the assumption that if you want information, it is stating a judgment that I have.

How do you account for the decisions of the State of New York, for example, holding the Amendment did not reach this question,[42] when there was a state where there was no problem of numbers, there were few Negroes, the court that last decided this was predominantly a Republican court, predominantly from upstate New York, where the underground railway had plenty of stations, all kinds of things to fight the war, a popular war.

How do you account for judges like that not understanding what this Amendment meant? The very section that promulgated it—it was a northern product, there was no getting away from that.

You studied the history of this a great deal. How do you account for those interpretations?

JUSTICE REED: May I ask this question before you answer that, also the question of the legislatures of the northern states on the Amendment, the same legislatures in some instances passed legislation which recognized segregation, allowed segregation amendments.

MR. RANKIN: Well, first, if I might answer in regard to the courts, apparently there was no detailed study of the history and background of the Fourteenth Amendment in connection with some of the decisions of the cases.

JUSTICE JACKSON: You can't say that of the New York case. It is one of the—

MR. RANKIN: And the Court will find that in later periods there was reliance placed upon *Plessy* against *Ferguson* and some of the earlier cases where the history was not reviewed in such detail, that will explain fully the decisions that the court made without examining the question in detail.

JUSTICE JACKSON: These men had lived with the thing. They didn't have to go to books. They had been through it. They didn't have to go to books any more than we have to read books on what is going on today.

MR. RANKIN: Well, if the Court is looking—

JUSTICE JACKSON: And the Grand Army of the Republic was the strongest force in that community, don't make any mistake about that.

MR. RANKIN: If the Court is looking for someone who knew, who lived through the period, to give it aid in regard to this problem, I think it has to look no further than its own decisions, and going back to the *Slaughter-House Cases* and the Strauder case, Justice Miller comments upon the fact in the *Slaughter-House Cases* that it was within five years of the time when all of this occurred and that

[42]Dallas v. Fosdick, 40 How. Pr. 249 (1896); People ex rel. Dretz v. Easton, 13 Abb. Pr. (N.S.) 159 (1872); People ex rel. King v. Gallagher, 93 N.Y. 438 (1883); People ex rel. Cisco v. School Board, 161 N.Y. 598 (1900).

they had the matter fresh in their minds, and then he reviews the background, the history and the detail and the reasons for the Amendment and what they were trying to reach in the greatest of detail, and we recommended to the Court something superior to anything else that can be found with regard to a fresh appraisal of the basis for the Fourteenth Amendment and the history back of it.

In the Strauder cases we have a later period, but we do have a period not too far removed, and a thorough consideration of what the Fourteenth Amendment means in all of its various reaches.

JUSTICE JACKSON: Then the assumption is that they didn't understand what it was about.

MR. RANKIN: Well, in those days—

JUSTICE JACKSON: That is what it comes to, isn't it?

MR. RANKIN: It was considered that education as such was a state matter, and we had the question of whether schools would be provided as public schools. We also had a good portion of the problem handled by private schools. We had areas where there were mixed separate schools and also where there was no restriction on attendance, and the two races did mix, but there was no provision legally for such mixture.

JUSTICE REED: So the very men that sat on the Plessy-Ferguson case on this Court were thoroughly familiar with all the history in that case.

MR. RANKIN: Well, the Court in that case was not giving any consideration to this particular situation. It was considering the question of segregation in public utilities and railroads.

JUSTICE REED: That is the difference, isn't it?

MR. RANKIN: There is a very material difference in the question of whether or not segregation is to be permitted in public schools furnished by the state itself and the monies of the state, although this Court has recognized that that may be and is a privilege, but that the state has no power to restrict that privilege based upon race in regard to the schools. If it is going to provide education at all, it must provide it equally to the citizens.

It does not have to provide education, and to that extent it is a privilege, but if it provides it at all, it must do it equally to all citizens.

Apparently that was not fully understood, the difference between it being privileged and the later decisions of this Court in regard to the requirement that even such a privilege had to be granted to citizens alike, but we think that question is now decided by this Court that it cannot be contravened at this time.

Regarding the question of the power of the Court, we do not think this is a matter that involves the right to abolish segregation in the public schools. It is a question whether or not the Fourteenth Amendment permits the state to determine that it shall have segregation as an order of the state in the conduct of its public education, and that we think is within the peculiar competency of this Court to determine.

It is a civil right to have education on the same basis as every other citizen.

When Congress deals with these matters, it must deal with them generally, and the courts deal with them specifically.

The courts deal with whether or not a certain litigant before it is entitled to relief, has not been permitted to have the rights he was entitled to by the wording of the Constitution, and this Court has never seen fit to determine that a man has been denied his constitutional rights, and then referred him to Congress to see what type of relief he should be granted from it.

JUSTICE DOUGLAS: The Department of Justice goes no further than to say that first we can decide this case, these cases, and second, we can decide them under what, on the basis of history?

MR. RANKIN: No, Your Honor, no. Our position is that the history helps the Court in showing that some of the conclusions that have been asserted from history are not borne out. The history as related by the *Slaughter-House Cases* and the Strauder case is the history that the Department of Justice found to be correct in its review of the entire matter.

That by reason of that history, it is shown that the pervading purpose of the Fourteenth Amendment was to establish that all men are equal, that they are equal before the law, that they are entitled to equal protection of the law, that no distinction can ever be made upon the basis of race or color, and that therefore this Court, in applying the rules it has laid down in many cases looking to that pervading purpose, can find only one answer to this case, and that is when they stand before the bar of this Court and say that "the reason that we want to segregate black children from white children is because of racism, just because of their color," that the Fourteenth Amendment does not permit that to happen, because if there was anything the Fourteenth Amendment tried to do for this country, it was to make it clear that no discrimination could ever by made, based upon race or color, and that is the position of the Department of Justice in this matter.

JUSTICE FRANKFURTER: That is your third conclusion on page 186 of your brief, isn't it?

MR. RANKIN: Yes. We think that the history is of great help to the Court in regard to the basic question of the rights of the parties, and this Court has the problem of deciding two things: First, whether or not the constitutional rights have been abridged, and we think that is clear. The history shows the pervading purpose.

JUSTICE DOUGLAS: The provision that Justice Frankfurter referred to doesn't say that, in my opinion. I am just inquiring to find out what it says.

You start on page 185, the Government brief reads as follows:

—The Government respectfully suggests to the Court that, if it holds school segregation to be unconstitutional, the public interest would be served by entering decrees in the instant cases providing in substance as follows:
(1) That racial segregation in public schools be decreed by this Court to be a violation of rights secured by the Constitution.

I would think that would be obvious, that if the Court holds segregation would be unconstitutional, that we would—and it was within the judicial competence, it would be within our duty to enter an appropriate decree to that effect. But my question went further than that. It was what are the merits, whether the Department of Justice had taken a position?

MR. RANKIN: Yes. I think Your Honor is correct in that regard, and the way I answered the question was due to the formulation of the question, but in order to answer your question specifically, it is the position of the Department of Justice that segregation in public schools cannot be maintained under the Fourteenth Amendment, and we adhere to the views expressed in the original brief of the Department in that regard. We did limit our brief in our—

JUSTICE DOUGLAS: I just wanted to clear up that confusion in my mind.

MR. RANKIN: Yes.

JUSTICE FRANKFURTER: You say this is the kind of a question where you are responding to the inquiry of the Court as to what the form of the decree should be. The Department has already in its prior brief and in this brief, if I can interpret the entire brief, made its position perfectly clear that it thinks segregation is outlawed by the Fourteenth Amendment, and on pages 186 and 187 you indicate the kind of a decree that should follow such a declaration, is that correct?

MR. RANKIN: That is correct. The problem about the questions that the Court presented that gave us the greatest trouble was the question of relief. Because of the statements of the Court, there are a number of decisions that when a person has had his constitutional rights abridged, that he had a present and personal right to immediate relief.

JUSTICE REED: Are you leaving the third question?

MR. RANKIN: I thought I had dealt with it, but I will be glad to try to answer any further questions.

JUSTICE REED: I did not quite understand what you were saying in regard to that. The third question is on the assumption the answers to question 2 (a) and (b) do not dispose of the issue, is it within the judicial power of the Fourteenth Amendment to abolish segregation. Now that is saying that the argument over history is inconclusive, as I understand it.

MR. RANKIN: That's right.

JUSTICE REED: Assuming that that is inconclusive, then does this Court through its own power have the right—is that the belief of the Government—have the power to declare segregation unconstitutional?

MR. RANKIN: The position of the Government is that the Court does have the power and that it has the duty.

JUSTICE REED: Where do we get that power, and how?

MR. RANKIN: By reason of the power given to it under the Constitution and by act of Congress and the—

JUSTICE REED: So far as the Fourteenth Amendment is concerned by the very words of the Fourteenth Amendment?

MR. RANKIN: Yes, by reason of section 1 which says that these rights shall not be denied by any state, and in the interpretation of that language the Court, in applying it, has the right to find, and according to its decisions will find, that the parties are entitled to this.

JUSTICE REED: Regardless of the view of Congress, regardless of the history of it, which you say is inconclusive, that the wording covers segregation?

MR. RANKIN: I think the best answer to that would be the history in regard to—

JUSTICE REED: Is that what we are trying to determine now?

MR. RANKIN: Yes.

JUSTICE REED: It could very well be. That is what is striking to me, if you lay aside the history, lay aside what has happened, and the intention as expressed in Congress, then we have nothing left except the bare words.

MR. RANKIN: That is correct.

JUSTICE REED: And those you say require the invalidation of all the laws of segregation?

MR. RANKIN: Yes. And the Court has in other cases seen fit to examine the question and not finding any specific language about, for instance, jury trials, has found that the Fourteenth Amendment would not permit any abridgement of those rights by reason of race or color.

And this Court has said many times that it does not have to find that a particular matter or subject was examined by Congress.

JUSTICE JACKSON: We have a statute on juries. Congress passed a statute on juries.

MR. RANKIN: Yes.

JUSTICE JACKSON: So it is clear that Congress acted on that subject.

MR. RANKIN: We don't have any statute, as I recall, about [petitions] or freedom of speech, but this Court has not hesitated to protect the provisions of the Constitution and the litigants before this Court in regard to them, and the history also does show that the framers of this constitutional amendment desired to avoid having it submitted to Congress, and they recognized that they might lose control of the Congress in the future, and they wanted to frame their change deliberately, section 1, in order to make certain that it wouldn't be a question for Congress, because you will recall the history that we relate.

Originally it was to empower Congress, in section 1, to take certain action, and they feared and they expressed the fears that Congress by that might change it and they would lose control and they said maybe they can get a majority, but two-thirds they will never get, and so they provided the specific right in such a form that it was like the provisions of the Bill of Rights. It was a declaration of a right that every citizen could look to and say, "That is mine, equality before the law."

JUSTICE REED: Which clause of the Fourteenth Amendment of the first section is that applicable to, to any person within its jurisdiction providing equal protection of the law?

MR. RANKIN: We think that there are two clauses that are controlling. One is the equal protection of the laws and the other is the depriving of any person of life, liberty or property without due process, both of them. Congress deliberately put the words so that no state could deny them.

JUSTICE REED: And is this a denial of liberty or property, segregation?

MR. RANKIN: Well, I would think it would be a denial of part of liberty rather than property.

JUSTICE REED: It has to be one or the other, or both, doesn't it?

MR. RANKIN: Yes, it could be a combination.
(A recess was taken from 2:00 p.m. to 2:30 p.m. this same day.)

AFTER RECESS

ARGUMENT ON BEHALF OF THE UNITED STATES—Resumed

by MR. RANKIN

MR. RANKIN: May it please the Court, I would like to deal briefly with the question of relief, and try to give to the Court our points on that problem.

THE CHIEF JUSTICE: Which problem is that, you say?

MR. RANKIN: The question of relief.
After the Court determines whether or not rights have been violated in these cases then there is the question of the relief that should be granted.

We do not regard lightly the question of presenting to this Court a policy of delaying at all the relief that should be granted to citizens of this country when constitutional rights are found to have been violated, as we feel that they have been in this case.

However, upon careful study of the entire problem, we do think there are considerations that we can recommend to this Court should be taken into account in the decision of these cases. These cases do not deal only with the particular plaintiffs. The Court knows that they deal with certain classes, in addition to these plaintiffs.

But beyond that, we think it is fair to take into account the fact that the precedents established by the Court in the decision of these cases will necessarily bear upon the educational systems of some seventeen states and the District of Columbia.

There have to be adjustments to take care of the children attending these schools, and to provide them a program of mixed schools that will be adequate; and there will also have to be the problems of the administration and the various financial problems involved. It seems unrealistic not to take into account those factors, and that some time may be involved in providing for them.

We, therefore, suggest that it should be—the burden should be—upon the defendants to present and satisfy the lower court as to the extent of time that is necessary to make such an adjustment in the school system, and that plan should be presented to the Court, not for the purpose of determining at all the wisdom of the plan, but only to determine and satisfy that court that, according to criteria presented and set out by this Court, that the plan satisfies the constitutional requirements of our Constitution and its amendments.

We, therefore, recommend to the Court, although we do not think it is squarely in point, the history of the Court in regard to the American Tobacco case[43] and the possibility that this decree may lay out, at least in a measure, a plan for handling these cases in returning them to the lower courts for final disposition.

We suggest a year for the presentation and consideration of the plan, not because that is an exact standard, but with the idea that it might involve the principle of handling the matter with deliberate speed.

JUSTICE JACKSON: Mr. Rankin, may I ask you a question or two about this remedy you suggest. We have no state before us, have we? We have several school districts.

MR. RANKIN: Yes, that is correct.

JUSTICE JACKSON: I suppose that even if we said that the state statutes or state constitutional provisions authorizing segregation were unconstitutional, local custom would still perpetuate it in most districts of the states that really want it; I assume that would be the case, would it not?

MR. RANKIN: We do not assume that once this Court pronounces what the Constitution means in this area that our people are not going to try to abide by it and be in accord with it as rapidly as they can.

JUSTICE JACKSON: I do not think a court can enter a decree on that assumption, particularly in view of the fact that for seventy-five years the "separate but equal" doctrine has prevailed in the cases that came before us within the recent past, indicating it still had not been complied with in many cases.

The only people we can reach with the judicial decree are the people who are before us in the case.

MR. RANKIN: That is correct.

JUSTICE JACKSON: So that if it is not acquiesced in and embraced, we have to proceed school district by school district, is that right?

[43]United States v. American Tobacco Co. 221 U.S. 106 (1911). The American Tobacco Co. was held to violate the Sherman Act by its monopolization of the tobacco industry. The District Court was given wide power to fashion an appropriate decree.

MR. RANKIN: Well, this Court traditionally handles each case as it comes before it.

JUSTICE JACKSON: Yes. It means that private litigation will result in every school district in order to get effective enforcement, and that is why, I suppose, this "separate but equal" doctrine has never really been enforced, because many disadvantaged people cannot afford these lawsuits. But the judicial remedy means just that, does it not, lawsuit after lawsuit?

MR. RANKIN: Well, it is probably true in every Fourteenth Amendment case that comes before the Court, each litigant has to come and say, "My rights have been infringed, and I have to be provided a remedy."

JUSTICE JACKSON: That is right; that is the nature of judicial process; that is why in some cases it has been necessary to set up something like the SEC to enforce individual rights in security transactions, and the Interstate Commerce Commission.

But what I do not get in your statement here are any criteria that we are to lay down to the lower court in your view to determine what shall be taken into consideration.

Now, you mention the antitrust cases, but we have been fifty years in interpreting the antitrust cases in this Court, laying down the criteria, the standards.

Some districts may have to have bond issues, some may have to submit to a vote; commissioners may resign; no commissioners would take the job—I wouldn't want it, to be caught between these forces.

What criteria are we going to lay down? I am all for having the district courts frame decrees and do all the rest of the work that we can put on them, but what are we going to tell them: "This is something different from antitrust? This is something that hasn't been before?"

What are we going to do to avoid the situation where in some districts everybody is perhaps held in contempt almost immediately because that judge has that disposition, and in some other districts it is twelve years before they get to a hearing? What criteria do you propose?

MR. RANKIN: If I may try to answer some of the questions that Your Honor—

JUSTICE JACKSON: It is all one question: What are the standards?

MR. RANKIN: In the first place, I do not think the country would ever be satisfied with anybody but the Supreme Court saying what the Fourteenth Amendment means; and, secondly—

JUSTICE JACKSON: We would not be, anyway.

MR. RANKIN: No. (Laughter)
Secondly, I think that this Court does not have the duty or the function to try to determine what is a wise educational policy for each one of the various school districts in the country.

JUSTICE JACKSON: I am with you there.

MR. RANKIN: It has the duty and the obligation to say that when the Constitution says that men shall be equal before the law, and the states shall regard them as equal in all of the various things that it does for them, that it cannot take one group of people and say, "You shall be separated just because of your color and from another group," and that is not equality.

JUSTICE JACKSON: That leads you squarely to Mr. Marshall's position that they have the right; children are getting older, they get out of school before they get this right and, therefore, it should be done, and then you say there are some conditions that should postpone that.

Now, what is to be taken, financial conditions, unwillingness of the community to vote funds? What are the conditions that the lower court should consider?

MR. RANKIN: I think that that problem will have to be tried as these matters are constantly before the lower courts and the federal courts in the determination as to whether or not the equities of the particular situation are such that the defendant has established the burden that it is unreasonable under those conditions to require them to act more rapidly than they propose, and those standards are well-established as a part of our judicial process and experience, and in the statements of this Court.

JUSTICE JACKSON: I forsee a generation of litigation if we send it back with no standards, and each case has to come here to determine it standard by standard.

MR. RANKIN: Well, experience has demonstrated that the common law procedure of trying to decide each case as it comes before the court has been very wise in the experience of mankind, and many of the decisions, problems, are handled by the lower courts in the federal system, and never reach this Court for final decision.

JUSTICE FRANKFURTER: Isn't there a difference between the applicable standard—it is one thing to talk about a standard—and another thing, the means by which this standard can be satisfied?

This Court might decree that as between state and state, one state is maintaining a nuisance; but how a nuisance should be abated is a very different question.

It does not bring into play what standards you apply, but what, in fairness to the public interest which determines their decree, should dictate as to the time or the circumstances under which that standard of equality has been caused, assuming that the standard of equality here requires what the Government says it requires.

Certainly the fact that local people do not like the result is not any condition that should influence or in any wise influence the court; but whether you actually have a building in which children can go to school, and what distances there are, and things like that, like questions of abating a nuisance which the local fellow has to determine is or is not an evasion of the requirements, are one of those facts of life that not even a court can overcome.

MR. RANKIN: That is right.

JUSTICE FRANKFURTER: If there is no appropriation by a legislature to build a school, the court cannot raise the taxes, the court cannot raise taxes by a court decree; or if a state makes a redistribution, the court cannot say, "You are indulging in educational gerrymandering."

MR. RANKIN: That is right.

JUSTICE FRANKFURTER: I am not suggesting that I have exhausted the difficulties because we still have them, but I do suggest that the standard is inherent in the very contention made by the Government, namely, that the standard of equality is not satisfied, indeed is violated by a separation based merely on color. Assuming that is so, then I do not see how you can escape some of the things which worry my Brother Jackson, and I know raise some questions.

JUSTICE JACKSON: They do not worry me; they will be worrying our children.

MR. RANKIN: May it please the Court, it is the position of the Government in this case, these cases are peculiarly those that deserve the most wise judgment of the members of this bench in the interests of this country.

We are dealing with a problem of equality before the law for little children. We are busy in the educational process throughout the country in saying to these children that our Constitution means that all men, regardless of race, color or creed, are equal. None are better, none are worse, and to do—

JUSTICE REED: I do not want to disagree with you on that, Mr. Rankin. But the problem we have here is how is that to be implemented if the case should be decided that segregation was unconstitutional? These parties in these several cases have asked us for a decree of court that they be admitted to certain schools. Are they entitled to that in case of segregation?

MR. RANKIN: It is our position that unless it can be shown by the defendants that that cannot be accomplished at once in accordance with the precedents of this Court of granting them their present and personal rights when their constitutional rights are invaded, that they should have them.

JUSTICE REED: Isn't it necessary in every school district at the present time that they have certain facilities, necessary facilities?

MR. RANKIN: That is right.

JUSTICE REED: They will be admitted, I suppose, tomorrow, if they wanted to take them.

MR. RANKIN: We also take the position that it is reasonable for this Court to remand the matter to the lower court and to take into consideration, as equity courts have for generations, the problems that have to be dealt with in any inequities that can be presented, and that the lower court can properly then determine how rapidly a plan can be achieved to come within the criteria established by this Court and the requirements of the Fourteenth Amendment, and that upon consideration of that, with all diligent speed, the lower court can enter a decree accordingly, and we visualize problems, but our courts have many problems, and they deal with those problems, and they weigh the various problems against the rights involved to accomplish the result in the best manner and as rapidly as possible.

JUSTICE REED: Mention one problem, mention just one.

MR. RANKIN: Well, the question is whether or not children should attend tomorrow or the next school term; and I do not see any great problem in that for the federal district court.

JUSTICE JACKSON: What is the criteria though; what considerations would you say would justify postponing it until next term, if he has a present right to enter?

MR. RANKIN: Whether or not it was a deliberate attempt to evade the judgment of this Court of equality or whether or not there are sound reasons that the action should be delayed because of transportation problems, whether or not the building is adequate, all of those matters—

JUSTICE JACKSON: Suppose you have two schools; you have a school that has been used by white pupils, a pretty good school; you have a pretty poor one that has been used by colored children. What are you going to do? How are you going to decide—you either have got to build a new school or you have got to move some white people into the poor school, which would cause a rumpus, or you have got to center them all in the good school. What would the court take into consideration?

MR. RANKIN: Well, time after time the courts have said that they were not going to be bothered by the worries and difficulties of the litigants about meeting the requirements of the Constitution or other principles laid down by this Court; and I think those are the problems that have to be dealt with by the local school districts, and they would have the obligation to bring in a plan to accomplish this in accordance with the order of this Court, as rapidly as could be obtained, and the details of it would not be a problem of the Court unless it found that the plan was unreasonable, that it was a deliberate attempt to evade the order of the Court, or that it was not equitably proper. Those standards—

JUSTICE JACKSON: This is the most definite one, what appears on page 186, being the most definite thing that you have been able to devise?

MR. RANKIN: We explored the possibility of more definite decrees, but experience seems to dictate that the more definite courts are, appellate courts, in trying to describe the activities of lower courts, the more often they are apt to not give them the opportunity to solve the problem in the best manner possible.

We conceived that the position and the duty of this Court is to establish the broad general principles of what could be obtained, what the Fourteenth Amendment meant with regard to equality in the attendance of schools; that there could not be a distinction because of race.

JUSTICE FRANKFURTER: Am I right in assuming, if not in inferring—I do not think I have the right to infer—but in assuming that the Government in its suggestions as to the kind of a decree, is not dealing with these cases on the assumption that what is involved are just these individual children, but you have indicated a while ago that underlying your suggestions lies the assumption that these cases will settle a widespread problem, as indicated by both Mr. Davis and Mr. Moore, involving, whatever it is, the relationship of ten million Negroes in seventeen states, and that it is not a question of putting one child in a school, but how to make a readjustment of an existing system throughout the states where this present practice prevails; is that right?

MR. RANKIN: Yes. We thought—

JUSTICE FRANKFURTER: Rather than looking forward to having endless lawsuits of every individual child in the seventeen states for the indefinite future.

MR. RANKIN: We felt that your question, Your Honor, reached that far and, further, for the Department of Justice of the United States to close its eyes to the effect of the precedent established by this Court, if it should so decide, was not the help that this Court was entitled to receive, and that we should view the extent of the reach that the decision might properly obtain and try to give the help that we could in regard to it.

THE CHIEF JUSTICE: Thank you, Mr. Rankin.
(Oral argument was concluded at 2:50 p.m.)

OLIVER BROWN, MRS. RICHARD LAWTON, MRS. SADIE EMMANUEL, ET AL.,
Appellants

vs.

BOARD OF EDUCATION OF TOPEKA, SHAWNEE COUNTY, KANSAS, ET AL.,
Appellees.

Case No. 1

Washington, D.C.,
Tuesday, December 8, 1953.

The above-entitled cause came on for oral argument at 2:50 p.m.

APPEARANCES:
On behalf of the Appellants:
ROBERT L. CARTER, ESQ.

On behalf of the Appellees:
PAUL E. WILSON, ESQ.

THE CHIEF JUSTICE: No. 1, Oliver Brown, Mrs. Richard Lawton, Mrs. Sadie Emmanuel v. Board of Education of Topeka, et al.

THE CLERK: Counsel are present, sir.

THE CHIEF JUSTICE: Mr. Carter.

ARGUMENT ON BEHALF OF APPELLANTS

by MR. CARTER

MR. CARTER: Mr. Chief Justice, the facts in this case are similar to those involved in the cases preceding.

The appellants are of elementary school age, of Negro origin, and they are required to obtain their elementary school education in segregated elementary schools maintained pursuant to the laws of the State of Kansas, and pursuant to the rules and regulations of the Topeka School Board.

The statute in question, whose constitutionality we are here attacking, is chapter 172 of the Kansas statutes of 1949.

JUSTICE FRANKFURTER: Is your case moot, Mr. Carter?

MR. CARTER: I hoped that I would get a little further into the argument before that question was asked. (Laughter.)

We take the position, Your Honor, that the case is not moot. The Government, the state, that is, takes the same position. We take that position because of the fact that although the plan which I had hoped to get to when I discussed questions four and five—but if you want me to discuss it now, I will—the plan which is presently in operation, and the resolution of the School Board of Topeka under which they have decided that they will eliminate segregation in the elementary schools in Topeka—under this plan, two schools have been desegregated, and the Negro children have been admitted.

However, with respect to the remaining schools, Negro children are still segregated.

The brief which the Topeka Board filed with this Court gives no indication as to how long they feel the plan which they now have in operation will take before the other Negro children will be able to go to an integrated school system.

We feel further that the case is not moot because the statute is still involved, and if the Court were without these problems being settled, we still have—while we have only one appellant here who has been admitted to the school, unsegregated school, pursuant to this plan—our position is that the case is not a moot case, and we have to address ourselves to the questions which the Court asked.

JUSTICE FRANKFURTER: Is Topeka here apart from—I understand the state takes a different view. Is the immediate respondent-appellee here?

MR. CARTER: If Your Honor will remember, last year the Topeka School Board did not appear.

JUSTICE FRANFKFURTER: No.

MR. CARTER: This year they did not appear. So far as I know, they have no intention of appearing, if I am right in that, Mr. Wilson?

JUSTICE FRANKFURTER: They have every intention of giving you what you want, is that it?

MR. CARTER: I beg your pardon?

JUSTICE FRANKFURTER: They merely have the intention of giving you what you want, and not contesting your claim?

MR. CARTER: That is right.

JUSTICE FRANKFURTER: That is what I call a moot case. (Laughter.)

JUSTICE JACKSON: Do I understand that the parties you represent here are now admitted to unsegregated schools?

MR. CARTER: No, sir. One of the appellants has been admitted to a school in the district in which he lives; that school has been opened to Negroes. Just one of the appellants has been admitted.

JUSTICE JACKSON: What about the others?

MR. CARTER: The others are still attending the four segregated schools.

JUSTICE JACKSON: You have clients then who are still subject to the rule of segregation?

MR. CARTER: Yes.

JUSTICE FRANKFURTER: But by the authorized pronouncement of the appellee, they will be admitted just as soon as it is physically or administratively or whatever the adverbs are—Topeka is able to admit them, and they do not contest your position.

MR. CARTER: That is true.

JUSTICE FRANKFURTER: Kansas does contest?

MR. CARTER: That is right.

JUSTICE FRANKFURTER: That is a different story. But Kansas is not a party.

MR. CARTER: Well, Kansas appeared in the court below as a party. It intervened in the court below as a party, specifically for the purpose of defending the constitutionality of the statute.

JUSTICE FRANKFURTER: Yes. But abstractly to defend a statute does not give this Court jurisdiction to pass upon it.

MR. CARTER: Well, frankly, Your Honor, my only feeling on this is that with respect to the plan which is in operation, the appellees have certainly indicated an intention—

JUSTICE FRANKFURTER: And you do not question the good faith?

MR. CARTER: I certainly do not.
But the point that I think that we need to, that we have to have in mind, one, I think, in so far as the plan itself is concerned, I have serious questions about—with respect to the plan; as to whether this is the forum to raise that, I do not know.

Also, I think in so far as the other appellants are concerned, as I indicated, I do not know when they will be free from the imprint of the statutes, and it does not seem to me that at this point in the litigation I can say that the case is moot, when the State of Kansas—

JUSTICE FRANKFURTER: Perhaps I ought to change my inquiry. I do not mean to shut off your argument. Having heard you before, it gives me pleasure to hear you again. But as I understand it, then, the position is that the respondent, the appellee, meets your claim, and you do not question the purpose is to meet it, and the question is whether, as a matter of formality, in fact, the concession of your claim would be appropriately carried out.

So I suggest what you ought to say to us is that we ought to enter a decree sending the case back to the district court to enforce that which the respondent or the appellee concedes. Therefore, it is a question of the terms of the decree, is it not, in your case?

I am sure that you must feel it is a welcome thing if a board of education accedes to your wishes and of its own volition stops—it has a desire not to oppose desegregation, and I am sure that is a welcome thing to you. I am not talking about the general question; I am talking about the specific thing, that the board of education has taken the position, and you just want to be sure that they will carry it out; is that right?

MR. CARTER: That is right. If that is the general view of the Court, I would certainly—

JUSTICE REED: What about the state? As I recall it, the state was admitted as a party.

MR. CARTER: Yes, sir; the state was admitted as a party.

JUSTICE REED: Or merely as a friend of the court.

MR. CARTER: No, they intervened as a party in the court below, defending the constitutionality of the statute under which the segregation was practiced and permitted and was, in fact, practiced in Topeka.
In the original—

JUSTICE REED: And is there authority in the State of Kansas for the Attorney General as intervenor in the litigation in which part of the state is involved or a city in the state or the board of education?

MR. CARTER: No.

JUSTICE REED: Has that been pointed out as to the Attorney General's right to intervene in the case and take charge of the case?

MR. CARTER: Well, that wasn't what occurred.

JUSTICE REED: They did not approach it on that basis?

MR. CARTER: No, sir. I will explain briefly what happened. We went before a statutory court, and we attacked the constitutionality of the statute.
The clerk of the court advised the Attorney General that a state statute was under attack.
The Topeka Board appeared and defended their action and the statute, and the state appeared separately in order to defend the constitutionality of the statute. They are in that position here. They appeared in the original argument, and they reappeared—

JUSTICE FRANKFURTER: They did not appear; we had to bring them in. We had to ask them whether they would let the thing go by default. They did not appear; they were not so anxious. They did not claim that they had a great right, that they had a right to defend here.

MR. CARTER: Well, I think—

JUSTICE FRANKFURTER: Perhaps "cajoled" is a better word.

MR. CARTER: If you are expressing—if that is the view of the Court, Your Honor—

JUSTICE FRANKFURTER: Mr. Carter, nobody knows better than you that I can speak only for one poor lone voice.

MR. CARTER: I certainly have no real desire to proceed with an argument.

JUSTICE FRANKFURTER: But, Mr. Carter, if all the appellants had been admitted—suppose all of them were in the position of this one child—

MR. CARTER: I would have no question about it.

JUSTICE FRANKFURTER: Then the state would not say "We want to be heard," could they?

MR. CARTER: No, sir. I would have no question about it if all the appellants had been admitted; I think that the question of mootness would have been clear. But my problem with respect to it is that some are admitted and some are not.

JUSTICE FRANKFURTER: I understand it then, that it is a question of whether Topeka will carry this out as quickly with these other children as they have with Leah—

MR. CARTER: Leah Carter, and I also have no way of knowing whether this would be so, because the appellees do not appear before the Court, and the state cannot speak for the appellees with respect to this question.

But if it is permissible, I would yield my time to the state, and see what the state has to say about this, and I would answer it, if that is permissible so far as the Court is concerned.

JUSTICE JACKSON: You have the privilege of rebuttal under our rules, if he says anything that you wish to answer.

THE CHIEF JUSTICE: Mr. Wilson, will you please address yourself to the question of whether it is moot or not.

ARGUMENT ON BEHALF OF THE STATE OF KANSAS

by MR. WILSON

MR. WILSON: If it please the Court, it is our position that the case is not moot from our standpoint for several reasons. In the first place, the appellant has pointed out that only one of the group of appellants that counsel represents has been admitted to the integrated public schools of Topeka.

JUSTICE REED: Why is that?

MR. WILSON: The Board of Education—may I preface this remark by pointing out that our statute is a permissive one. The local boards of education are authorized to make the determination on the local level as to whether separate or integrated schools shall be maintained in cities of the first class.

Now, as a matter of policy, and as a matter of policy only, and without reference to this case, the Topeka Board of Education has determined that segregation will be abandoned in the elementary schools of Topeka as soon as practicable. That is the language of their resolution.

Now, we think if they are simply exercising their prerogative under the statute, another city in the State of Kansas, the City of Atchison, has adopted a similar resolution that does not reflect at all on this case.

It was our view that the constitutionality of this statute is still under attack. We were permitted to defend the constitutionality of the statute in the district court.

We were asked to defend it in the Supreme Court a year ago, but we feel that we must, in order to maintain a position consistent with the expressed intent of this Court, answer the brief and the arguments that the appellants have supplied us.

JUSTICE FRANKFURTER: May I trouble you to tell me what are the cities of the first class in Kansas?

MR. WILSON Yes, sir. May I refer you to Appendix D in our brief, the very last page. There are set out in tabular form the nine cities of the first class where segregation is maintained on a complete or partial basis in the elementary schools.

Now, in addition to that, there are three cities, namely, Wichita, Hutchinson, and Pittsburgh, that do not maintain segregated elementary schools.

Two of those cities, as we point out in our brief, have completed a process of integration during the past two years. We feel that—

JUSTICE FRANKFURTER: Is there any litigation pending as to any of the other cities?

MR. WILSON: No, sir.

JUSTICE REED: Why did one of the parties, appellants, disappear from the case?

MR. WILSON: The plan adopted by the Topeka Board of Education was this: You will recall from the record last year and the arguments that the city then maintained within the entire district eighteen geographic areas. In each geographic area there was a school attended by the white students living within the limits of that area.

In addition to the eighteen white schools, there were four Negro schools spaced at wider intervals throughout the city. The first affirmative step taken by the Board of Education in carrying out its policy to abandon segregation as soon as practicable eliminated segregation in two of the geographic areas, namely, Randolph and Southwest.

There were nine Negro students living within the limits of those geographic areas. Consequently, they are admitted to the integrated schools, and one of these appellants is one of those children.

JUSTICE FRANKFURTER: As I understand it, the present situation is that the only litigation that is rife is the one now before the Court?

MR. WILSON: That is correct, if the Court please.

JUSTICE FRANKFURTER: As to which the educational authorities, with an authority not challenged by the state to stop segregated schools, in fact formally and officially announced that they are going to integrate their schools, and have begun the process of integration, is that correct?

MR. WILSON: I should point out that not only is the authority not challenged by the state, the authority is specifically granted by the statute that is here being attacked.

JUSTICE FRANKFURTER: So they are doing what they can do, no matter—

MR. WILSON: They are doing, as a matter of policy, as a matter of legislative policy, may I say, what they can do without reference to this case.

JUSTICE FRANKFURTER: But if they did what it wanted, the state cannot say "You are exceeding your authority," and no case could come here on that ground, could it?

MR. WILSON: Certainly not.

JUSTICE REED: If they were to reverse their position tomorrow, these children who seek admission would have no right to go unless it was unconstitutional?

MR. WILSON: That is right.

JUSTICE FRANKFURTER: Do you think it is an alarming assumption that in 1953 where a state has stopped segregation, and in the next year is going to begin segregation in Topeka, Kansas. Do you think we ought to do business on that assumption?

MR. WILSON: If the Court please, may I distinguish between the State of Kansas and the Board of Education of Topeka, Kansas, which is a separate municipal corporation.

The Board of Education of Topeka, Kansas, has announced its intention to abandon the policy of segregation. I think the Board is acting in complete good faith, and I have no notion that they will reverse that trend.

On the other hand, the State of Kansas is here to defend its statute, and I emphasize, and the Court emphasized, we came a year ago, at the express invitation of the Court, and there are other cities that are concerned, and, therefore, the State had hoped to be heard with respect to the questions that the Court submitted to it on June 8.

If the case is moot, obviously, after five or six hours, argument does reach a point of diminishing returns, and certainly we do not want to discuss a matter that is moot, if the Court deems that to be the case.

JUSTICE JACKSON: Is there anything that would distinguish your case and that would save your statute if the statutes in the other states went down?

MR. WILSON: I think not, Your Honor.

JUSTICE JACKSON: So that your case is governed by what—is there anything that you have to add that Mr. Davis or Judge Moore have not covered, in defense of your statute?

MR. WILSON: In preparing my argument, I examined the same authorities that both the other appellees and the appellants have examined. As a matter of fact, I cite both the same authorities that both the parties, as well as the Attorney General, have examined.

My conclusions, my interpretations, are substantially those that Mr. Davis and Judge Moore have presented to this Court.

MR. MOORE: That is Mr. Moore, I would just like to correct that.

MR. WILSON: I am not sure whether it is proper to apologize under the circumstances or not. (Laughter.)

THE CHIEF JUSTICE: You may proceed, Mr. Wilson.

MR. WILSON: In view of the comments by the Court, I shall proceed somewhat summarily. I shall not make an effort to review in detail the evidence that I base the conclusions that I shall present to the Court.

I think the facts—Mr. Carter started to state the facts in this case. Perhaps, in order to give proper perspective to my argument, some further statement would be proper.

We pointed out that the Board of Education in Topeka is a separate municipal corporation, is the party defendant in the court below; that the State of Kansas, with consent of the court below, intervened for the sole and only purpose of defending the statute that is under attack.

We further pointed out the permissive nature of our statute. It applies to cities of only—only cities of the first class, that is, cities of more than 15,000 population, of which there are twelve in the State of Kansas. It applies only on the elementary school level.

The school systems in the cities that are included in this group are divided generally into elementary, junior high, and senior high school levels. The elementary category includes only the kindergarten and the first six grades of instruction, and it is there only that the statute under attack applies, except in the single case of Kansas City where, under an exception in the law, the practice of segregation is authorized in the high school, in addition to the elementary grades.

Now, I emphasize that it is our position that the action of the Topeka Board of Education, which had been discussed here at some length, does not in any way alter the position or the status of the State of Kansas.

We are here as appellees; we are defending the constitutionality of the statute that is under attack.

The Board of Education of the City of Topeka, as a matter of policy and not—there is nothing in the record to indicate that it is a concession to the appellants in this case, but as a matter of policy—and exercising their power under the statute, the Board of Education has determined to abandon segregation as early as practicable.

JUSTICE BLACK: Do you think this is a case of a controversy between these people and the City of Topeka?

MR. WILSON: Sir?

JUSTICE BLACK: Do you think this is a case of a controversy between these people and the City of Topeka in the present situation? If so, what is it?

MR. WILSON: The appellants have denied the right of the Board of Education of the City of Topeka to maintain separate schools, pursuant to our statute. The City of Topeka has never agreed that it does not have such a right.

JUSTICE BLACK: It has been agreed to desegregate schools.

MR. WILSON: It has agreed as a matter of policy to put them in the schools. Now, there may be a controversy as to the means of accomplishing this stated intention.

The Board of Education has filed a separate brief here in which they point out numerous administrative difficulties that will be encountered, and in brief, they are asking for time, but they do not believe—

JUSTICE BLACK: You could not rest on that, could you?

MR. WILSON: I think we could not.

JUSTICE FRANKFURTER: To follow up Justice Black's question, is there any controversy between these appellants and the State of Kansas, any justiciable controversy?

MR. WILSON: These appellants allege and contend that a statute enacted by the legislature of Kansas is unconstitutional.

JUSTICE FRANKFURTER: Suppose I allege that a statute, an Act of Congress, is unconstitutional; and I have no secular damage of mine that is affected. I think such a profound Act of Congress, passed in this heedless way we have been told about, is unconstitutional. Can I go to court?

MR. WILSON: No, obviously not.

JUSTICE FRANKFURTER: Obviously not.

MR. WILSON: However, when you consider the peculiar circumstances under which the State of Kansas got into this case—

JUSTICE FRANKFURTER: Litigants sometimes get in, and then find themselves out. (Laughter)

MR. WILSON: Unless the Court desires, I do not wish to proceed with argument; that is, I have no intention to burden the already overburdened Court.

JUSTICE FRANKFURTER: That is not my question. There is no suggestion about your not arguing the appropriateness; it is just the question of whether it is one of those cases where you have to say there is no controversy in a judicial sense before the Court.

MR. WILSON: Well, to repeat my earlier statement, I think there still is a controversy because under the authority that the Board of Education presumes to exercise, it does maintain segregation in sixteen of its eighteen geographic areas, and it requires the children living in those areas to go to segregated schools.

THE CHIEF JUSTICE: I consider that a problem; I would like to hear some light on it anyway. I think when both parties to the action feel that there is a controversy, and invited the Attorney General to be here and answer these questions, I, for one, would like to hear the argument.

MR. WILSON: Thank you, sir.

At the outset I should point out—I have pointed out—that we are not here defending a policy, and the determination that has been made is one of policy.

We are here solely for the purpose of defending the right, the constitutional right, we contend, of the State of Kansas and of its own communities to make these determinations as to state and local policy on state and local levels.

We think that regardless of all that has been said, and regardless of the extreme difficulty of these cases, of the fact that they do involve great moral and ethical and humanitarian principles, there are still some very basic considerations, so basic in fact, that I am a little bit embarrassed to mention them to this Court after there has been so much argument.

But, nevertheless, they are so very important that I think I must suggest, in the first place, that this is a union of states that are sovereign, except for only those purposes where they have delegated their sovereignty to the national authority, and I think further to determine the scope of the national authority we must look at the intent and the purpose of the instrument by which the authority was delegated.

I think in these arguments we frequently lose sight of the historic doctrine of separation of powers. We fail to distinguish between the legitimate sphere of judicial activity and the legislative or policy-making function; and if I may presume, it may have been that the Court had these things in mind when it suggested to us last summer that we answer certain questions by way of reargument, for certainly my studies, and apparently the studies of other counsel, have reinforced these basic considerations that this is a federal union; the national Government only possesses power delegated to it, and that the legislative must always be distinguished from the judicial function.

Now, as to the specific intent of the framers of the Fourteenth Amendment, the evidence has been examined in detail and I should not wish to report that which has been said.

I can state generally, and I have stated generally, that we agree with the other appellees. We find the evidence to be persuasive that the Congress which submitted the Fourteenth Amendment did not contemplate that it would affect segregation in the public schools.

It may not be significant that all of the appellees in these cases—that is, all of the states, including the State of Delaware—have reached that conclusion working independently, but we do think it is significant that the Attorney General, in his brief, finds that the legislative history does not conclusively establish that Congress which proposed the Fourteenth Amendment specifically understood that it would abolish racial segregation in the public schools.

Now, we thought the question was rather specific. We thought the Court asked was it specifically understood. We contend it was not. The Attorney General agrees it was not. That should dispose of that question.

I think perhaps in the discussion here there has been too much emphasis on contemporary intent. I want to suggest very briefly that the concept of equality and equal protection was not something that originated with the 39th Congress.

For a long time prior to that the term "equal protection" had had a place in the understanding of the people and in the philosophy of government.

Equal protection, as we study the record, the aims and objectives of the abolitionist societies, equal protection was meant to include those very basic rights, rights for which governments are established, the right to life, to liberty and property, and we think that it is in that sense that the term "equal protection" is used in the Fourteenth Amendment.

We would point out that—we have pointed out in our brief—there is probably no occasion for pointing it out further—that there were specific denials in the Congress that civil rights and equal protection did comprehend the public schools and racial segregation therein.

Mr. Davis quite eloquently in his statement yesterday expressed to the Court the conviction that the thrust of the Fourteenth Amendment was toward the institution of slavery. We think that is the case, and nothing more.

The Fourteenth Amendment was intended to embody the rights that are cataloged in the Civil Rights Act, and they are cataloged rather specifically. They are set out in this language:

> That citizens will have the right in every State and Territory to make and enforce contracts, to sue, to be parties, to give evidence, to inherit, purchase, lease, sell, hold and convey real and personal property, and to the full and equal benefits of all laws and proceedings for the security of person and property as is enjoyed by white citizens.

Now, we think this is the fruition of the whole abolitionist movement and the most complete expression of the consensus of abolitionist aims.

We think that the only purpose of the Fourteenth Amendment was to give constitutional status and dignity to these aims and objectives expressed in the Civil Rights Act of 1866, and in them we find no place for the contention that racial segregation or the absence of racial segregation would be comprehended within their terms.

Turning to the states, we again find the same result, but our colleagues or at least the other appellees in these cases, have discovered—we were unable to find a single instance where it appeared to us that a state, by reason of deference to the Fourteenth Amendment had eliminated segregation from its public school system.

On the other hand, we found that some twenty-four of the states, either at the time of the adoption of the Amendment or within a few years thereafter, did legally sanction separate public schools.

We found that ten states, including my own State of Kansas, that by the same legislature in the same year and, I think perhaps in the same session, legislated with respect to segregated schools and ratified the Fourteenth Amendment.

Now, we think that is positive evidence that the states, of at least a majority of the states, did not contemplate, did not understand, did not comprehend that the Fourteenth Amendment would preclude segregation in the public schools.

Kansas is, perhaps, unique in this case because Kansas is a state with a pronounced abolitionist tradition. The other states, Virginia and South Carolina, were members of the Confederacy; Delaware, we are told by the Attorney General's brief, was sympathetic toward the Confederacy, although it remained in the Union.

On the other hand, Kansas was an abolitionist state. The settlement of Kansas was inspired and financed by the Immigrant Aid Society of Boston.

The first positive political influence in Kansas was the Free Soil Party, an offshoot of the abolitionists of the East.

Certainly, Kansas is not subject to the accusation that can be hurled, perhaps, at the other states that its tradition is rooted in the slave tradition.

But I mentioned a while ago the same legislature, and I might point out that this legislature was composed largely of Union veterans. Our historians tell us that Kansas contributed more troops to the Union armies in proportion to its population than any other state. Almost to a man, the legislature of 1867 was composed of those Union veterans, of men who had offered their lives for the cause of Negro freedom, and that legislature ratified routinely, as a matter of course, the Fourteenth Amendment.

We infer from the Governor's message that ratification was deemed desirable because it was a part of the national Republican program, and the Republicans were in the ascendancy in Kansas. That same legislature, within about six weeks, enacted a statute providing for separate education for children of white and Negro races in cities of the second class.

Prior thereto the statutes had provided for separate education, for optional separate education, in common school districts, that is, in the rural areas.

A little later, a statute had been enacted authorizing separate education in cities of the first class, which then was cities of more than 7,000.

Then you have the gap between the rural areas and the cities of more than 7,000, where segregation was not authorized.

By the action of the legislature of 1867, which ratified the Fourteenth Amendment, the picture was completed in Kansas. Segregation was then authorized on all levels.

Now, I point this out because it seems to me if we can infer any intention from our own legislative act, we must infer that the legislature recognized that within the State of Kansas there were areas where, by reason of lack of mutual understanding between the races, it would be impossible to provide equality of opportunity, assured by the Fourteenth Amendment in integrated schools.

Therefore, as a special benevolence, as a special device whereby equality to be assured in the Fourteenth Amendment could be complied with, the legislature of Kansas made it possible to establish separate schools in those areas.

Now, again that is only my inference. However, my adversaries infer also.

Now, to pass quickly to the other questions that are submitted, I think I have emphasized our position. We find that the Congress nor the state legislatures intended or comprehended or understood that segregation would be precluded by the Fourteenth Amendment.

The next question, of course, concerns the contemporary understanding of future intent, and again, we answer both questions in the negative.

We cannot understand, we cannot conceive, of how a Congress or how state legislatures, in ratifying an amendment, could contemplate that in the future the limitations that they imposed upon that amendment might be enlarged by any agency or any branch of the federal government.

The limitations were fixed by the intent that preceded and existed at the time of the adoption of the Amendment. We think those limitations were present in the minds of the Congress that submitted, and the states that ratified, the Amendment.

We do not believe that any member of Congress intended that the basic relationship between the states and the federal government should be altered by the Amendment. We do not think that they contemplated they were providing a means for amending the Constitution and giving it a meaning that it did not presently have.

We must admit that if we are impelled in this instance, and looking only at the intent, to choose between the judicial and the congressional power, the choice would necessarily be the congressional. My understanding is not, perhaps, mature on this phase of the question but, as I read these debates, there was throughout an emphasis on congressional power.

Undoubtedly the abolitionists had contemplated that Reconstruction might be affected by congressional action. The fact was that the Congress trusted neither the executive nor the judiciary to any extent, and so looking at the intent of the Congress and the intent of the legislatures, we must concede that should the issue before this Court be one within the Amendment, within the federal competence, that it was then the intent of the framers that the Congress and not the courts should supply the re-definition or the impetus by which the particular subject is comprehended within the terms of the Amendment.

With respect to the judicial power, our argument is limited pretty much by our conslusions with respect to the intended future effect of the Amendment. Certainly, in commenting upon the subject of judicial power, we are confronted with a considerable amount of difficulty.

Obviously, the judiciary has the power to determine the limitations of its power. Furthermore, any decision that this Court makes in this case will become the law of the case. In that sense, certainly the entire matter is within the judicial power.

However, when we consider the historic exercise of the judicial power, we are constrained to recognize a great deal of limitation and restraint upon that exercise.

There is a case in which Justice Holmes has commented on the judicial power and, particularly, on the judicial power to legislate, in these words. He says that:

I recognize, without hesitation, that judges do and must legislate, but they do so only interstitially. They are confined from molar to molecular motion.[44]

We think that, at least that is the key or that is the essence of our understanding of the judicial power, to move from molar, from mass, to molecular motions, to refine the broad and general concepts that are included in the statute and in the constitutional provisions that are presented to the Court.

[44]Southern Pacific Co. v. Jensen, 244 U.S. 205, 222 (1917).

Certainly, it is not moving from the molar to the molecular to move outside the original intention, and with a sweeping gesture to bring into the Constitution a meaning, a view that was not entertained by the framers and those that gave the Amendment its effect.

That disposes of our general arguments with respect to the first three questions.

The latter two questions of the Court deal with the remedy to be applied which, in this case, may be moot.

The State of Kansas, of course, is not concerned with the immediate problems that will confront the Board of Education in complying with whatever decree or order this Court may enter. We have taken the position that this Court need not concern itself in the Kansas case with a decree in detail, but should simply, in the event of reversal, remand the case to the district court with directions to form an appropriate decree.

There are a number of considerations which must be taken into the purview of that court, but they are not for consideration here.

We appreciate very much the opportunity to be heard somewhat summarily in the circumstances of a moot case, and we hope that in considering this matter, this matter of constitutional right, the Court will not be unmindful of the constitutional right of the State of Kansas to set up and maintain its own school system and to initiate and maintain there the policies that are most beneficial to all of its people.

Thank you.

THE CHIEF JUSTICE: Thank you, Mr. Wilson
Mr. Carter?

REBUTTAL ARGUMENT ON BEHALF OF APPELLANTS

by MR. CARTER

MR. CARTER: I would like to say this, Your Honors, I do still have doubt with regard to the question of mootness in this case.

However, as Mr. Justice Frankfurter pointed out, I would think it would not be likely that, having made this step, that Topeka would reverse itself, not in 1953.

I am also confident that the State of Kansas, if this Court declares the statute unconstitutional with respect to South Carolina and Virginia, that the State of Kansas would abide by that decision.

I might add that, in so far as I am concerned with respect to the arguments that have been urged by the Attorney General, since I do not feel he has opened any new avenues, it seems to me that in order to conserve the Court's time, I will not speak.

THE CHIEF JUSTICE: Thank you
(Whereupon, at 3:40 p.m., the argument was concluded.)

SPOTTSWOOD THOMAS BOLLING, ET AL.,
Petitioners,

vs.

C. MELVIN SHARPE, ET AL.,
Respondents

Case No. 8

Washington, D.C.
Tuesday, December 8, 1953.

The above-entitled cause came on for oral argument at 3:40 o'clock p.m.

APPEARANCES:
On behalf of the Petitioners:
GEORGE E. C. HAYES, ESQ., and JAMES M. NABRIT, JR., ESQ.

On behalf of the Respondents:
MILTON D. KORMAN, ESQ.

THE CHIEF JUSTICE: Number 8, Spottswood Thomas Bolling, et al., vs. C. Melvin Sharpe, et al.

THE CLERK: Counsel are present.

THE CHIEF JUSTICE: Mr. Hayes.

ARGUMENT ON BEHALF OF PETITIONERS

by MR. HAYES

MR. HAYES: May it please the Court, the case of *Bolling* v. *Sharpe* comes before this Court by reason of certiorari granted to the United States Court of Appeals for the District of Columbia, and the problems that we face are problems which are different from those which the Court has been hearing for the past two days; different, because of the fact of our federal relationship; different because of the fact that there are no state-federal conflicts; different because of the fact that in our case there is no question of equality of facilities.

It is probably proper that I should begin by saying something by way of background in order to acquaint the Court again of the problems, as we see it, that we face in this jurisdiction.

The minor petitioners in this case presented themselves to the authorities at the Sousa Junior High School, seeking admittance as students.

They were denied admittance, and expressly denied it for no other reason than because of their race and color.

They followed that up by going through each of the echelons with respect to the administrative authorities in the District of Columbia, and at each of the levels they were denied admission for no reason other than the question of their race or color.

This suit was then filed asking by way of injunction that they be admitted to these schools and that the Board of Education should not use as a means of excluding them the race and the color of these petitioners.

I have heard comment within the last few days about the concern that the seventeen states may have as to what this decision of this Court might be so as to know what they should do.

I respectfully submit to this Court that not seventeen states but the world at large is waiting to see what this Court will do as far as the District of Columbia is concerned, to determine as to whether or not the Government of the United States will say to these petitioners if they are not entitled to the same liberties as other persons, that they are denied it simply because of their race and color.

When my colleague, Mr. Nabrit and I—I should, perhaps, interrupt myself to say to the Court that it is our purpose to open our argument, divide fifty minutes of time between us, and then allow ten minutes for the closing—so I shall address myself to the feature with respect to the history as far as the statutes are concerned, and Mr. Nabrit will address himself to the things which seem pertinent to us by way of the inquiries made by this Court.

Turning then to this question of the history of the statutes, there has been a great deal said in the last few days about the statutes here in the District of Columbia having to do with the Fourteenth Amendment.

I do not need to say to this Court that we are not concerned primarily with the Fourteenth Amendment. We rely rather upon the Fifth Amendment because of the fact that that applies to our jurisdiction.

But a great deal has been said, as I have indicated to you, and as you will realize, with respect to the question of statutes here in the District of Columbia.

We find ourselves in the company of the distinguished Attorney General of the United States and his associates when we take the position that, as far as the statutes are concerned, as we conceive it, they are permissive and voluntary; they are not compulsory; and we believe that this Court can find, by looking at these statutes, or must find, either one of two things: either that they are permissive and voluntary, and that by so much, if they find that the Board of Education has construed them as being compulsory and has used them as a means of segregating Negroes, that then by its mandate this Court will say that the Board of Education is wrong in any such interpretation; or, if on the other hand, it were to be determined that they are, as a matter of fact, compulsory, that then this Court must, of necessity, say that they are unconstitutional if, as a matter of fact, they use as their yardstick nothing other than race or color.

It may, therefore, become important for us to look and see what was the atmosphere under which the statutes came upon the books.

JUSTICE REED: Whether they are permissive or mandatory, would they not be unconstitutional in either case?

MR. HAYES: If they are permissive and voluntary, the answer would be that they would be unconstitutional; but that the constitutional question—and this is where we think the issue is as we presently see it—that until the issue is raised, that then, of course, the question of constitutionality has not been passed upon, and it is our position that we are presently at the place where that issue, as far as this Court is concerned and as far as the statutes are concerned, is for the first time being raised and, therefore, Your Honor, to specifically answer your question, Justice Reed, the answer is, yes, we think it is unconstitutional in both instances, unconstitutional whether permissive and voluntary, unconstitutional whether by actual compulsion, and we think it is the present time when this Court should so determine.

JUSTICE FRANKFURTER: Mr. Hayes, may I ask what you mean by permissive? I am not talking about any legal implications, but am I wrong in thinking that Congress year after year passed appropriations for the maintenance of a system of segregation?

MR. HAYES: Your Honor is entirely correct with respect to the fact that they have passed appropriations.

It is our position that the fact that Congress, having found a certain situation and having acted upon it, and having supplementarily issued or allowed appropriations, that that inaction on the part of Congress or that acceptance of a situation on the part of Congress does not still avoid the fact of the unconstitutionality which we ask Your Honors to determine.

With respect to the history of these statutes I say there may be, therefore, some appropriate comment.

Slavery was abolished in the District of Columbia in April of 1862. In May of 1862, within approximately one month after the time of the abolition of slavery, two of these statutes that are presently on the books and under which the Board of Education is acting, were promulgated. Those are referred to, and they use the expression of "initiating education."

That was not an actual fact, because they amounted to nothing other than appropriations, appropriations to an existing situation.

What had happened had been that public education, as such, even among the whites at that time, had taken on no actual status.

As I have heard the suggestion within the last couple of days, I think it was from the Attorney General's office, from the Assistant there, that, as a matter of fact, from their point of view, what they were at that time attempting to do was to reach a situation which they found. It was not a question of them actually appropriating, of them actually initiating. It was the fact of their appropriating.

They found a situation existing. Public education was for the poor people. The persons who had money sent their children to private schools, and public education had no such concept as is the present concept with respect to public education; and so, what happened was that Congress, finding that situation and desiring, as it unquestionably did desire, that something should be done for the Negro, just emancipated from slavery, attempted to do something in the way of appropriating moneys.

It is to be noticed that what they did or attempted first to do was to tax Negroes for their properties, with an idea of Negro education in the public sense.

As I say, at that time it was not with respect to any public education but rather in the nature of appropriations. There were no public schools so far as Negroes were concerned.

It was not until 1864 that there was anything that purported to be a public school, as far as Negroes were concerned, and that was then in a private church, showing again that public education did not have the connotations that it presently has.

What they did was to attempt to give this Negro some opportunity for an education, and so it became a part of what the background was, that there was this appropriation for Negro education, and the things that happened subsequently, significantly, too, were that in 1864 there was a requirement of compulsory education.

Now, that takes on, too, a different aspect because as far as we are concerned, we find ourselves in a question of compulsory segregation, either announced, created or sanctioned by the federal government.

In 1864, I say then, they required compulsory education, and also provided that there might be the right of selection of persons who were white persons to send their children to a white school of their choice, and for Negroes to send Negro children to colored schools of their choice, the language at each time, if Your Honors please, being permissive in its character.

At no place in any of these enactments do we find language which specifically says, as they do in instances when the legislature feels disposed to say, "that this shall be a compulsory proposition as far as Negroes and whites are concerned," and the language in these statutes does not lend itself to anything other than permission rather than compulsion.

The enactments that came from that time forward, if Your Honors please—the question has been referred to of three lots which were to be given for the use of Negroes; another act which required that the money should be turned over to the Board of Education for Negro students because of the fact that moneys had been allocated and had not been properly applied.

Further along, the question of legislation having to do with assistant superintendents of the schools—there was that legislation—or with respect to the question of Boards of Examiners, all simply addressing themselves to a situation begun back in 1862, and which had been, shall I say, winked at and carried forward from that time forward, but not legislated upon, not made compulsory.

With respect to that situation, there has been, perhaps, some addressing of itself to the question as far as our courts are concerned, and I say our courts now, meaning the courts of the District of Columbia.

But I would call Your Honors' attention to the fact, in the first instance, the case of *Wall* v. *Oyster* that there was no question there raised of a character which is being raised before this Court.

What happened then was that the person who was the petitioner desired not to be placed in a colored school. She had taken a position that she would rather be held a part of the white race and, therefore, was asking not to be put into a colored school.

As Your Honors will see, that begins with the premise that the segregation in and of itself was all right; that all that the person wanted to do was to be put into a school which they believed would not put them among the Negroes, and so we say to you in that case there was no issue of the character that is here being raised.

My attention is called to the fact that as far as an interpretation of the statute was concerned—and this has significance which I want to bring to Your Honors' attention—that back in 1869, and I am reverting now—that back in 1869 there was an issue that was raised as to whether a colored child who had been given a permit to go to a white school should be allowed to go to that school, and that question was posed to the Office of the Corporation Counsel of the District of Columbia, who appears for the respondents in this case, and the Corporation Counsel at that time, in 1869, took the position that there was nothing in the statute that avoided this child being admitted to the white school, and the record seems to indicate that the child was admitted to this school, continued to go there until they finished the colored school.

We call Your Honors' attention to that not that we think it in any sense changes the situation, but rather to show the indecision that was a part of the picture, rather to show that even there then at the time of the early promulgation of the statute, there was the interpretation by the substantial office of the Government that it permitted of going into the white school and that that being the allowed circumstance, it was accepted as such, and no issue was raised further with respect to that.

JUSTICE FRANKFURTER: Mr. Hayes, in those days roughly what was the proportion of the colored population to the total population, just as a rough guess? Don't bother if you—

MR. HAYES: I would not like to give Your Honor an inaccurate statement. We did have calculations, and I think that somewhere—

JUSTICE FRANKFURTER: Don't bother.

MR. HAYES: Mr. Nabrit suggests there were in the District some 11,000 Negroes at that time. I do not know the proportion that there were, I mean, that held to the total population, but there were some 11,000 Negroes, and at that time, as I have indicated to Your Honors, the education which they were getting was that of the benign gentlemen who were the philanthropists, and that type of thing rather than any question of public education.

There was also at that time, as a part of the population situation which Your Honor has just asked me, after the time that slavery was abolished in the District, there was a great influx of freedmen into this area because of that circumstance, naturally because of that circumstance—there was this great influx.

I was addressing myself to the question of litigation in some sense that had come up. This litigation came again in the case of *Carr* v. *Corning,* and in that case—well, there were two cases, *Carr* v. *Corning* and *Browne* v. *Magdeburger,* and the two cases were combined because of the fact that inherent in them was the same proposition.

The *Browne* v. *Magdeburger* case—this proposition the question as to whether or not there was a violation of the constitutional right of a student because of the fact of being required to go into a school where there was the alleged inequality; that they were required to go where there was a double shift of students, so far as they were concerned, and the same proposition was raised in *Carr* v. *Corning,* but there was the additional proposition in the *Carr* v. *Corning* case, which we have raised in this case, and that was as to whether or not segregation as such, whether or not segregation per se, was unconstitutional.

That is the position which we are taking with respect to these cases, that segregation per se is unconstitutional, and that without regard to physical facilities, without regard to the question of curriculum, and that if, as a matter of fact, there is a designation that one must go to a particular school for no other reason than because of race or color, that that is a violation of the constitutional right, and as this Court has said, wherever the issue is raised with respect to color, then it is upon the Government to show that the reason for it—that there is a reason that is a justifiable reason. I shall address myself to that in a moment or two, if I have the time.

But with respect to this *Carr* v. *Corning* case, we take the position that as far as the *Carr* v. *Corning* case was concerned, it simply was decided incorrectly; that our Court of Appeals was simply wrong in its decision.

We call attention to the fact that there was in that case a dissenting opinion by Mr. Judge [Henry W.] Edgerton,[45] which we commend to this Court as being more nearly what the law should be with respect to that case.

In that case, Judge Edgerton went on to say that it was an improper concept to be able to have education based solely upon race or color.

Judge Edgerton in that case says, "Appellees say that Congress requires them to maintain segregation"—reading from page 48—page 48, Mr. Korman, in our original brief—"the President's Committee concluded that congressional legislation 'assumes the fact of segregation but nowhere makes it mandatory.' I think the question irrelevant, since legislation cannot affect appellant's constitutional rights."

That is the position which we urge upon this Court, that it cannot be affected—that the constitutional rights of these people cannot be affected by legislation of any character, and Mr. Judge Edgerton in that case was saying the thing which we say to this Court, that in his opinion there was not any such showing as made the Board of Education take such a step, but that from his point of view it was irrelevant as to whether they did or not, because if it purported to affect the constitutional rights of these persons, that then there was no alternative but that the Court should declare it to be unconstitutional.

I have heard the question asked today as to under what heading it should come. This Court has told us under what heading it should come. It should come under the heading of liberty because this Court in *Meyer* v. *Nebraska* said it was a violation of the liberty of the person, which is the language of the Fifth Amendment upon which we stand, to deny to him their constitutional right, and that constitutional right was then an educational right, just as has been indicated to Your Honors before.

May I say this final word: that we believe that this Court has already determined this proposition in the *Farrington* v. *Tokushige* case where, with respect to the Hawaiian legislation, this Court struck down legislation saying that it was a violation of the person's constitutional right, talking about education, and referred to *Meyer* v. *Nebraska, Bartels* v. *Iowa, Pierce* v. *Sisters,* saying, "Yes, admittedly, they come under the Fourteenth Amendment, but, as far as the Fifth Amendment is concerned, the same thing is to be adopted," and so we say to this Court that under whatever angle the situation is looked at in the District of Col-

[45]Henry White Edgerton (1888–   ). United States Circuit Judge for the District of Columbia Court of Appeals, 1938–   ; Chief Judge, 1955–1958.

umbia, from whatever aspect we take it, that this Court, as we conceive it, cannot say to a waiting world that we sanction segregation in the District of Columbia for no other reason than because of the fact that the skin of the person is dark. That, this Court has said, is suspect; that, you have said, is void; that, you have said, should not be sanctioned; that, we believe, must be your decision.

THE CHIEF JUSTICE: Mr. Nabrit.

ARGUMENT ON BEHALF OF PETITIONERS

by MR. NABRIT

MR. NABRIT: If the Court please, we have for the past two days been engaged continuously in a concentrated and thorough attempt to recapture the spirit and mood of a significant period in the history of our country.

The danger in this, as I see it, is that in a worthy attempt to project ourselves into the remote scenes of the 1860's and '70's, that we shall lack either the normal apperceptions of men of that day which, though inarticulate, nevertheless were a part of their own concept of day-to-day events, or we shall miss the motivations of legislators, though known then by all, though not set forth in specificity by any, which agitated both men and events eighty-eight years ago.

At best, I fear that we shall recapture only the overtones of these historical settings, the outlines of the broad sweep of events, but I hope at least we shall have grasped the general delineation of the primary purpose and objectives.

Men do not always set forth explicitly the motives which cause them to act as they do nor do congressmen always explain in detail either the objectives which they seek in proposed legislation or the reasons why they support or fail to support a particular bill.

In this posture of these cases then it seems to us that we need to be reminded of two facts of great importance and significance, as we consider the District of Columbia case.

First, none of this exhaustive discussion of history, however illuminating it may be, can conceal the blunt fact that under a system of legalized segregation millions of American Negroes live in this land of opportunity, equality and democracy as second-class citizens, suffering all types of civil disabilities imposed upon them in every aspect of their daily lives solely because of their race and color.

Today we deal only with one significant aspect of it, segregation in public school education.

In the second place, in this posture of the cases, we should single out the District of Columbia for different treatment, not alone because the District of Columbia brings this case under the Fifth Amendment, but because this is the federal government dealing with federal citizens. Here is no question of the delicate relationship of state and federal government. Here we are dealing with the capital of the free world.

In this framework we submit to the Court that the question before the Court is not merely the technical question of the construction of school statutes or the propriety or the reasonableness of the action of the respondents complained of here, but it is also the basic inquiry as to whether under our Constitution the federal government is authorized to classify Negroes in the District of Columbia as untouchables for the purpose of educating them for living in a democracy.

We say to the Court that this is not in line either with the principles of the Constitution of the United States, our ideals of democracy, nor with the decisions of this Court, nor with the executive orders of the President of the United States, nor with the orders of the Commissioners of the District of Columbia; and that so far as we have been able to find, with the exception of these school statutes, the training school in the District of Columbia and one or two other instances of that ilk, that there is in the District of Columbia no authority, no official, no body of responsible persons who takes the position that racial distinction should be imposed upon Negroes because of color, except for the respondents complained of here, and we say that these respondents do this in defiance of the decisions of this Court, the executive orders of the President of the United States, the policy of the District of Columbia Commissioners, and in that framework they violate federal policy, and that inconsistent position should lead this Court to deny these respondents the power which they claim to possess.

JUSTICE FRANKFURTER: Have the Commissioners of the District expressed themselves on this subject?

MR. NABRIT: They have expressed themselves, Mr. Justice Frankfurter, as not having authority over the school board and, therefore, it is one of the phases of the life in the District of Columbia to which the thrust of their power does not reach.

JUSTICE FRANKFURTER: Is the legislation of Congress clear that the school board is autonomous as to this question?

MR. NABRIT: I would like to—I will answer that, but I would like to answer it, instead of a yes or no—

JUSTICE FRANKFURTER: You do whatever you want to; you give that before you get through.

MR. NABRIT: Yes.

I want to answer that right now, Justice Frankfurter, because it is a peculiar situation.

In the District of Columbia the school board is not appointed by the President of the United States, it is not appointed by the District Commissioners, it is not chosen by the voteless inhabitants of the District of Columbia. Rather it is appointed by the District Court of the District of Columbia, and, as we understand the situation in the District of Columbia, we do not know to whom they are responsible. (Laughter) That is the status of the school board in the District of Columbia.

JUSTICE FRANKFURTER: They are appointed for a term?

MR. NABRIT: Of three years, and then they are either not reappointed or they are reappointed by the District Court of the District of Columbia.

JUSTICE FRANKFURTER: By the District Court you mean the whole bench of judges of the District, the United States District Court?

MR. NABRIT: Yes, sir; the United States District Court, a very unusual situation. (Laughter).

JUSTICE FRANKFURTER: Does the District Court define their powers or does the Code of the District of Columbia define their powers?

MR. NABRIT: Their Code—you know, under our setup in that area we have some adminstrative functions in the courts.

JUSTICE FRANKFURTER: Does the Code say anything about this problem, the segregation of the grade schools?

MR. NABRIT: No, sir.

JUSTICE FRANKFURTER: This is just a pronouncement by the board?

MR. NABRIT: That is right .

JUSTICE FRANKFURTER: And the board has pronounced—

MR. NABRIT: The board has pronounced it, although I notice—and this is something that the Court may reprimand me for, but I noted—in the brief and in the papers that counsel for the respondent is not certain as to what the positions of all his respondents are on this matter.(Laughter).
They are sued individually, you know.

JUSTICE FRANKFURTER: All you have to do is to read his brief; I do not know for whom he speaks.

MR. NABRIT: I neither, Mr. Justice Frankfurter.

JUSTICE FRANKFURTER: I take it he will tell us before we get through. (Laughter.)

MR. NABRIT: Yes, I hope so.
So, in this posture of the cases, we would like to say to the Court—and I say this primarily, if this is proper, so that the Chief Justice might have this because I said it to the Court—but I want it understood that our position is that, number one, the statutes governing the schools in the District of Columbia, which were passed immediately prior to and during the Civil War, without any thought of whether segregation was good or bad, when schools in the United States, public schools themselves, were at issue as to whether people ought not to educate their children privately or not—they were only thirty years old at that time—in the District of Columbia they were only six years old—and here were these Negroes; there were these three systems of schools, public schools for whites, Negroes excluded, a private school for Negroes, and a private school for whites—system of schools, these are all systems—Congress looked at these schools for Negroes getting no support, and authorized support for them from taxes from the Negroes themselves; that is the first bill. Obviously that did not do much good.

They then authorized taxes from all of the persons in the District to be used for that purpose, and in this four-year period, ending in the middle of the Civil War, all of the basic statutes governing the schools in the District of Columbia were enacted.

Under that circumstance and in that case, it is inconceivable that Congress would do anything but make a provision for people who had no schooling, no question of separate or anything else. It was just providing for schools that were found there.

Now, our position is that the Court should construe those statutes as voluntary, meaning by that what the congressman said in talking about them, and I do not cite him for history, but I cite him for the point, for his saying the point that I want to say on this point, that he said Negroes could go to the schools. That is all I need.

That is voluntary. If that be true, until somebody complains in this Court about the exertion of the power of government to compel him to go to one of these schools, there is nothing unlawful about that situation.

Therefore, we do not have a history of lawless action by people in the District of Columbia.

Now if the Court takes that view, it can dispose of the District of Columbia case simply by saying the statutes do not authorize compulsory segregation of races in the District of Columbia in the public schools, and your action complained of here is unlawful and violates the due process clause.

We don't have to go into any constitutional question. We just find they don't have the authority.

Now I suggest that this Court has always done that when it was faced with the statute which it had not interpreted, and one interpretation would be to a constitutional result, and the other interpretation would lead to a non-consititutional result.

And since we suggest to you that if these statutes compel it, they would violate our federal policy, they would violate the due process clause of the Fifth Amendment, the liberty aspect of it, it would violate section 41 and 43 of Title 8 of the Civil Rights Act, that under these circumstances the Court should construe these as merely voluntary statutes, and that in the event the Court doesn't agree, it has still to deal with the question of whether they are not in the nature of bills of attainder. So we suggest as our line of argument that the Court say there is no authority for the actions complained of. It is out of line with the District of Columbia. Now the counsel for the respondents—

JUSTICE REED: On whose part was the complaint?

MR. NABRIT: On the part of the pupils and the parents. Here are two systems of education. Everybody has been going in there without any complaint for sixty or seventy years.

JUSTICE FRANKFURTER: Who has kept these children out of this?

MR. NABRIT: Before this?

JUSTICE FRANKFURTER: Now.

MR. NABRIT: Oh, these respondents, these people—we have got them named. We have them all pointed out.

JUSTICE FRANKFURTER: Do they make a justification for that?

MR. NABRIT: They do.

JUSTICE FRANKFURTER: What do they say?

MR. NABRIT: On the grounds of race and color and that "we are compelled by these statutes."

JUSTICE FRANKFURTER: Do they say the statutes compel them or the statutes authorize them?

MR. NABRIT: Oh, no. They say they are compelled to do it. They don't make any technical differential between authority and compel. They say they are compelled by these statutes to do it.

JUSTICE FRANKFURTER: Suppose we say the statutes do not compel them and then they say it is a matter of discretion, "We ourselves think it is a matter of discretion"?

MR. NABRIT: Well, all we would do—

JUSTICE FRANKFURTER: Start a new suit?

MR. NABRIT: I was just going to tell you, we would file suit that day. (Laughter.)

JUSTICE FRANKFURTER: I am merely suggesting it is multiplying litigation instead of subtracting it.

MR. NABRIT: Well, at least we are going along with the line that the Court follows of restraining itself from engaging in decisions of constitutional questions when it may resolve the problem by a step less than that.
One other thing the Court may do, and I like the Schneiderman[46] case because the Court did something there that I think we don't use enough.

JUSTICE FRANKFURTER: You are for opinions that you like, is that it?

MR. NABRIT: That's right. I like this Schneiderman opinion, Mr. Frankfurter, because in that case the Congress passed, you will recall, an attachment statute in 1906. An alien was naturalized in 1927. About 1919, I believe, Mr. Justice Holmes enunciated that clear and present danger doctrine.
In '42 when this Court passed on that statute for the first time, they read into that statute the intent which Mr. Holmes first discovered—I won't say discovered—announced, twenty years almost after the statute was passed.
Now why can't the Court in this case read into these statutes an intent on the part of Congress not to segregate Negroes by compulsion following the Schneiderman case?

[46]Schneiderman v. United States, 320 U.S. 118 (1943). The government sought unsuccessfully to denaturalize the defendant (represented in the Supreme Court by Wendell Willkie) for failing to disclose that he was a Communist in 1927 when he secured his citizenship papers. The Court found that the defendant could have believed in the Constitution in 1927 despite his Communist associations.

JUSTICE FRANKFURTER: That is easier than worrying about what they debated in '66.

MR. NABRIT: Precisely. That is precisely our position.

Now I would say, I want to say—I want to save ten minutes, but I want to say one thing on this matter of due process, because it seems to me the Court has had a remarkable record in dealing with the exertions of power by the federal government on its citizens where it was faced solely on race or color, and if I am correct, the only instances where the Court has permitted that to be done since Dred Scott has been in the case where war power was involved, and implied power essential to effectuate the war power. With great reservations the Court has permitted the federal government to make racial distinction.

Now I think that that establishes the fundamental principles upon which our case rests, and that it is in line with the policy of this Court, and we would there urge the Court under these considerations to hold that the respondents are without power in the District of Columbia to discriminate or segregate the Negro pupils solely on the basis of race and color.

THE CHIEF JUSTICE: Mr. Korman?

ARGUMENT ON BEHALF OF RESPONDENTS

by MR. KORMAN

MR. KORMAN: Mr. Chief Justice, may it please the Court, at the outset I should like to state the position of the corporation counsel of the District of Columbia in this matter. I stand before the Court to defend acts of Congress which we believe to be lawful and constitutional. I stand before the Court to assert that this is not the forum wherein laws should be attacked because change is wanted. I stand before the Court, as we stood before the Court on May 1 of this year, to defend legislation which we think is valid legislation and constitutional legislation. I refer to the Thompson Restaurant case.[47]

At that time, we found statutes enacted in 1872 and 1873 which required service to all well-behaved persons in any restaurant, hotel, or other place of assembly in the District of Columbia, irrespective of race and color.

For seventy-five or eighty years no one had attempted to enforce those laws. They were believed to be dead. They were called to our attention; we looked into the history of them; we studied the statutes and acts of legislatures thereafter. We studied the Constitution of the United States and the decisions of this Court, and we came to the conclusion that those statutes were valid, even though lying dormant for all those years, and that they were constitutional, and we came here to defend them.

Now, we say to the Court that there are statutes enacted by the Congress of the United States which provide for separation of races in the schools; that they have not lain dormant for seventy-five or eighty years, but they have been repeatedly legislated upon by the Congress of the United States. It appears that they are still valid, that it is still the policy of the Congress to maintain separate schools for

See note 40, *supra*.

the races in the District of Columbia, and we are here to defend the validity and the constitutionality of those laws.

JUSTICE FRANKFURTER: When you say "we," am I to infer that means the Board of Education of the District of Columbia?

MR. KORMAN: You are, sir. I speak for the Board of Education of the District of Columbia, although I admit very frankly in our brief that I have not talked to the individual members so far as their position on the sociological issue is concerned.

JUSTICE FRANKFURTER: I do not know what that means.

MR. KORMAN: It means this: (Laughter) From public statements that I have seen in the press, it appears that at least some members of the Board of Education are strongly convinced at this time that the time has come for a change in the system; that the time has come to integrate the schools of the District.

Indeed, I concede that there is a strong movement in the District of Columbia from a number of sources to strike down segregation in all fields. The President of the United States has made the pronouncement that he expects to use all the power of his office to accomplish that end. The Commissioners of the District of Columbia have made a pronouncement that they intend to try to implement the statement of the President, and they have, in fact, taken action in that direction.

I say that there are many people in the District of Columbia who feel that way.

By the same token, statements have come to me from a number of sources that there are others who think otherwise; indeed, I am constrained to believe that some members of the Board of Education believe otherwise.

But as we see it, that issue, which is the one I called the sociological issue, is not the one involved here.

JUSTICE FRANKFURTER: But my question is to elicit, not by anything other than what I read in your own brief, that this is a strictly legal position which you take as an officer of the Court. I supposed the corporation counsel must represent appellants or respondents before the Court.

MR. KORMAN: That is right.

JUSTICE FRANKFURTER: And it becomes relevant to know whether the Board of Education of the District maintains and has instructed the corporation counsel to maintain the position which you are putting and which you now plead before the Court.

MR. KORMAN: Yes, Your Honor.

JUSTICE FRANKFURTER: Then you do speak for the Board of Education?

MR. KORMAN: Yes, I do.

JUSTICE FRANKFURTER: All right.

MR. KORMAN: I speak for the Board of Education in that the position we take here today is the same position that we took here one year ago, and slightly more than a year ago, when we filed the original brief, and we have not changed our position on that. We advised the Board of Education what the law is; they do not tell us what the law is.

JUSTICE FRANKFURTER: No, but clients do not have to pursue their rights under the law. They may take a position in advance of the law, and lawyers do not maintain positions. They merely maintain their clients' positions.

MR. KORMAN: May I say this to the Court: that the Board, while it is sued individually, is sued individually because it is not an entity, as a matter of law.

The petition in this case asserts, and it is a fact, that the Board of Education itself denied these petitioners entry into the school that they claim they have a right to enter into.

JUSTICE FRANKFURTER: I do not want to take needless time. It is a simple question. You tell the Court that you are here, as other counsel are here, under instructions appropriately given by their clients, and, of course, I will accept your word for it.

MR. KORMAN: At the time this case was first filed, the corporation counsel was asked by the Board of Education to defend it in the district court. We were definitely apprised of the position of the Board of Education.

The case arose in 1950. Since that time there has been a decided change in the personnel of the Board of Education. There are some eight of the nine members who have been replaced. Only one, Mr. Sharpe, still remains of the original defendants in the district court.

There has been no notification to us that the new Board—the Board as now constituted, and which denied to these petitioners the entry into the school which they claimed the right to enter, has changed its position in that regard.

We have seen some statements in the press by some members of the Board which have been alluded to in the briefs.

JUSTICE FRANKFURTER: I do not care about that, and the reason why I think it is important is—I hope this is not improper for stating my own individual responsibility—to the extent that problems of this sort are settled outside a court of law, to that extent, in my opinion, the public good is advanced; and if, by any chance, settlements are made in various jurisdictions through the power of those who have power to settle it, I call it all to the good, without the need of litigation and adjudication and controversy.

Therefore, I raised the question. If you will give me assurance that you are here by the same right by which the State of South Carolina is represented by its counsel, and the State of Virginia, and the Commonwealth of Virginia by its, of course, I repeat, I will accept your word.

MR. KORMAN: We are here on that condition; yes, sir.

JUSTICE FRANKFURTER: Very well.

JUSTICE BLACK: May I ask you, I do not quite understand you, because you stated—when was it, a year ago that you said the Board had changed? Will you let us know in the morning, when the case comes up, whether the Board wants you to defend this case. It has raised some question in my mind, and I think—

MR. KORMAN: I do not know whether I can or not, Your Honor.

The Board is composed of nine members; I do not know whether it is possible to get them together tonight or not.

JUSTICE JACKSON: Isn't the corporation counsel by law made the representative of the Board?

MR. KORMAN: That is right.

JUSTICE JACKSON: I think that settles it. You may have a row with your own clients, but that is not our business.

JUSTICE FRANKFURTER: The question is, your client at the moment—

MR. KORMAN: My client is the Board of Education.

JUSTICE FRANKFURTER: Yes, but they do not know it, apparently.

MR. KORMAN: There are a number of other respondents, who are the superintendents of schools, and some of the assistant superintendents of schools, and the principal of the Sousa Junior High School.

They are all respondents in this case, and we were directed to represent them by order of the Commissioners of the District of Columbia specifically because there were other respondents or defendants in the case, as originally filed than the actual members of the Board of Education, and in those instances we get an order from the Commissioners of the District of Columbia to represent the parties. We have such an order.

(Whereupon, at 4:30 p.m., the Court arose.)

(Oral argument was resumed at 12:07 p.m. December 9, 1953.)

THE CHIEF JUSTICE: No. 8, Spottswood Thomas Bolling, et al, v. C. Melvin Sharpe, et al.

THE CLERK: Counsel are present.

THe CHIEF JUSTICE: Mr. Korman.

ARGUMENT ON BEHALF OF RESPONDENTS, resumed

by MR. KORMAN

MR. KORMAN: May it please the Court, when the Court rose on yesterday, we were having some discussion concerning the right of corporation counsel to appear here as counsel for the respondents. On yesterday I made certain statements to the Court. I should now like to document those statements to some extent.

Section 1301 of the Code of Law for the District of Columbia provides that the corporation counsel "shall be under the direction of the Commissioners and shall have charge of the conduct of all law business of said District among other things."

And it provides further that "he shall perform such other professional duties as may be required of him by the Commissioners."

I said to you on yesterday that the last action of the respondent members of the Board of Education as set forth in the complaint filed in this case below was to deny to the petitioners admission to the Sousa Junior High School which is set apart for the instruction of white students. You will find that statement on page 7 of the record.

I have in my hand a copy of a letter sent by Mrs. Elise Z. Watkins, the secretary of the Board of Education, to Mr. George E. C. Hayes, with copies to Mr. Merican and Mr. Nabrit under date of November 6, 1950. I shall not read the whole letter.

It acknowledges receipt of a letter from Mr. Hayes, Mr. Merican and Mr. Nabrit under date of October 31, 1950, requesting admission of the petitioners to the Sousa Junior High School. The letter continues:

> In reply to your letter, you are advised that the following motion was passed by the Board: 'That the Board feels it has fulfilled its obligation as far as it is capable and that the request to send children to the Sousa Junior High School be denied.'

On the bottom of that is this certification by Mrs. Watkins:

> I hereby certify that this letter embodies the action of the Board of Education taken at its meeting on November 1, 1950. I am familiar with all of the actions of the Board of Education since that time, and the Board of Education has taken no action to rescind or change in any manner its action on November 1, 1950, as reflected in this letter to Mr. George E. C. Hayes, dated Nobember 6, 1950.

I said to you on yesterday that the Board of Education—

THE CHIEF JUSTICE: What was the date of that certificate, sir?

MR. KORMAN: That certificate is dated—it is not dated, Your Honor. It was signed yesterday evening. It is a copy of a letter written November 6 with an up-to-date certification as of today.

THE CHIEF JUSTICE: Thank you.

MR. KORMAN: I said to you on yesterday that the Board of Education had requested the Commissioners to direct the corporation counsel to represent them in this action, and that the Commissioners had so directed us.

I have in my hand a copy of a letter prepared by Mrs. Watkins, the secretary of the Board of Education, and I have also in my hand a duplicate original of that letter dated November 13, 1950, which came to the office of the corporation counsel.

The letter is to the Board of Commissioners of the District of Columbia, and without burdening the Court to read the whole thing, it asks the Commissioners to direct the corporation counsel to represent all of the respondents in two civil actions, one of which is *Bolling* v. *Sharpe*. Mrs. Watkins has put this certification as of last evening on a copy of that letter:

> I hereby certify that the foregoing is a true and correct copy of the letter sent by me to the Board of Commissioners, D.C., under date of November 13, 1950, at the direction of the President of the Board of Education.
>
> This is the usual letter which is sent to the Board of Commissioners whenever the Board of Education or its members or its public school officers have been sued, and is in accordance with Chapter 1, Article 9, section 1 of the rules of the Board of Education which provide when legal advice or service as counsel is desired by the Board of Education upon matters relating to the administration of school affairs, application shall be made to the Commissioners, D. C., for the services of the corporation counsel of the District of Columbia.

Mrs. Watkins continues:

> I am familiar with all of the actions of the Board of Education since the date of the letter of which the foregoing is a copy, and certify that the Board of Education has taken no action to rescind the request of the president of the Board of Education that the board members, the superintendent of schools, and the public school officers be represented by the corporation counsel of the District of Columbia in regard to the civil actions enumerated in the foregoing letter.

In the case of *Denney* v. *Callahan* in 294 Federal 992, it was held that the rules of the Board of Education have the force and effect of law.

I have in my hand a certification by Mr. G. M. Thornett, secretary for the Board of Commissioners, D. C., prepared last evening certifying—I shall read it:

> I hereby certify that the following is a true and exact excerpt from the minutes of the meeting of the Board of Commissioners of the District of Columbia on November 14, 1950.

I shall not read the whole order, but I say to the Court that it contains a direction to represent the various members of the Board of Education and the various school officers named as respondents in this case denominated *Spottswood Thomas Bolling, et al* v. *C. Melvin Sharpe, et al*. There has been no withdrawal of any of that, and I should be very glad if the Court desires to file these copies with the clerk of this Court, with sufficient copies for each member of the Court, if required.

I may say to you further that on last evening Mr. West, the corporation counsel, Mr. Gray, the assistant corporation counsel, and I held what might be called a four-way telephone conversation with Mr. Sharpe, the president of the Board of Education, and we were assured by him that we have the right to stand before you and say that we represent the members of the Board of Education in this controversy.

This morning Mr. Sharpe telephoned me about ten thirty to say that of his own volition he had contacted all the members of the Board of Education and that he could say to me that, in his own words, 100 per cent they say that I have the right to stand before you to represent them in this controversy; that they want decided the question of the constitutionality and the validity of the acts of Congress under which the dual school system in the District of Columbia is being maintained.

JUSTICE BLACK: May I ask you then this question? The reason I asked you the question yesterday was not that I doubted your right as corporation counsel to defend them if they wanted the case defended. You say they want the constitutionality decided.

MR. KORMAN: And the validity of these acts.

JUSTICE BLACK: I understand that. The thing that disturbed me, more from what had been said, I gathered the impression there is the implication that perhaps the majority of the board were going to change the rules; and, if so, I did not think that the Court should be called upon to decide the constitutionality of the rules.

MR. KORMAN: May I say this, Mr. Justice Black. I do not understand that there is a majority of the board that has such a feeling. I am not sure. It may be that that is the case.

JUSTICE BLACK: That was the cause of my interest in the question I asked you. That was the point in my mind.

MR. KORMAN: But I may say to you further, sir, that our position as legal advisers to the board is that they have not the right to make any change in the system, because we believe firmly, and I hope to establish to you in argument today, that the acts of Congress require the maintenance of separate schools for white and colored children in the District of Columbia, and that those acts of Congress are constitutional.

I may say to you further that that has been passed on indirectly by this Court in the case of *Plessy* v. *Ferguson* in 1896, directly by the United States Court of Appeals for the District of Columbia in 1910 in the case of *Wall* v. *Oyster,* and directly and specifically in the cases of *Carr* v. *Corning* and *Browne* v. *Magdeburger* in 1950 by the United States Court of Appeals for the District of Columbia Circuit, holding in so many words that the acts of Congress required the maintenance of separate schools for white and colored children, and that those acts of Congress are constitutional.

It does not lie in my mouth to say to the members of the Board of Education that they have a right to fly in the face of such decisions and I say to you that they could not make any change as we understand the law, and I think as they understand the law, however much any of them might want the law to be otherwise.

JUSTICE BLACK: Of course, that would be a different lawsuit. I don't suppose that the corporation counsel would have a right to defend the board or require them to appear as defendants if a majority of them decided that they wanted to change the rule.

Now I can understand mandamus might be filed againt them or something of that kind.

MR. KORMAN: I would think that under those circumstances, sir—I don't know whether we would be called on to represent them or not, but if we were, I would feel constrained to go before the Court and confess error, because we believe the law is otherwise.

As I said to the Court on yesterday, we stand here to maintain the validity of these acts of Congress, just as we stood before this Court in May and asked this Court to sustain the validity of other legislative enactments in the Thompson Restaurant case. That in the one case segregation is inveighed against and that in the other it is required, is to us a legal immateriality.

We say that Congress has a right and that the legislature which enacted the other laws had the right to pass such laws, and they are in effect in the District of Columbia.

I should like to touch on the question of the kind of decree which might be entered by the Court in the event of unconstitutionality. I take this up at this point because I believe that the Court will not reach that point, but I think that in respect of the Court's wishes, I should say something about it, because the question was asked.

JUSTICE DOUGLAS: Are you going to reach the legal questions, whether the District of Columbia statutes—

MR. KORMAN: I expect to cover that further.

JUSTICE DOUGLAS: —are mandatory or are merely permissive?

MR. KORMAN: Yes, I expect to reach that. We have suggested in our brief on reargument that the Court should not enter any detailed decree.

On page 17 of our brief we merely make this suggestion:

The soundest suggestion that counsel for respondents can make to the Court concerning the nature of the order, if unconstitutionality is to be decreed, is that the Court make recognition of the necessity for proper preparation and changes which appear essential to perfect integration in all jurisdictions and remand the cases to the respective District Courts with instructions for such courts to prepare decrees directing the immediate commencement of such preparation, with periodic investigation by the District Courts of the progress thereof, with direction that, in accordance with the principle of unconstitutionality of separation of races in schools, integration be commenced at the earliest possible date, and that complete integration be accomplished by a definite future date, not to exceed in any jurisdiction more than a maximum period of time.

And we do not suggest any maximum period of time.

JUSTICE JACKSON: If you can't, how are we going to? How are we going to be better informed on that than you?

MR. KORMAN: I don't know that you can be, Your Honor, and I don't know that I can help, and I don't know that any counsel here can help the Court, for the reason that it appears in the District of Columbia and in many of these States legislation may be necessary, as has been suggested by members of the Court.

Some officers may move slower than others, some may resign, not want to serve at all, and so forth. Those are contingencies which I frankly don't know how the Court can deal with.

Perhaps it might be better—and I know that my friends on the other side will disagree with this—that no positive future date be set, but that the matter be left to the District Courts, because I don't think that anyone can now determine what those lengths of time will be. Certainly I can't predict what time may be required to get Congress to act on something.

THE CHIEF JUSTICE: Mr. Korman, is there any legal question involved in remanding this to the District Court of the District of Columbia, in view of the fact that the District Court itself appoints the members of the Board of Education who are the appellees in this case?

MR. KORMAN: I don't think so, sir. I may say, sir, that there have been many cases that have come before that court involving the Board of Education since the organic act of 1906, when they got the authority to appoint members of the Board of Education, and the record will show that they have dealt quite firmly and severely with the members of the board when necessary.

I don't think there is any tie between the members of the bench and the members of the board so that it would be at all embarrassing in any way for them to take positive and firm action if necessary, even in opposition to wishes of some of the members of the board. I don't anticipate that that would ever come up.

Indeed, my thought is that the matter would be worked out quite amicably. I am inclined to believe that the Board of Education, if there should be a mandate from this Court that segregation is unconstitutional, would take immediate steps to try to plan and work out the desegregation of the schools of the District of Columbia as quickly as possible.

I have made some suggestions in the brief concerning things that I believe are necessary to be done before the actual reshuffling of children takes place. I don't believe that my opponents agree with me.

Indeed, I am not at all sure that all of the members of the Board of Education, from some public statements I have seen in the press, agree with some of the things that I have said, but I assure the Court that I did not pluck them out of the air.

I consulted with the chief executive of the Board of Education, the Superintendent of Schools at some length. I consulted with representatives of the United States Government, in the United States Department of Education. I consulted with others, and I have read on the subject, and I am firmly of the belief that some preparation and indoctrination of the teachers to handle integration is a prime prerequisite.

My friends on the other side take me to task for this, and they say that these things are not necessary, but yet there is a strange situation developed. In their reply brief on page 17 and on page 16, they have an indication that the American Friends Service Committee has conducted courses of instruction for some 120 enrollees in four classes or seminars extending from last March until November of this year.

It is not shown whether the 120 enrollees were thirty who enrolled four times in each of the four seminars. There are, however, 3,500 to 3,600 teachers in the public school system. I should like to call the Court's attention to the fact that in the appendix to the brief which we have filed on reargument, there is a letter from the Superintendent of Schools of the District of Columbia which shows that instructional courses have been provided for recreation workers, so that they will be properly indoctrinated in the handling of integration in recreation areas, and we find that those courses were put on on a voluntary basis, and at the expense of these organizations:

The National Conference of Christians and Jews, the Jewish Community Council of Greater Washington, the American Friends Service Committee, the Washington Interracial Workshop, the Washington Federation of Churches, the Catholic Interracial Council, the Washington Urban League, and the Unitarian Fellowship for Social Justice.

Now strangely enough in this yellow-backed brief which was filed as a friend of the Court last year, before this case was argued, we find these organizations among others that are advocating the striking down of segregation in the District Court:

The Catholic Interracial Council, the Commission on Community Life of the Washington Federation of Churches, the Friends Committee on National Legislation, the Jewish Community Council of Washington, the Unitarian Fellowship for Social Justice, the Washington Interracial Workshop, the Washington Urban League.

And so we see that the organizations that are urging this Court to strike down segregation are conducting courses to instruct teachers and workers in the proper way to handle integration, and if that is not an acknowledgment that it is necessary, then I don't know what is.

May I say one thing further. The complaint in this case asks for a declaratory judgment that the acts of Congress under which separate schools are conducted in the District of Columbia are unconstitutional. It would seem to me that a decree by this Court that segregation is unconstitutional would require the lower court to enter such declaratory judgment, and that would indeed cover the whole situation in the District of Columbia, and not just this handful of students who have brought this suit, and so I don't think we have the problem that was suggested by Mr. Justice Jackson, that the decree would only go to the immediate petitions.

JUSTICE JACKSON: You have all of your authorities here?

MR. KORMAN: Sir?

JUSTICE JACKSON: All of your authorities are in this litigation, aren't they?

MR. KORMAN: Yes.

JUSTICE BLACK: The petition asks that we enter a declaratory judgment, or the Court does, stating that the defendants are without right, construing the statutes having to do with public education, as requiring the board to do this. That is the first question that has to be decided, isn't it?

MR. KORMAN: I think so, sir.

JUSTICE BLACK: And I would assume that it should be construed in a way possible so that we don't reach a constitutional question.

MR. KORMAN: That has been the policy of this Court, but by the same token it has been the policy of this Court as expressed in the Butler[48] case, every presumption is to be indulged in favor of faithful compliance by Congress with the mandates of the fundamental law.

Courts are reluctant to judge any statute in contravention of them, but under the frame of our government, no other place is provided where the citizen may be heard to urge that law fails to conform to the limit set upon the use of a granted power.

When such a contention comes here, we naturally require a showing that by no reasonable possibility can the challenged legislation fall within the wide range of discretion permitted to the Congress.

Now I realize that that is not completely apposite, because it does not go to the constitutionality but to construction, which is a different thing, but I believe I can demonstrate to you that these acts of Congress do require the maintenance of separate schools.

JUSTICE BLACK: Has it been construed by the local District Court or the local Court of Appeals—

MR. KORMAN: Yes, sir.

JUSTICE BLACK: —in this respect?

MR. KORMAN: In this respect. They have been twice so construed, in the case of *Wall* v. *Oyster* in 1910, and in the combined cases which were consolidated for argument and consolidated opinion, *Carr* v. *Corning* and *Browne* v. *Magdeburger,* decided in 1950.

JUSTICE FRANKFURTER: Did Judge Prettyman[49] in the Carr case explicitly deal with this problem? He sustained the segregation and he sustained the constitutionality, but was it an issue in that case, whether the segregation was to be sustained, because that was the system which the board enforced, or that segregation was sustained because the statutes compelled the court to enforce them?

MR. KORMAN: The question was raised in that case, and Judge Prettyman—

JUSTICE FRANKFURTER: Did he discuss that problem, Mr. Korman? That is what I want to know.

MR. KORMAN: He reviewed all of the statutes, and then he said—

JUSTICE FRANKFURTER: And said segregation is constitutional?

---

[48]United States v. Butler, 297 U.S. 1 (1936). The Agricultural Adjustment Act, one of the more important New Deal enactments, was declared unconstitutional.

[49]Judge E. Barrett Prettyman (1891–   ). United States Circuit Judge for the District of Columbia Court of Appeals, 1945–   ; Chief Judge, 1958–1960.

MR. KORMAN: No. He said this. It is set forth more fully in the brief we filed last year. I have this quote in my notes. After citing the various statutes, he said:

These various enactments by Congress cannot be read with any meaning except that the schools for white and colored children were then intended to be separate.

That was his conclusion, and I think I can demonstrate that to you by reviewing the statutes, which I should like to do.

JUSTICE FRANKFURTER: I am not questioning that, but as I remember his opinion and as I remember Judge Edgerton's dissent, they did not clinch, if I may use a vulgarism, on that question.

MR. KORMAN: I am quite in agreement with you that Judge Prettyman and Judge Edgerton did not clinch on that question.

JUSTICE FRANKFURTER: That is all I am trying to find out, the scope of the decision on that question.

MR. KORMAN: But Judge Clark[50] clinched pretty well on that.

JUSTICE FRANKFURTER: In that case?

MR. KORMAN: Yes.

JUSTICE FRANKFURTER: Was there an opinion by Judge Clark?

MR. KORMAN: No. He joined Judge Prettyman in the majority.

JUSTICE FRANKFURTER: How can a concurring judge go beyond what he concurs with, unless he says so? I don't understand that.

MR. KORMAN: Well, my understanding—

JUSTICE FRANKFURTER: He may have done so from the bench, but so far as my reading goes, which is all I have in these matters, I did not see that that issue was in contest between the judge who wrote the majority opinion and the judge who wrote the dissent.

MR. KORMAN: I don't think it was in contest between those two, no.

JUSTICE FRANKFURTER: All right, that is all there is in the books. I have no private edition of their opinion.

MR. KORMAN: Well, sir, Judge Clark joined with Judge Prettyman—

JUSTICE FRANKFURTER: But he could not join more than what Judge Prettyman wrote.

[50]Judge Bennett Champ Clark (1890–1954). United States Democratic senator from Missouri, 1933–1945; United States Circuit Judge for the District of Columbia Court of Appeals, 1945–1954.

MR. KORMAN: No, but he joined that much, and Judge Prettyman wrote—

JUSTICE FRANKFURTER: So I read Judge Prettyman's opinion—

MR. KORMAN: And I think it bears out my opinion.

JUSTICE FRANKFURTER: Very well.

MR. KORMAN: May I then proceed to a review of these enactments? I think it should be said to the Court that in 1862 Congress passed an Act on April 16 by which the slaves in the District of Columbia were freed, and slavery was abolished.

At that time there was in the District of Columbia two cities and a county, all of which were ruled by Congress. There was the City of Washington and the City of Georgetown, and the county which was ruled, governed, by a levy court, and the legislation for all of them was by Congress. About a month later, on May 20, Congress provided for schools for the county. Up to that time there had been no schools at all in the county.

There had been for some years public schools in the cities for white children, but not for colored children.

In the Act of May 20 setting up the colored schools, setting up the schools in the county, there was a law enacted, some thirty-six sections, and in one of those sections, section 35, as I recall, they provided schools, separate schools, equal schools, for the colored children. May I refer to the Act itself and read you some of the—

JUSTICE DOUGLAS: What act is this?

MR. KORMAN: This is the Act of May 20, 1862.

JUSTICE DOUGLAS: That was the first one?

MR. KORMAN: Yes, sir. That was the one which set up schools in the county for white and colored children.

JUSTICE DOUGLAS: Is this in your brief?

MR. KORMAN: No, this is in the petitioners' brief on page 23. It is set out in extenso, and we did not set it out again.

And be it further enacted, that the said levy court may in its discretion, and if it shall be deemed by said court best for the interest and welfare of the colored people residing in said county, levy an annual tax of one-eight of one per cent on all the taxable property in said county outside the limits of the cities of Washington and Georgetown, owned by persons of color, for the purpose of initiating a system of education of colored children in said county.

Discussions on this indicate that there were not many colored people in the county.

—levy an annual tax of one-eighth of one per cent on all the taxable property in said county outside the limits of the cities of Washington and Georgetown, owned by persons of color, for the purpose of initiating a system of education of colored children in said county, which tax shall be collected in the same manner as the tax named in section 13 of this Act. And it shall be the duty of the trustees elected under section 9 to provide suitable and convenient rooms for holding schools for colored children, to employ teachers therefor, and to appropriate the proceeds of said tax to the payment of teachers' wages, rent of school rooms, fuel and other necessary expenses pertaining to said schools, to exercise a general supervision over them, to establish proper discipline, and to endeavor to promote a full, equal and useful instruction of the colored children in said county.

I think I might skip down to the last sentence at the bottom of that page:

And said trustees are authorized to receive any donations or contributions that may be made for the benefit of said schools by persons disposed to aid in the elevation of the colored population in the District of Columbia.

And so you see that here is Congress setting up a system of schools in the County of Washington for white children, and in one section of the same Act, setting up separate schools for colored children, and saying that they shall be equal in all respects. It seems to me that that is the beginning of the "separate but equal" doctrine.

Now, then, on the next day, May 21, 1862, the Congress set up schools for colored children in the cities, the cities of Washington and Georgetown, and therein they provided a tax of 10 per cent on the property of colored persons for the maintenance of these colored schools.

Now unusually enough—and I have to burden the Court with reading—but that is an Act of four sections.

My friends yesterday spoke about the striking down of the Black Codes, and here we see in one Act the establishment by the Congress in the District of Columbia, of separate schools for Negro children and the striking down of the Black Codes, all in one Act:

Be it enacted by the Senate and House of Representatives of the United States of America in Congress assembled, that from and after the passage of this Act it shall be the duty of the municipal authorities of the cities of Washington and Georgetown, in the District of Columbia, to set apart 10 per centum of the amount received from taxes levied on the real and personal property in said cities owned by persons of color; which sum received for taxes, as aforesaid, shall be appropriated for the purpose of initiating a system of primary schools, for the education of colored children residing in said cities.

This is section 2:

And be it further enacted, That the boards of trustees of public schools in said cities shall have sole control of the fund arising from the tax aforesaid, as well as from contributions by persons disposed to aid in the education of the colored race, or from any other source, which shall be kept as a fund distinct from the general school fund; and it is made their duty to provide suitable rooms and teachers for such a number of schools as, in their opinion

—not classes but such number of schools as in their opinion—

will best accommodate the colored children in the various portions of said cities.

Section 3. And be it further enacted, that the board of trustees aforesaid shall possess all the powers, exercise the same functions, have the same supervision over the schools provided for in this Act as are now exercised by them over the public schools now existing in said cities by virtue of the laws and ordinances of the Corporation thereof.

Obviously they mean the setting up of separate schools for the Negroes. Now, section 4, and this strikes down the Black Codes in the same Act:

And be it further enacted, That all persons of color in the District of Columbia, or in the corporate limits of the cities of Washington and Georgetown, shall be subject and amenable to the same laws and ordinances to which free white persons are or may be subject or amenable; that they shall be tried for any offenses against the laws in the same manner as free white persons are or may be tried for the same offenses; and that upon being legally convicted of any crime or offense against any law or ordinance, such persons of color shall be liable to the same penalty or punishment, and no other, as would be imposed or inflicted upon free white persons for the same crime or offense; and all acts or parts of acts inconsistent with the provisions of this Act are hereby repealed.

So it seems to me that thereby is a positive demonstration that Congress wanted to do something for these newly freed slaves, but at the same time while giving them these rights of the white man, the right to be tried in the same courts, the right to be subject only to the same punishments and so on, all of these things in the same Act, and sets up for him separate schools.

JUSTICE REED: What act is that?

MR. KORMAN: That is the Act of May 21, 1862, 12 Stat. 394, page 407.

JUSTICE REED: Is that in here?

MR. KORMAN: The citation is in there but the full text is not in my brief.

JUSTICE DOUGLAS: It is 12 what?

MR. KORMAN: 12 Stat. 407.

Now, then, that was on May 21. On July 11, in the same year, Congress established a board of trustees for colored schools. You see, these schools had been set up under the existing board of trustees which handled the white schools, and they established a separate board of trustees for the colored schools, and they transferred the authority from the board of trustees of the schools as set forth in the Act of May 21 to the new board of trustees for colored schools, and in that connection may I read to the Court something that was said by Senator Grimes[51] on the Senate Floor at the time that was being considered:

I am instructed by the Committee on the District of Columbia to whom was referred the bill of House of Representatives No. 543, relating to schools for the education of colored children in the cities of Washington and Georgetown in the District of Columbia, to report it back and recommend its passage.

[51]Senator James W. Grimes (1816–1872) of Iowa. Governor of Iowa, 1854–1858; Republican senator, 1859–1869.

And then, after something further which is not concerned here, he said this: "The motion was agreed to—" this is from the Congressional Globe—

> The motion was agreed to and the bill was considered as in the Committee of the whole. It provides that the duties imposed on the board of trustees of the public schools of the cities of Washington and Georgetown in the District of Columbia, by virtue of an Act entitled 'An Act Providing for the Education of Colored Children in the Cities of Washington and Georgetown, District of Columbia, and for Other Purposes' approved May 21, 1862 be transferred to Daniel Breath, Zales J. Brown, and Zena C. Robbins and their successors in office who are now to be created a board of trustees of the schools for colored children in those cities who are to possess all of the powers and perform all the duties conferred upon and required of the trustees of public schools in Washington and Georgetown by the Act referred to.

> These trustees—

And I am still quoting—

> are to hold their offices for the respective terms of one, two, and three years to be determined by lot, and it is to be the duty of the Secretary of Interior on the first day of July, 1863 and annually on that date thereafter to appoint from among the residents of those cities a trustee in place of the one whose term has expired.

And so on. The bill became law.

The next enactment that we find with reference to the schools in on June 25, 1864, which established a board of commissioners of primary schools in the county, and that provided for the purchase of sites, for the erection of schools, for the regulation of the number of children, the fixing of tuition and so on. That contained in section 16 this provision:

> That any white resident of said county shall be privileged to place his or her child or ward at any one of the schools provided for the education of white children in said county he or she may think proper to select, with the consent of the trustees of both districts and any colored resident shall have the same rights with respect to the colored schools.

But I can't see how possibly anyone could think that Congress intended otherwise than that those schools should be separate.

Section 18 provided funds to be set up or collected for the maintenance of those schools according to the census, the proportion of colored children to white children of school age. Now in that connection I would like to read to you something that was said by Representative Patterson[52] in the House when that bill was being considered. He said this:

> In the twentieth section we have endeavored to give efficiency to the system by requiring attendance at school under a penal enactment. This is in accordance with the school laws in most of our northern cities, and would seem to be especially necessary here.

[52]Representative James W. Patterson (1823–1893) of New Hampshire. Republican representative, 1863–1867; Republican senator, 1867–1873.

And then further on he said this:

But the most important feature of the amendment is to be found in the seventeenth and eighteenth sections, and in the proviso of the nineteenth section which provides for separate schools for the colored children of the District. To accomplish this, we have provided that such a portion of the entire school fund shall be set aside for this purpose as the number of colored children between the ages of six and seventeen bear to the whole number of children of the District.

Now let us follow the chronology of some of the things done by Congress, and I should like to point out to you, which I think probably is rather well known to the Court, that because of its plenary legislative power over the District of Columbia, the Congress, if I may use the expression, frequently uses the District for testing purposes. They put through bills here which they later enact into national policy, and I find in Bryan's *History of the National Capital,* page 133, this statement:

Some years prior to the attempt to commit the Government to a national policy of internal improvements through a District measure, the District had been made the battleground upon which for nearly four decades the contest over slavery was waged. The field of action was chosen not because of concern in the District, but because there the Congress had the power of exclusive legislation and could at a stroke do away with the entire system.

And so we find that in 1862 they struck down slavery in the District, but it was not until three years later that they proposed the Thirteenth Amendment which accomplished it for the rest of the nation. And so it was with other things, as I shall demonstrate to you.

And further on in this same book, at page 259, we find this statement. It is only indicative of the thinking of the time:

In Alexandria, the loss of the banks was especially felt and there was great anger and excitement. At a town meeting held in that place, resolutions were adopted declaring that if Congress looked upon the District as a 'field of legislative experiment' the people of the several states are called upon to relieve us of political bondage.

That was the attitude of the people in those times, and that was what Congress did. And so it seems to me that when you find the Congress making these enactments for the District of Columbia, setting forth as they abolish slavery here, later on for the whole country as I shall show you, giving the right of suffrage to the Negroes in the District, later on for the whole country, the District of Columbia is the testing ground, and it seems to me it should lend weight to some of the arguments that were made here earlier concerning the intention of Congress in framing the Fourteenth Amendment, but I won't touch on that. I think that has been fully covered.

On February 1, 1865, there was a resolution proposing the Thirteenth Amendment abolishing slavery. I have already pointed out to you that that was done for the District in '62.

In March of '65 there was the right of the Negro to ride on street cars. The act of July 23, 1866, was—that was right at the time the same Congress was proposing the Fourteenth Amendment—passed an act enforcing the payment of the proportionate share of the taxes for the colored schools, which had been provided for earlier, as I read you.

Apparently it wasn't being paid on time, and they put some teeth in it, and put a 10 per cent penalty in it if it wasn't paid on time.

And then on July 28, 1866, that same Congress which proposed the Fourteenth Amendment passed this act transferring certain lots, and this was the language.

For the sole use of the schools for colored children.

And further on in the act,

To be used for the colored schools.

And providing that if they were not so used,there should be reversion to the United States. Then, as I told you earlier, on January 8, 1867, the right to vote in elections in the District was given to the Negro. And in 1869 there was the bill to abolish the separate school boards and transfer all of this to one school board, and it passed, but it was vetoed because the President said the Negroes here did not want that, and it was not passed over the President's veto. It died.

And then my friends refer to a memorial by the City Council of Washington to the Congress. They refer to that on pages 44 and 45 of their brief, that the City Council of Washington memorialized Congress to strike down segregation in the schools, and that is true.

The City Council of Washington did memorialize Congress to strike down segregation in the schools, but it was a fruitless gesture. It was a vain effort. Nothing came of it. So that we see that the Congress, in spite of the memorialization by the Council of the city, refused to take such action and it seems to me that that definitely establishes the intent of Congress.

But my friends made one mistake in their brief when they cited the memorial by the City Council to the Congress to change the school system. They cited a page, and I thought I had better look at it, and so if you will refer to—and I shall not take the time to read it, because I see my time is running out—the Washington, D. C., Council, 67th Council, 1869–1870, at pages 828 and 829, and later on—

JUSTICE JACKSON: Are those set forth in your brief?

MR. KORMAN: No, Your Honor.

JUSTICE JACKSON: I wonder if you are going to rely on our memory?

MR. KORMAN: I shall be very glad to submit these references in writing, if the Court would permit. These are things which I found only recently.

JUSTICE JACKSON: It is pretty hard to—I would think you would file a supplemental brief setting forth this. It would be advisable if you think it is important, because it will all be out of mind.

MR. KORMAN: Well, let me say this: I shall briefly refer to what this says.

JUSTICE JACKSON: All right, I am not trying to stop the argument. I am simply suggesting—

MR. KORMAN: Yes, I understand that. The Council of the City of Washington took to task rather severely by a resolution a member of the school board who had issued a certificate to a colored girl to enter a white school. They quoted a report, and opinion by the corporation counsel. There was no corporation counsel at that time. There was an opinion by some lawyer for the District of Columbia Government then that once having got the ticket, they couldn't deny this girl the right to enter this school, and the Council takes that very much to task and says that the man ought to be fired for doing such a thing.

On February 21, 1871, the legislative assembly of the District was created combining the cities of Washington and Georgetown and the county into one, but there was no integration of the schools provided for. In the 41st Congress, there was the specific bill by Senator Sumner to integrate the schools, and there was a great deal of debate found in the Congressional Record, but the bill did not pass.

In the 42nd Congress, in 1872, there was a bitter debate on a similar bill to integrate the schools, but it failed of passage. And then the Legislative Assembly passed the acts which I mentioned earlier which gave to the Negro the right to enter all restaurants and places of public assembly, but they did not legislate on this subject of schools, because they knew they could not.

They gave the Negro all sorts of rights and powers in the District, but they did not legislate on schools because they couldn't, and that was at the time when Mr. Sumner, the Senator from Massachusetts, was a member of the District Committee in the Senate, and I have no doubt that they acted under his prodding, and yet they took no action because they knew that the schools were intended to be separate.

And then in 1900 a school board was provided for of seven paid members of the school board, a superintendent and two assistant superintendents, one of whom under the direction of the superintendent shall have charge of the schools for colored children and the organic act of 1906 came along when they reorganized the whole school system, and the reason, Mr. Nabrit, why they provided for the appointment for the Board of Education by the judges was because they felt that the judges were incorruptible and that the school board appointed by them would not be subject to the vagaries of politics and pressure groups. And you will find that in discussion on the subject.

Then I should like to call your attention to the Teachers' Salary Act of 1945, and of 1947, which says essentially the same thing. May I read some of those provisions to the Court:

> There shall be two first assistant superintendents of schools, one white first assistant superintendent for the white schools who, under the direction of the superintendent, shall have charge of general supervision over the white schools, and one colored first assistant superintendent for the colored schools who shall have direction of those schools.

And so on through enactments right up to the present day. Each year, as has been pointed out, Congress appropriates for this separate system of schools and provides so much money for the colored schools, so much money for the white schools, as is set up in the requests for appropriations.

I might call your attention further, in addition to the appendix which was filed and which is the order of the Commissioners of the District of Columbia striking down segregation in certain areas and which contains in it a recognition by them that there are certain areas in which they have no power to act because it has been taken care of and provided for by the Congress of the United States, and with that I shall leave it to the Court and ask the Court to take into account the arguments which were set forth in our brief filed in 1952.

JUSTICE REED: Mr. Korman.

MR. KORMAN: Mr. Justice?

JUSTICE REED: The matter referred to here as being acts of the Congress for the benefit of the District of Columbia Government, are they stated in your brief?

MR. KORMAN: The Act of the Congress relating to the District of Columbia?

JUSTICE REED: Yes.

MR. KORMAN: All of the Acts?

JUSTICE REED: That you referred to this morning. For instance, 12 Stat. 407.

MR. KORMAN: Yes, sir, they are referred to in my brief. They are not set out in extenso, but they are referred to and those citations of statutes are set forth in the brief.

JUSTICE REED: Which brief is that?

MR. KORMAN: That is the 1952 brief. The brief that was filed this time touched only upon the fourth and fifth questions asked by the Court. We took the position—

JUSTICE REED: There is a section called "The Acts of Congress providing for education of children in the District of Columbia," which is section 2 of your brief.

MR. KORMAN: The latest brief?

JUSTICE REED: No. This is the 1952 brief.

MR. KORMAN: Yes, sir. That contains those acts, the reference to them. You will find at the bottom of page 12 the list of these enactments.

JUSTICE REED: That you referred to this morning?

MR. KORMAN: That's right, sir.

THE CHIEF JUSTICE: Thank you. Mr. Nabrit.

REBUTTAL ARGUMENT ON BEHALF OF THE PETITIONERS

by MR. NABRIT

MR. NABRIT: If it please the Court, counsel for respondents in answer to the question of referring the decision as to action to be taken, if the Court would find that segregation in the District of Columbia is not authorized, to the district court as satisfying some inquiries upon the Court, he quoted from the act in which the authority for the judges to do this—in which it was stated that the purpose was to confer the power of appointment in a group of persons who were noncorruptible.

Under American jurisprudence, however, we would suggest to the Court that in considering due process, we have not let the incorruptibility or noncorruptibility of the persons involved permit us to entrust to them both the appointive and reappointive power of boards, and then the judicial power to distinguish between litigants who are contesting the rights of the board and the board on the basis that their incorruptibility satisfies the requirements of due process.

We don't suggest in any way or question the corruptibility or the impeccability or the character of the judges. All we suggest to the Court is that there appears to be an impropriety in the District of Columbia where the District judges appoint the members of the board, and if they don't like them, they don't reappoint them, and when I say "don't like them," I mean it in the high sense. They don't reappoint them. And yet when we sue the Board of Education, these same judges pass upon the actions of the board.

Now we merely suggest to the Court that there appears to be some impropriety in that. And again counsel for respondents take the position that the attitude of Congress with respect to racial distinction in the District of Columbia can be gathered by reading certain phrases in these statutes. Now, counsel neglects some very important things in doing that.

Number one, out of the eleven basic statutes governing the control of schools of the District of Columbia, nine of those statutes were passed between 1862 and 1866. Of those nine, seven of them were passed before 1864 by the end—between 1862 and 1864.

At that stage of history in this country two things ought to be borne in mind by the Court. One, we were on the verge of the Civil War in 1862. We were in the midst of the Civil War thereafter until 1864. I merely speak of that period because the war continued.

Number two, during that period public education itself was in an elementary stage of development. The public education for anybody in the District of Columbia, even the whites, was in such a fragmentary and rudimentary situation as not to be dignified by the name of public educational system.

Now, in that historical framework, where Congress provided funds, and Mr. Grimes said in both of these Acts to which Corporation Counsel referred your attention, that these were revenue acts to give to systems—I should not use the word "systems"—to Negro schools some financial support in a situation where there were three types of schools, a so-called public school system for whites, private schools for whites, and private schools for Negroes.

Now, without using the word "separate," without using any words of compulsion, when Congress provided that sort of system, to say that the intent of

Congress was to provide for racial distinctions in education, when at the same time in every other Act of Congress beginning with the Emancipation Act which he referred to, the elimination of the Black Codes which he referred to, the Civil Rights Act, the Acts giving the District of Columbia Negroes electoral rights, the Acts enacted immediately after the enactment of the Fourteenth Amendment, those dealing with restaurants, public places in the District of Columbia, those in the Civil Rights Act of 1875, every one of those Acts of Congress provided against any distinction on the basis of race or color with respect to Negroes.

It is inconceivable that in this type of fragmentary educational system the Congress there intended to manifest an intention to impose a racial distinction. There is no basis for such a supposition. So that we must read these statutes if we are going into history in the light of the historical background where we find it.

Now, we suggest to the Court, however, if it does not agree, that it is not necessary to do that. They can look in these statutes in vain for any language which provides any type of penalty or punishment or disability for the mixing of Negroes and whites in the public schools in the District of Columbia.

In *Ex parte Endo* this Court has said this: that when the Government, the federal Government, imposes restraints upon its citizens based upon race, or when it restrains its liberty, I think we can say the Court went that far, that the restraint must be justified by the language used in specificity. The justification for the restraint must be found in the words used, and we suggest to the Court that no such condition exists with respect to these statutes.

Now, in the third place we say with respect to these statutes that the Court does not agree with that, that the Court should give these statutes an intent which is in conformity with the decisions of this Court, the policy of the Government, both executive and legislative as we have indicated.

I think it also highly important to call this to the attention of the Court: that the President of the United States, President Truman, the Attorney General of the United States during Mr. Truman's Presidency, President Eisenhower, the Attorney General now under President Eisenhower, Attorney General Brownell, both of the executive officers of the highest position in this country of the major political parties, including the highest legal officers of the United States, have stated: 1. These statutes do not compel or authorize segregation. 2. That segregation is unlawful and unconstitutional in the District of Columbia.

Now I suggest that under those circumstances that is much more persuasive than the position taken because some statute authorizes the corporation counsel to represent the Board of Education. Those statutes do not authorize him to determine, contrary to all of the legal opinion, that these persons must compel segregation in the public schools. He says that is his opinion and he cites for that *Carr* v. *Corning*.

Now, in *Carr* v. *Corning*, the Court decided that these statutes in the framework with which we have been dealing with them, indicated that Congress did not intend to lift the question of segregation in education out of the hands of Congress, and under the facts in that case they found equality.

The Court did not reach the question which we ask the Court to decide here, whether or not the Government has the power to impose racial distinction in affording educational opportunity to citizens in the public schools in the District of Columbia solely on the basis of race or color, so that *Carr* v. *Corning* is no help;

and if *Carr* v. *Corning* had decided that there would be no doubt about our position, that would have no binding effect on this Court when, for the first time, this Court is called upon to decide as to the lawfulness of this type of action by the federal government.

Now, as far as *Wall* v. *Oyster* is concerned, that was the case in which a Negro girl was admitted to the white schools. Shortly after she was admitted it was found out that some far ancestor of hers in the past had a few drops of Negro blood, but it could not be discerned by looking at her.

They put her out, and she tried to get back, and the issue was on the basis of classification, and the court said that the District had the power to classify, and that their classification of you as a Negro could not be contested.

Now, the court said that, well, underlying that wasn't there an assumption that this was a proper separation of the races in the District? I would say yes, but that was not the issue.

Furthermore, *Wall* v. *Oyster* points out the basic thing that is wrong in this whole situation, and that is there is no justification for the separation of these races except on a basis of inferiority, because in *Wall* v. *Oyster* this girl was in the school, no question being raised about her, the same person. When they found out she had this drop of Negro blood in her, she became unfit to associate with the others in the classroom, and she was put out not because of anything that was wrong, other than that she possessed this Negro blood.

That, we say, is inconsistent with the Constitution of the United States, and nothing has been said by the corporation counsel in this Court in the last argument or this, which offers to this Court any suggestion of any reason or any justification for this separation of races by the exertion of governmental power, save and except there is something in the nature of the Negro which makes him unfit to associate with the whites in the public schools. And that, we say, is against the policy of the federal government and against the Fifth Amendment of the Constitution of the United States.

Now, I did want, if I have a minute or two, to say something to the Court about this matter of relief and about the question of—well, I did not mean to say anything about the power of the Court.

My answer to the question about the power of the Court is, of course, the Court has its power under its equitable power to give any type of relief which the Court thinks is desirable, and with that we have no quarrel.

We think, however, that the Court might raise a question itself as to whether it should exercise the power in these cases so as to give any type of gradual relief.

In the District of Columbia we go further, we say to the Court that the District of Columbia itself does not ask for any gradual relief. We assert no gradual relief is necessary.

Under those circumstances we would think that the Court, having no reason to give gradual relief of itself, would consider gradual relief not to be involved in the District. If that be sound, that would leave the question of what type of decree the Court should enter. In our judgment, the Court should not enter a detailed decree.

In our judgment, we have a time within which we think the Court should require the respondents to grant the relief requested, and that is that the Court enter a decree that these respondents be restrained from operating and managing these schools in the District of Columbia on the basis of racial distinctions alone, by the beginning of the next school term succeeding the issuance of the decree.

So that if the decree were issued—it is a supposition contrary to fact—if the decree were issued in January, the next term would be September; if it were issued in May, the next term would be September.

Now, if it were issued in June, the last day, it would still be September. In our judgment, there would then be sufficient time for whatever normal administrative problems arise in the adjustment of an integrated system to be resolved in the District.

We like to point that out to the Court: Number one, they talk about the reshuffling of students. There are 105,000 students. A normal administrative procedure would take the cards of all the students in the elementary grades, group them, group those cards of the students in junior high, group those in the senior high, so that you have your school populations in your cards; get maps for your areas in the District of Columbia divided for convenience; select either five or ten or whatever number of students you want represented by a pin, and put a pin in that map to show the number of students in each area.

You have the capacity of every school building in the area in each of the categories, and it is a simple proposition to distribute them; so simple is it that in the District of Columbia they do it every year, if not every other year, for the separate Negro system, and for this separate white system which they impose on us.

Now, in order to do it for both, all you do is to coalesce this mechanical action.

The second thing they say that is so difficult is that they have some teachers with different seniorities, and that when you get two lists together of these eligibles, you do not have any way to do that.

This Court has decided in any number of these labor cases that where we have collective bargaining agreements, and you have seniority and these lists, in the decision of the Court these lists are put together and there is no difficulty.

As a matter of fact, the superintendent of schools has announced that they are going to combine the lists for all teachers of physical education this year. It is just as simple to combine lists for all else; so there is no difficulty as to that.

The next thing they say it is difficult because you have got to indoctrinate the teachers. We know it is much better, the more the teachers have some training in intercultural relations, the better it is. We do not dispute that.

But in the District of Columbia 85 per cent of the teachers of the 3,500 teachers have served and are serving today on integrated committees, so they have not been isolated in a vacuum. All of the officers operate that way, largely groups of students operate that way. All of that is in our brief.

In addition to that, over two hundred of them will have been trained for intergroup living and activities and work before March, so that we have a nucleus if we only use those trained or if we only use those who belong to their amalgamated or integrated teachers union, to furnish a nucleus of teachers experienced enough to do this.

All of that calls for simply administrative judgment.

So that these evils and obstacles which the corporation counsel—although he takes the position that gradualism is not necessary, he postulates to this Court in a form to require the same time that gradualism requires—seems to have no substantial basis or merit and, therefore, we suggest to the Court that these respondents be required to conform to a mandate of this Court, assuming the Court decided that segregation is unconstitutional, that this or that that action is not lawful, that they do this at the beginning, by the beginning of the next succeeding school term; and, to be specific, since we hope the decision will come some time during this next year, that it be September, 1954, at the beginning of the school year.

I would like to say as one final sentence, if I may, that America is a great country in which we can come before the Court and express to the Court the great concern which we have, where our great government is dealing with us, and we are not in the position that the animals were in George Orwell's satirical novel *Animal Farm,* where after the revolution the dictatorship was set up and the sign set up there that all animals were equal, was changed to read "but some are more equal than others."

Our Constitution has no provision across it that all men are equal but that white men are more equal than others.

Under this statute and under this country, under this Constitution, and under the protection of this Court, we believe that we, too, are equal.

(Whereupon, at 1:20 p.m., the argument was concluded.)

FRANCIS B. GEBHART, et al.,
Petitioners,

vs.

ETHEL LOUISE BELTON, et al.,
Respondents.

Case No. 10

FRANCIS B. GEBHART, et al.,
Petitioners,

vs.

SHIRLEY BARBARA BULAH, et al.,
Respondents.

Washington, D.C.,
December 9, 1953

The above-entitled cause came on for oral argument at 1:20 p.m.

APPEARANCES:
On behalf of Petitioners:
H. ALBERT YOUNG, ESQ.

On behalf of Respondents:
JACK GREENBERG, ESQ., and THURGOOD MARSHALL, ESQ.

THE CHIEF JUSTICE: No. 10, Francis B. Gebhart, et al, v. Ethel Louise Belton, et al.

THE CLERK: Counsel are present.

THE CHIEF JUSTICE: Mr. Young.

ARGUMENT ON BEHALF OF PETITIONERS

by MR. YOUNG

MR. YOUNG: The petitioners in this case, Your Honors, seek review of final judgments of the Supreme Court of the State of Delaware affirming orders of the Court of Chancery.

The petitioners are members of the Board of Education of the State of Delaware, and the boards of the Claymont Special School District and the Hockessin School District.

The provision from which the petitioners seek relief is the same in both cases:

That the defendants, and each of them, are enjoined from denying to infant plaintiffs and other similarly situated, because of colored ancestry admittance to the public schools.

In the Court of Chancery the respondents urged the proposition that segregation in and of itself is contrary to the Fourteenth Amendment and prayed for a declaratory judgment to that effect.

The petitioners appealed from other rulings of the chancellor which enjoined the petitioners from refusing admittance to the plaintiffs to schools maintained for white children.

The basis of these rulings was that the physical and educational facilities of the schools maintained for Negro children were inferior.

Simultaneously the respondents appealed from the denial of a declaratory judgment, and the Delaware Supreme Court affirmed the decrees of the Chancellor.

The petitioners applied for certiorari to this Court on the narrow issue, namely, the type of relief which should have been granted, the form and shape of the decree, and asked for an opportunity to equalize the facilities.

The respondents did not file a cross petition nor did they seek any review of the decision that segregation in and of itself is not contrary to the Fourteenth Amendment.

The basic question then of segregation per se is, therefore, not before this Court in the Delaware case, but the respondents, however, take a different view, and because of this position taken by the respondents and the importance of the questions raised, and the wishes of this Court, and a sense of duty, we have attempted to answer the questions that are posed to counsel.

There is no evidence that Delaware refused to ratify the Fourteenth Amendment because of a belief that it would require the state to admit Negroes into its public schools on a mixed basis.

The respondents draw from the historical facts in Delaware the remarkable conclusion that the General Assembly, in a series of discriminatory statutes, demonstrated that it fully understood that equality before the law demanded non-segregation, and that school segregation in Delaware is based upon white superiority.

A few important facts, taken out of the pages of history from the State of Delaware, will throw some light on its position with respect to the Fourteenth Amendment and segregated schools.

Delaware did not secede from the Union nor did it join the Confederacy.

Its geographic position alone was sufficient to assure Delaware's loyalty to the Union. Its situation on the Wilmington-Philadelphia-Baltimore Railroad and the Delaware Railroad, along which troops could be moved south, and on the Delaware River, controlled by the Union fleet which lay off Hampton Roads in Virginia, would have made resistance hopeless. In addition, the material prosperity of the state had become increasingly dependent upon Northern markets.

Reinforcing the material ties was a long Delaware tradition of loyalty to the Constitution, and pride in having been the first state to ratify it.

Delaware's adherence, however, to the Union cause was a reluctant one. Attempts to obtain from the legislature a resolution of adherence to the Union failed. There were many manifestations of Southern sympathies throughout the state, throughout the war, and although slave-owning was clearly on the decline, particularly in Wilmington and other sections of New Castle County, one of the three counties of the State of Delaware, and although a vast majority of the Negroes were no longer slaves, it was pretty clear that slavery was a part of the social and economic life of the citizens of the remaining two counties, Kent and Sussex, as it was a part of the lives of the citizens of the Southern states.

Throughout the Civil War, the Democrats maintained firm control of the state government. It proclaimed itself the White Man's Party, and was in power until the late eighties or early nineties. It disapproved of suffrage or political or social equality for Negroes.

The dominant mood in Delaware, both during and after the Civil War, was opposed to abolitionism and equality for the Negroes, and in our own state legislature, in a joint resolution of the House and Senate opposing the Freedmen's Bureau Bill, the Civil Rights Bill, the Negro Suffrage, we witnessed the expression of the feeling that equality cannot be sanctioned under the laws of God or nature, and Senator Saulsbury[53] at that time stated that he was proud that his state was the last to abolish slavery.

The Thirteenth Amendment was unqualifiedly rejected by the legislature in 1865. The legislature expressed its unqualified disapproval of the Fourteenth and Fifteenth Amendments, and refused to adopt them in 1867 and 1869, respectively.

After the passage of the Fifteenth Amendment, poll tax laws in Delaware, designed particularly to disfranchise the Negroes, were adopted with great effect.

In the meantime, Negroes' education in Delaware had made small progress. In the Constitution of 1792 we provided for a public school system; in 1829 we provided for schools for white children by statute, and by the Constitution of 1831 we reaffirmed what we had said in our Constitution of 1792 and provided for a public school system. This was all before any consideration of the Fourteenth Amendment by the State of Delaware.

In 1875 there was a statute imposed upon Negro property-holders, and the funds that were obtained were used to supply and furnish education to the Negroes through a Delaware Society for the Advancement of Negro Education.

It was in 1881, for the first time, that Delaware did make some appropriation from its treasury for the education of Negroes, but the provision was rather meager and rather inadequate, but it is significant that it was the first step and the first stride forward in helping the Negro in his education in the State of Delaware.

In 1897 the Constitution that was rewritten and now under attack by our friends, and now in force in the State of Delaware, provided for segregated schools on an equal basis in the State of Delaware.

That section read as follows:

> In addition to the income of investments of the public school funds, the General Assembly shall make provision for the benefit of the free public schools which shall be equitably apportioned among the school districts of the state; provided, however, that in such apportionment no distinction shall be made on account of race or color, and separate schools for white and colored children shall be maintained.

In the late eighties or early nineties, a political revolution took place in the State of Delaware. The Republicans began to be a serious threat to the control of the Democrats, who proclaimed themselves as the White Party.

This was partly due to the activities and the financial contributions of a political adventurer, John Addicks by name, who was a wealthy stock manipulator from Pennsylvania, and reading of the contest for the United States senatorship

[53]Senator Willard Saulsbury (1820–1892) of Delaware. Democratic senator, 1859–1871.

in 1889, came to Delaware and stated he was available, and because of his contributions to the party at that time, the Republicans got in control, and he also accomplished the enfranchisement of a great many of the Negroes by paying their poll tax.

JUSTICE FRANKFURTER: To an outsider it does not appear as one of the great social reforms of this country, does it?

MR. YOUNG: That is correct, Your Honor.

And by 1898 the Republican Party, through his efforts, however, had upset the Democrat control so that the white supremacists in the State of Delaware had been overthrown. It was against this background that the Constitution of 1897, now in force, was adopted.

It is evident that the constitutional provision and its statutory counterpart in Delaware were in the cause of education of the Negroes, a long stride forward.

The attitude of the people of Delaware had undergone a change, for the slogan "White Man's Party" had finally lost its political potency, and the ineffaceable stamps of superiority were no longer present, and the doctrine of Negro inequality was no longer a guiding force in the framing of the statute.

The change may be said to have been formalized on February 12, 1901, when the Delaware legislature, without a dissenting vote, accepted and ratified the Thirteenth, Fourteenth, and Fifteenth Amendments.

In Delaware we ratified those three Civil War amendments thirty years after they had been submitted for ratification. Thus, the argument of the respondents to the effect that school segregation in Delaware is based on the doctrine of white superiority is refuted.

The resolutions about white superiority cited by the respondents in support of their argument belong to an era in Delaware history that had passed when the present school law and the present school system were enacted.

The constitutional provision for a separation of the races in the public schools in Delaware was not based upon any declaration of natural or God-made inequality or inferiority of the Negro. It was adopted in the light of the history and tradition of the people of the State of Delaware as the wisest and most workable and most acceptable method of educating the youth in that state, both white and colored.

Now, in answer to Question 1, I do not want to burden the Court—I know much argument has been presented—but it seems to me that in connection with Delaware's position, in order for the Court to obtain some idea of what the thinking was in the Congress at the time, I would like to touch upon some of the action and debates, although briefly, if I may, of Congress.

JUSTICE REED: May I ask a question whether there is any other case in the courts of Delaware? I should like to be informed.

MR. YOUNG: No, Your Honor.

JUSTICE REED: Just for my information.

MR. YOUNG: This is the only case.

JUSTICE REED: This is the only case?

MR. YOUNG: This is the only case, the first case of its kind.

JUSTICE REED: We know nothing then as to the federal performance?

MR. YOUNG: No, this is the only case.

In attempting to evaluate the understanding of Congress, of course, we have got to consider the debate in Congress and the actions of Congress, the action of Congress, for example, on the bill to enlarge the Freedmen's Bureau; the Civil Rights Act of 1866, the Fourteenth Amendment, and also the debates on the Civil Rights Act of 1875.

The debates in Congress on legislation of a similar character afford strong evidence that the Fourteenth Amendment was considered to have no effect on public school segregation.

A majority of the Senate and House came from the states which had segregated school systems. I have no doubt that Senator Sumner and Representative Stevens wanted to include in the Fourteenth Amendment mixed schools for white children and colored children.

I have no doubt that those who opposed the amendment attempted to stigmatize the bill, and made every effort they could to see to it that the Negroes received no rights, civil, political or social; but I do believe that between the proponents of those measures and the opponents of those measures there was that responsible majority that saw the distinction between civil and political rights and social rights.

The members of Congress, I respectfully submit, would not have remained silent if they thought it would invalidate segregation in the schools in the states which they represented and which held to segregation of public education.

The suggestions that it would do so came from the white supremacists who sought to stigmatize the bill; they sought to present a parade of horror to the existing state of public opinion, and their expressions should be taken cautiously.

Much has been said about the legislation in the District of Columbia at the time when they provided for a segregated school system and, at the same time, also abolished certain acts of discrimination, and did so both prior to any consideration of the Fourteenth Amendment, and also took up the question of the Negroes' rights during a consideration of the Fourteenth Amendment, and after a consideration of the Fourteenth Amendment. But at no time did they change the system in the District of Columbia with respect to segregated schools.

Mr. Grimes or Senator Grimes of Iowa, in reporting the bill, had this to say in offering an amendment, and if Your Honors would permit me I would like to read from it because it illustrates that Congress did not sit by nor was Congress asleep, apparently, or that this act of providing segregated schools in the District of Columbia was not just a perfunctory or routine matter about which no one knew anything.

Mr. Grimes. Before the bill is read, I wish to propose some amendments on which the question can be taken altogether. In line 7 of section 9, after the word 'the' and before the word 'taxable,' I move to insert the word 'white'; in line 19 of section 9 before the word 'inhabitants,' insert the word 'white'; in line 30–3 of section 9, after the word 'District,' insert the words 'owned by white persons.'

and so forth and so on; and then he concludes:

> The purpose is to make the bill conform to the view of the committee—the bill was not printed in consonance with their views—and to confine the levy of taxes to white persons in the District, and to open the schools to the admission of white children.

It does not seem likely that with this language, and with this introduction with respect to the provision for segregated schools in the District of Columbia, the window of the Republic at that time, that such equalitarians as Ben Wade of Ohio[54], and Senator Sumner and Senator Sprague[55], and Representative Stevens and all the other equalitarians would have sat by and said nothing.

The amendment was adopted and another amendment offered by Senator Grimes to provide separate schools for Negroes in the county, without any dissent, and it is interesting to know that these amendments were adopted without any opposition, even though twenty-three members of the 39th Congress that considered the Fourteenth Amendment, served in the Senate at that time, and not a single member of the House raised his voice against segregation in schools in the District of Columbia.

In the 40th Congress no suggestion was made to abolish segregation in schools in the District of Columbia when a bill to transfer the duties of the trustees of the colored schools for the cities of Washington and Georgetown came under consideration, and this bill was passed after the Fourteenth Amendment was declared and ratified; and again the 41st and 42nd Congresses, in those Congresses attempts were made to abolish segregation in the public schools, and in 1874 Congress reaffirmed its segregation policy in the District of Columbia.

It is hardly conceivable that the Congress which proposed the Fourteenth Amendment was attempting to prohibit the states a type of school which it had endorsed and failed or refused to change in the District of Columbia.

It is clear that the Fourteenth Amendment was not intended, as contended by the respondents, to write into the Constitution the principle of absolute and complete equality so as to include the prohibition by the states against school segregation.

Thaddeus Stevens realized that this notion of equality had not been achieved in the passage of the Amendment when, at the opening of the debate on the Fourteenth Amendment, he had this to say:

> This proposition is not all that the Commission desired. It falls far short of my wishes. But it fulfills the present state of public opinion. Not only Congress but the several states are to be consulted. Upon a careful survey of the whole ground we do not believe that nineteen of the loyal states could be induced to ratify any proposition more stringent than this.

---

[54]Senator Benjamin F. Wade (1800–1878) of Ohio. Whig and Republican senator 1851–1869. He was President pro tempore of the Senate, 1867–1869 and would have succeeded to the Presidency of the United States if Andrew Johnson had been found guilty of the impeachment charges against him. Wade refused to disqualify himself and voted against Johnson.

[55]Senator William Sprague (1830–1915) of Rhode Island. Republican senator, 1863–1875. He married Katherine Chase, daughter of Chief Justice Salmon P. Chase.

Then at the close of the debate on July 13,1866, he said this:

We may perhaps congratulate the House and the country on the new approach to the completion of a proposition to be submitted to the people for the admission of an outlawed community into the privileges and advantages of a civilized and free government. When I say that we should rejoice at such a completion, I do not thereby intend so much to express joy at the superior excellence of the scheme as that there is to be a scheme, a scheme containing much of positive good as well, I am bound to admit, as the omission of many better things.

I am going to skip some of it, but he concluded:

Do you inquire why, holding these views and possessing some will of my own, I accept so imperfect a proposition?

He is talking about the Fourteenth Amendment.

I answer because I live among men, and not among angels; among men as intelligent, as determined and as interested as myself,who, not agreeing with me, do not choose to yield their opinions to mine. Mutual concession, therefore, is our only resort or mutual hostilities.

There is no doubt that one of the things which Stevens at that time found lacking was a provision to compel the elimination of school segregation, and that he thought then, as we urge now, that it is a matter of policy for the states, within their police power.

The debates and the absence of reference to school segregation in the House led to the conclusion that the House understood that the Fourteenth Amendment did not affect the right of the state to educate the Negro in segregated schools. Of the 183 or so congressmen, 129 came from states which either had mandatory segregation or no education for the Negroes, and at least six others from states which had segregated school systems.

It is unlikely that they would have ignored the consequences of such measures on the school systems of their own states if they believed that they were abolishing school segregation.

The respondents state that the debates which followed the bill to enlarge the power of the Freedmen's Bureau amounted to a forthright assault on the idea that there could be racial segregation in the public schools, and then they rely upon Representative Hubbard of Connecticut, who made no mention of racial segregation in public schools; they rely on Representative Rousseau of Kentucky, who opposed the bill because he said the Bureau would take over all the schools used by white children; and they rely upon Representative Dawson, a white supremacist who, every time the occasion arose, castigated the extreme radicals and suggested that the bill would permit white and Negro children to sit side by side.[56]

In the debates on the Civil Rights bill, Representative Rogers of New Jersey

[56]Representative Richard D. Hubbard (1818–1884) of Connecticut; Democratic representative, 1867–1869. Representative Lovell H. Rousseau (1818–1869) of Kentucky; Major General in the Union Army during the Civil War, Republican representative, 1865–1867. Representative John L. Dawson (1813–1870) of Pennsylvania; Democratic representative, 1851–1855 and 1863–1867.

and Kerr of Indiana stated that the bill would outlaw segregation in the common schools of the various states.

However, Representative Wilson of Iowa, chairman of the Judiciary Committee and floor leader of the bill in the House, stated that it did not mean that Negro children would attend the same schools as white children, these not being civil rights or immunities.

In the amendment to the Freedmen's Bureau bill proposed by Representative Donnelly of Minnesota[57] to require the Commissioner to provide common school education to all refugees and freedmen who shall apply therefor, was defeated—not a single reference or quotation by any proponent of the bill to support the statement that this was an assault on the idea that there could be racial segregation in the public schools.

In the debates in the Civil Rights bill in the Senate, only Senator Cowan of Pennsylvania suggested that the bill would abolish segregation in the school systems in his state. No such suggestion appears to have been made in the Senate with respect to the Freedmen's Bureau or the Fourteenth Amendment.

The silence in the Senate on the school question leads only to the conclusion that it was the understanding of the Senate that the measures would not affect segregated education. The senators and representatives were not oblivious to the effect of these measures on the school systems in their own states, nor would they have failed to discuss the consequences if they believed that segregation would be outlawed.

The respondents state on page 91 of their brief that none of the bill's supporters in the House, except Wilson, deny that the bill had any effect of ending all caste legislation, including segregated schools, and that this was the view of the Senate.

Well, the significant thing is not that no one contradicted the white supremacists, such as Rogers and Kerr and Cowan, but that no one contradicted Wilson, the man responsible for the bill, on the floor of the House, who specifically stated that the bill did not mean that Negro children would attend the same school as white children, holding that these were not civil rights or immunities.

Wilson's statement constituted an official interpretation, and neither Stevens nor Conkling[58] nor Bingham nor Donnelly nor any other radical Republican contradicted him; and the respondents have produced nothing to explain the silence of the proponents of the bill with respect to segregation in schools.

The actions of a majority of the state legislatures which ratified the Fourteenth Amendment, in re-enacting school segregation laws or allowing such laws to stand, demonstrate the understanding of those legislatures, that the Fourteenth Amendment did not abolish such segregation, and we agree with the appellants' statement on page 140 of their brief that if there was any authorization or requirement of segregation in state school laws, and after ratification, the legislature took

[57]Representative Ignatius Donnelly (1831–1901) of Minnesota. Republican representative, 1863–1869.

[58]Senator Roscoe Conkling (1829–1888) of New York. Republican representative, 1859–1863 and 1865–1867; senator, 1867–1881. A leading figure in the Grant and Hayes Administrations, he also declined nomination as Chief Justice of the United States in 1873 and as Associate Justice in 1882.

no action to end this disparity, undoubtedly it would appear that this state did not understand the Amendment to have the effect which appellants urge, and all the more reason, we state, that if the state legislature actually took action to continue or to compel school segregation, the legislature must have understood the Fourteenth Amendment not to abolish such segregation.

In some of the cases the legislatures which ratified the Fourteenth Amendment provided for segregation; others permitted segregation; others had no segregation.

In some instances the segregation in schools was declared invalid under state laws, but not under the Fourteenth Amendment.

In some cases, as in the case of New York, of ringing declarations that Negroes shall have full equality and the enjoyment of all civil and political rights, segregation was not regarded as a violation of such rights. Wherever segregation was abolished, whether by statute or by court decisions, there is no evidence that the Fourteenth Amendment entered into the question.

As to the action by future Congresses under section 5, we state that the enforcement clause, section 5, was inserted in order to give Congress the power to supplement any civil remedies or other protection which might be available or through the courts by providing penalties for violation of the Amendment.

The provisions of the Fourteenth Amendment do not permit Congress to broaden the Amendment, but merely provides for more effective remedies than those which might be obtained through the normal judicial process.

It cannot logically be argued that although the Amendment was properly understood to be broad enough to eliminate segregation in public schools at the time it was enacted, that it was, nevertheless, understood that Congress might in the future make segregation illegal.

In answer to question three, we take the position that the problem obviously is a legislative one and not a judicial one.

To construe the Amendment as requiring the abolition of segregation in the public schools would be to give the Amendment a meaning and an effect directly contrary to the understanding of the framers.

It was clearly understood by both Congress which submitted, and the states which ratified, the Amendment that it was to have no effect on the public school system of the state.

The Court, if it should abolish segregation, would not be interpreting the document to meet new conditions, but would be meeting a problem which existed at the time of the Fourteenth Amendment—the time the Fourteenth Amendment was adopted—in a manner directly contrary to the intent of those who proposed and adopted the Amendment.

The wisdom of abolishing segregation in public schools of the states was considered by Congress at and about the time the Fourteenth Amendment was adopted.

Congress consistently, whenever the matter arose, decided to leave this problem to the states.

This Court is not in a position to judge to what extent the prejudices and tensions which gave rise to the segregation laws and the Congressional decision to leave those matters to the states, have abated in any particular state or district, or to judge the wisdom of abolishing segregation in public schools of that state.

The matter should be left where Congress originally left it, in the state legislatures.

The problem before the Court is whether the people of those states, providing for a segregated school system, in the exercise of their judgment, based on first-hand knowledge of local conditions, decide that the state objective of free public education is best served by a system of separate but equal schools; and if I may borrow from—

THE CHIEF JUSTICE: General, may I ask you what is the situation in Delaware today as of this moment?

MR. YOUNG: In Delaware, in the high school district which is the Claymont School District—and I might say it is the northern part of the state, almost on the borderline of Pennsylvania—there are nineteen school children in that school out of twenty-two eligible Negro children. The total enrollment, you might be interested in knowing, is five hundred in the high school, but about eight hundred in the entire school; it is a combination elementary and high school.

Now, in the other district, which is the elementary school district, and which is referred to as the Hockessin School District, there are six out of forty-six that are attending that school, and that is also in New Castle County and on—near the Pennsylvania border, but more towards the west, the southwest; and I might add here that I heard the statement from—one of counsel, our adversaries, said that he was very happy to report that they were in those schools.

Well, I do not know to what extent he is happy, but I might say, if I am permitted to say it outside the record, that in a recent survey there was an indication that there was not too much happiness in the district, in the school, particularly where the six out of the forty-six are attending, and that situation is not solved in that particular district in New Castle County.

JUSTICE JACKSON: At any rate, Mr. Attorney General, we have no question in your case of shaping the remedy? I suppose the questions accidentally went to you as well as to the other counsel?

MR. YOUNG: That is right, yes.

JUSTICE JACKSON: But in your case we have no problem of a decree?

MR. YOUNG: If segregation per se is declared invalid, that is the end of it.

JUSTICE JACKSON: It goes to the state courts?

MR. YOUNG: That is right.

JUSTICE JACKSON: So we have nothing to do with that?

MR. YOUNG: That is right.

JUSTICE JACKSON: So that those questions should not really have been addressed to you, I think.

MR. YOUNG: It would have been very much appreciated if they had not been. (Laughter.)

JUSTICE FRANKFURTER: We have had the benefit of your observations.

MR. YOUNG: Thank you, Justice Frankfurter.

JUSTICE REED: In that county are there still existing segregated schools?

MR. YOUNG: Yes.

JUSTICE REED: All except in two districts?

MR. YOUNG: Just the two districts are affected.

JUSTICE REED: And they are maintaining segregated schools?

MR. YOUNG: They are maintaining segregated—

JUSTICE REED: There are Negro residents and it is—

MR. YOUNG: That is right.

If I may borrow from a statement made by the venerable Mr. John W. Davis, and quote from his brief this statement, he said:

> An emotional approach to this question is a poor substitute for a rational discussion of the problem at hand, which is to be judged by the application of well-settled principles governing the effect of the Fourteenth Amendment on the police power of the state.

The arguments, I respectfully submit, such as I have heard in this courtroom for three days by our adversaries, have great emotional appeal, but they belong in an entirely different forum and in a different setting.

Any change in state policy is for the legislature. The Fourteenth Amendment is a pact between the federal government and the individual states.

The intention of the parties was clear at the time it was adopted and ratified. In order to make that provision in the Constitution cover the question of public school segregation, it must be done within the framework of the Constitution, for as between providing for integrated or mixed schools in those states, where it is deemed best to maintain separate but equal schools, and preserving the meaning and intent of the provision of the Fourteenth Amendment, and the sanctity of the. pact between the federal government and the states, it is more important that this problem, however worthy, be dealt with within the meaning of our Constitution.

As author Stanley Morrison, in conjunction with Charles Fairman, in a very scholarly article which appeared in the Stanford Law Review on "The Judicial Interpretation of the Fourteenth Amendment" aptly put it:

> No matter how desirable the results might be, it is of the essence of our system that the judges must stay within the bounds of their constitutional power. Nothing is more fundamental, even the Bill of Rights. To depart from this fundamental is, in Mr. Justice Black's own words, 'to frustrate the great design of a written Constitution.'

I would like to reserve the balance of my time for rebuttal.

THE CHIEF JUSTICE: Mr. Redding.

ARGUMENT ON BEHALF OF RESPONDENTS

by MR. GREENBERG

MR. GREENBERG: Mr. Greenberg.

If it please the Court, Mr. Redding and I shall argue only briefly in support of our position.

In this case, as the Attorney General of Delaware has indicated, plaintiffs prevailed in the courts below. The plaintiffs and members of their class, are now in schools to which they sought admission, but the Attorney General is trying to get them out, and we appear here in an effort to keep them in the schools permanently.

As respondents here, we urge that the decision of the court below did not give respondents all that the Constitution guaranteed. Therefore, in this Court we urge that the decision below should be affirmed on grounds other than those given by the court below, and that segregation in elementary and high schools in the State of Delaware should be declared unconstitutional.

At the argument last term we submitted it was clear that the decision below could be affirmed on independent state grounds, and that this Court need not reach the constitutional question. But since this Court has seen fit to address two respondents in this case the same questions which it addressed to petitioners in Nos. 1, 2, and 4, we inferred that this Court believed that the constitutional question may be reached in this case.

JUSTICE FRANKFURTER: I do not quite understand the general invitation to counsel to submit arguments on a certain point changes the relevant issue within a controversy; I do not quite understand that.

MR. GREENBERG: I do not believe it changes the relevant issues, but we thought, perhaps, the Court was interested in the question of the constitutionality of segregation in the Delaware case.

JUSTICE FRANKFURTER: As with the Attorney General of Delaware, I am glad to get his observations; and I am glad to get yours, but I do not see that something which is not in issue before we asked specific questions in a group of cases, becomes the issue because we had asked them.

MR. GREENBERG: We submit that although the decision below may be supported on an independent state ground, that in reality, equal protection of the laws will not be given to the respondents unless the constitutional question is reached because, in truth and in fact, they are attending the schools in which they now are, so to speak, under a cloud. They are not like the rest of the students in the school, they are under—

JUSTICE FRANKFURTER: I think you should have cross-appealed.

JUSTICE JACKSON: You have not cross-appealed.

JUSTICE FRANKFURTER: I understand you can sustain a decision below on any ground, but I do not understand that you can object to a decision below on a ground that you have not appealed from.

MR. GREENBERG: Well, we did not cross-appeal, Mr. Justice Frankfurter, because we believed that we could urge other grounds for the affirmance of the judgment below.

JUSTICE FRANKFURTER: You can urge any ground you please that will justify the decree below; but you cannot go outside of the decree below.

MR. GREENBERG: Well, it is our understanding—

JUSTICE FRANKFURTER: I am glad to get your observations, but I might suggest I do not think the nature of the issues has been changed.

JUSTICE JACKSON: I think the question was addressed in this case along with all the others, so if there were any variations they could be called to your attention.

I do not think that we—speaking for myself—took into account the fact or expected in this case to deal with the problem of the decree and the relief or questions addressed to those things, because we cannot direct the state court as to what decree it shall enter. All we can say is, "You shall not go beyond a certain point," which we say is the constitutional limit. Here affirmance is as far as we can go. We could not order them to shape their decree.

MR. GREENBERG: It is our position, Mr. Justice Jackson, that the decree below does not give equal protection of the laws.

JUSTICE JACKSON: You did not appeal.

MR. GREENBERG: No, we did not.

JUSTICE JACKSON: So far as this case is concerned, the most that we can do would be to affirm the decree, but you probably will have the benefit of anything said in any other case that is helpful.

(Whereupon, at 2:00 p.m., a recess was had.)

AFTER RECESS

ARGUMENT ON BEHALF OF RESPONDENTS—resumed

by MR. MARSHALL

MR. MARSHALL: May it please the Court, during the luncheon recess counsel in this case conferred, and it was agreed among at least, so far as we are concerned, that instead of going into the main part of the argument, that we would merely make a brief statement on it.

And, in the first point we wanted to make it clear the reason that we did not file cross-petitions in the court, and we have set out in our brief on the argument,

322

the small one, on page 2, three cases, *Helvering* v. *Lerner,* and *Langnes* v. *Green*[59], and we gathered from those cases that in the situation such as this where we were not opposed to the decision of the lower court and merely wanted to urge other grounds for the decision in the case, that we should proceed with the case and merely urge in argument the point, specifically the point as to the validity of the segregated school statutes.

We are afraid that in that particular posture of the case, if the Court should rule that we should have cross-applied, it could be interpreted that we have waived the other part of the case, and I merely wanted to briefly state our position on the main part, and that is that our primary responsibility here is to urge the Court not to reverse the judgment of the Supreme Court of Delaware, and not to take the position urged by the Attorney General to reverse and send the matter back.

In other words, so far as we are concerned, we are asking that the Court affirm the decision of the Supreme Court of Delaware.

The other point we wanted to urge upon the Court was even if the Court is of the opinion that they should not pass upon the validity one way or the other of the Delaware statutes, because we did not cross-appeal or for some other reason, it appears to us that these cases are all consolidated, the state cases in particular, and that if the Court, in the Virginia and the South Carolina cases in particular, should make it clear that the state was without power to enforce such statutes in the State of Virginia and the State of South Carolina, then merely affirm the decision of the Delaware case, I have no doubt at all that the Supreme Court of Delaware would follow the rationale of the decisions in the Virginia and South Carolina cases, so that if, as has been urged over and over again—and as I understand the position of the Attorney General of Delaware—that when these physical facilities become equal they will then either put the colored children out or take some proceedings to have them removed, that if the Court goes the way I have just suggested, I have no doubt that at that time the same Supreme Court of Delaware, having considered the decision in the Virginia and South Carolina cases, would hold that the Attorney General could not have the children removed because as of that time it would clearly be the decision of this Court that in such instances the State of Delaware as well as the State of Virginia and South Carolina are without power to enforce such statutes.

So it seems to me to narrow down to the position that in this case if the Court merely affirms the decision of the Supreme Court of Delaware, the first task that we have before this Court is to urge this Court to affirm that decision, at least go that far, because to us the decision in the Supreme Court of Delaware is the minimum that we could expect on our theory of what the Fourteenth Amendment

[59]Helvering v. Lerner Stores Corporation, 314 U.S. 463 (1941). A taxpayer unsuccessfully challenged the federal government's system for determining capital stock tax liability on the ground that it was an unlawful delegation of legislative authority since the taxpayer was free to choose any valuation he desired for the capital stock. The constitutional point was considered by the Court although no appeal on that issue had been taken. Langnes v. Green, 282 U.S. 531 (1931) was an action to limit liability of a shipowner following a collision at sea. He was allowed to raise a question decided adversely below although he did not appeal that issue.

requires. And with that I don't need the McLaurin or any of the other cases to urge that upon the Court.

I go all the way back to the Gaines case, where Chief Justice Hughes said that the laws segregating the races depend upon their validity on the equality that is offered under it. So I think in that case, and despite all Mr. Young said earlier about what was peculiar to Delaware and what have you, I do not find anything that says that this Court should reverse the decision which said merely that in the absence of equal physical facilities the colored children have to be admitted to the existing facilities.

So on that very narrow basis, it seems to me that the judgment of the Delaware court should be affirmed, at least on that narrow basis.

Our other ground that we urged, which was that in the decision and opinion of this Court, the expression be—or rather not, instruction—but that it should be made clear to the Delaware court that they are not required as they thought by the prior decisions of this Court to uphold the validity of the statutes so that at future times it can be applied to the same plaintiffs in this case.

Furthermore, I do not think that we should reply in detail to the Attorney General of Delaware's argument about the meaning of the Fourteenth Amendment, because our argument in the other cases has been full, and I do not know anything to add to our other argument, and I do not see anything that has been added by Mr. Young's argument, which would require us to meet it, except the peculiar situation in Delaware.

He thinks it is peculiar, we think it is peculiar. We have both dealt with it in great detail in our briefs, and I think that is as far as I would like to go on that.

I agree that the remedy point is most certainly not involved in this case. I think, as in the South Carolina and Virginia cases, the only points involved are the points as to the Congressional intent and the reliance that I understand from Mr. Young's argument runs the same as the others.

We have the segregation in the schools of the District of Columbia, that they did not intend to exclude—rather, they did intend to exclude—school segregation.

All of the lawyers have repeatedly argued that since the states had segregation statutes when they ratified the Fourteenth Amendment, we would gather something from that, when in truth and in fact, this Court in the case of *Neal* v. *Delaware*[iii] and specifically—of course, they were speaking of the jury situation—in that case the Court said specifically, this Court:

> The Fourteenth Amendment was intended to strike the word 'white' out of all those statutes.

So it seems to me when you pick up one point or another point it will do the Court no good.

The other point urged by the Attorney General is on the power argument and what this Court can do in the situation, and as I understand the power argument, it is, so far as we are concerned, that the authority of this Court is clear, and no one disputes that.

[iii]Neal v. Delaware, 103 U.S. 370 (1881). The Delaware Constitution permitting only white men to serve on juries was declared unconstitutional.

The real question involved is as to whether or not the states involved as of now, today, do or do not have power to use race and race alone for the basis of segregation, and that applies, our theory, that the states have been effectively deprived of that power hold as true—Mr. Young emphasized this—in Delaware, which is just beside Pennsylvania.

It applies as well there as it applies in South Carolina and Virginia, and therefore, unless there are questions, we submit this case and urge the Court to affirm the judgment of the Supreme Court of Delaware.

Thank you, sirs.

JUSTICE FRANKFURTER: Might I ask General Young whether the specific judgment we have before us is the final order that was entered by the Chancellor which was adopted by the court? Is that your understanding?

MR. YOUNG: That is right. There is nothing in rebuttal.

(Whereupon, at 2:40 p.m., the Court adjourned.)

FINAL DECISION ON THE MERITS

BROWN ET AL. v. BOARD OF EDUCATION
OF TOPEKA ET AL.

NO. 1. APPEAL FROM THE UNITED STATES DISTRICT COURT
*FOR THE DISTRICT OF KANSAS.**

Argued December 9, 1952.—Reargued December 8, 1953.—
Decided May 17, 1954.

347 U.S. 483

MR. CHIEF JUSTICE WARREN delivered the opinion of the Court.

These cases come to us from the States of Kansas, South Carolina, Virginia, and Delaware. They are premised on different facts and different local conditions, but a common legal question justifies their consideration together in this consolidated opinion.[1]

---

*Together with No. 2, *Briggs et al.* v. *Elliott et al.*, on appeal from the United States District Court for the Eastern District of South Carolina, argued December 9-10, 1952, reargued December 7-8, 1953; No. 4, *Davis et al.* v. *County School Board of Prince Edward County, Virginia, et al.*, on appeal from the United States District Court for the Eastern District of Virginia, argued December 10, 1952, reargued December 7-8, 1953; and No. 10, *Gebhart et al.* v. *Belton et al.*, on certiorari to the Supreme Court of Delaware, argued December 11, 1952, reargued December 9, 1953.

[1] In the Kansas case, *Brown* v. *Board of Education*, the plaintiffs are Negro children of elementary school age residing in Topeka. They brought this action in the United States District Court for the District of Kansas to enjoin enforcement of a Kansas statute which permits, but does not require, cities of more than 15,000 population to maintain separate school facilities for Negro and white students. Kan. Gen. Stat. § 72-1724 (1949). Pursuant to that authority, the Topeka Board of Education elected to establish segregated elementary schools. Other public schools in the community, however, are operated on a nonsegregated basis. The three-judge District Court, convened under 28 U.S.C. §§ 2281 and 2284, found that segregation in public education has a detrimental effect upon Negro children, but denied relief on the ground that the Negro and white schools were substantially equal with respect to buildings, transportation, curricula, and educational qualifications of teachers. 98 F. Supp. 797. The case is here on direct appeal under 28 U.S.C. § 1253.

In the South Carolina case, *Briggs* v. *Elliott*, the plaintiffs are Negro children of both elementary and high school age residing in Clarendon County. They brought this action in the United States District Court for the Eastern District of South Carolina to enjoin enforcement of provisions in the state constitution and statutory code which require the segregation of Negroes and whites in public schools. S.C. Const., Art. XI § 7; S.C. Code § 5377 (1942). The three-judge District Court, convened under 28 U.S.C. §§ 2281 and 2284, denied the requested relief. The court found that the Negro schools were inferior to the white schools and ordered the defendants to begin immediately to equalize the facilities.

In each of the cases, minors of the Negro race, through their legal representatives, seek the aid of the courts in obtaining admission to the public schools of their community on a nonsegregated basis. In each instance, they had been denied admission to schools attended by white children under laws requiring or permitting segregation according to race. This segregation was alleged to deprive the plaintiffs of the equal protection of the laws under the Fourteenth Amendment. In each of the cases other than the Delaware case, a three-judge federal district court denied relief to the plaintiffs on the so-called "separate but equal" doctrine announced by this Court in *Plessy* v. *Ferguson,* 163 U.S. 537. Under that doctrine, equality of treatment is accorded when the races are provided substantially equal facilities even though these facilities be separate. In the Delaware case, the Supreme court of Delaware adhered to that doctrine, but ordered that the plain-

---

But the court sustained the validity of the contested provisions and denied the plaintiffs admission to the white schools during the equalization program. 98 F. Supp. 529. This Court vacated the District Court's judgment and remanded the case for the purpose of obtaining the court's views on a report filed by the defendants concerning the progress made in the equalization program. 342 U.S. 350. On remand, the District Court found that substantial equality had been achieved except for buildings and that the defendants were proceeding to rectify this inequality as well. 103 F. Supp. 920. The case is again here on direct appeal under 28 U.S.C. § 1253.

In the Virginia case, *Davis* v. *County School Board,* the plaintiffs are Negro children of high school age residing in Prince Edward County. They brought this action in the United States District Court for the Eastern District of Virginia to enjoin enforcement of provisions in the state constitution and statutory code which require the segregation of Negroes and whites in public schools. Va. Const., § 140; Va. Code § 22–221 (1950). The three-judge District Court, convened under 28 U.S.C. §§ 2281 and 2284, denied the requested relief. The court found the Negro school inferior in physical plant, curricula, and transportation, and ordered the defendants forthwith to provide substantially equal curricula and transportation and to "proceed with all reasonable diligence and dispatch to remove" the inequality in physical plant. But, as in the South Carolina case, the court sustained the validity of the contested provisions and denied the plaintiffs admission to the white schools during the equalization program. 103 F.Supp. 337. The case is here on direct appeal under 28 U.S.C. § 1253.

In the Delaware case, *Gebhart* v. *Belton,* the plaintiffs are Negro children of both elementary and high school age residing in New Castle County. They brought this action in the Delaware Court of Chancery to enjoin enforcement of provisions in the state constitution and statutory code which require the segregation of Negroes and whites in public schools. Del. Const., Art. X, § 2; Del. Rev. Code § 2631 (1935). The Chancellor gave judgment for the plaintiffs and ordered their immediate admission to schools previously attended only by white children, on the ground that the Negro schools were inferior with respect to teacher training, pupil-teacher ratio, extracurricular activities, physical plant, and time and distance involved in travel. 87 A. 2d 862. The Chancellor also found that segregation itself results in an inferior education for Negro children (see note 10, *infra*), but did not rest his decision on that ground. *Id.,* at 865. The Chancellor's decree was affirmed by the Supreme Court of Delaware, which intimated, however, that the defendants might be able to obtain a modification of the decree after equalization of the Negro and white schools had been accomplished. 91 A. 2d 137, 152. The defendants, contending only that the Delaware courts had erred in ordering the immediate admission of the Negro plaintiffs to the white schools, applied to this Court for certiorari. The writ was granted, 344 U.S. 891. The plaintiffs, who were successful below, did not submit a cross-petition.

tiffs be admitted to the white schools because of their superiority to the Negro schools.

The plaintiffs contend that segregated public schools are not "equal" and cannot be made "equal," and that hence they are deprived of the equal protection of the laws. Because of the obvious importance of the question presented, the Court took jurisdiction.[2] Argument was heard in the 1952 Term, and reargument was heard this Term on certain questions propounded by the Court.[3]

Reargument was largely devoted to the circumstances surrounding the adoption of the Fourteenth Amendment in 1868. It covered exhaustively consideration of the Amendment in Congress, ratification by the states, then existing practices in racial segregation, and the views of proponents and opponents of the Amendment. This discussion and our own investigation convince us that, although these sources cast some light, it is not enough to resolve the problem with which we are faced. At best, they are inconclusive. The most avid proponents of the post-War Amendments undoubtedly intended them to remove all legal distinctions among "all persons born or naturalized in the United States." Their opponents, just as certainly, were antagonistic to both the letter and the spirit of the Amendments and wished them to have the most limited effect. What others in Congress and the state legislatures had in mind cannot be determined with any degree of certainty.

An additional reason for the inconclusive nature of the Amendment's history, with respect to segregated schools, is the status of public education at that time.[4] In the South, the movement toward free common schools, supported by general taxation, had not yet taken hold. Education of white children was largely in the hands of private groups. Education of Negroes was almost nonexistent, and practically all of the race were illiterate. In fact, any education of Negroes was forbidden by law in some states. Today, in contract, many Negroes have achieved outstanding success in the arts and sciences as well as in the business and profes-

[2]344 U.S. 1, 141, 891.

[3]345 U.S. 972. The Attorney General of the United States participated both Terms as *amicus curiae.*

[4]For a general study of the development of public education prior to the Amendment, see Butts and Cremin, A History of Education in American Culture (1953), Pts. I, II; Cubberley, Public Education in the United States (1934 ed.), cc. II–XII. School practices current at the time of the adoption of the Fourteenth Amendment are described in Butts and Cremin, *supra,* at 269–275; Cubberley, *supra,* at 288–339, 408–431; Knight, Public Education in the South (1922), cc. VIII, IX. See also H. Ex. Doc. No. 315, 41st Cong., 2d Sess. (1871). Although the demand for free public schools followed substantially the same pattern in both the North and the South, the development in the South did not begin to gain momentum until about 1850, some twenty years after that in the North. The reasons for the somewhat slower development in the South *(e. g.,* the rural character of the South and the different regional attitudes toward state assistance) are well explained in Cubberley, *supra,* at 408–423. In the country as a whole, but particularly in the South, the War virtually stopped all progress in public education. *Id.,* at 427–428. The low status of Negro education in all sections of the country, both before and immediately after the War, is described in Beale, A History of Freedom of Teaching in American Schools (1941), 112–132, 175–195. Compulsory school attendance laws were not generally adopted until after the ratification of the Fourteenth Amendment, and it was not until 1918 that such laws were in force in all the states. Cubberley, *supra,* at 563–565.

sional world. It is true that public school education at the time of the Amendment had advanced further in the North, but the effect of the Amendment on Northern States was generally ignored in the congressional debates. Even in the North, the conditions of public education did not approximate those existing today. The curriculum was usually rudimentary; ungraded schools were common in rural areas; the school term was but three months a year in many states; and compulsory school attendance was virtually unknown. As a consequence, it is not surprising that there should be so little in the history of the Fourteenth Amendment relating to its intended effect on public education.

In the first cases in this Court construing the Fourteenth Amendment, decided shortly after its adoption, the Court interpreted it as proscribing all state-imposed discriminations against the Negro race.[5] The doctrine of "separate but equal" did not make its appearance in this Court until 1896 in the case of *Plessy* v. *Ferguson, supra,* involving not education but transportation.[6] American courts have since labored with the doctrine for over half a century. In this Court, there have been six cases involving the "separate but equal" doctrine in the field of public education.[7] In *Cumming* v. *County Board of Education,* 175 U.S. 528, and *Gong Lum* v. *Rice,* 275 U.S. 78, the validity of the doctrine itself was not challenged.[8] In more recent cases, all on the graduate school level, inequality was found in that specific benefits enjoyed by white students were denied to Negro

[5]*Slaughter-House Cases,* 16 Wall. 36, 67–72 (1873); *Strauder* v. *West Virginia,* 100 U.S. 303, 307–308 (1880):
"It ordains that no State shall deprive any person of life, liberty, or property, without due process of law, or deny to any person within its jurisdiction the equal protection of the laws. What is that but declaring that the law in the States shall be the same for the black as for the white; that all persons, whether colored or white, shall stand equal before the laws of the States, and, in regard to the colored race, for whose protection the amendment was primarily designed, that no discrimination shall be made against them by the law because of their color? The words of the amendment, it is true, are prohibitory, but they contain a necessary implication of a positive immunity, or right, most valuable to the colored race,—the right to exemption from unfriendly legislation against them distinctively as colored,—exemption from legal discriminations, implying inferiority in civil society, lessening the security of their enjoyment of the rights which others enjoy, and discriminations which are steps towards reducing them to the condition of a subject race."
See also *Virginia* v. *Rives,* 100 U.S. 313 318 (1880); *Ex parte Virginia,* 100 U.S. 339, 344–345 (1880).

[6]The doctrine apparently originated in *Roberts* v. *City of Boston,* 59 Mass. 198, 206 (1850), upholding school segregation against attack as being violative of a state constitutional guarantee of equality. Segregation in Boston public schools was eliminated in 1855. Mass. Acts. 1855, c. 256. But elsewhere in the North segregation in public education has persisted in some communities until recent years. It is apparent that such segregation has long been a nationwide problem, not merely one of sectional concern.

[7]See also *Berea College* v. *Kentucky,* 211 U.S. 45 (1908).

[8]In the *Cumming* case, Negro taxpayers sought an injunction requiring the defendant school board to discontinue the operation of a high school for white children until the board resumed operation of a high school for Negro children. Similarly, in the *Gong Lum* case, the plaintiff, a child of Chinese descent, contended only that state authorities had misapplied the doctrine by classifying him with Negro children and requiring him to attend a Negro school.

students of the same educational qualifications. *Missouri ex rel. Gaines* v. *Canada*, 305 U.S. 337; *Sipuel* v. *Oklahoma*, 332 U.S. 631; *Sweatt* v. *Painter*, 339 U.S. 629; *McLaurin* v. *Oklahoma State Regents*, 339 U.S. 637. In none of these cases was it necessary to re-examine the doctrine to grant relief to the Negro plaintiff. And in *Sweatt* v. *Painter, supra,* the Court expressly reserved decision on the question whether *Plessy* v. *Ferguson* should be held inapplicable to public education.

In the instant cases, that question is directly presented. Here, unlike *Sweatt* v. *Painter*, there are findings below that the Negro and white schools involved have been equalized, or are being equalized, with respect to buildings, curricula, qualifications and salaries of teachers, and other "tangible" factors.[9] Our decision, therefore, cannot turn on merely a comparison of these tangible factors in the Negro and white schools involved in each of the cases. We must look instead to the effect of segregation itself on public education.

In approaching this problem, we cannot turn the clock back to 1868 when the Amendment was adopted, or even to 1896 when *Plessy* v. *Ferguson* was written. We must consider public education in the light of its full development and its present place in American life throughout the Nation. Only in this way can it be determined if segregation in public schools deprives these plaintiffs of the equal protection of the laws.

Today, education is perhaps the most important function of state and local governments. Compulsory school attendance laws and the great expenditures for education both demonstrate our recognition of the importance of education to our democratic society. It is required in the performance of our most basic public responsibilities, even service in the armed forces. It is the very foundation of good citizenship. Today it is a principal instrument in awakening the child to cultural values, in preparing him for later professional training, and in helping him to adjust normally to his environment. In these days, it is doubtful that any child may reasonably be expected to succeed in life if he is denied the opportunity of an education. Such an opportunity, where the state has undertaken to provide it, is a right which must be made available to all on equal terms.

We come then to the question presented: Does segregation of children in public schools solely on the basis of race, even though the physical facilities and other "tangible" factors may be equal, deprive the children of the minority group of equal educational opportunities? We believe that it does.

In *Sweatt* v. *Painter, supra,* in finding that a segregated law school for Negroes could not provide them equal educational opportunities, this Court relied in large part on "those qualities which are incapable of objective measurement but which make for greatness in a law school." In *McLaurin* v. *Oklahoma State Regents, supra,* the Court, in requiring that a Negro admitted to a white graduate

[9]In the Kansas case, the court below found substantial equality as to all such factors. 98 F. Supp. 797, 798. In the South Carolina case, the court below found that the defendants were proceeding "promptly and in good faith to comply with the court's decree." 103 F. Supp. 920, 921. In the Virginia case, the court below noted that the equalization program was already "afoot and progressing" (103 F. Supp. 337, 341); since then, we have been advised, in the Virginia Attorney General's brief on reargument, that the program has now been completed. In the Delaware case, the court below similarly noted that the state's equalization program was well under way. 91 A. 2d 137, 149.

school be treated like all other students, again resorted to intangible considerations: ". . . his ability to study, to engage in discussions and exchange views with other students, and, in general, to learn his profession." Such considerations apply with added force to children in grade and high schools. To separate them from others of similar age and qualifications solely because of their race generates a feeling of inferiority as to their status in the community that may affect their hearts and minds in a way unlikely ever to be undone. The effect of this separation on their educational opportunities was well stated by a finding in the Kansas case by a court which nevertheless felt compelled to rule against the Negro plaintiffs:

"Segregation of white and colored children in public schools has a detrimental effect upon the colored children. The impact is greater when it has the sanction of the law; for the policy of separating the races is usually interpreted as denoting the inferiority of the negro group. A sense of inferiority affects the motivation of a child to learn Segregation with the sanction of law, therefore, has a tendency to [retard] the educational and mental development of negro children and to deprive them of some of the benefits they would receive in a racial [ly] integrated school system." [10]

Whatever may have been the extent of psychological knowledge at the time of *Plessy* v. *Ferguson*, this finding is amply supported by modern authority. [11] Any language in *Plessy* v. *Ferguson* contrary to this finding is rejected.

We conclude that in the field of public education the doctrine of "separate but equal" has no place. Separate educational facilities are inherently unequal. Therefore, we hold that the plaintiffs and others similarly situated for whom the actions have been brought are, by reason of the segregation complained of, deprived of the equal protection of the laws guaranteed by the Fourteenth Amendment. This disposition makes unnecessary any discussion whether such segregation also violates the Due Process Clause of the Fourteenth Amendment. [12]

Because these are class actions, because of the wide applicability of this decision, and because of the great variety of local conditions, the formulation of decrees in these cases presents problems of considerable complexity. On reargument, the consideration of appropriate relief was necessarily subordinated to the primary question—the constitutionality of segregation in public education. We

[10]A similar finding was made in the Delaware case: "I conclude from the testimony that in our Delaware society, State-imposed segregation in education itself results in the Negro children, as a class, receiving educational opportunities which are substantially inferior to those available to white children otherwise similarly situated." 87 A. 2d 862, 865.

[11]K. B. Clark, Effect of Prejudice and Discrimination on Personality Development (Midcentury White House Conference on Children and Youth, 1950); Witmer and Kotinsky, Personality in the Making (1952), c. VI; Deutscher and Chein, The Psychological Effects of Enforced Segregation: A Survey of Social Science Opinion, 26 J. Psychol. 259 (1948); Chein, What are the Psychological Effects of Segregation Under Conditions of Equal Facilities?, 3 Int. J. Opinion and Attitude Res. 229 (1949); Brameld, Educational Costs, in Discrimination and National Welfare (MacIver, ed., 1949), 44–48; Frazier, The Negro in the United States (1949), 674–681. And see generally Mydral, An American Dilemma (1944).

[12]See *Bolling* v. *Sharpe, post,* p. 497, concerning the Due Process Clause of the Fifth Amendment.

have now announced that such segregation is a denial of the equal protection of the laws. In order that we may have the full assistance of the parties in formulating decrees, the cases will be restored to the docket, and the parties are requested to present further argument on Questions 4 and 5 previously propounded by the Court for the reargument this Term.[13] The Attorney General of the United States is again invited to participate. The Attorneys General of the states requiring or permitting segregation in public education will also be permitted to appear as *amici curiae* upon request to do so by September 15, 1954, and submission of briefs by October 1, 1954.[14]

It is so ordered.

[13]"4. Assuming it is decided that segregation in public schools violates the Fourteenth Amendment

"*(a)* would a decree necessarily follow providing that, within the limits set by normal geographic school districting, Negro children should forthwith be admitted to schools of their choice, or

"*(b)* may this Court, in the exercise of its equity powers, permit an effective gradual adjustment to be brought about from existing segregated systems to a system not based on color distinctions?

"5. On the assumption on which questions 4 *(a)* and *(b)* are based, and assuming further that this Court will exercise its equity powers to the end described in question 4 *(b)*.

"*(a)* should this Court formulate detailed decrees in these cases;

"*(b)* if so, what specific issues should the decrees reach;

"*(c)* should this Court appoint a special master to hear evidence with a view to recommending specific terms for such decrees;

"*(d)* should this Court remand to the courts of first instance with directions to frame decrees in these cases, and if so what general directions should the decrees of this Court include and what procedures should the courts of first instance follow in arriving at the specific terms of more detailed decrees?"

[14]See Rule 42, Revised Rules of this Court (effective July 1, 1954).

BOLLING ET AL. v. SHARPE ET AL.

CERTIORARI TO THE UNITED STATES COURT OF APPEALS FOR THE DISTRICT OF COLUMBIA CIRCUIT.

No. 8. Argued December 10–11, 1952.—Reargued December 8–9, 1953.—Decided May 17, 1954.

347 U.S. 497

MR. CHIEF JUSTICE WARREN delivered the opinion of the Court.

This case challenges the validity of segregation in the public schools of the District of Columbia. The petitioners, minors of the Negro race, allege that such segregation deprives them of due process of law under the Fifth Amendment. They were refused admission to a public school attended by white children solely because of their race. They sought the aid of the District Court for the District of Columbia in obtaining admission. That court dismissed their complaint. The Court granted a writ of certiorari before judgment in the Court of Appeals because of the importance of the constitutional question presented. 344 U.S. 873.

We have this day held that the Equal Protection Clause of the Fourteenth Amendment prohibits the states from maintaining racially segregated public schools.[1] The legal problem in the District of Columbia is somewhat different, however. The Fifth Amendment, which is applicable in the District of Columbia, does not contain an equal protection clause as does the Fourteenth Amendment which applies only to the states. But the concepts of equal protection and due process, both stemming from our American ideal of fairness, are not mutually exclusive. The "equal protection of the laws" is a more explicit safeguard of prohibited unfairness than "due process of law," and, therefore, we do not imply that the two are always interchangeable phrases. But, as this Court has recognized, discrimination may be so unjustifiable as to be violative of due process.[2]

Classifications based solely upon race must be scrutinized with particular care, since they are contrary to our traditions and hence constitutionally suspect.[3] As long ago as 1896, this Court declared the principle "that the Constitution of the United States, in its present form, forbids, so far as civil and political rights are concerned, discrimination by the General Government, or by the States, against any citizen because of his race."[4] And in *Buchanan* v. *Warley,* 245 U. S. 60, the Court held that a statute which limited the right of a property owner to convey his property to a person of another race was, as an unreasonable discrimination, a denial of due process of law.

Although the Court has not assumed to define "liberty" with any great precision, that term is not confined to mere freedom from bodily restraint. Liberty under law extends to the full range of conduct which the individual is free to pur-

---

[1]*Brown* v. *Board of Education, ante,* p. 483.

[2]*Detroit Bank* v. *United States,* 317 U.S. 329; *Currin* v. *Wallace,* 306 U.S. 1, 13–14; *Steward Machine Co.* v. *Davis,* 301 U.S. 548, 585.

[3]*Korematsu* v. *United States,* 323 U.S. 214, 216; *Hirabayashi* v. *United States,* 320 U.S. 81, 100.

[4]*Gibson* v. *Mississippi,* 162 U.S. 565, 591. Cf. *Steele* v. *Louisville & Nashville R. Co.,* 323 U.S. 192, 198–199.

sue, and it cannot be restricted except for a proper governmental objective. Segregation in public education is not reasonably related to any proper governmental objective, and thus it imposes on Negro children of the District of Columbia a burden that constitutes an arbitrary deprivation of their liberty in violation of the Due Process Clause.

In view of our decision that the Constitution prohibits the states from maintaining racially segregated public schools, it would be unthinkable that the same Constitution would impose a lesser duty on the Federal Government.[5] We hold that racial segregation in the public schools of the District of Columbia is a denial of the due process of law guaranteed by the Fifth Amendment to the Constitution.

For the reasons set out in *Brown* v. *Board of Education*, this case will be restored to the docket for reargument on Questions 4 and 5 previously propounded by the Court. 345 U.S. 972.

It is so ordered.

[5] Cf. *Hurd* v. *Hodge*, 334 U.S. 24.

INDEX